The Islamic Law of Personal Status

Series General Editor

Dr Mark S. W. Hoyle

Forthcoming Titles in the Series

Islamic Family Law, Chibli Mallat and Jane Connors (eds)

Arab and Islamic Laws Series

The Islamic Law of Personal Status

Second Edition

Jamal J. Nasir, B.A. (Hons), Ph.D. (Lond)

Barrister (of Lincoln's Inn)
Former Minister of Justice of Jordan
Senior Counsel on all questions of International, Arab and African Laws
Member of the Jordan Bar and entitled to practise before other Arab Bars
Member of the Federal Supreme Court of Nigeria
Counsel on Islamic Law
One time Lecturer on International Law
Advocate

Graham & Trotman
A member of the Kluwer Academic Publishers Group
LONDON/DORDRECHT/BOSTON

Graham & Trotman Ltd.
Sterling House
66 Wilton Road
London SW1V 1DE

Kluwer Academic Publishers Group
101 Philip Drive
Assinippi Park
Norwell, MA 02061 USA

First Published in 1986
Second Edition Published in 1990

British Library Cataloguing in Publication Data

Nasir, Jamal J. (Jamal Jamil)
The Islamic law of personal status – 2nd edn.
1. Islamic personal law
I. Title
342.61

ISBN 1-85333-280-1 Series ISBN 1-85333-414-6

Library of Congress Cataloging-in-Publication Data

Nasir, Jamal J.
The Islamic law of personal status / Jamal J. Nasir. – 2nd edn.
p. cm.
Includes bibliographical references (p.).
ISBN 1-85333-280-1 Series ISBN 1-85333-414-6
1. Status (Islamic law) I. Title.
LAW
340.5′9—dc20 89-28721
CIP

Typeset in Baskerville by Acorn Bookwork, Salisbury, Wilts
Printed and bound in Great Britain by Billing & Sons Ltd, Worcester

CONTENTS

FOREWORD

It was with diffidence that I agreed to write this brief Foreword to Dr. Jamal Jamil Nasir's learned work on *The Islamic Law of Personal Status*. Although as a comparatist I have, of course, an interest in Islamic law, my knowledge of the great legal tradition embodied in the Sharia is both limited and superficial. Accordingly, I can only discuss in general terms Dr. Nasir's valuable work.

Dr. Nasir writes with the practitioner particularly in mind. The very nature of the Islamic legal tradition requires that the contemporary law of personal status found in Arabic countries be presented against the background of the Quran and the Sunna as explicated by the several Juristic Schools. The Sharia—resting on Allah's commands for Muslim society—was, and remains, a divine law.

Accordingly, Dr Nasir begins with an Introduction which treats the historical development of Islamic Jurisprudence, the Islamic Schools of Law, and the Methodology used by Islamic jurists. Turning then to particular topics such as marriage, dower, dissolution of marriage, inheritance, and wills, he begins the discussion in each instance with a consideration of the subject in Sharia law. The legislation and contemporary views of particular Arabic countries are then presented for each topic.

This approach emphasizes the continuity of the Islamic law respecting personal status; at every point, the influence of the Sharia on contemporary practices and solutions is evident. This is not to say that contemporary legislation and practices exhibit no differences from the Sharia. However, at least to a non-Muslim, the differences seem, by and large, to take the form of evolutionary developments from—rather than sharp breaks with—the Sharia tradition.

The task Dr. Nasir set for himself being the presentation of the personal law of various Arabic countries to practitioners, he does not pursue the question of how faithful this contemporary legislation is to Islamic tradition. Doubtless no simple answer can be given, although the issue is one of considerable cultural and political importance in many parts of the Middle East.

For a variety of reasons, in the past the presentation of Islamic law to Western lawyers has been to a considerable extent through the writings of non-Muslims. These writers have, for the most part, been deeply learned in the Arabic language and in Islamic culture and history. However, a non-Muslim's perception and understanding of an area such as personal status is informed by a sensibility that is different from that of a Muslim.

Accordingly, a treatment of *The Islamic Law of Personal Status* by an Arab with Dr. Nasir's distinguished credentials is particularly welcome. Member of the Jordan Bar and former Minister of Justice of that country, he practised before the Federal Supreme Court of Nigeria and appeared before International Tribunals. His present practice at the English Bar includes questions of Islamic law. His book is an important contribution. Although intended primarily for the practitioner, it contributes as well to general understanding of an area of law that is of special significance in Arabic society.

Arthur Taylor von Mehren
Story Professor of Law
Harvard University

PREFACE

This edition, like its predecessor, is a systematic account of personal status provisions under both the traditional Sharia Law and the modern enactments of Middle Eastern and North African States.

Since the first edition of this book was published, an enactment of personal status provisions has occurred in Kuwait, and this has been give adequate coverage in the relevant chapters of this edition, in order to complete the chain of modern enactments in most Arab States.

The encouraging reception of the first edition by legal practitioners and those concerned with the development of Islamic Law (especially in Muslim communities abroad), has been an incentive to undertake a revision, taking account of the Kuwaiti enactment and other amendments that have taken place since its publication.

It is my hope that the publication of this second edition in paperback may offer direct access particularly to students and universities, as well as to other institutions and interested persons. Both editions contribute to a general understanding in an area of law that is of special significance to the lives of millions of those of the Islamic faith throughout the world.

Dr Jamal J. Nasir
December 1989

Dedicated in gratitude and affection to my late father Jamil, as all his friends knew him, to my son, Khaled, in recognition of his distinguished academic achievements, and to my family

Chapter 1

Introduction

1. HISTORICAL DEVELOPMENT OF ISLAMIC JURISPRUDENCE

Islam is a major religion, promulgated by the prophet Muhammad in the 7th century AD. Within a century of the Prophet's death in 632 AD, early generations of Muslims of the Arabian Peninsula had spread, through conquest, the system of values of this nascent religion over a great part of the then known world. The boundaries of the new Islamic empire reached from Spain to India, through Central Asia.

Islam, which in Arabic literally means "surrender", provides that man should give himself to God, surrender his soul completely to Him, and leave everything in His Hands. This message fundamentally was the message revealed to every prophet, to be delivered to his own people throughout the history of mankind.

Today there are more than six hundred million Muslims,[1] drawn from a vast variety of races and cultures, extending West from the heartland of Islam to the shores of the Atlantic and East to the shores of the Pacific, bound by a common faith and a sense of belonging to a single community (*Umma*), a bond which dates back to the very beginnings of Islam.

From the days of the Prophet, Islam was not just a religion, but a complete code for living, combining the spiritual and the temporal, and seeking to regulate not only the individual's relationship with God, but all human social relationships.

The Prophet was at the same time a religious mentor, military commander, social reformer and political leader. In the words of the Quran, the Word of God was revealed to His Messenger for the guidance of mankind, to provide the heart of the Islamic faith and to lay the foundations of Islamic law and social order. The Quran sets down only

1 Art. "Islam" in *Encyclopaedia Britannica*, Vol. 9 (1979).

general rules and provisions, leaving elucidation and detailed judgments to the Prophet, as explained in the Quranic verse: "And we have sent down unto thee the Message that thou mayest explain clearly to men what is sent for them."[2]

Islamic legislation, or the Sharia, can be traced back to the migration (*hijrah*) of the Prophet and his followers in 622 AD from Mecca to Medina, where the nucleus of the Islamic state was formed. The Islamic calendar dates from the beginning of the hijrah, 1 AH, being 622 AD. At that time, the answers to particular questions or statements of legal decisions were made in the form of Quranic provisions as revealed to the Prophet. These provisions embraced matters related to ritual and worship concerning the next world, as well as rules related to this world, and dealing with domestic relations, civil obligations and punishments.

The Prophet and his Companions used *ijtihad*, that is, independent and informed opinion on legal or theological issues. These did not constitute *per se*, a juristic source, as they were always subject to confirmation or amendment through revelations, the sole source at that time.

The death of the Prophet (in 9 AH, 632 AD) ushered in the second phase of the development of Islamic law, covering the era of the Patriarchal Caliphs (9–40 AH, 632–661 AD). This was the heroic age of Islamic conquest, bringing the Muslim Arabs into contact with peoples of other races and cultures, thus posing questions to which no answers had previously been devised or sought. From personal status to the international level, questions arose concerning private matters of the family, contracts and obligations, and matters of public interest, whether political or administrative.

Since revelation as a source of legislation was no longer available after the Prophet's death, the Patriarchal Caliphs and the Prophet's Companions (*Sahaba*) used reasoned personal opinion in three ways:

(i) through the interpretation of texts, i.e. the Quranic verses and the Prophet's practices and sayings known as the *Sunna*;
(ii) analogy (*qiyas*), that is deriving judgment from similar cases ruled upon under the Quran, Sunna or previously established ruling by unanimity;
(iii) deduction from the spirit of the Divine Law in the absence of any text or analogy.

This gave rise to some divergence of opinion due to subjective and regional differences, e.g. the people of Medina settled disputes on the evidence of one witness and an oath of the plaintiff, while the people of

2 Sura Nahl, XVI, verse 44.

Egypt, Syria and Iraq would only allow the evidence of two men or a man and two women.[3] Nevertheless, such differences remained narrow.

An important feature of the reasoned opinion (*ijtihad*) made in this period was its empiricism. The pious Companions, conscious of the burden of responsibility involved in making legal judgments on any but factual questions, left aside all hypothetical issues. A leading early Kufi jurist, Ibn Abi Leila, is quoted as saying: "I met one hundred and twenty of the Prophet's Companions, and each one of them who narrated a saying of the Prophet wished that another Sahabi had narrated it, and each of them who gave an opinion wished that it had been given by another."[4]

Throughout the period of the first Islamic polity, in the city state of Medina, under the Prophet and the Patriarchal Caliphs, the fundamental unity between the spiritual and the temporal remained unscathed.

The advent of the Umayyads, the first dynasty in Islam (41–132 AH, 661–750 AD), saw the first distinction between the religious and the secular. The Caliphate, although retaining its spiritual title, gave way to the empire-state and the era of the formation of juristic doctrines and the recording of legal principles and general rules.

Islamic juristic thought reached its peak during that period, starting with the death of the last Companion in the last days of the Umayyad Dynasty and spanning the whole of the Golden Abbassi Era (from the 2nd to the 4th centuries AH, the 7th to the 10th centuries AD). Islamic jurisprudence became a discipline in its own right to which a new class of jurists devoted their lives, recording the general discursive rules and codifying the various juristic doctrines, based either on political grounds, as with the Shias and the Kharijites, or on scholarly research, as with the Hanafis and the Shafiis. Their rulings were derived from the texts of the Quran, the Sunna of the Prophet and from the specific circumstances of their regional environments.

Thriving juristic thought of this period went hand-in-hand with the development of other disciplines: the exegesis of the Quran, arranged and collected in a single book (the *Mus-haf*); the compilation of the Prophet's Traditions (*Hadith*) under stringent rules, to sort out the authentic from the forged; and the translation of Greek texts on philosophy and logic.

Various schools of Islamic juristic thought flourished, producing systematic doctrines which differed from one another according to their interpretation and knowledge of texts, their customs, social environments and their political allegiances. It must be stressed, however, that the founding fathers of these doctrines presented them as plausible, non-

3 Ibnu Qayyim Aljouzia, *Aalaam-ul-Muwaqqeen*, Vol. 3, p. 84.
4 Ibn Hazm, *Al-Ahkam*, Vol. 2.

binding opinions which ought not to be followed blindly or fanatically, and recognized the existence of other equally valid interpretations.

Unfortunately, this advice went unheeded in the next stage of juristic thought, known as the era of imitation (*taqlid*) and rigidity (*jumud*), from the middle of the 4th to the 13th centuries AH, the early 10th to the 19th centuries AD.

Independent juristic thought ceased and it was said then that "the door of ijtihad was closed". The imitative jurist became bound to a single doctrine from which he could not convert to another. A Hanafi scholar (*faqih*), Al-Karkhi, went so far as to say that "every Quranic verse or Tradition of the Prophet that goes against the opinion of our School shall be deemed liable to interpretation or altogether abrogated."[5]

Eventually the door of the ijtihad was re-opened during the 13th century AH, the 19th century AD, as the impact of the West was felt in Muslim society. The Traditionalists of the previous phase were regarded as being out of touch with the times. Modern juristic thinkers, such as Jamal-ud-din Al Afghani (1838–98) and his Egyptian disciple Muhammad Abdu (1849–1906), rebelled against stagnation and called for social and legal reforms. They disputed any paramount or exclusive authority of the basic doctrine of taqlid as embodied in the law recorded in the medieval manuals and claiming to represent the interpretation placed by the early jurists upon the Quran and the Sunna of the Prophet. Contemporary jurists claimed the right to interpret independently the original divine texts in the light of modern social circumstances. What classical jurists interpreted as a moral exhortation, e.g. in polygamy, was regarded by modern Islamic law-makers as a positive legal condition to be enforced by the courts.

A new pluralistic eclectic juristic stream developed, with the aim of choosing, from among the various schools, that best suited to the needs of modern Islamic society. This trend culminated in the compilation and enactment of the Mejelle or Ottoman Civil Code (1293 AH, 1876 AD). Made up of 1851 articles, it was based, in principle, on the Hanafi juristic school. It was not, however, restricted to that doctrine since it adopted provisions from the other schools which were deemed best suited to the people's interests and the spirit of modern times. It remained, until recently, the written civil code of Syria, Jordan and Iraq. Even with the enactment of new civil codes in these countries, the merit of the Mejelle lies in its concentration into 99 articles the essence of Islamic jurisprudence. These articles will be discussed in a later section under the heading of Islamic Legal Maxims.[6]

5 Ibn-ul-Atheer, *Al Kamil Fil-Tarikh*, Vol. 8, p. 106.
6 See p. 35 *et seq.*

Although the Islamic law courts, known as the Sharia Courts, have been abolished as a separate entity in Egypt and Tunisia, the original Islamic law, known simply as Sharia, is still applicable in its entirety in the Arabian Peninsula. It is Sharia law which is still in force in matters of personal law, including the law of succession and religious endowment (*waqf*) in all states with Muslim majorities except Turkey. New penal and civil codes based on European models have replaced the Sharia, which remains, nevertheless, a source of guidance to the secular courts in the absence of any specific legal provisions. Although there is no theory of contract proper in the Islamic Sharia, the principal rules implicit in a contract are compiled in general juristic rules upon which Western style modern civil codes are based.

The Scope of this Book

This book has been designed first of all as a practical manual for the practising lawyer. According to the definition in the Mejella, Islamic jurisprudence is "the knowledge of the precepts of the Divine Legislator in their relation to human affairs". It follows that its aim is to regulate the life of the individual, as a member of society and a citizen of the state. Therefore, Islamic jurisprudence falls into two major parts: worship and ritual (*ibadat*) and civil obligations (*muamalat*). The philosophy of ibadat provisions is that they are held to be perennial, immutable and valid for all societies and all times. They comprise the Five Pillars of Islam, namely: the profession of faith (*shihada*), the five congregational prayers in a day (*salat*), payment of the religious tax (*zakat*), fasting in the month of Ramadan (*siyam*) and the once in a lifetime pilgrimage to Mecca (*hajj*). They also embrace family law, namely that concerning marriage, divorce, parentage and inheritance.

The other major part of Islamic jurisprudence concerning civil obligations (muamalat) deals with the relationships between individuals and states and is considered liable to change according to custom, times and environment. It therefore corresponds to the civil and penal codes, constitutional, administrative and financial law and private and public international law.

These divisions were all treated on an equal footing in the classical works on Islamic jurisprudence and were deemed the most important and comprehensive concepts of Islam at the practical level. However, it transpires from historical surveys that the Islamic provisions dealing with civil obligations have been superseded in practically all contemporary Islamic States by new, positivist legislation, and are consequently now only of academic relevance.

Since the questions of worship and ritual are hardly relevant to a practical work on Islamic law such as this, there remains only family law and such other legal questions as are still governed, in modern legislation, by the Sharia, namely the will and religious endowments.

As a background to the detailed treatment of these subjects, it is necessary to give a glimpse of the Islamic juristic schools and the methodology of a *sui generis* system of legal thought.

This book shall, therefore, start with a section on the Islamic Schools of Law, followed by a section on Methodology. Family or Personal Status Law will be presented under the headings of Marriage, Dower, Maintenance, Dissolution of Marriage, The Iddat, Parentage, Rights of Children, Maintenance for Descendants, Ascendants and Collaterals, Guardianship and Rules of Inheritance. The last chapters will be devoted to the Will, the Religious Endowment (*waqf*) and Gifts (*hiba*) respectively.

2. THE ISLAMIC SCHOOLS OF LAW

A. The Origins of the Juristic Schools

During the lifetime of the Prophet, no controversy ever arose over either general principles, or the detailed particulars. Every question was decided either on the basis of Revelation or the personal opinion of the Prophet, later confirmed or rectified by Revelation.

The first controversy to arise concerning a principle related to the death of the Prophet himself. This had not been accepted by some until Abu Bakr, the first Patriarchal Caliph, read them the Quranic verse: "Lo! thou wilt die, and lo! they will die."[7]

The first controversies concerning practical matters related to the succession of the Prophet and the abstention by some tribes from payment of the religious tax (zakat). Both issues were settled through consensus and reasoned opinion.

The Companions of the Prophet, after his death, followed two separate trends when deciding on new questions from the Islamic legal point of view. The first trend, known as the Traditionalists, or the School of *Hadith*, adhered to the Quran and the Prophet's Sunna, refraining from judging any hypothetical problem. The other, known as the School of Personal Opinion (*Al-Raay*), advocated the interpretation of the texts and analogy derived from precedents.

These two trends developed into two major schools of juristic thought following the transition from the city-state to the empire, and contact with

7 Sura Zumar, XXXIX, verse 30.

other non-Arab cultures. The Traditionalists, concentrated mainly in the Hijaz – but also with minor centres in Kufa, Egypt and Syria – would never venture beyond the texts, often taken literally, and would consider any personal opinion as heretic. They used to decide on any question by recourse to the Quran, then the Sunna of the Prophet. When they came across conflicting rulings by the Prophet, they would opt for those attributed to the most authentic narrator, failing which they would refrain from judgment. This school did not survive its founder, Az-Zahiri, who died 270 AH (880 AD).

The School of Personal Opinion (*Al-Raay*) flourished mainly in Iraq, which was also the birth-place of the Shia and the Kharijis. Their thesis was that the Divine Law, the Sharia, was completed before the death of the Prophet, by which time it had been completed and made clear, and that it is a rational system based on solid principles and logical causes which explain and regulate the Sharia rulings. They set themselves to the task of identifying those principles and causes to infer judgment on problems whether actual or hypothetical. On the other hand, they were meticulous to ascertain the authenticity of the Prophet's precedents lest they would found any ruling on a false tradition.

Although the jurists agreed broadly on the four sources of the Sharia, namely: the Quran, the Sunna, analogy and consensus, they differed widely in their interpretation of the texts, in the value they attached to analogy and in their definition of consensus, e.g.:

(i) a word in a text may mean different things;
(ii) it may be taken literally or metaphorically;
(iii) there may be some conflict between textual rulings in which case the jurist would adopt the later ruling, if known, or opt for one and dismiss the other, according to his personal discretion;
(iv) a text may be made absolute or confined to certain circumstances or conditions.

As for analogy, the jurists differed on its value in relation to a saying of the Prophet of which there was only one report. They also differed on its pemises derived from the savings and acts of the Prophet's Companions, as to whether they were desirable or in the public interest.

They also differed on the definition of consensus, whether it was that of the jurists of Medina at a given time or the jurists of the Islamic Community (Umma) as a whole at a given period.

Custom and social environment also had a role in the controversy between jurists. But perhaps the most important factor was the political differences which gave rise to the three main doctrines of Islamic legal thought, namely: the Sunnis, the Shias and the Kharijis.

B. The Islamic Juristic Schools

(1) Introduction

After the death of the Prophet, one group of Muslims maintained that His successor should be His cousin and son-in-law, Ali ibn Abi Talib, and that succession should remain in the Prophet's family. However, on the order of Ali himself, they accepted the Caliphate first of Abu Bakr and after him of Omar. The dispute was renewed on the election of Uthman, and after his assassination, war broke out between the supporters of Ali and their opponents who supported Muawiya, then Governor of Syria. Ali himself was assassinated and Muawiya founded the first royal dynasty in the history of Islam, the Umayyads. The disputes between the various groups moved to the realm of logical arguments and speculation which centred to begin with on the principles of the faith, giving rise to such philosophical doctrines as the *Jabria* (Determinism), the *Salafia* (Traditional Fundamentalism) and the *Mutazila*, the rationalist Islamic philosophers. These, especially the latter, represented the most authentic Islamic philosophy, but precisely because of their almost exclusively theological bearing, they fall outside the scope of the present work.

Clearly related to our subject matter, however, are the polemics, dealing with essential juristic provisions, connections with those political events, such as the *Imamat* (leadership of the community) the qualifications of the *Imam* (leader) and rulings on dissidents, sinners and belligerents – leading to fully developed juristic schools.

In the following sections, we shall start with those schools which owe their origins to the political disputes, namely the Kharijis, the Abadis and the Shias, and then deal with the mainstream of juristic Islamic thought, namely the Sunni schools, born of methodical research, inference or meticulous observance of the traditional texts.

(2) Kharijis

In the war between Ali and Muawiya, Ali's army consisted mainly of undisciplined and anarchic tribesmen, while Muawiya commanded the best and most disciplined army of the empire. Facing defeat in the Battle of Siffin, Muawiya ordered his troops to raise copies of the Quran on their spears, pleading for arbitration. The majority of Ali's followers opted for acceptance, as the war was for the upholding of the Word of God. A minority refused, believing this to be a military ploy. When Ali, under pressure, agreed to arbitration with his enemy, the defiant troops, the Kharijis (Seceders) left his party to oppose both him and Muawiya, on the grounds that accepting arbitration would imply that the justice of their cause was in doubt, while they fought in the firm belief that it was just.

The Kharijis founded a revolutionary party on the religious precept "to enjoin what is just and forbid what it evil"[8] both in word and in deed, is the duty of every Muslim. Their doctrine may be summed up by two fundamental tenets:

(i) The theory of caliphate: The Caliph shall be elected freely by all Muslims, regardless of his race, even if he is a slave. There shall be as many Caliphs as the countries they rule. The elected ruler shall have no right to abdicate or resort to arbitration. Should he err or deviate from the religious precepts, he shall be dismissed. Their theory of the state derives from the principle that political power belongs to God and therefore cannot be passed on by any person to his heirs. The Kharijis constitute the Islamic sect most rigorously against monarchy and hereditary rule.
(ii) The observance of the religious imperatives is an integral part of the Islamic faith. Those who believe in God and in the mission of His Prophet, but who fail to obey the religious injunctions, are deemed to be infidels.

The Kharijis further maintain that ritual purity, which is a precondition for performing religious rites, should be both physical and spiritual. A lie, slander or malice would render one's ablution void, causing one to be ritually unclean.

The Kharijis are the only Islamic sect to reject the stoning to death of adulterers, confining the penalty to flogging, pursuant to the general Quranic ruling: "the adulteress and the adulterer, flog each of them with a hundred stripes."[9]

On marriage, they confine the prohibited degrees on grounds of fosterage (suckling a child) to foster-mothers and foster-sisters as decreed in the Quran,[10] and on *unlawful conjunction* (see Chapter 7.1.b.(1).(b).) they allow a man to be married to his wife's maternal or paternal aunt, a relationship forbidden under all the Sunni schools, but permitted subject to the aunt's consent, according to the Shias.

(3) The Abadis[11]

The majority of historians and writers on Islamic sects and doctrines consider the Abadis a sect of Kharijis, albeit the most moderate and the nearest to the Sunnis. Modern European orientalists and Arabists

8 Sura Tauba, IX, verse 71.
9 Sura Nur, XXIV, verse 2.
10 Sura Nisaa, IV, verse 23.
11 Spelt normally by modern European Scholars as Ibadis, *cf.* T. Lewicki, Art. al-Ibadiyya, in *Encyclopaedia of Islam.*

subscribe to this opinion, pointing out that the Abadis are the only surviving Kharijis. This claim, however, is most emphatically denied and even considered a libel by the Abadis themselves, who denounce the Kharijis as dissidents and heretics. True, like the Kharijis, they objected to arbitration in Siffin, but on different grounds. They maintained then that Ali, whom they considered the Legatee of the Prophet (*wasi-ya-nubouwwa*), by accepting the arbitration of men, abdicated the imamat, leaving a vacancy for which they elected Abdullah ibn Wahb Al-Rasi as the new Imam.

They derived their name from Abdullah ibn Abad At-Tamimi, who died in Basra, in the year 85 or 86 AH (702 AD). Theirs is the reigning doctrine in Oman and they have a considerable following in Tripolitania (the Djabal Nafusa), in Tunisia (the island of Djerbe), in Algeria (the Mzab) and in Zanzibar on the East coast of Africa.

They base their doctrine on the Quran, the Sunna and the consensus. They extend the Sunna beyond the sayings and deeds of the Prophet to include those of the first two Patriarchal Caliphs, Abu Bakr and Omar. To those three overriding sources they add analogy and inference where no text exists.

They believe that the Imamat is not an exclusive perogative of the Prophet's clan, Quraish, quoting the Quranic ruling: "The noblest of you, in the sight of God, is the best in conduct."[12] What they require of the Imam is justice, piety and strict observance of the edicts of the Quran and the teachings of the Prophet and his first two successors. Therefore the Abadis do not recognize the Immat of the Umayyad or Abbasi Caliphs, with the only exception of the pious Umayyad Caliph Omar ibn Abdil Aziz, whose son Abdullah is said by some Abadis to have been himself an Abadi. They acknowledge the multiplicity of the Imamat in various countries.

In theology, they are strongly against anthropomorphism, and adhere to the most abstract concept of God, under the Quranic verse, "Naught is as His likeness".[13]

They preach tolerance in war and in peace. Their conduct in victory over their foes is exemplary, observing strictly the edicts of Islam: no looting, no hot pursuit, no torture and no killing of the wounded. Unlike the Kharijis who deemed all their opponents as infidels, the Abadis allow marriage and inheritance between their members and the followers of other Muslim sects. The Abadis' independence of opinion, progressive thinking and tolerance towards their opponents are all epitomized in His Majesty Sultan Qaboos bin Said, the fourteenth monarch in the Al bu

12 Sura Hujurat XLIX, verse 13.
13 Sura Shura, XLII, verse 11.

Said dynasty, under whose inspiring leadership the Sultanate of Oman is making tremendous strides to achieve the best of western civilization and the revival of its glorious traditions.

The Zanzibar Abadi law of divorce allows a wife to apply to the court for the dissolution of her marriage on the ground of cruel treatment by the husband.

The Abadis allow a bequest to an heir subject to the consent of the other heirs. They order the mandatory bequest, i.e. a share of orphans in the estate of their grandparent, a reform adopted in the modern laws of Egypt, Syria, Morocco, Tunisia, Jordan, Iraq, Algeria and Kuwait.

They prohibit religious endowments except to mosques.

In general, they differ from the four Sunni doctrines only on comparatively trivial legal issues.

(4) The Shia

The Arabic word Shia literally means: followers, party, partisans or supporters. It occurs a number of times in the Quran with these meanings. Later, it came to mean the followers of Ali and the people of his House, as contradistinct from the Sunnis, who consider themselves the "orthodox" Muslim denomination, and regard the Shia the "heretical" denomination. Sunni historians and jurists trace the advent of Shiism as a religious movement to the war between Ali and Muawiya over leadership of the Islamic community which led to the establishment of the Muawiya's Ummayad dynasty in power. The Shias themselves trace their origins back still further to the controversy over the succession of the Prophet, in what is called the Al-Saqifa affair, when allegiance was paid to Abu Bakr as the first Patriarchal Caliph. Some Companions of the Prophet maintained that Ali, the Prophet's son-in-law, was the most suitable successor, relying on various arguments which included, *inter alia*, that Ali was appointed by the Prophet as the standard-bearer at many wars, and that he was the Prophet's deputy at Medina during the expedition to Tabuk when Muhammad said to Ali: "You are to me what Aaron was to Moses except that there will be no Prophet after me." Then, in his last public address to the largest gathering before his death three months later, Muhammad took Ali by the hand and declared: "He of whom I am the mawla (patron), of him Ali is also the mawla. O God, be the friend of him who is his friend, and be the enemy of him who is his enemy."[14] Ali's partisans, in order to preserve the unity of the community, reluctantly swore allegiance to Abu Bakr. The most distinguished among them were the so-called four pillars of the first Shia, namely Abu

14 Ibn Hisham: *Siratu Rasul Illah* (Cairo 1936).

Dharr ul-Ghifari, one of the earliest followers of Muhammad, an extremely pious ascetic; Ammar ubn Yasir, an early convert to Islam; Al Miqdad ubn Amr, one of the seven early converts to Islam; and Salman ul-Farisi, a Persian whom the Prophet ransomed from slavery and adopted as his mawla and member of his family.[15]

The term Shia was first used in the document of arbitration at Siffin, the last battle fought between Ali and Muawiya to denote the "party of Ali" (Shiat Ali or al-Alawiyya), their opponents the "party of Uthman" (Shiat Uthman or al Uthmaniyya) and the Syrians (ahl ash-Sham or Shiat Muawiya). Shiat Ali consisted of Ali's small personal following who always considered him the most worthy person to lead the Community after the death of the Prophet, together with other groups who supported him for other than religious reasons. Later, Shia scholars classified Ali's supporters into four ranks: Al-Asfiyaa, "the sincere friends"; Al-Awliyaa, "the devoted friends"; Al-As-hab, "the Companions"; and Shurtat al-Khamis, "the chosen ones". A zealous personal party, fervently believing that in Ali was to be found truth and guidance, and which had sworn "to befriend those whom Ali befriended and to antagonize those to whom he was hostile", secured the survival of Shiism in spite of the numerous political defeats inflicted on the movement over the years.[16]

The Shias maintain that Islam has, from the very beginning, been both a religious discipline and a serious political system. The Imamat is believed to be a pillar of the faith based (according to Jafar al-Sadiq, the first elaborator of the Shia Ithna-Ashari doctrine and after whom the Jaafria or Ithna-Ashari school was named) on two fundamental principles: explicit designation (*nuss*) and knowledge (*ilm*). According to the first principle, the Imamat is a prerogative bestowed by God upon a person chosen from the family of the Prophet, who before his death and with the guidance of God, transferred the Imamat, by explicit designation, to a named individual descended from Ali and Fatima, the Prophet's daughter. According to the second principle, an Imam is a divinely inspired possessor of a special source of knowledge of religion, which can only be passed on before his death to the succeeding Imam. Thus, the Imam of the time becomes the sole authoritative source of knowledge in religious matters.[17]

The Shias are unanimous that the first Imam, as explicitly designated by the Prophet, was Ali, from whom the Imamat passed in a similar way to Hassan, then Hussein, then Hussein's son, Ali Zain el-Abedeen. Thereafter the Shias diverge into a number of sects: the Zaidia, Ithna-Ashari and Ismailiyya.

15 Jafri, *The Origin of Shia Islam*, pp. 52–53.
16 *Ibid.* p. 97.
17 *Ibid.* pp. 290–292.

(a) The sect of Zaidia maintains that the Imam of their time was Zaid, son of Ali Zain el-Abedeen and great grandson of Ali. Of all the Shia Schools, they differ least from the Sunnis, only diverging on certain matters. For example, they consider the animal slaughtered by a non-Muslim ritually unclean; and they prohibit marriage of a Muslim male to a Christian or Jewish woman, quoting the Quranic prohibition: "Hold not to the guardianship of unbelieving women."[18]

Unlike the other Shias, they do not allow *muta* (temporary) marriage.

On the Imamat, they allow the validity of the proclamation of an Imam, even if another candidate appears to be better. Unlike the Ithna-Ashari, they do not require any explicit designation. To them, a sufficient qualification for any eligible Imam is to be descended from Fatima, the Prophet's daughter, to be an independent scholar, and courageous enough to revolt against the ruler claiming the Imamat for himself. They also differ from the Ithna-Asharis in that there is no specified number of Imams, and the Imam must be identified by his description and attitudes.

The Zaidi are mainly concentrated in the Yemen where their Imams combined both spiritual and temporal leadership until they were ousted in the 1961 revolution.

(b) The Ithna-Ashari. By far the largest Shia denomination, they derive their name (the Twelvers) from their belief in twelve Imams who were, in chronological order:

(i) Ali ibnu Abi Talib (d. 40/661)
(ii) Hassan (d. 49/669)
(iii) Hussein (d. 61/680)
(iv) Ali ibn-ul-Hussein (Zainul Abideen) (d. 95/714)
(v) Muhammad ul-Baqir (d. 115/733)
(vi) Jafar us-Sadiq (d. 148/765)
(vii) Musa al-Kazim (d. 183/799)
(viii) Ali ar-Rida (d. 203/818)
(ix) Muhammad ul-Jawad at-Taqi (d. 220/835)
(x) Ali an-Naqi (d. 254/868)
(xi) Al-Hassan ul-Askari (d. 260/874)
(xii) Muhammad ul-Mahdi (al-Quaim and Al-Hudjdja) (entered major occulation in 329/940)

The twelfth Imam is believed to be still alive to return towards the end of time to fill the world with truth and justice.

A main methodological difference between the Shias and the Sunnis, which reflects the difference between their idealism and pragmatism

18 Sura Mumtahana, LX, verse. 10.

respectively, is their attitude towards consensus and analogy. The Shias, unlike the Sunnis, do not recognize qiyas as a source of legislation. This is related to their Imamat doctrine. The Shia Imam has three functions:

(i) the rule over the Community of Islam;
(ii) to explain the religious sciences of the law; and
(iii) to be a spiritual guide to lead men to an understanding of the inner meaning of things.

Because of this triple function, he cannot be elected as a spiritual guide and can only receive his authority from above. The Imam must be infallible (*masum*) in order to be able to guarantee the survival and purity of the religious tradition.[19]

The Imams acted directly when they were living among their followers to instruct them directly. During the major occulation of the last hidden Imam, the Shia Divines, on his behalf and under his putative guidance, interpret the law and doctrine.[20]

The Shias differ from the Sunnis on the details of inheritance. Some differences are major, others are minor and there is total agreement on certain topics. On divorce, the Ithna-Asharis consider that for it to be valid, a divorce should be pronounced in the presence of two honest witnesses, according to the Quranic ruling: "Either take them back on equitable terms or part with them on equitable terms and take for witness two persons from among you endowed with justice".[21]

Moreover, three pronouncements of divorce in the same sitting are regarded by the Ithna-Asharis as a single pronouncement.

On contracts, they stipulate them to be in Arabic for those who know the language.

On inheritance, they allow a Muslim to inherit from a non-Muslim, but not vice versa.

On marriage, they allow the marriage of a Muslim male with a Christian, Jewish or magi woman, although they consider it detestable (*makruh*). They allow the muta, or temporary marriage, to a woman free of any legal impediment, under a binding contract and for a fixed dower, giving effect to entitlement of the offspring to inheritance and the wife counting her *iddat* (waiting period) on the expiry of the contract during separation or before it.

The Ithna-Ashari doctrine has been the state religion in Iran since the 16th century AD (10th century AH). It has considerable following in Iraq, Lebanon, Syria, Pakistan and Afghanistan.

19 Art. "Ithna-Ashari" in *Encyclopaedia of Islam*.
20 *Ibid*.
21 Sura Talaq, LXV, verse 2.

(c) The Ismailiyya. Of all the minor Shia sects, the most important is that of the Ismailis who broke away from the Shias during the 8th century AD (2nd century AH) over the successor to the Imamat. They agree with the Ithna-Ashari on the first six Imams, but differ on the seventh Imam. They uphold the claims of Ismail, who was the elder brother of the main Shia Imam, the seventh Imam, Musa al-Kazim ibn Jafar, and whom the Twelvers disqualified for drinking wine. They introduced into Islam a number of esoteric doctrines, such as the belief in the successive incarnations of God and in the transmigration of souls. They hold that these beliefs are matters of faith and above human discussion. Like the Twelvers, they hold the Imam to be infallible. During the 10th century AD (4th century AH), the Ismaili Fatimid Dynasty established a prosperous empire in Egypt. Today, the Ismailis owe religious allegiance to the Agha Khan, a descendent of Ismail, and they are now found in Pakinstan, Eastern and Southern Africa, and in parts of the Middle East. Although the penultimate Agha Khan (1887–1957) took steps to bring his followers closer to the main body of the Muslims,[22] there is a peculiar dearth of Ismaili legal texts available, and their practices will not be dealt with in this book.

(5) The Sunnis

The Sunnis, the "Traditionalists" or the "orthodox Muslims", constitute the mainstream of Islamic theology and jurisprudence. They believe they are the exponents of the original and unadulterated Islamic orthodoxy as revealed in the Quran and in the traditions and precedents set by the Prophet and his Companions, and as elaborated by the great early Islamic thinkers. Under this broad paradigm, two trends have been already referred to (see above) namely the two schools of reasoned opinion and of the manifest text, with a broad spectrum of doctrines between the two systems.

During the Heroic Age of Islamic Juristic Thought, numerous schools flourished, but others disappeared. Only four Sunni Schools have survived to this day. They are the Hanafis, the Malikis, the Shafiis and the Hanbalis.

(a) The Hanafis. Named after Abu Hanifa Al-Numan, (80–150 AH circa 700–767 AD), this doctrine spread during the Abbasid Dynasty and was the official doctrine under the Ottoman Empire and thereafter in Egypt, Syria, Jordan, Palestine, Lebanon and the Sudan. It is followed by the Muslim population of Turkey, Albania, the Balkans, Caucasus, Afghanistan, Pakistan, China, India and Iraq.

22 Art. "Islamic Theology and Philosophy" in *Encyclopaedia Britannica*.

Abu Hanifa was meticulous about the ascertaining of the authenticity of any tradition attributed to the Prophet, making ample use of analogy and "Istihsan", i.e. giving preference to a rule other than the one reached by the more obvious form of analogy. His juristic research was not confined only to factual questions, but included hypothetical cases. "Legalistic devices" (*Hiyal Shariya*) are an essential characteristic of his doctrine used in an attempt to compromise between the legal, the ideal and the real, to bridge the gap between jurisprudence and reality, stressing the fundamental pragmatism of his own doctrine and that of the Sunni doctrines in general.

Abu Hanifa refused the highest judicial office in spite of tremendous pressures from the Caliphs. But his closest disciple Abu Yusuf Yaqub bin Ibrahim Al-Ansari (113–183 AH, circa 730–798 AD) reached the office of the Chief Justice. He amalgamated the Hanafi School of Opinion and the Hijazi School of Tradition, his judicial experience providing the link between theory and practice and helping to propagate the Hanafi doctrine within the judicial offices, until then almost exclusively monopolized by Hanafi jurists. He was the author of many books of which two are still available: *A Critique of Auzaii*, an exponent of the School of Tradition, and *A Treatise of Kharaj* (the land tax) written on the orders of the Caliph Harun ur-Rasheed.

Muhammad bin al-Hassan Ash-Shaybani (132–189 AH, circa 750–805 AD) was another eminent Hanafi scholar who understudied Abu Hanifa. He then studied jurisprudence and traditions with Malik in Medina for over three years. Like his teacher, Abu Yusuf, he combined the two schools of personal opinion and tradition. He also benefited from his judicial career, contributing most to the compilation of the Hanafi system of jurisprudence in spite of differences of opinion between the three scholars within the school.

Later jurists referred to Abu Hanifa and Abu Yusuf as "the two masters" (*ash-shaikhan*) and to Abu Hanifa and Muhammad as "the two extremes" (*at-tarafan*) and Abu Yusuf and Muhammad as "the two friends" (*as-sahiban*).

(b) The Malikis. This doctrine was named after its founder, Malik bin Anas, (93–179 AH, circa 712–195 AD). The Maliki doctrine is today widespread in Egypt, the Sudan, North and West Africa and the eastern central part of Arabia. At one time it was followed in Andalusia, Spain, due to the fact that most of Maliki's disciples were Egyptian scholars who attended his lessons in Medina and after returning to Egypt, moved later to North Africa and then to Spain.

Although Medina lost its political importance when the seat of government moved first to Damascus and later to Baghdad, it retained its predominance as a seat of learning since it was the original domicile of the Prophet's Companions, Ansar and Muhajireen, and the dwelling place of the traditionalists of whom the most eminent were 'Aisha, the Prophet's widow, and his Companions Abdullah bin 'Abbas, Abdullah bin Omar and Zaid bin Thabit.

The sources of the doctrine were the Quran, the Prophet's Traditions, consensus and analogy. The Malikis' conception of consensus differed from that of the Hanafis, in that they construed it as the consensus of the community represented by the people of Medina. They held precedents set by the Medinites above the single source traditions and analogy, to which they also preferred the ruling by the Companion deemed to be an authority on the subject.

Malik made extensive use of sayings (Hadith) and did not assign to analogy the status accorded thereto by the Hanafis, often deriving his rulings from the principles of public interest (*istislah*), the Hanafi (*istishab*), and a strong pragmatism. Maliki reasoned opinion was not, therefore, confined to analogy.

The difference between the doctrines of the Malikis and the Hanafis is one of degree, not of nature. They both used tradition and reasoned opinion, but with variable stress and to differing extents. Both schools tolerated divergence of opinion within their doctrines.

(c) The Shafiis. The doctrine of the Shafiis was named after Muhammad ibn Idris Ash-Shafii (150–204 AH, circa 767–820 AD). The Shafii was the first juristic system to be based on clear principles and distinct methods. It represents a middle course between those renouncing personal opinion and those who follow it blindly, with a slight preference for the traditions. It spread in Jordan, Palestine, Syria, the Lebanon and Yemen, and has a large following in Egypt, Indonesia, the Philippines, Brunei, Darussalam, Singapore, Malaysia, Thailand, Sri Lanka and the Maldives.

Ash-Shafii, a pupil of Malik, wrote the first book ever on the principles of Islamic jurisprudence called *Ar-Risala* (The Epistle). To him, the paramount sources are the Quran and the Sunna, failing which it is analogy thereon. Should a tradition of the Apostle of God be narrated as authentic by generation after generation, then it is the conclusive ruling. Consensus overrules a tradition narrated by a single authority. A tradition shall have its manifest meaning attributed to it and, if liable to multiple interpretations, the nearest to its manifest purpose shall prevail. Of conflicting traditions of apparently equal validity, the most authentically attributed shall prevail.

(d) The Hanbalis. Named after Ahmad ibn Hanbal (164–241 AH, circa 780–850 AD), some historians did not consider this doctrine a juristic

system, but described ibn Hanbal as a Traditionalist. Yet, considering the answers he gave to juristic questions put to him, compiled in a book entitled *Masail* (Questions), these do reveal a juristic doctrine with an independent method and original principles.

Although fundamentalist to the extreme in its rigidity in matters of ritual, this doctrine is equally noted for its tolerant approach to transactions, advocating allowance or non-prohibition in the absence of any text to the contrary.

The Hanbali School did not enjoy the popularity of the preceding three Sunni doctrines for a combination of reasons, among them the exclusion of its exponents from power and judicial office, a reluctance to give personal opinion, a rejection of analogy (which they only used as a last resort when all other sources failed) and their fanatic intolerance towards other doctrines.

Later, some Hanbali leaders, such as Ibn Taymiyya (died 728 AH, circa 1328 AD) and Ibn Qayyim Al-Jouzia (died 751 AH, circa 1350 AD), did exhibit tolerance and gave personal opinion. They made Hanbali teachings known to the people, especially in matters of transactions.

During the 12th century AH, 19th century AD, Muhammad Ibn Abdul Wahhab revived the Hanbali doctrine in Najd and spread it in Hijaz in the Arabian Peninsula. The Hanbali teachings are today the official doctrine of the Kingdom of Saudi Arabia.

Hanbalism derives its provisions from the Quran and the Sunna, prevailing over any consensus, opinion or inference. It acknowledges without question an opinion given by a Companion of the Prophet if there is no dissention, otherwise the opinion of a Companion nearest to that of the Quran or the Sunna shall prevail. Quite often the Hanbalis do not indicate a preference where there were conflicting rulings by the Companions, but declare them all potentially valid. Traditions of the Prophet, according to the Hanbalis, are either valid or exhibit varying weaknesses which are nevertheless acknowledged.

3. THE METHODOLOGY OF ISLAMIC JURISPRUDENCE

A. The Usul and the Fiqh

Islamic Jurists distinguish between the *usul* and the *fiqh* proper. The usul (singular: *asl*) are the "roots" or theoretical bases of Islamic law which lay down the method to be followed by scholars to infer judgment from their premises and to assess the degree of strength and weakness of the premises. The fiqh is the body of legal provisions based on those methods. The Maliki jurist Ahmad bin Idris al-Qarafi (died 684 AH, 1300 AD) distinguishes between two sections of the principles of Sharia, the methodology defined above and the universal legal rules which are a body of the analogous maxims inferred inductively from particular legal provisions, as the common principle or legal criteria from which they are derived.

In this section, we deal first with the roots of Islamic law, followed by an enumeration of the general legal maxims.

B. The Roots of Islamic Law

These roots have been repeatedly referred to in connection with the historical development of Islamic law and schools of Islamic legal thought. They are the Quran, the Sunna, consensus and personal opinion. They are believed by jurists to be shown in their entirety in the Quran. The first source, the Quran, is referred to in the verse: "So judge between them by what God hath revealed."[23] The Sunna as a source is referred to in the verse: "Whatsoever the Apostle giveth you, take it, and whatsoever he forbiddeth, abstain from it."[24] Consensus is mentioned as a source in the verse: "And whoso opposeth the Apostle after guidance hath been revealed to him and followeth other than the believers' way."[25] Personal opinion and reasoning are implied in the verse: ". . . that thou mayest judge between mankind by what God showeth thee."[26] One specific form of personal opinion, Istihsan, is referred to in the verse: ". . . therefore give good tidings to my bondmen who hear advice and follow the best thereof."[27] General usage is advised in the verse: "Hold to forgiveness and enjoin general usage. . . ."[28]

While generally accepted by virtually all schools of Islamic juristic thought, these sources are interpreted differently, especially the sayings (Hadith) and consensus (*Ijma*), as we will show in the following detailed sections on each source:

(1) The Quran

The Quran is believed by Muslims to be the living word of God revealed to His Prophet. Its wording is as sacred as the meanings it conveys.

23 Sura Maida, V, verse 49.
24 Sura Hashr, LIX, verse 7.
25 Sura Nisa, IV, verse 115.
26 *Ibid.* verse 105.
27 Sura Zumar, XXXIX, verses 17/18.
28 Sura Afar, VII, verse 199.

Therefore no translation, however thorough, bears the same weight as the Arabic original: at best it can only be an honest rendering of the meaning. The Quran's conclusive authority and infallibility are beyond question, as is its status as the first and most highly esteemed source of Islamic law.

The Quran was revealed to the Prophet, who was illiterate, in Mecca and Medina, over a period of 23 years, as pronouncements of precepts or replies to questions. It consists of 114 suras of 6342 verses, of which only 500 verses deal with the provision of law (*al-ayat-ush-shariya*); the remainder deal with beliefs and moral conduct. The Mecca suras, brief and concise, concerned cosmology, faith and moral education. The Medina suras, long and detailed, concerned legislation.

The wording of a Quranic ruling is either conclusive and binding (*qati*) allowing only one meaning, for example "a sixth" in the verse "and to his parents a sixth of the inheritance"[29] or contingent (*zanni*) as, for example, in the verse: "Women who are divorced shall wait, keeping themselves apart, three courses",[30] where the Arabic word for courses "*quroo*" could mean either menstrual periods or periods of menstrual purity.

The text may be taken literally or interpreted metaphorically. Literal interpretation is again divided into detailed (*mufassal*) and general (*mujmal*). The detailed enunciations are either perennial (*muhkam*) or abrogate (*mansukh*). The passage abrogating an earlier one is called *nasikh*. By these means, jurists were able to solve some of the contradictions in the Quranic precepts, the later revelations abrogating the earlier. The basic rule remains that only a Quranic statement may overrule another.

(2) The Tradition

The Tradition or Sunna is the second most authoritative source of Islamic legislation. Etymologically, the Sunna is the path trodden, beaten and made evident by the forefathers. It can be used in several connotations: there is the pre-Islamic Sunna, i.e. the precedent of normative custom which the Arabs were bound to observe and imitate, any deviation from which constituted an innovation that should be discarded (*bida*); there is the Sunna of the Patriarchal Caliphs, i.e. their administrative and legal acts which some jurists dispute as binding precedents. But the Sunna which is the second source of Islamic legal standards is, according to the Sunnis, the Sunna of the Prophet (*sunnatu-n-Nabi*) which, according to the Shia Ithna-Ashari, is extended, in addition to the Prophet's precedents, to the *Nahdj-al-Balagha* of the Imam Ali and the *Sahifa Sadjdjadiyya* of the Imam Ali Zayn al-Abideen.

The Prophet's Sunna is divided into: (i) verbal utterances of the Prophet (*sunna qualia* or Hadith); (ii) acts of the Prophet (*sunna filia*); and

29 Sura Nisaa, III, verse 1.
30 Sura Baqara, II, verse 228.

(iii) the tacit assent of the Prophet, i.e. his refraining from expressing disapproval on hearing or observing certain things said or done (*sunna taqririyya*).

Unlike the Quran, whose wording is binding and immutable, the wording of the sayings (Hadith) may change, although the meaning is binding and attributed to divine revelation. Here a distinction must be made between the content or subject matter of a Hadith and its authenticity – the source from which it derives its authority. Islamic jurists classify the Prophet's traditions into three degrees of certitude:

(a) Mutawatir, i.e. a tradition handed down through an uninterrupted chain of trustworthy witnesses. This is absolutely certain and recurs mostly in the Acts of the Prophet (sunna filia) but is seldom found in the verbal sayings. One such rare Hadith is "whoever deliberately tells a lie about me shall occupy his place in Hell."

(b) Mash-hoor, i.e. widespread. This differs from mutawatir in that a link in the chain by which it is handed down is missing. An example is a Hadith narrated by 'Umar and later cited as such by a chain of narrators: "Acts are judged by intention, and each shall receive according to intentions." Mash-hoor is a strong legislative source, carrying high probability if not certitude. Such example is the ruling on the bequest left unspecified in the Quran but later limited by the jurists under the Hadith: "One third and it is a lot."

(c) Khabar Al-Ahad, i.e. a Hadith attributed to the Prophet by a single witness. This constitutes the bulk of the sunna. The jurists differ over adopting this class of Hadith, but it is generally accepted subject to certain criteria. Ash-Shafi would reject any such tradition attributed by a single authority with the exception of Said ibn il-Musayyab. Malik would accept a one-source tradition if it were in conformity with legal use and custom in Medina, a position disputed by the majority of scholars. For the Hanafis, a one-source Hadith must fulfil three conditions:

(i) that the narrator himself shall abide therewith in his conduct;
(ii) that it shall not cover a recurrent topic, as it should then have been narrated by many Companions; and
(iii) that it shall conform with the Sharia precepts.

The rulings of the Sunna may be confirmatory, explanatory or complementary to the Quranic precepts.

(3) Consensus

Jurists differ on the definition of consensus as a source of legislation. The Ithna-Asharis and other Imami Shias restrict it to the agreement of their infallible Imams. The Kharijis would accept consensus only within their own community where they require unanimity. Some Hanbalis and their contemporary descendants, the Wahhabis of Saudi Arabia, together with the Zahiris, limit consensus to the agreement of the Companions of the Prophet. The Malikis define consensus as agreement, firstly of the Companions of the Prophet, and secondly of the two following generations, i.e. the scholars of Medina, known as "the followers" (*tabi-oun*) and "the followers' followers" (*tabiout-tabieen*), since these are held to be the most thoroughly acquainted with revelation.

However, common orthodox doctrine maintains that consensus is simply the general agreement of all scholars of the Islamic community living in a certain period after the era of the Prophet's revelation, without the requirement that this agreement is unanimous. This doctrine relies on a famous tradition of the Prophet which says that "My community will never agree to what is wrong." According to this definition, consensus must comply with four conditions:

(i) that it shall be the consensus of scholars, an essential requirement for whom is moral purity;
(ii) that the majority of such scholars shall agree to the legal opinion, allowing for a dissenting minority;
(iii) that the object of their agreement shall be a legal matter liable for reasoned opinion, relating to permissibility, prohibition, validity or nullity. It cannot relate to a secular matter such as the affairs of war, or to a matter settled by revelation, such as the life beyond, or a religious matter that has already been conclusively proven;
(iv) that it shall occur long after the death of the Prophet, since, had he agreed on the opinion in question, it would have become a tacit agreement (*sunnatu taqrir*), or had he disagreed it would have invalidated the consensus.

Consensus may be verbal, or by practical example, or by tacit agreement (*ijma-us-sukut*) which is acknowledged by the majority of Hanafis and Hanbalis but dismissed by the Malikis, Shafiis, most theologians and a minority of Hanabalis.

Consensus derives from the Quran, such as in the unanimous consideration of the grandmother as a prohibited degree under the Quranic ruling that mothers are a prohibited degree; or from the Sunna, such as granting the grandmother a sixth share of the estate, relying on a similar ruling by the Prophet; or from analogy, such as agreeing to the succession of Abu Bakr by analogy of the Caliphate to the leading of Muslims in prayers; or from the public interest, such as agreeing to the compilation of the Quranic texts in one volume.

In general, consensus is a conclusive argument in proving the existence of a law, or interpreting or abrogating it.

(4) Reasoning by analogy (qiyas)

While the previous sources are essentially conventional, deriving from divine revelation (the Quran and the Sunna) or by consensus (ijma), analogy (qiyas) is a process of individual logical reasoning, sometimes being referred to as personal opinion (*raay*) or reasoned inference (ijtihad). Islamic jurists define analogy as the deduction of a ruling on a case for which no provision is found in the Quran or the Sunna from a similar case for which there is such a provision, on the strength of a common factor. It has, therefore, four essentials (*arkan*): (i) the known case, the root (*asl*); (ii) the unknown case, the derivative (*fara*); (iii) the common factor, the reason (*illa*); and (iv) the known ruling on the root under a text or by consensus, extendable to the derivative (*hukm-ul-asl*). For analogy to be valid, it has to comply with three conditions: (i) that the common factor is the ground for the ruling; (ii) that the reason is identical in both cases; and (iii) that the ruling is general and not exceptional.

The authority of analogy is a matter of controversy among jurists. Some jurists reject it entirely, and even trace it back to the Devil who argued with God:

> "Then we bade the angels: Fall ye prostrate to Adam! And they fell prostrate, all save Iblis who was not of those who made prostration. He said 'What hindered thee that thou didst not fall prostrate when I bade thee?' Iblis said 'I am better than him. Thou createdst me of fire while him Thou didst create of clay.' "[31]

Among this school were the Zahiris and Al Bukhari, who included in his collection of Traditions two chapters devoted to "Those which adhere to the Quran and to the Sunna" and "Traditions relative to the disapproval of opinion (raay) and to the practice of qiyas".[32] The advocates of analogy, on the other side, invoked the Hadith when the Prophet sent Muadh ibu Jabal to the Yemen as the judge, and asked him: "How will you decide when a question arises?" The dialogue ran as follows:

> "According to the Book of God.
> And if you do not find the answer in the Book of God?
> Then according to the Sunna of the Apostle of God.
> And if you do not find the answer in the Sunna of His Apostle?
> Then I shall come to a decision according to my own opinion without fail."

31 Sura Araf, VII, verses 11 and 12.
32 *Saheeh-ul-Bukhari*, Vol. 9, pp. 113–126.

The Propet was delighted and said: "Praise be to God who guided the apostle of the Apostle of God to what pleases God and His Apostle."[33]

The bulk of Islamic jurists acknowledge analogy as a source of legislation although in varying degrees, the champions being the Hanafis, the least enthusiastic being the Hanbalis, who use it as a last resort, while the Malikis and Shafiis steer a middle course. The Ithna-Asharis accord analogy much more freedom, maintaining that the gate of ijtihad – reasoned personal opinion – is always open, although only to the scholars who, acting as the representatives of the absent Imam, re-interpret the Sharia in every generation according to its immutable principles and the actual situation of the community.

C. Islamic Legal Rules and Practices

Apart from the Usul, the basis from which Islamic law is inferred, Muslim jurists compiled a number of universal rules of jurisprudence (*al qaw-aid al-kullia al-fighiyya*), from which particular legal provisions may be deduced. The earliest Hanafis compiled 17 such rules, which were subsequently increased to 37 by al-Karkhi, who died in 340 AH (951 AD); then to 86 by ad-Dabbousi who died in 430 AH (1038 AD). The Egyptian Hanafi jurist, Ibn u-Nujaim, who died in 910 AH (1563 AD) reduced all universal legal rules to 6 fundamental maxims.

In order to provide the newly created tribunals with an authoritative statement of the Islamic law in matters of contracts and obligations, the Mejellet ul Ahkam al-Adliyya, that is the Compendium of Legal Provisions, referred to for brevity as the Mejelle, was codified in 1293 AH (1876 AD) as the Ottoman Civil Code. In the explanatory memorandum, the Drafting Commission, citing Ibn Nujaim, but remarking that his work was not followed up by later Islamic jurists and that many of the universal Islamic maxims were scattered in the various Islamic legal texts and often mixed with particular provisions of law, decided to compile the most general legal maxims by way of an introduction to the Code. The Mejelle contains 99 of such maxims of Islamic jurisprudence.

These maxims must be distinguished from general theories. They are simply yardsticks for the deduction of particular precepts within the general theories, such as those dealing with the contract, ownership, obligations and the like, which were not treated by the ancient Islamic jurists but are now the subject of research by contemporary scholars.

Although the Mejelle has been superseded by the national Civil Codes

33 Abu da'ud Sijistani, *Sunan-ul-Mustafa* (which is known as *Sunanu Abi Da'ud*) (Cairo, 1952).

of Syria, Iraq and Jordan, the general legal maxims constituting Articles 2–100 inclusive of the Mejelle are mostly included in the new Codes. We shall now deal with the most important of these maxims in the Mejelle, avoiding their overlapping, and showing, where applicable, when they appear in the respective Civil Codes. They can be grouped under five headings:

(1) Intention
(2) Proof
(3) Flexibility
(4) Injury
(5) Custom

(1) Intention

A matter is determined according to intention, that is to say, the effect to be given to any particular transaction must conform to the object of such transaction (Art. 2).[34] This is based on an authentic tradition that: "Deeds are judged by intentions and each shall get what he intends." It follows that should there by a discrepancy between the intention and the appearance, intention, if known, shall prevail. A particular application of this rule is Article 3: "*In contracts, effect is given to intention and meaning and not to words and phrases.*" The Mejelle cites the example that a contract for sale and subject to the right of redemption shall have the force of a pledge.

(2) Proof

Certainty is not dispelled by doubt (Art. 4). This is the general principle of proof and becomes Article 74 of the Jordanian Civil Code and 445/l of the Iraqi Civil Code. From this general rule the Islamic jurists derived the principle of *istis-hab* whereby "*A state of affairs known to have once existed is regarded as having persisted unless the contrary can be proven*" (Art. 10; Arts. 4, 75, Jordanian and 447, Iraqi).

Other Articles related to the same rule are: "*Freedom from obligation shall be deemed the original state of things*" (Art. 8; Arts. 73, Jordanian and 444, Iraqi). This fundamental principle finds a specific application in an authentic saying of the Prophet: "*Evidence is for him who affirms; the oath for him who denies*", a provision which forms Article 76 of the Mejelle (Arts. 77, Jordanian and 448/1, Iraqi). This principle is further elaborated in Article 77: "*The object of evidence is to prove what is contrary to appearance*; the object of the oath is to ensure the continuance of the original state" (Arts. 78, Jordanian and 448/2 Iraqi).

34 Mejelle. In this section the first Article in brackets refers to the Mejelle.

Under the same rule of certainty fall several other provisions:

"*No attention shall be paid to inferences in the face of obvious facts*" (Art. 13);

"*Where the text is clear, there is no room for interpretation*" (Art. 14; Arts. 215, Jordanian and 2, Iraqi).[35]

"*One legal interpretation shall not destroy another*" (Art. 16);

"*No statement is imputed to a man who keeps silence, but silence is tantamount to a statement where there is an absolute necessity for speech*"[36] (Art. 67; Arts. 95, Jordanian; 81, Iraqi; and 44/1 Kuwaiti);

"*No weight is given to mere supposition*" (Art. 74), supposition (*tawahhum*) being deemed weaker than doubt.

(3) Flexibility

Difficulty begets facility (Art. 17). The same rule is worded differently as "*Latitude should be afforded in the case of difficulty*" (Art. 18). The basic provision is derived from the Quran in various verses, e.g. "God intends every facility for you; He does not want to put you to difficulties."[37]

Several rules are inferred from this basic one:

"*Necessity renders prohibited things permissible*" (Art. 21; Arts. 222, Jordanian and 212, Iraqi);

"*Necessity is estimated by the extent thereof*" (Arts. 22; Art. 212, Iraqi);

"*Necessity does not invalidate the right of another*" (Art. 33; Arts. 63, Jordanian and 213/1, Iraqi); e.g. if a hungry person eats bread belonging to another, such a person must later pay the value thereof on being able so to do.

"*An act allowed by law cannot be made the subject of a claim to compensation*" (Art. 91; Arts. 3, Syrian; 61, Jordanian; 6, Iraqi; 4, Egyptian; and 4, Libyan).

Schacht describes this tendency as the "concerted action of interested parties", which is, according to the sociology of law, a primary source of law. While respecting the orthodox Sharia, it bestows on it a greater

35 The same principle is adopted, albeit in a different form, in the Civil Codes of Egypt, Syria, Libya, Kuwait and Algeria (Article nos. 150, 151, 152, 193, 111, respectively) reading as follows: "When the wording of a contract is clear, it cannot be deviated from in order to ascertain by means of interpretation the intention of the parties."

36 The same principle is again expressed in the Civil Codes of Egypt, Syria, Libya and Algeria. In a case in which an offerer could not, by reason of the transaction, in accordance with commercial usage, or on account of other circumstances, have anticipated a formal acceptance, the contract is deemed to have been concluded if the offer is not refused within a reasonable time. Failure to reply is equivalent to acceptance when the offer relates to dealings already existing between the two parties or when the offer is solely in the interests of the offeree. (Egyptian 98; Syrian 99; Libyan 98; Algerian 68).

37 Sura Baqara, II, verse 185.

flexibility and adaptability and supplements it in many respects. It allowed the use of *hawala*, or bill of exchange, and in general the hiyal, or legal devices, which is the use of legal means for extra legal ends that could not be achieved directly with the means provided by the Sharia.[38]

(4) Injury

"*No injury shall be committed nor shall be met by injury*" (Art. 19). This is an authentic saying of the prophet explaining the Quranic ruling "The recompense for an injury is an injury equal thereto, but if the person forgives and makes reconciliation, his reward is due from God."[39] Ideally there should be no injury, but should any injury be committed, it shall entail compensation equal in degree to the injury suffered. This is adopted in the Iraqi Civil Code (Art. 216) and the Jordanian Civil Code (Art. 62). From this general rule, many others follow:

"*Injury is removed*" (Art. 20; Art. 62, Jordanian);

"*An injury cannot be removed by the commission of a similar injury*" (Art. 25);

"*A private injury is tolerated in order to ward off a public injury . . .*" (Art. 26);

"*Severe injury is removed by lesser injury . . .*" (Art. 27; Arts. 65, Jordanian and 213/1 and 214/1, Iraqi);

"*Repelling an evil is preferable to securing a benefit*" (Art. 30; Arts. 64, Jordanian and 6, Iraqi).

A particular application of this provision is that "*When prohibition and necessity conflict, preference is given to the prohibition*" (Art. 46; Art. 4/1, Iraqi).

This is the basis of the whole concept of *Maslaha* which is defined as "the procurement of benefit and the avoidance of injury within the spirit of the Sharia", and sets concern for human welfare high above the logic of formal principles of deduction.

(5) Custom

Custom is an arbitrator (Art. 369). By custom here is meant current usage among people in their transactions. It is acknowledged by the Sharia, and jurists allow conventional conditions in contracts, even if they were not explicitly mentioned, provided that the custom in question does not conflict with the Sharia. This rule is cited in the explanatory memorandum of the Jordanian Civil Code, in comment on Article 2/3 dealing with custom and guideline to be followed by courts in the absence of a legal text and a Sharia enunciation. Several rules follow:

"*Public usage is conclusive evidence which must be observed in action*" (Art. 38);

38 Schacht, J. *An Introduction to Islamic Law* (Oxford, 1979), p. 210.
39 Sura Shura, XLII, verse 40.

"*No doubt that judgments shall vary with the change in the times*" (Art. 39; Art. 5, Iraqi);

"*In the presence of custom no regard is paid to the literal meaning of a thing*" (Art. 40);

"*Effect is only given to custom where it is of regular occurrence or when universally prevailing*" (Art. 41);

"*Effect is given to what is of common occurrence, not to what happens infrequently*" (Art. 42);

"*A matter recognized by custom is regarded as though it were a contractual obligation*" (Art. 43; Arts. 100, Jordanian; 186, Iraqi; 95, Egyptian and Libyan; and 96, Syrian);

"*Matter recognized by merchants is regarded as being a contractual obligation between them*" (Art. 44);

"*A matter established by custom is like a matter established by law*" (Art. 45).

Chapter 2

Personal Status in the Arab States

1. WHAT IS PERSONAL STATUS?

Personal Status, *Al-Ahwaal Ash-Shakhsiya*, is a recent legal term in Arabic, unknown to the classical Islamic jurists, and non-existent in all classical texts of Islamic jurisprudence. As recently as 1880, when the first version of the Sharia Courts Bill was issued, the Egyptian legislator used the phrase "matters of the Sharia", *Al-Mawaad-dul-Shariyya*, to refer to questions of personal status.

In fact, the very concept seems to have been unknown to the early Islamic jurists to whom the Sharia consists of two major divisions, beliefs on theology and human acts. The latter was divided again into rites and transactions to regulate acts between persons, such as contracts, marriage and kindred institutions, or acts dealing with property, e.g. sale and rent. The Shafiis make marriage and matters related thereto a category in its own right, alongside three other categories: rites, transactions and penology.[1]

The term was first known in Egypt in the 1890s in the title of a book *Sharia Provisions on Personal Status* by Muhammad Qadri Pasha, then an Egyptian Minister of Justice who had earlier compiled two other books on civil transactions and the questions of waqf, all three books based on the Hanafi doctrine. It was first used in Iraq in the Courts Bill of 28 November 1917, then in the Sharia Courts Act 1923 and the Basic Iraqi Law (Constitution under the Monarchy).[2]

The first definition of personal status was given on 21 June 1934 by the Egyptian Court of Cassation as follows:

1 As-Shafii, *Al Umm*, Vol. 5, *The Book of Marriage* (Cairo).

2 M. Naji, *Sharh Qanoon il Ahwal-ish-Shakhsiyya* (Baghdad, 1962), pp. 10–22; A. Karam, *Al Ahwal-ush-Shakhsiyya* (Baghdad, 1979), p. 5.

> "Personal Status is the sum total of the physical or family descriptions of a known person which distinguish him from the others and give legal effects under the law in his social life, such as being male or female, married, widowed or divorced, a parent or a legitimate child, being of full legal capacity or defective capacity due to minority, imbecility or insanity, being of absolute or limited legal capacity.
>
> As for matters related to property, they are all by nature real status questions. But the Egyptian legislator, finding that waqf, gift and will, all being contracts without consideration, are based on the religious concept of charity, includes them in the personal status issues. . . ."[3]

The verdict seems to defeat its own purpose for setting an objective criterium to distinguish personal from real status matters. It also fails to distinguish the status and the legal capacity which is in fact a consequence of the status.

The Iraqi legislator refrained from any definition of the personal status, and instead enumerated the questions related there in a limitative way. Inductively these questions are:

(i) the waqf: conditions; beneficiaries of their allocation; administration; and the guardian;
(ii) status, including being alive, dead, missing or absent;
(iii) legal capacity and the accidents thereto;
(iv) betrothal, marriage, prohibited degrees, registration and proof;
(v) marital rights and duties, dower and maintenance;
(vi) repudiation of marriage;
(vii) parentage and degrees of kinship;
(viii) custody and fostering;
(ix) maintenance of descendants, ascendants and other kin;
(x) guardianship, wills, acts taking effect after death and questions of inheritance.[4]

Many legislative provisions on the above (e.g. inheritance) are left to the classical Sharia texts.

The Tunisian Presidential Decree of 26/11/1376 AH, 26/6/1957 AD, Raid 51-57-19 enumerates the personal status questions as follows:

> "Personal Status shall include disputes over the status of the persons and their legal capacity, marriage, property dispositions between spouses, mutual rights and duties of the spouses, divorce, repudia-

3 Civil Cassation on 21/6/1934, Appeal No. 40J. Year 3, Published in *Al Muhamat*, year 13, p. 87.
4 M. Naji, *op. cit.* pp. 27–28.

tion and judicial separation, parentage, acknowledgement or disavowal of paternity, family and descendants relationships, maintenance duties among relatives and others, rectification of parentage, adoption, tutelage, guardianship, interdiction, attainment of majority, gifts, inheritance, wills and other acts taking effect subsequent to death, the absent person and the declaration of a missing person to be dead" (Art. 2).

2. THE PRESENT STATE OF LEGISLATION ON PERSONAL STATUS IN THE ARAB STATES

In the majority of modern Arab Islamic states, there is as yet no legislative enactment on personal status. The Sharia Law as compiled in the traditional legal manuals, is still formally applied in its entirety in most Arab Gulf States, Saudi Arabia, Yemen, Libya and the Sudan. We shall come back to that after a brief outline of the state of legislation in the rest of the Arab world.

In Egypt, as previously mentioned, the eminent jurist Muhammad Qadri Pasha compiled in 1893 *The Sharia Provisions on Personal Status*, a book of 646 Articles on marriage, divorce, gift, interdiction, wills and inheritance, all based on the Hanafi doctrine. For a long time the book was the standard textbook for Egyptian Islamic law students and a manual for the Sharia Courts, although it did not acquire the official acknowledgement of the State. A commission of Islamic law scholars published in 1916–1917 a draft code on marriage and divorce which met with a strong opposition and was shelved. Two decrees were promulgated: 26/1920 and 25/1929, which parted from the then adopted Hanafi law and adopted the rulings of other doctrines on some questions related to maintenance, iddat, divorce and separation on grounds of insolvency, absence of the husband and injury to the wife. A Presidential Decree No. 44/1979 was issued introducing new rulings on divorce, polygamy, maintenance, arbitration between the spouses, custody and guardianship of the children, thus giving the woman improved rights to divorce and maintenance. The Constitutional Court on 4 May 1985 declared that the said Decree was unlawful on the grounds that the State President had no lawful right to issue such a decree since there was no urgency to enact it. The People's Assembly, therefore, promulgated Act No. 100/1985 to take effect on the same date of publication of the Constitutional Court ruling of the non-constitutionality of Decree No. 44/1979, with only minor changes thereto. For some years now, the People's Assembly has been considering a draft law on marriage and divorce, but no decision has been taken yet.

In the Lebanon, with its complicated sectarian structure, each denomination has been accorded an autonomous juristic personality. Article 9 of the Lebanese constitution asserts:

> "The freedom of belief is absolute. The State, while paying homage to the Almighty God, shall respect all religions and doctrines, shall guarantee the freedom to conduct religious rites under the State's protection provided it shall not contravene the public order, and shall also safeguard for the citizens of whatever religion or sect, due respect of their Personal Status Code and their spiritual interests."[5]

The Lebanese Law recognizes the three major religions and their subdivisions. The Islamic sects include the Sunnis, the Shia Jaafari, the Shia Alawites, the Ismailis and the Druzes. Of these, only the Druzes have a Codified Personal Status Act of 1948 amended in 1959. For the Sunni and Jaafari sects Decree No. 241 of 4/11/1942 regulated the Constitution, the procedures and the judiciary of the Sharia Courts. One Article, 111, of the Decree specified the relevant applicable law as follows:

> "The Sunni judge shall give judgement according to the most authoritative opinion of the Hanafi Doctrine except in those cases specified in the Family Rights Act, promulgated on the 8th of Muharram 1336 AH, the 25th of October 1917, in which case the rulings of the said act shall be applied by the Sunni judge. The Jaafari judge shall give judgement in accordance with the Jaafari Doctrine, and the relevant provisions thereto of the Family Rights Act."

This latter Act had been promulgated by the Ottoman Sultan Muhammad Rashad on 25 October 1917, shortly before the collapse and the termination of sovereignty of the Ottoman Empire in the Arab countries and was never, therefore, enforced. Article 111 was thus a revival thereof. Although the above-mentioned Decree of 1942 was subsequently amended and then abrogated, the latest Act of 16 July 1962 retained the full text of Article 111 in a new Article 242.[6]

In Syria, a compendium of personal status provisions was promulgated under the Presidential Decree No. 59 on 17/9/1953. According to the Explanatory Memorandum thereof, the new legislation derived from five sources:

(i) the Customary Family Rights Law, on which court rulings were based;
(ii) the Egyptian law modified to suit the local conventions;
(iii) Qadri Pasha's *Sharia Provisions of Personal Status Questions*;

5 Quoted by Baylani, *Personal Status Laws in the Lebanon*, p. 12, n. 1.
6 *Ibid.* pp. 17–18.

(iv) an eclectic adoption by the Legislative Committee of rulings under doctrines other than the Hanafi;
(v) A Personal Status Law Draft by the Damascus Judge.

The Presidential Decree No. 59/1953 covered the subjects of marriage, divorce, parentage, custody, legal capacity, wills and inheritance. It was amended by the Law 34 on 31 December 1975 in respect of polygamy, the dower, fostering, custody, maintenance and guardianship. The said laws apply to all Syrians except the Druzes (Art. 307), and the Christian and Jewish Communities who shall apply their own religious provisions governing betrothal, marriage conditions and conclusions, wife's obedience, wife's maintenance, minor's maintenance, declaration of voidance and dissolution of marriage, dower and custody (Art. 308).

In Iraq the Sharia remained the general law of the land without any distinction between the personal status and the civil cases, until the last days of the Ottoman Empire, with the promulgation of the Mejelle, the Civil Code, which separated civil from personal status although it remained subject to the Sharia and especially the Hanafi School. Personal status matters were defined for the first time in the Provisional Sharia Procedures Act of 1336 AH (1917 AD) which made them the subject of the exclusive jurisdiction of the Sharia Court, to be decided according to the Sharia provisions. In 1917, a Declaration by the C-in-C of the British Army of Occupation, later amended in 1921, put personal status matters for the Jaafaris under the jurisdiction of the civil courts to be decided on according to the Jaafari doctrine, while retaining the jurisdiction of the Sharia Courts for the personal status cases of the Sunnis, again applying the Hanafi teachings.

In 1923 the personal status matters of the Jaafaris were referred to the jurisdiction of the newly formed Jaafari Sharia Courts, applying the Jaafari Doctrine.[7]

On 30 December 1959, the Personal Status Act No. 188/1959 was promulgated as the Universal Personal Law for all the Iraqis, except those for whom special legislation was made, the exceptions being the Christians and the Jews for whom special religious courts were established under the Religious Courts for the Christian and Mosaic Denominations Act No. 32/1947.

In the Explanatory Memorandum for the 1959 Act, it was noted that:

"the Sharia Provisions of Personal Status have never been compiled in a single code, selecting from the jurists' opinions those most acceptable and convenient for the times, with the Sharia judiciary basing their judgments on the classical jurisprudence texts, inferred

7 M. Naji, *op. cit.* pp. 14–15.

opinions on controversial issues and the decisions of the Courts in Islamic States."

This attitude was retained in the 1st Article of Act No. 188, asserting that:

2. "In the absence of any legislative provision to be applied, judgment shall be given under the principles of the Islamic Sharia most suitable to the provisions of this Act.
3. The Courts shall be guided by the rulings established by the judiciary and Islamic Jurisprudence in Iraq and the other Islamic States whose laws are akin to the Iraqi laws."

Act No. 188/1959 has since been amended by Acts No. 11/1963 and No. 21/1978.

In Jordan, the Personal Status Law was promulgated on 5 September 1976 as provisional law No. 61/1976 abrogating the previous Jordanian Law of Family Rights No. 92/1951 (Art. 186/1). It is provisional in the sense that it was issued under Article 31 of the Constitution in the absence of the National Assembly.

It refers to the most authoritative Hanafi opinion for recourse in matters not covered in the said Law (Art. 183). It deals with marriage and betrothal, marriage contract, the dower, repudiation, dissolution by order of the Court, iddat, parentage, fosterage, custody, maintenance for kin, and provisions concerning the missing person and the will. It leaves the details of inheritance provisions to the classical texts.

In Morocco, a royal commission was briefed in August 1957, to elaborate a Code of Islamic Law. The Commission decided unanimously to present a project of such a Code which was promulgated by a number of Royal Decrees, issuing a series of books dealing with personal status, the whole of which would constitute "The Code of Personal Status and Succession". The first two books on marriage (Arts. 1–43) and the dissolution of marriage (Arts. 44–82) were issued under Decree No. 1/57/343 of 22 November 1957, to take effect as from 1 January 1958. The same date was set for the application of the provisions of Book III on parentage and the consequences thereof, namely custody, fosterage and maintenance both for the wife and the relatives (Arts. 83–132) under Decree No. 1/57/379, followed by Book IV on legal capacity and proxy under Decree No. 1/58/019 of 25 January 1958, Book V on Wills (Arts. 173–216) under Decree No. 1/58/073 on 20 February 1958, and finally, Book VI on Succession (Arts. 217–297 under Decree No. 1/58/112 of 3 April 1958. These provisions apply throughout the Kingdom of Morocco, to the exclusion of any other rulings. Recourse is ordered to the most authoritative or best known and widest applied opinion of the Maliki jurisprudence in all cases which are not covered by the Code.

In Tunisia, personal status questions are governed by the Personal Status Mejelle promulgated on 6/1/1376 AH, 13/8/1956 AD, Raid 66-56, amended by Law No. 40 of 2/3/1377 AH, 27/9/1957 AD, Raid 19, to abrogate a separate personal status law for Jewish and non-Muslim Tunisians who are now subject to the same legislation. It deals with marriage (later amended by Act 1/1964), divorce (with additions under Act 41/1962 and 7/1981), iddat, maintenance, custody (as amended under Acts 49/1966 and 7/1981), parentage, the missing person, inheritance, majority and interdiction (as amended under Act 7/1981), wills (added under Act 77/1959), and gifts (added by Act 17/1964).

A decree of 20/12/1376 AH, 18/7/1957 AD, regulates the administration of estates. Act No. 27 of 12/8/1377 AH, 4/3/1958 AD, was issued in respect of public guardianship, sponsorship and adoption, and was later amended by Act No. 69/1959.

In Algeria, the Family Law No. 84/1984 was promulgated on 9 June 1984 dealing with marriage, maintenance, guardianship, inheritance, wills, gifts and waqf. It applies to all Algerian citizens and those residents in Algeria subject to the provisions of the Civil Code relating to conflict of laws (Art. 221).

Four weeks later, on 7 July 1984, in Kuwait, Law No. 51/1984 in the matter of Personal Status was promulgated by the Emir. Before that, the courts in the State of Kuwait used to apply the provisions of the Maliki doctrine in cases of personal status. The new Law is divided into three main parts: marriage (Arts. 1–212), wills (Arts. 213–287) and succession (Arts. 288–336). Under Article 343, recourse should be made to the most authoritative opinion of the Maliki doctrine in the absence of any provision, then to the general principles thereof. It applies to those who were governed by the doctrine of Imam Malik and to the non-Muslims of different religions or denominations; non-Maliki Muslims shall be subject to their respective doctrines (Art. 346).

As for the other countries, where so far no legislation has been enacted on personal status, e.g. in the Kingdom of Saudi Arabia, the Hanbali doctrine reigns supreme. In the absence of any formal act on personal status, the courts apply the Hanbali provisions according to classical works on jurisprudence.

In the Yemen Arab Republic, that is Northern Yemen, the Zaidi doctrine reigns and is applied by the courts without, again, any formal compendium.

In the People's Democratic Republic of Yemen, that is Southern Yemen, Family Act No. 1/1974 was promulgated, containing some provisions on marriage and dissolution of marriage which are not in conformity with the provisions of the Islamic Sharia.[8]

8 As-Sabooni, *The Family Institution*, etc., p. 26.

In the Socialist People's Libyan Arab Jamahiriyya, the Maliki doctrine is applied by the Sharia Courts. However, the authorities are now in the process of compiling a Personal Status Act to be eclectically based on all the doctrines of Islamic jurisprudence.

The State of the United Arab Emirates has drafted comprehensive legal provisions on transactions, criminal offences, procedures, labour, companies and personal status, all based on the Islamic Sharia. This constitutes the first legislative effort to see the light of day, although it has not yet been promulgated in the Arab States, in spite of less earnest attempts in some Arab countries to codify the Islamic Sharia.

The Personal Status Draft Act includes 555 Articles, and covers provisions on marriage, repudiation, parentage, fosterage, custody, wills, inheritance and maintenance. Although this draft has been ready since 1979, it has been referred to the Council of Ministers in 1982 with other draft Acts. Each draft is accompanied by an explanatory note to show the source of every Article, and the reference to be consulted to interpret such provisions in the Islamic jurisprudence of all doctrines. The last Article of the Personal Status Draft Act provides that, in the absence of any legal text, the Maliki doctrine shall apply, failing which the Hanafi doctrine.[9]

In the Sudan, although the people follow the Maliki doctrine, it is the Hanafi doctrine that is applied in the matters of personal status, except those specified under legislative circulars from the Chief Sharia Judge, in which other doctrines shall apply. Now, the Court of Appeal has replaced the Chief Sharia Judge under Article 6 of the Sharia Court Act for the year 1967, whereby the Sharia Court there shall rule according to the most authoritative opinion of the Hanafi jurists, except in matters on which the Supreme Sharia Court of Appeal issues judicial circulars to apply the Hanafi or other opinion in legislation. It is worthwhile to mention that the Sudanese Sharia Court are competent to rule on matters other than those of personal status according to the Islamic Sharia, if so requested by the litigants. The Chief Sharia Judge issued various circulars on marriage, divorce, gift, waqf, and inheritance, without there being a comprehensive compendium of all the provisions of personal status.[10] The former Sudanese President Numeriy tried to apply the provisions of Islamic Sharia in all matters, including penology. However the situation is vague now after another military take-over.

As early as 1977, endeavours have been made to codify a united Personal Status Law for all the members of the League of Arab States. After several congresses and committee meetings of the Arab Ministers of Justice, a draft Unified Personal Status Law for all the member states was

9 *Ibid.* pp. 26–27.
10 *Ibid.* p. 25.

worked out as a first step to promulgate it as a law by the individual states. It is mainly based on the Sunni, especially the Hanafi doctrine, with some additions in line with the latest legislations, especially in the matter of the mandatory will.

In view of the importance of such a project, although it has not yet been promulgated as a law, the complete translation of the draft with the Presentation Memorandum is included in an Appendix at the end of this book.

3. CONFLICT OF LAWS

Apart from Tunisia, conflict of laws in personal status matters is dealt with in the Civil Codes of Arab States which have modern personal status laws.

The Tunisian Legislative Order of 26/11/1376 AH, 24/6/1957 AD, Raid 51-57-19 as amended by Law No. 40 of 2/3/1377 AH, 27/9/1957 AD, Raid 19 rules under Article 1 that "Foreigners shall be governed by their National Law in matters of personal status". Under Article 4, it specifies the applicable law to settle a dispute between two ligitants of different nationalities according to the subject matter in the following manner:

(i) The respective personal status law of each party in matters of status, legal capacity and conditions of marriage.
(ii) The personal status law of the husband at the time of marriage in matters of mutual rights and duties of the spouses, property dispositions between spouses, divorce, repudiation and judicial separation.
(iii) The personal status law of the person liable for payment in matters of payment of maintenance.
(iv) The personal status law of the minor or person placed under interdiction in matters of tutelage, guardianship interdiction and majority.
(v) The personal status law of the father in matters of parentage, rectification of parentage, acknowledgement or disavowal of paternity.
(vi) The personal status law of the adopter and adoptee in matters of adoption.
(vii) The personal status law of the adopter in matters of effects of adoption.
(viii) The personal status law of the deceased, the donor and the testator in matters of inheritance, gifts, wills and other acts taking effect subsequent to death.

(ix) The personal status law of the absent person or missing person deemed to be dead in the matter of absence and the missing deemed tantamount to death.

Egyptian, Syrian, Iraqi, Jordanian, Libyan and Algerian Civil Codes, and the Kuwaiti Law No. 5/1961 in respect of Legal Relations Containing a Foreign Element, contain identical provisions, similar to the Tunisian, as for the applicable law in any case of conflict in the following fashion:

(i) The fundamental conditions relating to the validity of marriage are governed by the national law of each of the two spouses (Arts. 12, Egyptian; 13, Syrian; 19, Iraqi; 13/1, Jordanian; 12, Libyan; 11, Algerian). However, both the Iraqi and Jordanian Civil Codes (Articles 19/1 and 13/2 respectively) add that a marriage between two foreigners or a foreigner and a native citizen shall be deemed valid in form if it is concluded according to the law of the country where it is made or the laws of each of the two spouses. This provision has been adopted from Articles 6 and 7 of the Hague Convention of 13 June 1902.[11] The Kuwaiti law distinguishes between the material conditions for the validity of marriage, e.g. the legal capacity, the validity of consent and the conditions of freedom from any marriage impediments, which shall be governed by the national law of the spouses if they are of the same domicile, otherwise by their respective national law (Art. 36) and the formal conditions for marriage, such as solemnization and religious rites, which are governed by the law of the country where marriage was contracted, or by the national law of each spouse (Art. 37). The same Article adds that the said national law must be observed in respect of notice or publication of marriage, although the absence of such a notice or publication shall not render the marriage void in countries other than those whose regulations have been violated.

(ii) The effects of marriage, including its effects upon the property of the spouses are regulated by the law of the country to which the husband belongs at the time of the conclusion of the marriage (Arts. 31/1, Egyptian; 14/1, Syrian; 19/2, Iraqi; 14/1, Jordanian; 13/1, Libyan; 12, Algerian; 36, Kuwaiti).

(iii) Repudiation of marriage is governed by the law of the country to which the husband belongs at the time of repudiation, whereas divorce and separation are governed by the law of the country to which the husband belongs at the time of commencement of the legal proceedings (Arts. 13/2, Egyptian; 14/2, Syrian; 14/2, Jordanian; 13/2, Libyan; 12, Algerian). Iraqi Article 19/3 makes re-

11 Explanatory Notes to the Jordanian Civil Code, p. 45.

pudiation, divorce and separation subject to the law of the country to which the husband belongs either at the time of repudiation, or of commencement of the legal proceedings. Under Kuwaiti Article 40/5/1961, divorce is governed by the latest common nationality of both spouses during marriage and before divorce or separation action; otherwise, the husband's national law at the time of marriage shall prevail.

(iv) Notwithstanding the above provisions, the national law alone shall apply if one of the two spouses is a native citizen (Arts. 14, Egyptian; 15, Syrian; 19/5, Iraqi; 15, Jordanian; 14, Libyan; 13, Algerian; 36, Kuwaiti).

(v) Obligations as regards payment of maintenance to relatives are governed by the national law of the person liable for such payment (Arts. 15, Egyptian; 16, Syrian; 21, Iraqi; 16, Jordanian; 15, Libyan; 14, Algerian). Kuwaiti Article 45 adds that the Kuwaiti law shall govern temporary maintenance to such relatives.

(vi) The national law of a person who is to be protected shall apply in respect of all fundamental matters relating to natural and legal guardianships, receiverships, and other forms of guardianship of persons without legal capacity and of absent persons (Arts. 16, Egyptian; 17, Syrian; 20, Iraqi; 17, Jordanian; 16, Libyan and 15, Algerian; 46, Kuwait).

(vii) Inheritances, wills and other dispositions taking effect after death are governed by the national law of the deceased (the propositus), the testator, or the person disposing of property at death (Arts. 17/1, Egyptian; 18/1, Syrian; 18/1, Jordanian; 17/1, Libyan; 16, Algerian). Articles 47 and 48 of the relevant Kuwaiti Act concur, adding that the form of the will and other dispositions taking effect after death shall be governed by the law of the disposer at the time of disposition or of the country where it occurred. The same ruling applies to the gift (Art. 49). Iraqi Articles 22 and 23, while ruling that the law of the deceased or the propositus at the time of his death shall apply to the questions of inheritance and wills, make the following provisos:

(a) Difference of nationality shall not bar inheritance of movable and real property but no foreigner shall inherit from an Iraqi unless the foreign law allows an Iraqi to inherit from him.

(b) A foreigner who leaves no heir shall have his property in Iraq devolved to the Iraqi State notwithstanding any provision to the contrary under the law of the foreigner (Art. 22).

(c) The Iraqi law shall apply as to the validity of the will for and succession to the immovable property situated in Iraq and owned by a deceased foreigner (Art. 23).

(viii) As for legal capacity and status, the laws of all the above-mentioned Arab States are unanimous that it shall be governed without any exception by the law of the country to which the persons belong by reason of their nationality (Arts. 11/1, Egyptian; 12/1, Syrian; 18/1, Iraqi; 12/1, Jordanian; 11/1, Libyan; 10, Algerian; 36, Kuwait). This provision is valid even for the legal capacity for marriage, notwithstanding the case when one spouse is a native citizen as under (iv) above.

(ix) Under the Sharia, betrothal is not a binding contract between the two parties, it being only a promise to marry. This attitude is adopted by all Arab States except Kuwait, where Article 35 of Act No. 5/1961 reads as follows:

> "Betrothal shall be considered a matter of personal status, and shall be governed in terms of validity by the domicile law of the male suitor, in terms of effects by the domicile law of the suitor at the time of betrothal, and in terms of cancellation by the domicile law of the suitor at the time of cancellation".

4. THE METHOD FOLLOWED IN THIS WORK

It is quite clear from the above that the Sharia Law has not been abrogated even in those states which introduced recent legislative enactments. These recent texts sometimes referred to Sharia rules, e.g. on inheritance under the Iraqi Law. In other instances they selected the rules of a specific Sharia doctrine, e.g. the Hanafi in Syria and the Malakis in Morocco. Even in certain innovations, e.g. the prohibition of polygamy in Tunisia, some Sharia texts were quoted in support. The majority of Arab Islamic States still apply the Sharia Law in its entirety.

Therefore in the following chapters we shall deal with the basic Sharia rulings and cite the relevant legislative enactment where appropriate. In the light of the definition and enumeration of personal status questions, we shall treat the following subjects even if some are relegated in some countries to the respective Civil Codes:

> Marriage, Dower, Maintenance, Dissolution of Marriage, The Iddat, Parentage, Rights of Children, Maintenance for Descendants, Ascendants and Collaterals, Guardianship, Rules of Inheritance, Wills, the Religious Endowment (waqf) and Gifts (hiba), in that order.

Chapter 3

Marriage

1. DEFINITION

Marriage, according to the classical juristic definition, is a contract prescribed by the legislator, and it denotes the lawful entitlement of each of the parties thereto to enjoy the other in the lawful manner.[1]

The Tunisian Code omits the definition altogether. The Syrian, Iraqi and Jordanian Codes give an almost identical definition:

"Marriage is a contract between a man and a woman who is lawfully eligible to be his wife with the objective of joint life and procreation." (Arts. 1, 3/1/2, respectively).[2]

The Moroccan Decree elaborates more on the definition:

> "Marriage is a legal pact of association and solidarity between a man and a woman, meant to last, the objective thereof being to maintain chastity and lawful wedlock, multiplying the nation through founding a family under the patronage of the husband, on solid grounds, to ensure for the contracting parties the discharge of the responsibilities related thereto in security, peace, love and respect" (Art. 1).

The Kuwait Law No. 51/1984 defines marriage as "A contract between a man and a woman who can lawfully be wed to him, to the end of tranquillity, chastity and the strength of the nation" (Art. 1). In a similar vein, Algerian Article 4 reads "Marriage is a contract lawfully concluded between a man and a woman, the ends of which are, *inter alia*, the formation of a family based on love, compassion, co-operation, chastity of the two spouses and the preservation of legitimate lineage".

Marriage is therefore a civil contract, without the Christian notion of

1 Abu Zahra, *On Marriage*, p. 17; Abdullah, *Personal Status*, p. 23.

2 Unless otherwise stated, all Articles mentioned refer to the Arab Codes of Personal Status described in the previous chapter.

sacrament.[3] Still, it is a unique contract in that:

(i) the rights and obligations which derive from it are dictated by the legislator, and shall not be subject to any agreement to the contrary between the parties; and
(ii) in spite of their civil character, marriage contracts are mostly regulated under religious jurisdiction to impart upon their effects a character of sanctity.

There are substantial differences in the provisions of marriage between the two major streams of Islamic jurisprudence, the Sunna and the Shia, which we shall point out as we deal with the various headings.

2. PRELIMINARIES OF MARRIAGE

The prelude to the marriage contract is the betrothal (*khutba*), which is the request by the man for the hand of a certain woman in marriage, and the approach to her, or to her kin, with a view to describe his status, and to negotiate with them the subject of the contract and their respective demands in that connection.[4] For the betrothal to be valid, both parties should be aware of the circumstances of the other, and should know the potential spouse's character and behaviour in order that the contract may be valid, and the union it establishes be viable; the means of obtaining this information is through enquiries, investigations, consultations, and the meeting of the couple, provided that it shall not be without the attendance of a chaperon.

If the man's offer is accepted by the woman, or those who are legally entitled to act on her behalf, the betrothal shall take place, and would be a reciprocated promise of the man and the woman to marry in the future. Once betrothal has taken place, no other man shall be allowed to approach the woman with a view to betrothal knowing that the woman

3 Art. 1 of the Oriental Church Act 1949 for Syria and Lebanon reads as follows: "Marriage is a contract raised by The Lord Jesus to the sublime status of a sacrament. Therefore a valid marriage between two baptized persons is both a contract and a sacrament." An eminent Roman Orthodox Jurist Ibn-ul-Assal, wrote, "A marriage contract shall not be made or solemnized except with the presence of a Priest, his prayers for the two parties thereof, and his bestowing Eucharist upon them at the time of the Muptial Service whereby they are united and become one body. Otherwise it shall not be marriage. It is the prayer which renders women lawful for men and men for women . . ." *Al-Majmuu As-Safawi*, p. 40.

4 Betrothal is used in preference to the word engagement because it is a more conventional arrangement and, unlike the latter, does not entail, *per se*, damages on the breach thereof as will be explained in more detail later in the text.

has already been betrothed. This restriction is lifted should the previous betrothal be cancelled.

A. Conditions of Betrothal

Since the betrothal is a preliminary to a marriage contract, no betrothal shall be valid unless the woman is eligible forthwith for marriage. Therefore no betrothal can take place of a married woman, as it will then constitute the violation of the husband's right. The woman revocably divorced cannot be betrothed explicitly or implicitly as her married status still holds, and the husband has the right during the iddat[5] period to return at any time without her consent.

The widow, during her period of iddat, may be betrothed implicitly but not explicitly. An explicit request of betrothal is a phrase like "I would like to marry you" or "I request you to be my wife". An implicit request of betrothal is such a phase as "I would like to marry a good or a beautiful woman" or "I intend to marry (or I wish to find) a suitable wife for me." The irrevocably divorced woman cannot be engaged implicitly or explicitly until the end of the iddat. Any other impediment of marriage, as we shall see later, shall also prohibit any betrothal. Such impediment could be permanent, as in the case of a prohibited degree, or temporary, such as the betrothal of a sister while the man still has her sister as wife. We shall deal later with the subject of the prohibited degrees.

It should be pointed out that a forbidden betrothal is considered a religious sin, but if a man asks a woman who is already betrothed, or is still in her iddat, to marry him, and their marriage takes place after the iddat, such a marriage shall be deemed legally valid and binding if it fulfils all the legal requirements.

B. Breach of Betrothal

Betrothal, like other marriage preliminaries, is merely a mutual promise of marriage between the two parties. It does not constitute a marriage contract, and therefore is not binding on either party. Classical Islamic jurists and modern legislators are unanimous that either party has an unquestionable right to break the betrothal, otherwise it would be entering, under coercion, into a contract meant ideally to be for a lifetime. There are explicit provisions to that effect in modern Personal Status Codes recently passed in Islamic countries, e.g. Tunisian Personal Status Mejelle of 60/1956, Article 1: "Every promise of marriage shall not be

5 *Iddat* (literally "the counted period"): A period of continence following the dissolution of marriage by death, divorce or otherwise. See Chapter 7.

deemed marriage and shall not be binding."; Moroccan Article 2: "Betrothal and other customary preliminaries of marriage are a promise of marriage and do not constitute a marriage. . . ."; Article 3: "Both parties to the betrothal may break it. . . ."; Jordanian Article 3: "No marriage shall be solemnized by just a betrothal. . . ."; Article 4: "Each party to the betrothal may break it."; Article 2 of the Syrian Personal Status Code and Article 3 of the Iraqi Code read: "Betrothal, marriage promise, reading the Fatihah . . . shall not constitute a marriage." The Syrian Legislator adds: "Each of the fiancé and fiancée may break the betrothal."

While the breach of betrothal is an unconditional right of each party according to the jurists and under the law, an injury may befall the party who has not committed the breath. Some Islamic jurists of all schools rule out any amends in such a case under the general Sharia rule that "An act allowed by law cannot be made the subject of a claim to compensation." Other modern Islamic jurists, e.g. Professor Abu Zahra of Egypt, relying upon the general rule that "There shall be no injury, no injury shall be met with an injury, and injury shall be removed", maintain that the injured party shall be entitled to amends to make good a breach of betrothal on grounds other than betrothal *per se*, e.g. if furniture was bought or accommodation secured at the request of the declining party.[6]

The Egyptian Court of Cassation, the highest court of the land whose judgments are binding interpretations of the law, has ruled that:

> "betrothal is only a preliminary step towards marriage contract, a mere promise that is not binding on either party who are lawfully free to end it at anytime, especially as in the marriage contract the two parties must enjoy absolute liberty to enter into it, in view of its paramount importance to society, which freedom of action shall be hindered if either party is under the threat of being liable to damages. However, if the promise to marry and the subsequent withdrawal therefrom are accompanied by other acts entirely independent thereof, of such a nature as to cause material or moral injury to one of the parties, such acts shall give rise to a lawful suit for damages against the party from whom they emanate on the ground that such acts, apart from the mere breach of promise, shall constitute tort that requires redress."[7]

The Jordanian provisional Act mentioned above does not contain any provisions in such a case. Following the Maliki School, Article 3 of the said

6 Abu Zahra, *On Marriage* (Cairo, 1950), p. 38; O. Abdullah, *Islamic Sharia Personal Status* (Alexandria, 1968), pp. 53–55.

7 Cassation Hearing of 14/12/1939, Appeal No. 13, Year 9J., *Compendium of Legal Rules (Civil)*, Vol. 1, p. 118.

Moroccan Decree rules that the man may recover any gifts unless he is the party who committed the breach, a position also maintained by the Tunisian Act (Article 2) in the absence of any condition to the contrary. The Syrian Personal Status Act rules in Article 4 that:

> "1. Should the fiancé pay dower in cash and the woman uses it to buy furniture and then the fiancé withdraw, the woman shall have the option either to refund the dower or hand over the furniture.
> 2. Should the woman break the betrothal, she shall return the dower or the equivalent thereof.
> 3. Presents shall be subject to the provisions of gifts."[8]

The Shafiis rule that the gift shall be recovered under all circumstances; the Hanafis, whose opinion is generally upheld by the courts in most Islamic states, take the view that any betrothal gifts, like gifts in general, are recoverable as the donor is entitled to revoke such donations, if they have not increased in value, been disposed of or destroyed.[9]

3. PILLARS AND CONDITIONS OF MARRIAGE CONTRACTS

A. Pillars

Like any other contract, a marriage contract can only be concluded through the two essentials or pillars (*arkan*) of offer and acceptance by the two principals or their proxies (Arts. 5, Syrian; 14, Jordanian; 4, Iraqi; 8, Kuwaiti; and 4, Moroccan).

Jordanian Law stipulates that offer and acceptance shall be through explicit words of marriage, *inkah*, *tazweej* (Art. 15), a position adopted from the Shafii School. In other Arab countries, words denoting marriage linguistically or according to custom are allowed (Arts. 6, Syrian; 4, Iraqi; 4-1, Moroccan; 10, Algerian; and 9, Kuwaiti). This position derives from the Hanafis, who also admit metaphorical words, which may be:

(i) Words denoting taking possession instantly without consideration such as gift and charity, which are unanimously deemed by the Hanafis to mean an offer of marriage. This position is confirmed by the Quran and the Prophet's Tradition: e.g. "And a believing woman if she give herself unto the Prophet and the Prophet desire to take her in marriage a privilege of Thee only not for the rest of believers" found

8 See Chapter 15 on Gifts.
9 Abiani, Commentary on the Sharia Provisions, p. 9.

in a verse beginning: "Oh, Prophet we have made lawful unto thee Thy wives unto whom thou has paid their dowries, and those whom thy right hand possesseth of those whom Allah hath given thee as spoils of war."[10]

(ii) Words that denote immediate ownership for a consideration like buying and selling. If the metaphor for marriage is corroborated, some Hanafi jurists accept such words as a valid offer of marriage. Others refuse it. But words denoting taking possession of the usufruct immediately are unanimously denied to constitute an offer of marriage.

The three Imams, Abu Hanifa, Malik and Ibn Hanbal agree that Islamic marriage can be solemnized in languages other than Arabic. But Al Shafii stipulates that an Islamic contract of marriage shall be concluded only in Arabic for those who know it, on the analogy with the prayers which can only be performed in Arabic.[11]

Marriage can also be concluded by the language of signs for those who cannot speak or write (Arts. 10, Syrian; 4/2, Moroccan). It may be in writing if one party is absent (Articles 7, Syrian; 6/2, Iraqi). Both rulings are included in Kuwaiti Article 9.

Offer and acceptance must occur at the same meeting. If the meeting is over after the offer and before the acceptance, the offer becomes void (Arts. 11, Syrian; 6/1a, Iraqi; 5/1, Moroccan).

The offer shall not be withdrawn by the offerer after it is accepted by the other party. But the offerer may withdraw before acceptance, in which case there is no contract nor any obligation, which can only result from the concordance of the two essentials of offer and acceptance (Syrian Art. 11/1).

If the offer is made through a messenger or a written letter, the acceptance shall be required at the meeting where the message is delivered or the letter is read. An acceptance at a later meeting shall not be valid. Article 10, paragraph c. of the Kuwaiti Law No. 51/84, sets, in such a case, a delay of three days, starting from the offeree reading the content of the letter or hearing the message, unless the offer sets another adequate delay or the recipient indicates rejection.

Mutual hearing and understanding of the offer and acceptance are essential to establish a marriage contract, even if such understanding is only in broad outline and not necessarily in detail. Without hearing and understanding, there shall be no contract linking offer and acceptance (Arts. 11/1, Syrian; 15, Jordanian; 6/1b and c, Iraqi; 10/e, Kuwaiti).

10 Sura Ahzab, XXXIII, verse 50.

11 Shafii, *Al UMM*, Vol. 5, p. 33.

B. Conditions of Legal Capacity

(1) Legal capacity

Both parties must possess legal capacity. The contract shall be deemed void if either or both parties are devoid of legal capacity. Full legal incapacity of either party shall render the contract null. A person possessing partial legal capacity may act as a proxy for a third party in a marriage contract, while his own marriage shall be subject to the approval of the person possessing the power thereto. A person of full legal capacity can conclude a marriage contract as a principal or as a proxy. For the purposes of marriage, a wastrel is deemed of full legal capacity as interdiction, if any, affects only his financial dispositions.[12]

(2) Puberty and majority

The legal capacity for marriage is not always the same as the full civil legal capacity. The Tunisian Law (Art. 5) stipulates that no marriage can be contracted between a man under 20 years of age and a woman under 17 without special court permission which shall not be given unless there are serious grounds and it is unquestionably to the welfare of the two spouses. The same law sets the age of full civil capacity at 20 years for both sexes (Art. 157). The marriage of persons under the legal age is subject to the guardians' consent. The matter is referred to the court if such a consent is withheld, and the spouses-to-be persist (Art. 6).

In Egypt, all persons attaining majority in possession of their mental faculties and not under legal disability have full legal capacity to exercise their civil rights. The majority of a person is fixed at 21 years completed in accordance with the Gregorian Calendar (Art. 44 of the Egyptian Civil Code No. 131/1948). Yet, the legal age of marriage is indirectly suggested under the Sharia Court Act No. 78/1931, Article 99 as amended by the Law No. 87/1951, which bars "the judicial consideration of any matrimonial suit if the wife's age is less than 16 lunar years or if the husband's age is below 18 lunar years without special permission."

In the Lebanon, there are different provisions for the Sunnis, the Shias and the Druzes. Article 4 of the Family Rights Act which governs the Sunni personal status stipulates for the bridegroom to possess legal capacity for marriage to be at least 18 years old, and for the bride to be 17. Articles 5, 6 and 7 of the same Act give the court the power to sanction the marriage of adolescents below the set ages should their condition so

12 Aub Zahra, *op. cit.* pp. 58, 59; Abdullah, *op. cit.* pp. 97, 98.

warrant. The Jaafari doctrine requires puberty for the parties to be proven, provided that no marriage shall be allowed for a boy under 15 years or a girl under 9. Under the Druze Personal Status Act of 1948, the bridegroom shall possess legal capacity for marriage on reaching 18 years of age and the bride on reaching 17 years (Art. 1). The Sectarian Judge may give marriage permission to an adolescent boy who is over 16 years but below 18 years, should his condition so permit, subject to the consent of his guardian (Art. 2). The same licence may be given to an adolescent girl who is over 15 but under 17, subject to the same provisos (Art. 3). Without the guardian's consent, each adolescent may apply for the annulment of marriage within six months as from the date of reaching the age fixed in Article 1 (Art. 4). Any marriage of a boy under 16 or a girl under 15 is categorically prohibited (Art. 5).

The Moroccan Decree fixes the age of legal capacity for marriage at 18 for the boy and 15 for the girl (Art. 8) while allowing marriage for parties under the statutory age of majority subject to the consent of the guardian with the right of appeal to the court (Art. 9).

The Jordanian Law stipulates that the bridegroom shall have reached 16 years and the bride 15 years to possess the legal capacity for marriage (Art. 5), while fixing the age of majority at 18 years according to the Gregorian Calendar (Civil Code Act 43-2).

The Syrian Legislator requires the attainment of puberty as a precondition for the capacity of marriage (Art. 15-1) setting the respective age at 18 for the boy and 17 for the girl (Art. 16). The age of full legal capacity, or the age of majority, is 18 full calendar years (Art. 46 of the Syrian Civil Code). However, an adolescent boy having completed 15 years, or a girl having completed 13 years, claiming to have reached puberty, may apply for marriage to the Judge, who shall grant them permission subject to the realization of their truthfulness and their physical capabilities (Personal Status Act, Art. 18/1).

The Iraqi Personal Status Act fixes the age of legal capacity for marriage at 18 years (Art. 7/1 as amended by Art. 1 of the Act 21/1978), which is the legal age of majority (Civil Code, Art. 106). A minor of 15 years may be granted permission by the court, subject to his proving physical ability and to his guardian's consent, which can be waived by the court if it is unreasonably withheld (Art. 8 of the Personal Status Act No. 188/1959 as amended by Art. 2 of Act No. 21/1978). The Kuwait law simply stipulates sanity and puberty as conditions for the marriage legal capacity (Art. 24a). The judge may allow the marriage of an insane or imbecile male or female, if a medical report certifies that such a marriage would help recovery, and the other party accepts (Art. 25b). It prohibits the notarization or the ratification of a marriage contract unless the girl has reached 15 and the boy 17 years of age at the time of notarization (Art. 26).[13]

An innovation in the Syrian, Jordanian and Moroccan Codes regulates the age gap between the two spouses-to-be. Under the Syrian Article 19, if they are disproportionate in age, and no good is seen to be forthcoming, the judge may withhold permission for them to marry. The Jordanian Article 7 is more categorical and precise, ruling that "No marriage contract shall be solemnized for a woman under 18 years of age if the husband-to-be is over 20 years older than her, unless the judge makes sure of her consent and free choice, and that the marriage is in her interest." Article 15 of the Moroccan Personal Status Decree simply leaves the harmonious proportioning of the ages of the spouses to the discretion of the wife solely.

(3) Sanity

Legal capacity requires, besides age, being of sound mind (Arts. 15/1, Syrian; 5, Jordanian; 7/1, Iraqi; 6, Moroccan). However, the court may grant an insane person or an imbecile permission to marry on the strength of a medical report certifying that marriage would help the patient's recovery (Arts. 15/2, Syrian; and 8, Jordanian). The Iraqi and Moroccan Laws add that this shall be subject to the other party's awareness of the fact and consent thereto (Arts. 7/2 and 7, respectively). Under the Sharia, a marriage contract shall be null and void if either party to the contract is insane, an indiscriminating imbecile or an indiscriminating minor, due to the absence in this case of the will and consent.[14] The Druze sect rules out the marriage of the insane under any circumstances.[15]

13 An emotionally charged problem with which practitioners are frequently faced is the child marriage. As seen in our review, the minimum age for a wife-to-be is 15 years unless special permission is granted by the court. But it cannot be denied that various subterfuges are often used, especially in rural and bedouin areas, to present prospective brides to the authorities as being older than they really are. A case in point are two studies reported in the Article "Iranian Cultures" in the *Encyclopaedia Britannica*, Vol. 9, p. 865, revealing that the median age of women's marriage in four villages near Shiraz was between 13 and 15 years, and 80 per cent of working class wives of Ispahan were married between the ages of 9 and 16 years of age inclusive. Against this background, the Iranian law makes the marriage of any person under the minimum legal marriage age (of 15 years for women) an offence that renders the person responsible liable to six months' to two years' imprisonment, rising to two to three years' if the girl is below 13. However, permission may be granted by the court for the marriage of a girl of 13 years.

14 Abdullah, *op. cit.* p. 71.

15 Lebanon Druze Personal Status Act, Art. 5.

C. Guardianship in Marriage and Marriage by Proxy

(1) Guardianship

(a) Guardianship of persons and property is dealt with separately in a later chapter, following the Islamic Sharia and legislation. At this stage we shall only treat guardianship in marriage.

Guardianship in marriage falls under two categories in respect of the ward, according to the classical Sharia tenets:

(i) Guardianship with the right of compulsion (*wilayat-ul-ijbar*) is exercised over a person of no or limited legal capacity wherein the guardian may conclude a marriage contract which is valid and takes effect without the consent or acceptance of the ward;

(ii) Guardianship without the right of compulsion (*wilayat-un-nadb*) is exercised when the woman, whether a virgin or previously married, possesses full legal capacity, but in deference to social customs and traditions, delegates the conclusion of her marriage to a guardian. In fact, this is more of an authorization of agent than guardianship. Some Islamic jurists call it joint guardianship when the woman has been previously married.

Nevertheless, the general consensus of jurists is that the woman shall not conduct her own marriage contract, whether she is a virgin or previously married, even when she possesses full legal capacity. Only the Hanafis do not require a guardian to conclude the contract on behalf of the woman unless she is of no or limited legal capacity.

According to the Sunni schools, marriage guardians shall be agnates[16] in the following order:

(i) descendants, i.e. the son and the son's son how-low-soever;

(ii) ascendants, i.e. the father and the true[17] grandfather, how-high-soever;

(iii) the full brothers and the agnate brothers and their male descendants, how-low-soever;

(iv) the agnate uncles and their sons.

In the absence of agnates, guardianship shall be vested in relatives according to proximity; otherwise it shall be vested in the Head of State and his delegate, notably the judge.

16 Agnate (*asaba*): person whose relation to the ward can be traced without the intervention of female links. See also the chapters on Guardianship of the Person and Inheritance.

17 The agnatic grandfather. See also Chapter 12 on Inheritance.

According to the Shia Ithna-Asharis, the guardian is indispensable in order for the marriage of minors and majors of defective or no legal capacity to be valid. The guardian is always the father or the agnatic grandfather how-high-soever, failing which the legal guardian, otherwise the judge. Marriage guardianship shall never pass to the mother, the father's mother, any agnate or cognate in the absence of a father, an agnatic grandfather or a legal guardian, but shall be vested in the judge. Only the judge shall have the power to act as the marriage guardian for an adult who has reached the age of majority in a sane state, then later becomes insane.[18]

These are the general Sharia rules on marriage guardianship. Recent legislations adopt most of them. The order of guardians is strictly followed in Jordan (Art. 9), in Morocco (Art. 11), in Tunisia (Art. 8), and in Syria (Art. 21). The judge is declared the guardian for whoever has no guardian (Arts. 24, Syrian; 12, Jordanian; 8, Tunisian). The same rule is specified under Article 11 of the Algerian Personal Status Law which rules that the marriage of a woman shall be conducted by her guardian, who is the father, failing which a close agnate relative of hers, and under Article 29 of the Kuwaiti law which briefly adopts the order of inheritance.

However, the guardianship with the right of compulsion is expressly prohibited in Morocco under Article 12/4 which reads:

> "The guardian, even if he is the father, shall not compel his daughter who has reached puberty even if she is a virgin to marry without her permission and consent unless temptation is feared, in which case the judge shall have the right to compel her to marry in order that she may be under the protection of an equal husband who will take care of her."

In a similar vein, Articles 12 and 13 of the Algerian Law rule that no guardian can stop his ward from marrying if she so wishes, and if it is in her interests. Should he prevent her from doing so, the judge may give her permission without prejudice to the provisions of Article 9 aforesaid. However, the father may prevent his virgin daughter from marrying if that prevention is in her interests. But no guardian, whether a father or otherwise, can compel his ward to marry, nor can he get her to marry against her consent.

The Iraqi legislation goes even further, ruling, under Article 9 as amended by Article 3 of Law No. 21/1978 that:

> "No kin or stranger may compel any person whether male or female to marry against his/her consent. A marriage contract under compulsion is void if no consummation has occurred. Similarly no kin or

18 Al-Hilli, *Jaafari Personal Status Provisions*, p. 10.

stranger may prevent the marriage of anyone who has the legal capacity for marriage under this law."

The Kuwaiti legislator steers a middle course – a virgin between puberty and 25 years of age needs a marriage guardian, who shall be an agnate in his own right (*asaba bin-nafs*) in the order of inheritance, failing whom, the judge (Art. 29); the previously married or the female of 25 or over, has the choice in marrying, but shall delegate the entering into contract to her guardian (Art. 30).

In the Lebanon, the Sunnis distinguish between the male and female minors. The boy does not need the consent of his guardian but permission by the court is to be granted only on his proving that he has reached puberty and can afford to marry. Under no circumstances may a boy under 17 years of age be made or allowed to marry (Art. 7 of the Family Rights Act). No girl may be married under 9 years of age. Between 9 and 17 she may marry by court permission, which may be granted if she claims to have attained puberty, is of a condition suitable for marriage and she obtains the consent of her guardian. Above 17 her guardian's consent shall still be required for a minor to marry, but the judge may allow her to avoid this consent if the guardian's refusal is unfounded.

Guardianship with the right of compulsion was practised by the Lebanese Sunnis observing the Hanafi law until the coming into force of the Family Rights Act, which prohibited the marriage of the minor in all but a few exceptional cases and confined the exercise of the right of compulsion to the marriage of the insane (male or female), provided that such marriage is necessary for them and is permitted by the Sharia judge (Arts. 4–7).

However, this right is retained by the Lebanese Jaafaris. The guardian may make the minor marry regardless of his consent. But the minor may choose between continuing the marriage or applying for its annulment on reaching majority, should he deem such a marriage to his disadvantage. The Jaafari Doctrine makes no distinction between male and female minors who both need the consent of the guardian and the judge's permission for their marriage. On the other hand, if the father or the grandfather refuses to give the minor in marriage, no other relative or judge may do so, regardless of the grounds for the father's or grandfather's refusal. Should the minor be given away in marriage by a judge, the marriage shall be subject to his/her approval on reaching majority.[19]

For the Lebanese Druzes, refer to paragraph 3. B. (2) above (Puberty and majority).

In Syria, Jordan and Morocco, all forms of compulsion to marry are

19 *Ibid.* p. 11.

excluded. The guardian still retains the right to object to the marriage of his ward, but can be overruled by the judge.

(2) Marriage by proxy

A person of full legal capacity, whether a man or a woman, may authorize another person to conduct the marriage on his or her behalf. Likewise, a marriage guardian may appoint an agent for that purpose. Such authorization may be given orally or in writing, and it shall not require evidence, although this is desirable.

The authorization shall be effective and binding on the principal if it conforms with the principal's instructions, otherwise it shall be subject to the principal's consent.

The marriage proxy is merely acting on behalf of the principal in respect of concluding the marriage contract, and his mission shall be deemed accomplished once the marriage contract is made. Therefore, the husband cannot require the wife's proxy to enforce his wife's obedience, nor can the wife demand that the husband's proxy, as such, should pay her the dower unless he has guaranteed it, in which case he shall be liable to pay it to her, by virtue of the guarantee not of the marriage proxy.

These are the general rules of Sharia on proxy which generally apply in Muslim states with certain restrictions. The Moroccan Law restricts the power to appoint a proxy for marriage to the guardian in respect of his female ward, and the husband-to-be (Art. 10/1); a judge shall not solemnize his own marriage or that of any of his ancestors or descendants to his ward (Act. 10/2). Under the Syrian Law (Art. 8/2) a proxy may not marry his female principal unless he is explicitly empowered to do so in the power of attorney, a ruling similarly adopted by the Kuwaiti Law, Article 27/b. While not requiring any conditions to be fulfilled in the marriage proxy, the Tunisian Law (Art. 10) rules that the proxy shall not appoint any other agent without permission of his male or female principal. It also stipulates that the authorization of agents shall be through a legal document to include expressly the designation of both spouses, otherwise it would be void. The Jordanian and Iraqi Laws simply allow offer and acceptance to be made either by the principals or their proxy or proxies (Arts. 14 and 4, respectively).

4. CONDITIONS OF VALIDITY OF THE MARRIAGE CONTRACT

Apart from complying with the provisions regarding offer and acceptance, marriage capacity and sanity, etc., the marriage contract has to fulfil other requirements to be valid according to Sharia and/or modern laws. Those relate to witnesses, eligibility of the woman, and form of contract.

A. Witnesses

Sunni jurists throughout the ages are unanimous that the presence of witnesses is essential to ensure publicity which makes the division between lawful wedlock and fornication. They rely on proven traditions by the Prophet: "Publicize marriage even with timbals", "There is no marriage without witnesses." Aisha, the wife and narrator of the Prophet, quotes him also as saying: "There can be no marriage without a guardian and two honest witnesses. If there is any dispute between them, the Ruler is the Guardian of the person who has no Guardian." The first Patriarchal Caliph, Abu Bakr, is reported as saying: "Marriage in secret is not allowed until it is publicized and witnessed."

The witnesses must be two men or a man and two women, adult, sane and free. They must hear and understand offer and acceptance. If both parties of the marriage are Muslim, the witnesses must be Muslim. If the wife to be is a Kitabi (a believer in Christianity or Judaism, literally a member of the people of Scriptures), the jurists Muhammad, Zafar, Shafei and Ahmad do not accept the witnesses to be Kitabis; Abu Hanifa and Abu Yussof accept such witnesses. The Hanafi School does not stipulate that the witnesses must be righteous, arguing that the philanderer is as good for publicity purposes as the righteous, that he can enter into a marriage on his own or his ward's behalf and that he is eligible to hold public office, therefore, *a fortiori*, he must be acceptable as a witness. Shafei and Ahmad dissent, on the ground that, apart from publicity, a witness must also serve the purpose of proof in the event of a denial, and no philanderer's evidence is admissible.

The modern Arab laws observe these provisions collectively. In Syria, "It is a condition for the validity of a marriage contract that it be witnessed by two men, or a man and two women, who are Muslim, sane and adult and shall hear offer and acceptance and understand the intention thereof" (Art. 12). In Iraq, Article 6/1 reads: "No marriage contract shall be concluded if any of the following conditions for conclusion of validity is missing: . . . d. The witness of the marriage contract by two witnesses possessing legal capacity." The Jordanian legislator virtually repeats (in Article 16, under the heading "Conditions for the valid conclusion of the marriage contract") the text of the Syrian Article 12 with the qualification that the witnesses must be Muslim if the spouses are, and adding that the witnesses of the contract may be the ancestors or descendants of the parties. In Morocco, "It is a condition for the validity of the marriage contract that it be witnessed by two righteous men who shall hear at the same meeting the offer and acceptance from the husband or his deputy and from the guardian after the wife's consent and her authorization to him to act on her behalf" (Art. 5/1). The Tunisian Code simply requires for the validity of a marriage contract, the presence of two reputable witnesses (Art. 3). Article 9 of Algerian law reads as follows: "A marriage contract shall be concluded on the consent of the two spouses and in the presence of the wife's guardian and two witnesses, and on an agreed dower." Article 11 of the Kuwaiti law requires for the validity of the marriage "the presence of two Muslim witnesses who are male, adult and sane, who shall hear the speech of the contracting parties and understand the meaning thereof"; it also allows two Kitabi witnesses if the wife is a Kitabi.

On the other hand, the Shia do not require the presence of two witnesses for the validity of a marriage contract. Their presence is not a condition of validity, but it is at best desirable (*marghub*) as a precaution against denial. It is preferable that the witnesses be in possession of the requirements for acceptability, but the contract shall remain valid even if they are libertines, and even if they lacked all other requirements for acceptability.[20]

The Druzes of Lebanon require the presence of witnesses who may be of the ascendants or descendants of the two parties, provided that there shall be no less than four witnesses (Art. 14 of the Lebanese Law of 24/2/1948).

B. The Eligibility of the Woman

The woman who is the object of the marriage must be immediately eligible for marriage to the person who proposes. There must be no impediments on the grounds of kindred, affinity or fosterage, or on grounds of the social status (being already married, or during an iddat, or equality) or because of difference in religion. In view of the importance of the subject, we shall deal with this condition in a later section under the heading of "Impediments of Marriage".

C. The Form

The Sharia jurists require that the marriage contract form shall have immediate effect, and shall not be suspended or deferred to the future. It may include conditions for either or both spouses which must be observed if they are advantageous to either party. Examples of such conditions are: that the woman retains the right to dissolve the marriage; that neither

20 Al-Hilli, *op. cit.* p. 5.

party may leave the town they agree to settle in; that the husband may not marry another.

Concurring with these provisions, the Shias do not allow any marriage which is conditional on a non-existent condition or a non-existing occurrence. But they acknowledge a marriage on an irregular condition, in which case the marriage is valid and the condition is void, e.g. non-payment of dower. They acknowledge for both parties *Khiyar-ush-shart*, i.e. the stipulated right of cancellation, e.g. if the wife is not a virgin or not free from physical deformity.[21]

The Hanafis, on the contrary, deem this last condition null and void while the contract remains valid.[22]

It seems that the Hanbalis adopt the fairest and closest doctrine to the Sharia spirit and the one most likely to serve the interests of both spouses. They maintain that any condition agreed between the parties, orally or in writing, must be honoured and given effect, and any party who made that condition shall retain the right of cancellation if the condition is broken, unless there is a Sharia proof of its being void. They cite the Quranic verse "And fulfil every engagement for it will be enquired into (on the day of Reckoning)"[23] and the Prophet's Tradition "The worthiest conditions to be honoured are those that make women lawful for you." If any condition could be proven void under the Sharia, it should not be stipulated at all, and if made, must be deemed null and void, e.g. a condition by a wife to have a previous wife divorced.[24]

The Tunisian Code upholds the stipulated right of cancellation if an agreed condition is not honoured or is violated without any liability if divorce takes place before consummation (Art. 11).

In Iraq, the legitimate conditions stipulated in a marriage contract must be honoured (Art. 6/3). The wife is granted the right to apply for cancellation if the husband does not comply with any such condition in the contract (Art. 6/4).

In Jordan, an advantageous condition for either party that does not conflict with the marriage aims, does not involve anything unlawful, and is recorded in the contract, shall be honoured according to the following guidelines:

(i) If the wife stipulates a condition apt to secure her a lawful interest and not to infringe on a third party's right, e.g. not to be removed from her town, or to reserve the right to divorce herself at will, or to live in a given locality, or for the husband not to marry another

21 *Ibid.* p. 6.

22 Al Abiani, *Sharia Personal Status Provisions*, p. 17.

23 Sura Israa, XVII, verse 34.

24 Abul-Naja, *Hanbali Jurisprudence*, p. 60; ibn Qayyim al Jouzia, *Zaad-ul-Maad*, Vol. 4, p. 4; Ibnu Qayyim Aljouzia, *Ilam*, Vol. 2, p. 246.

woman, the condition shall be valid and binding, and the failure to honour it shall give the wife the right to apply for cancellation without prejudice to any of her marital rights.

(ii) A condition by the husband that secures him a lawful advantage without infringing on a third party's right, e.g. for the woman not to work outside the matrimonial home, or for her to live with him at the town where he works, shall be valid and binding, and any violation thereof shall entitle the husband to apply for divorce and to be discharged of her deferred dower and iddat maintenance.

(iii) A condition included in the contract that conflicts with its purpose or involves anything unlawful, e.g. a condition by one party that the other party shall not share the matrimonial home, shall not live as man and wife, shall drink alcohol or shall alienate a parent, shall be deemed void but the contract shall remain valid (Art. 19/1/2/3).

Likewise, the Syrian Legislator deems any condition in the marriage contract that contravenes its legal order or intentions and involves any illegality, to be void without affecting the validity of the contract (Art. 14/1). A condition that secures the wife a lawful interest without jeopardizing the rights of a third party or restricting the husband's freedom in his lawful business shall be valid and binding (Art. 14/2). A condition that restricts such freedom of the husband or infringes on the rights of a third party shall be valid but not binding to the husband and shall entitle the wife making the condition, if the husband does not honour it, to apply for divorce (Art. 14/3). The Kuwaiti legislator (Art. 40), electively distinguishes between three kinds of marriage contract conditions: (a) a condition that violates the very roots of marriage, e.g. for the husband not to touch the wife, shall render the contract void; (b) a condition that runs against the implications of marriage without contravening its principles, e.g. that there will be no mutual inheritance between the spouses, shall be void while the contract remains valid; (c) a condition that contravenes neither the roots nor the implications of marriage and is not prohibited, e.g. for the wife to complete her studies, shall be binding and enforceable, under pain of the beneficiaries applying for rescission. Such a condition must be recorded in the marriage document (Art. 41). The right to apply for cancellation shall be lost if the beneficiaries thereof drop it expressly or implicitly (Art. 42).

5. PERMANENT AND TEMPORARY MARRIAGE

The Sunnis and Shia part ways on the form of marriage contract dealing with the duration of marriage.

The Sunni jurists are unanimous that the form of the marriage contract must not include or imply any time limit, in the belief that the aim of marriage is the establishment of a lawful and permanent partnership, the founding of a family and the caring for and bringing up of children, all being aims attainable only with a life-time contract dissolved only by death. On these grounds, they prohibit the form of timed marriage which was known in paganism and remained in the early days of Islam until it was firmly prohibited by the Prophet six times on six occasions. This is known as the muta (temporary) marriage. The Shia deny the abrogation of this form of marriage as explained below.

The Sunni jurists further argue that even under the Shia doctrine, muta marriage is not marriage proper since it established no maintenance nor inheritance rights for the woman.

While the muta is unanimously deemed null and void by the Sunnis, a Hanafi jurist, Zafar ibn ul-Hudhail stands alone in considering a temporary marriage a valid contract which remains effective and binding while the time limit is a void condition to be dropped. This argument is adopted by some other Sunni jurists in some forms of offer and acceptance. An example is when a man says to a woman: "I want to marry you on condition that I divorce you after a month" and she replies: "I accept". The marriage is valid but the condition is void, and the contract shall be permanent.[25]

Of all the modern Arab legislation on personal status, muta and temporary marriage are mentioned explicitly only in the Jordanian Law. Article 34/6, deems it irregular, not void, having no effect if there is no consummation and establishing certain effects after consummation (see below "Effects of Marriage"). The Sharia (Sunni) provisions apply in other codes which fail to mention temporary or muta marriages.

The Shias maintain that the muta marriage has not been abrogated. They cite a verse of the Quran: "And those of whom you seek *content*, give unto them their portions as a duty".[26]

A Shia male may contract a muta marriage with a Muslim, Christian, Jew or magi (fire-worshipping) woman, but not with a woman professing any other faith. A Shia woman shall not contract a muta marriage with a non-Muslim.[27]

For a muta marriage contract to be valid, two conditions must be met: the term of cohabitation should be fixed and may be a day, a month, a year or a number of years; and a dower should be specified.

If the term is fixed but the dower is not specified, the contract would be void. In the converse case, i.e. if the dower is specified but the term is

25 Abu Zahra, *op. cit.* p. 48.
26 Sura Nisaa, IV, verse 24.
27 Al-Hilli, *op. cit.* p. 32.

omitted, the contract shall be void as a muta, but may operate as a permanent marriage.

No right of divorce is recognized in a muta marriage which is dissolved *ipso facto* by the expiry of the term. However, the husband may, at his will, terminate the contract verbally by "making a gift of the term to the wife" even before the completion of the term.

The wife is entitled to full dower if the muta marriage is consummated, even if the husband puts an end to the contract in the manner described above, but he is entitled to deduct a proportionate part of the dower if the wife leaves him before the expiry of the term. If the muta marriage is not consummated, the wife shall be entitled to half the dower.

A muta wife shall not be entitled to maintenance.

Although a muta marriage does not create mutual rights of inheritance between the man and the woman, the children conceived while it exists are legitimate and entitled to inherit from both parents. Where the cohabitation of a man and a woman commences in a muta marriage, with no evidence as to the term for which the marriage was contracted, the proper inference would be, in absence of evidence to the contrary, that the muta continued during the whole period of cohabitation and the children conceived during that period are legitimate and entitled to inherit from their father.

6. MARRIAGE EQUALITY

Equality between the two spouses in certain matters is a condition for the validity of marriage according to the Hanafi doctrine, applied in Egypt, or for the marriage contract to be binding in Syria (Art. 26), Jordan (Art. 20), Morocco (Art. 14/a) and Kuwait (Art. 34). It is a right to be exercised by the wife and the guardian, according to the Sharia and the laws of Syria (Art. 29), Morocco (Art. 14/a) and Kuwait (Art. 34).

Equality, which can be defined as parity of status, is considered by the Hanafis in six matters: lineage, Islam, freedom, property, trade or craft, and piety.

The Malikis consider equality in religious piety, freedom from defects, and lineage in that the husband should have a known father and should not be a foundling whose parents are unknown.

The Shafiis require for equality, freedom from defects, lineage, chastity, craft and solvency.

The Hanbalis consider religious piety, lineage, solvency and craft.

The Jordanian Law simply requires for the marriage contract to be binding that the man shall be equal to the woman in the property, explaining that this means for the man to be able to afford the advance dower and the wife's maintenance (Art. 20). Both the Syrian and the Moroccan Laws make equality a matter of convention and custom (Arts. 28, 14/b, respectively). Kuwaiti Article 35 sets religious piety as the criterion of equality; Article 36 grants the wife exclusively the right to decide on the age suitability.

Equality must be considered at the time of the marriage contract (Arts. 20, Jordanian; 14/6, Moroccan; 34, Kuwaiti).

The Syrian Law entitles the guardian to apply for the annulment of the marriage if the woman marries a person who is not her equal without the guardian's consent (Art. 27).

The Jordanian Law distinguishes between two cases: (i) if the guardian gives in marriage his ward, whether she is a virgin or previously married, with her consent to a man whose equality is known to neither of them, and then it becomes known that he is not an equal, neither shall have the right to object; (ii) if equality is stipulated at the time of marriage or if the husband declares he is an equal and then it transpires that he is not, both the wife and the guardian may apply to the court for the dissolution of marriage (Art. 21), similar to Kuwaiti Art. 38.

This right shall not apply if the woman is pregnant (Arts. 30, Syrian; 23, Jordanian).

The Shia Ithna-Asharis also consider equality in marriage from the husband's side, who must be at least equal to the woman in lineage, Islam, property, piety and craft. All except Islam are considered the woman's rather than the guardian's right. They are considered at the time of the contract and are not a condition of validity. Islam of the husband is a condition for the marriage to be valid: no Muslim woman may marry a non-Muslim. Islam is considered for the husband himself regardless of his ancestors and the prestige of learning is above that of lineage. For craft, the Shias also refer to custom. The right to apply for a separation is denied on the consent of the woman or on discovering lack of equality after the contract.[28]

7. MARRIAGE IMPEDIMENTS

It is an essential condition for the validity of marriage that the woman must be eligible forthwith to marry the man who proposes. In other words, there must be no impediment under the Sharia or the law against the marriage of a certain woman to a certain man.

Marriage impediments are either permanent or temporary. Permanent prohibition is based on three grounds: kindred, affinity and fosterage.

28 *Ibid.* pp. 16–17.

Temporary prohibition is based on existing marriage, irrevocable divorce or difference of religion. Impediments are mostly temporary because once the impediment is removed, marriage can be solemnized. In this section, impediments are dealt with in the order stated above.

A. Permanent Prohibition

(1) On grounds of kindred

Permanent prohibited degrees for marriage on grounds of kindred are ordained in the Quranic verse "Prohibited to you are your mothers, daughters, sisters; father's sisters, mother's sisters, brother's daughters, sister's daughters."[29] These include directly or by implication the man's ancestors and descendants, the descendants of his first ascendants, and the first descendants of every ancestor how-high-soever (Art. 33, Syrian; 14/1, Iraqi; 25, Moroccan; 15, Tunisian; 13, Kuwaiti). The Jordanian Law is much more specific: the prohibited degrees for marriage fall in four categories:

(i) mothers and grandmothers;
(ii) daughters and granddaughters how-low-soever;
(iii) sisters and sisters' and brothers' daughters how-low-soever.
(iv) Paternal and maternal aunts (Art. 24).

The same prohibitions apply for the Jaafaris.[30]

(2) On grounds of affinity

There are four categories for these prohibited degrees:

(i) The wife of any ascendant how-high-soever, whether agnate, as the father's father, or consanguines as the mother's father, *whether there is or is not consummation.* This is ordained by the Quranic verse "And marry not women whom your fathers married; except what is past: it was shameful and odious and abominable custom indeed."[31]
(ii) The wife of any descendant how-low-soever, *whether marriage thereto is consummated or not*, and whether an agnate, like the son's son, or consanguine like the daughter's son. This is ordained under the Quranic verse ". . . wives of your sons proceeding from your loins."[32]
(iii) Ascendants of the wife how-high-soever *regardless of consummation*,

29 Sura Nisaa, IV, verse 23.
30 Al-Hilli, *op. cit.* p. 8.
31 Sura Nisaa, IV, verse 22.
32 *Ibid.* verse 23.

under the Quranic verse "Prohibited to you . . . and your wives' mothers."[33]

(iv) Descendants of the wives how-low-soever, *provided that marriage is consummated*, under the Quranic verse ". . . and your step-daughters under your guardianship, born of your wives to whom you have gone in – No prohibition if you have not gone in."[34] The Jordanian Law explicitly adds in this category the daughters of the wives' children, provided consummation has taken place (Art. 25/4).

These are the Sharia provisions according to the Malikis, Shafiis and Hanbalis, and to the laws of Iraq (Art. 15), Jordan (Art. 25), Morocco (Art. 27), Tunisia (Art. 16), Algeria (Art. 26), Kuwait (Art. 14), the Druzes of Lebanon (Art. 13), and the Jaafaris.[35]

Following all the doctrines except the Shafii, the Syrian law includes in the prohibited degrees in this category, in addition to the wife of the ascendant or descendant or any woman with whom either had sexual intercourse, and in addition to the ascendants of the wife, the ascendants and descendants of any woman with whom the man had sexual intercourse (Art. 34/1–2). The Kuwaiti legislator follows suit (Art. 15).

The Shia Ithna-Asharis likewise add to the prohibited degrees in this section the ascendants and descendants of a woman with whom a man committed adultery. The adulteress shall be a prohibited degree to his ascendants and descendants, but not her ascendants and descendants.[36]

(3) On grounds of fosterage

The general rule is that any prohibited degree on grounds of kindred is also prohibited on grounds of fosterage (suckling), under the Quranic verse ". . . And your foster mothers who gave you suck and your foster sisters."[37] and the Prophet's saying "fosterage shall create the same prohibited degrees as kindred", a provision adopted by all schools and modern Arab legislation (Arts. 35/1, Syrian; 26, Jordanian; 16, Iraqi; 28/1, Moroccan; 17, Tunisian; 27, Algerian; 16/a, Kuwaiti).

However, there are exceptions to this general rule referred to in general in the above-mentioned Articles of the Syrian, Iraqi and Jordanian Laws, save for exceptions under the Hanafi Doctrine or enumerated in detail in Articles 17 (Tunisian), 28/2 (Moroccan) and 28 (Algerian). The last three Articles sum up those exceptions, ruling that "only the suckling

33 *Ibid.*
34 *Ibid.*
35 Al-Hilli, *op. cit.* p. 8.
36 *Ibid.*
37 Sura Nisaa, IV, verse 23.

baby, excluding his brothers and sisters, shall be deemed a child of the foster mother and her husband".

For fosterage to create a prohibited degree, it must take place in infancy and reach a certain number. The jurists differ on both these points. The Hanafis, followed by the Malakis, maintain that even one suck is enough. The Shafiis and Hanbalis require five feeds for certain fosterage to be established, a position adopted by the laws of Syria (35/2), Morocco (28/3), and Kuwait (17). No limit is set in Joran, Iraq or Tunisia.

As for the time of fostering, the Hanafis make it 30 lunar months, on the strength of the Quranic verse "In pain did his mother bear him and in pain did she give him birth and his bearing to his weaning is thirty months".[38] The Malikis, Shafiis and Hanbalis make it two lunar years, quoting two Quranic verses, "The mothers shall give suck to their offspring for two whole years if the father desires to complete the term"[39], and "In years twain was his weaning".[40] This is the position adopted in Syria (35/2), Tunisia (17) and Morocco (28/3). Algerian Article 29 maintains that fostering shall create a prohibited degree only if it occurs before weaning or during the first two years of life, regardless of the quantity of the milk sucked.

According to the Jaafari doctrine, for suckling to create prohibited degrees, the following four conditions must be fulfilled:

(i) that the woman's milk shall flow as a result of a legitimate birth;
(ii) that the baby shall suck from the woman's breast directly;
(iii) that it shall suck milk during the first two years of life;
(iv) that it shall suckle from the breast of the same woman for a day and a night or 15 sucklings without being separated by any other feed. The same Shia exceptions apply.[41]

There is no prohibited degree on ground of fosterage for the Druzes of Syria (Art. 307/c) nor Lebanon (Chapter 2, Druze Personal Status Law 1948).

B. Temporary Impediments

Temporary impediments to marriage are based on (i) existing marriage; (ii) irrevocable divorce; (iii) religion. Except for a few cases due to divorce, these impediments could theoretically be removed to allow for a valid marriage. We shall deal with each in turn.

38 Sura Ahqaf, XLVI, verse 15.
39 Sura Baqara, II, verse 233.
40 Sura Luqman, XXXI, verse 14.
41 Al-Hilli, *op. cit.* pp. 97/99.

(1) Existing marriage

An existing married status is an impediment to a valid marriage in three situations: (a) woman married or in her iddat; (b) unlawful conjunction; (c) polygamy. There is a fourth case, unique to the Kuwaiti law.

(a) A woman who is validly married or is observing her counting period (*iddat*) subsequent to a revocable or irrevocable divorce or death of the husband cannot marry another man until the marriage is lawfully dissolved or the iddat is over, under the Quranic verses "Prohibited to you . . . women already married"[42] and "Divorced women shall wait concerning themselves for three monthly courses"[43] and "If any of you die and leave widows behind, they shall wait concerning themselves four months and ten days."[44] *Iddat* will be treated in a separate section.

Jurists are unanimous that such a marriage is irregular and the parties should separate of themselves or by a court order if no consummation occurred. But if it did, jurists differ: Hanbalis and Shafiis rule that the spouses should be separated, but the man can marry the woman again on completing her iddat. The Malikis maintain that they must be separated and that the woman shall be permanently prohibited to him.

This provision prohibiting the marriage to a married woman or a woman in her iddat is adopted in the Laws of Syria (Art. 38), Jordan (Art. 27), Iraq (13), Morocco (29/6), Tunisia (Art. 20) and Kuwait (Art. 19). The Jaafaris concur.[45]

A special case in this context is that of the absent or missing person. Under the most authoritative provisions of the Sharia adopted in the Egyptian Law No. 25/1929 such a person shall be deemed dead after four years of his going missing in circumstances which make it likely to presume his death. In all other circumstances, the court shall have the discretion, after ordering enquiries and investigations by all the possible means, to fix the time at which he shall be deemed dead (Art. 21). After the court's ruling in this manner, the wife shall observe the iddat of death (Art. 22). The same provisions are indicated in the Kuwaiti Articles 146 and 147.

The Jordanian Law follows closely those provisions. It elaborates on the circumstances which make it likely to presume death as follows; an earthquake disaster, an air raid, collapse of public security, commotion and the like, when the court shall rule on his death one year after his going missing. If he went missing in a known location and is likely to have

42 Sura Nisaa, IV, verses 23/24.
43 Sura Baqara, II, verse 228.
44 Sura Baqara, verse 234.
45 Al-Hilli, *op. cit.* p. 9.

perished, the court shall rule on his death four years later. Otherwise, the judge shall have the discretion to determine the time of the missing person's death after ordering all the necessary investigations to find out whether he is alive or dead (Art. 177) whereupon the missing person's wife shall observe the iddat of death (Art. 178).

If the missing person appears or is proven to be alive after a court ruling on his death in the above manner, the Egyptian legislation ordains that his wife shall be his unless she was married to a second husband unaware of the first husband's being alive, in which case she shall belong to the second husband unless the said iddat was not observed (Maintenance and some Personal Status Provisions Act No. 25/1920, Art. 8). The same ruling is adopted in Kuwaiti Article 148. According to the Jordanian Article 179, the marriage to a second man of the woman whose husband was deemed dead and then appeared to be alive shall remain valid if consummation had occurred; but it shall be annulled if there was no consummation. The Tunisian Law simply requires the wife of the missing person to observe the iddat of death as from the date of the court order deeming her husband dead (Art. 36). The Jaafaris concur.[46]

In Syria, the missing person's definition is "every person of whom it is not known if he is alive or dead or who is known for sure to be alive but his whereabouts are unknown" (Art. 202). His being missing comes to an end on his return, or under a court ruling declaring him dead, having reached 80 years of age, or four years after his going missing in war or similar cases listed in military laws in force (Art. 205).

(b) Unlawful conjunction. This is an impediment which forbids a Muslim to have two wives at the same time who are related to each other by kindred, affinity or fosterage such that had either of them been a male, they would have been prohibited from marrying each other under the Quranic verse listing the prohibited degrees ". . . and two sisters in wedlock at one and the same time except for what is past".[47] This is supplemented by the authentic tradition of the Prophet, "There shall be no marriage at the same time to a woman and her paternal or maternal aunt, nor a woman and her brother's or sister's daughter."

The Sunni and Shia jurists are unanimous on this impediment with the exception of some Kharijis who allow simultaneous marriage to women so related apart from the sisters, sticking to the literal text of the Quranic verse. Again, the jurists are unanimous that the prohibited degree in unlawful conjunction holds whether the ground is kindred, affinity or fosterage. The only exception is the two Hanbali scholars, Ibn Taymiya and his disciple Ibn-ul-Qayyim, who allow such a conjunction between

46 *Ibid.* p. 141.
47 Sura Nisaa, IV, verse 23.

prohibited degrees on account of fosterage in the absence of a Quranic text on this impediment.

Unlawful conjunction is removed on one of the women being divorced, and after the lapse of her iddat.

The Jordanian, Iraqi, Syrian and Kuwaiti Laws adopt this impediment in its widest connotations (Arts. 31, 13, 39, and 20 respectively).

The Moroccan Law includes an exception, allowing simultaneous marriage to a woman and her step-mother or step-daughter (Art. 29/1), contrary to the definition given above.

This impediment is unthinkable in the Tunisian and the Syrian and Lebanese Druze Laws, where polygamy is forbidden, as we shall discuss in the next section.

(c) Polygamy. Under the Sharia, both according to the Sunnis and the Shias, a Muslim man can have up to four wives at the same time, subject to certain conditions, in accordance with three major sources: The Quran, the Tradition and Concensus. The Quran rules "Marry women of your choice, two or three or four; but if ye fear that ye shall not be able to deal justly then only one."[48] As for the Sunna, the Prophet on several occasions ordered the newly-converted to Islam who had many wives to keep four and discharge the rest. As for consensus (Ijma), Muslims from the days of the Prophet until now have approved, both in words and in deeds, the simultaneous marriage to four wives.

This ruling has been strictly adhered to in the Laws of Syria (Art. 37), Jordan (Art. 28), Iraq (Art. 13), Morocco (Art. 29/2) and Kuwait (Art. 21), under which no man can marry a fifth wife until one of the existing four is divorced and has completed her iddat.

Under the Tunisian Law, polygamy is forbidden, and constitutes a criminal offence, rendering a man who marries before his previous marriage is dissolved liable to a penalty of one year's imprisonment and/or a fine of 240,000 francs, even if the new marriage is unlawful (Art. 18). Polygamy is also prohibited among the Druzes of Lebanon (Act of 24/2/1948, Art. 10), and of Syria (Art. 307/6).

The controversy over polygamy started in the early 20th century, with Egypt and the Middle East opening to Europe. Modern religious reformers, led by Sheikh Muhammad Abdou (died 1905), advocated restrictions of polygamy, considering it an injustice to the woman. Other reformers argued that polygamy must be prohibited, quoting verse 129 of Sura Nisaa, IV (the same Sura which allowed polygamy): "Ye shall not be able to deal in fairness and justice between women however much ye wish", in addition to the earlier verse ". . . but if ye fear that ye shall not be able to deal justly then only one" (verse 3).

48 *Ibid.* verse 3.

The fundamentalists reacted strongly, arguing that such an interpretation would render the Quranic allowance for up to four wives absurd and inoperative, and that in order to honour it, a distinction must be made between justice in verse 3 which would mean equality between wives in material and tangible matters, and justice in verse 129 which would then mean inner feelings over which man has no control. They quoted traditions of the Prophet to substantiate their opinion.[49] For a while, the fundamentalists in Egypt won their case, forcing legal reformations on the subject during the 1920s, 1940s and early 1950s to be shelved.

But the trend seems now to be in favour of restricted polygamy if not monogamy forthright.

In Iraq, marriage to more than one wife is allowed ony by permission of the judge, who shall not give it until he makes sure of fulfilment of two conditions:

(i) that the husband is financially capable of supporting more than one wife;
(ii) that there is a legitimate interest (Art. 3, para. 4).

The judge has also the discretion to rule that wives would not be treated in fairness and equity, whereupon he shall not permit polygamy (*ibid.* para. 5). Any man who contravenes the two said paragraphs shall be liable to a penalty of one year's imprisonment and/or a fine of Iraqi Dinars 100.

The Syrian legislation is less categorical while following the same course. The judge has the power to forbid a married man from taking another wife unless there is a legitimate justification and the financial capability to support both wives is proven (Art. 17).

Although the Jordanian Law imposes no obvious restrictions on polygamy, it allows the wife to stipulate in the marriage contract that the husband shall not take another wife and entitles the wife to sue for divorce if such a condition is not honoured (Art. 19/1).

The same allowance for the wife is repeated in the Moroccan Law (Art. 31). There is also a provision prohibiting polygamy if injustice among wives is feared (Art. 30/1). Marriage to a second wife is not allowed unless she is made aware of the fact that the husband is already married, and the first wife is entitled to apply to the court to assess any injury inflicted on her as a result of a second wife, even if there is no stipulation against it (Art. 30/2).

The Egyptian Act No. 100/1985 follows the same trend, adding to Act No. 25/1929 Article 11 *bis* which requires the husband to declare in the marriage document his social status, stating in his declaration the name of the wife or wives living with him in matrimony. The Notary Public is

49 *Cf.* Abu Zahra, *op. cit.* pp. 89–96.

required under the law to notify her or them of the new marriage by registered mail with recorded delivery. The new law entitles the wife whose husband has married again to apply for divorce if she suffers a material or moral injury that renders continued marital life between their likes difficult, even if she has not stipulated in their marriage contract that he may not marry another. The judge shall try to effect a reconciliation, failing which he shall order an irrevocable divorce. The wife shall lose the right to apply for divorce on this ground on the lapse of one year from her knowledge of the marriage to another, unless she has consented thereto whether expressly or by implication. This right shall be renewed whenever the husband marries again. If the new wife does not know that her husband is already married until after her marriage to him, she may also apply for divorce.

(d) Kuwaiti Article 23. Article 23 of the Kuwaiti Personal Status Act No. 51/1984 prohibits the marriage of a man to a woman whom he stirred viciously against her husband, unless she is remarried to her previous husband who later repudiates her or dies, leaving her a widow. This provision, unique to the Kuwaiti law, is introduced to safeguard the family "rendering futile the action of those who try to break the union of the spouses, by inciting the wife to harm her husband or luring her by money or otherwise, in order to be able to marry those women who have been tricked by them", according to the Explanatory Memorandum to the Law. It derives from the Maliki Doctrine which treated such incidents by prohibiting the second marriage and rescinding it if it was concluded. Some Malikis rule such a prohibition to be permanent. Others consider it to be only temporary, to be removed on the first husband divorcing the woman again or leaving her a widow. The Kuwaiti law adopted the latter ruling, considered to be the most authoritative Maliki opinion, according to the Jurist Zarqani.

(2) Irrevocable repudiation

A specific form of irrevocable repudiation is meant here, namely a third pronouncement of repudiation following two previous ones. During a first or a second pronouncement, the husband may withdraw his pronouncement and the marriage continues without new dower or contract, or even without the woman's consent before the expiry of the iddat period. But after a third pronouncement, she becomes temporarily prohibited to him until she marries another husband after completing her iddat and is later duly separated from him through death or divorce. The authority is two Quranic verses: "Divorce must be pronounced twice and then (a woman) must be retained in honour or released in kindness."[50] And a little later, "And if he hath divorced her (the third time), then she is not lawful unto him thereafter until she had wedded another husband."[51]

This is the universal Sharia provision, followed by both the Sunnis and the Shias. It has been included in all modern Arab legislations, except Tunisia (Arts. 36, Syrian; 30, Jordanian; 29, paras. 3 and 4, Moroccan; 13, Iraqi; 22, Kuwaiti).

In Tunisia, this becomes a permanent impediment. The husband is prohibited to marry his divorcee after three pronouncements (Art. 19). Although the fundamentalists consider this is a violation of an honoured provision, the Tunisian commentator, Muhammad Al-Tahir As-Senoussi bases it on a Tradition by the Prophet in which he cursed such a marriage, and a Tradition by the Second Patriarchal Caliph, Omar, that "If a man is reported to me to have done that I would stone him", both quoted by Ibn Qayyim al Jouzia, a Hanbali fundamentalist himself who considered such an arrangement as a distorted Sharia which it is the duty of every Muslim, and especially those in power, to stop.[52]

Another form of irrevocable divorce, by mutual cursing, "mulaana", constitutes a permanent marriage impediment, unless the husband admits perjury.[53] Some Hanafi jurists, on the authority of a Tradition of the Prophet, rule that the impediment shall stay for ever.[54]

According to the Druzes, any divorce shall render the divorcee permanently prohibited to the husband (Lebanese Druze Personal Status Act/1948, Art. 11, Syrian Personal Status Act, Art. 307-G).

(3) Difference of religion

The Sharia makes a distinction between men and women in respect of the impediment of difference in religion. The Sunni and Shia jurists are unanimous that no Muslim woman can marry a non-Muslim under the two Quranic verses, "and give not your daughters in marriage to polytheists till they believe"[55] and "O ye who believe! When believing women come into you as fugitives, examine them. Allah is best aware of their faith. Then, if ye know them for true believers, send them not back unto the infidels. They are not lawful for the infidels nor are the infidels lawful for them."[56]

50 Sura Baqara, II, verse 229.
51 *Ibid.* verse 23.
52 Muhammad Al-Tahir As-Senoussi, *Mejelle of Personal Status* (Tunis, 1958), pp. 28–29.
53 Abu Zahra, pp. 98–99; Abdullah, pp. 403–404; Al-Hilli, pp. 85–86.
54 Abu Zahra, p. 346.
55 Sura Baqara, II, verse 221.
56 Sura Mumtahana, LX, verse 10.

This universal prohibition shared by the Shia,[57] has been incorporated in the modern personal status laws of Syria (Art. 48/2), Jordan (Art. 33/1), Iraq (Art. 17), Morocco (Art. 29/5), and Kuwait (Art. 18/2). It also applies even where it is not explicitly mentioned. The marriage of a Muslim woman to a non-Muslim man shall be void unconditionally, regardless of being consummated or not. The two parties have to be separated.

As for the Muslim men, they are prohibited to marry a non-Kitabi woman. These include those who do not believe in any prophets or holy scriptures, the atheists, the idolaters and the worshippers of the sun or stars. A magi woman, i.e. a worshipper of fire, may marry a Muslim man according to the Shias, who consider her an equivalent to the "People of the Book", "Ahlul-Kitab", meaning the Jews and the Christians.[58] The Sunnis include the magis among the prohibited infidels. This provision is based on the Quranic verse "Wed not polytheists till they believe".[59] The authority allowing the Muslim man to marry a woman of the "People of the Book" is the Quranic verse:

> "This day are all good things made lawful to you. The food of those who have received the Scripture is lawful for you and your food is lawful for them. And so are the virtuous women of the believers and the virtuous women of those who received the Scripture before you (lawful to you) when you give them their marriage portion and live with them in honour, not in fornication, nor taking them as secret concubines."[60]

8 MARRIAGE FORMALITIES

Under the strict Sharia provisions, for both the Sunnis and the Shias, a marriage contract shall be valid, effective and binding if it fulfils all the previous requirements. The Sharia proper does not require either or both parties to be adults, since minors, having reached puberty may marry. It does not even stipulate that a marriage contract shall be written down in a formal or informal document, nor even to be written at all. This is the position held in all Islamic states where there is no codified legislation.

In Egypt, however, while the above position is not disputed, the legislator has laid certain rules both to prove marriage and to hear matrimonial

57 Al-Hilli, p. 16.
58 *Ibid.* p. 9.
59 Sura Baqara, II, verse 221.
60 Sura Maida, IV, verse 5.

disputes before the courts. Under the Decree No. 78/1931 in respect of the regulation of the Sharia Courts, Article 99, paragraphs 4 and 5, lays two conditions for hearing a matrimonial case before the court:

(i) that matrimony be proven by a formal marriage certificate;
(ii) that the ages of the wife and the husband shall not be below 16 and 18 years of hijra respectively.

Nevertheless, it must be stressed again that the Egyptian Law did not dispute the validity, effectiveness or binding of a marriage contract concluded under the Sharia, but only prevented judges from hearing matrimonial cases in which the parties have not reached the prescribed ages, and from hearing a matrimonial case if matrimony was denied if there is no written formal document.

Some formalities must be complied with in the case of marriage of an Egyptian Muslim man and a non-Muslim or a foreign woman. Under Article 27 of the Mazun regulations of 1915, the Mazun (that is the public officer authorized to solemnize marriages) shall not conclude either the marriage of an orphan who has no guardian, nor contracts in which one party is a foreign citizen or is not a Muslim, as this shall be left to the courts. Moreover, the Egyptian Ministry of Justice has prepared a special document in Arabic, English and French containing the most important terms, rights and duties of marriage under the Islamic Sharia; namely, that the husband may marry more than one wife, that he may divorce his wife, that his children by a Kitabi wife shall be Muslim like the father, and that there shall be no inheritance between the spouses if they differ in religion.

In the Lebanon, according to the Family Rights Act and the Sunni and Jaafari Sharia Judiciary Act regulating the personal status of the Lebanese Sunni and Jaafari denominations, the Sharia Court of the jurisdiction of the domicile of either party has exclusively the power to solemnize marriage contracts for Muslims. Likewise, the personal status officer can only record marriage contracts duly solemnized and bearing the authentication of the spiritual chief by whom a contract was solemnized. Again, these legal texts do not invalidate a Muslim marriage that does not observe these rules. But the civil and spiritual authorities would not recognize such a marriage unless the competent Sharia Court rules that it is proved.

As for the Druzes of Lebanon, it is a condition for the validity of a marriage contract to be solemnized by a Sheikh Aql (i.e. the local Druze religious chief), or the denominational judge or their duly delegated deputies (Art. 16 of the Lebanese Druze Personal Status Act of 1948).

For the Syrian Druzes, the judge must ascertain the legal capability of the parties, and the validity of marriage before the contract (Art. 307/a).

As far as the other Syrians are concerned, the law (Art. 40) lays elaborate regulations:

(i) The marriage application shall be submitted to the district judge accompanied by the following documents:
  (a) a certificate of the local chief of the names of the parties to be married, their age, their domicile, the name of the guardian, and a declaration that there is no legal impediment to the marriage;
  (b) a certified extract of the birth and personal status records of the parties;
  (c) a medical certificate by a physician chosen by the parties to the effect that they are free from contagious diseases or medical impediments to the marriage. The judge may ascertain these particulars by a physician he appoints;
  (d) marriage permission for the military and those of national service age;
  (e) the approval of the Public Security Directorate if either party is a foreigner.

(ii) No marriage concluded outside the court shall be confirmed before these formalities are complied with, without prejudice to any penal clause.

The judge shall forthwith allow the marriage contract to be solemnized once these documents are submitted. In the event of doubt he may order a delay of 10 days to publicize the marriage in whatever way he deems suitable (Art. 41). If the contract is not concluded within six months, the court's permission shall be deemed void (Art. 42). The judge or any legal assistant authorized by him shall solemnize the contract (Art. 43). The marriage certificate shall include the following particulars:

(i) the names of the two parties in full and their respective domiciles;
(ii) solemnization of the contract and the date and the place thereof;
(iii) the names of the witnesses and agents and their respective addresses in full;
(iv) the amount of the prompt and the deferred dower and whether the prompt was received or not;
(v) the signature of the parties concerned, the mazun and the confirmation by the judge (Art. 44).

The court's assistant shall record the fact of the marriage in his special register, and shall send a copy thereof to the civil status department within 10 days of the marriage date, which copy shall spare the parties the notification of the marriage to the said department, with the court's assistant held liable for negligence should he fail to send the said copy (Art. 45). All these marriage formalities are free of any charge (Art. 46).

In Jordan (Art. 17) the following rules are laid down:

(a) The man desirous to marry shall refer to the judge or his deputy to solemnize the contract.
(b) The marriage contract shall be solemnized by the judge's mazun as per a formal document. The judge as such shall perform this formality personally in exceptional cases by permission of the Chief Sharia Justice.
(c) A marriage entered into without a formal document, shall render the person who makes it, the spouses and the witnesses, liable to the penalty under the Jordanian Penal Code and to a fine of no more than 100 dinars for each.
(d) Any Mazun who fails to record the contract in the official document after payment of the dues shall be liable to the two penalties of the previous paragraph, and shall be dismissed.
(e) The Sharia judge shall appoint the marriage contract Mazun, on the approval of the Chief Sharia Judge who may issue whatever instructions he deems suitable to regulate the functions of the Mazuns.
(f) (sic) The Muslim consuls of the Hashemite Kingdom of Jordan abroad shall solemnize marriage contracts and hear the divorce pronouncements of Jordanian citizens abroad, and shall record these documents in special registers.
(g) "Consuls" shall include the Hashemite Kingdom of Jordan Ministers, Plenipotentiaries, Chargés d'Affaires, Counsellors and their deputies.

In Iraq, Article 10 enumerates the formalities for the registration and proof of marriage contracts. The marriage contract must be registered with the competent court free of charge in a special register under the following conditions:

(i) Submission of a statement free of fiscal stamp, of the identity of the parties, their age and the amount of dower, with a declaration that there is no legal impediment against marriage, the said statement being signed by the contracting parties and certified by the local chief or two dignitaries of the locality.
(ii) Enclosing a medical report certifying that the spouses are free from epidemic diseases and other medical impediments, together with other documents stipulated by the law.
(iii) The contents of the statement shall be recorded in the register to be signed by the contracting parties, or stamped with their thumb prints in the presence of the judge who shall certify it, and give the

spouses that marriage document which shall be valid without any further evidence, and enforceable in respect of the dower unless disputed before a competent court. Any man who contracts his marriage outside the court shall be liable to imprisonment for not less than six months and not more than a year, or to a fine of not less than three hundred and no more than a thousand dinars. The penalty shall be increased to no less than three years' and no more than five years' imprisonment in the event of the man contracting marriage outside the court while he is already married.

In Morocco under Article 41, the marriage contract shall require two honest witnesses, and must be preceded by filing three documents:

(i) a certificate by the representative of the administrative authority of the names of both parties, their age, domicile and the name of their guardian;
(ii) a statement of the husband's personal status; and
(iii) a proof of the dissolution of marriage where the woman has previously married to ascertain that she has completed her iddat and has no legal impediment.

The marriage certificate under Article 42 should include:

(i) The names of the spouses and their parents, their respective domiciles, age, identification, e.g. nationality, and the name of the guardian.
(ii) The fact of solemnization of the contract, its date and place, showing whether it is done by the spouses and the guardian.
(iii) A full statement of the status of the wife showing whether she is a virgin or previously married, an orphan, or has a father alive with or without a natural or a legal guardian appointed by the judge, and if she has been previously married, if she is divorced or widowed and the completion of her iddat.
(iv) Reference to the certificate by a representative of the administration authority quoting the number thereof.
(v) The amount of the dower specifying the prompt and the deferred parts thereof and whether it was received in hand or by admission.
(vi) The signature of the two honest witnesses certified by the judge and under his seal.

Under Article 43, the text of the contract shall be recorded in the court marriage register and a copy thereof shall be sent to the department of civil status, and the original shall be given to the wife or her representative within a delay not exceeding 15 days from the date of the contract. The husband is entitled to a copy thereof.

In Tunisia, it is simply stated that only a formal document shall prove the marriage under a special law (Art. 4). The Civil Status Act No. 3/1377 AH (1957 AD) as amended by Acts Nos. 71/1958, 20/1962, 2/1964 and 12/1964, requires (Art. 31) that the marriage contract inside Tunisia shall be solemnized before the local religious Shaikhs or the civil status officer, together with two honest witnesses.

The marriage of Tunisians abroad shall be solemnized before the Tunisian diplomats or consuls or according to the laws of the country in which it takes place.

Under Article 32 of the same Act, the marriage contract shall include the following particulars:

(i) The spouses' names, family names, professions, ages, dates and places of birth, domicile and residence and nationality.
(ii) The names, family names, profession, domicile and nationalities of their parents.
(iii) A declaration by the witnesses that each spouse is free from any marriage commitment.
(iv) Names and family names of the previous spouse of each spouse, together with the date of death or divorce dissolving the previous marriage contract.
(v) Where applicable, the consent or permission required under Article 3 of the "Personal Status Mejelle" and the specification of dower.

Under Article 33 the local shaikhs must send within a month from the date of the contract to the civil status officer of their area, a notification of the marriage before delivering a copy of the marriage contract to the parties concerned.

Under Article 34, the civil status officer of the area where the contract was solemnized shall record the marriage notification in a special register immediately on being informed thereof, and shall inform the civil status officer of the place of birth of the spouses of the fact of marriage. The latter officer shall record on the marriage contract the particulars of the birth of each spouse (Art. 35).

Any marriage contracted contrary to the provisions of Article 31 above shall be deemed void (Art. 36), nevertheless giving the following three effects:

(i) establishment of parentage;
(ii) the starting of the iddat from the date of the voidance declarations; and
(iii) the creation of prohibited degrees on grounds of affinity (Art. 36 *bis*).

The Tunisian spouses married abroad according to the laws of the country in which their marriage was solemnized shall record their marriage in the marriage register of the nearest Tunisian Consulate within three months (Art. 37).

Foreigners in Tunisia shall marry in accordance with the Tunisian Laws on the strength of a certificate by their Consul that they can marry. Two foreigners of the same nationality may marry before the diplomatic or consular representatives of their country in Tunisia, who shall inform the civil status officer of the locality where marriage took place (Art. 38).

9. EFFECTS OF MARRIAGE

The effects of marriage depend on the quality of the marriage contract. Classical Islamic jurists and some modern Islamic legislators classify the marriage contracts into valid, irregular and void. The Shias consider the irregular equivalent to the void.

The valid contract (*sahih*) is a contract which fulfils all its essentials and conditions of conclusion and validity. This is the Sharia definition, also adopted in Syria (Art. 47), Jordan (Art. 32), Morocco (Art. 32/1) and Kuwait (Art. 43/b). Under the Sharia, a valid contract may be either effective (*nafith*) if both spouses possess full legal capacity, i.e. adult, sane and of discretion and act on their own, or suspended (*mauquf*) if either lacks full legal capacity or is represented by a voluntary agent (*foudouli*), in which case the contract shall be subject to the approval of the guardian or the principal. This distinction is retained in the Syrian Law, Article 52, which makes the suspended marriage equivalent to an irregular marriage.

The irregular (or defective) marriage (*fasid*) is a contract which fulfils its essentials and conditions of conclusion but lacks a condition of validity, e.g. the presence of witnesses (for the Sunnis), or the marriage of a man to his foster sister without either of them knowing of the fact.

The Syrian Article 48/1 gives a similar definition of the irregular marriage as "every marriage which satisfies its essentials of offer and acceptance but lacks some conditions".

Rather than giving a definition, The Jordanian legislator enumerates inclusively the cases of irregular marriage as follows:

(i) if either or both parties lack conditions of marriage capacity at the time of the contract;
(ii) if there are not witnesses;
(iii) if the contract is entered into under coercion;
(iv) if the witnesses do not comply with the Sharia descriptions;
(v) the case of unlawful conjunction on grounds of affinity or fosterage; and
(vi) the muta and temporary marriages (Art. 34).

The Tunisian Mejelle defines the irregular marriage as one which is subject to a condition that conflicts with the substance of the contract or which contravenes the conditions laid down earlier (Art. 21).

The void marriage (*batil*), under the Sharia, is a marriage defective in its essentials or in any condition of conclusion or of validity. The marriage contract shall be void if the formula does not denote its establishment, if a contracting party is lacking capacity, if acceptance does not conform with offer, and if the woman was a prohibited degree to the man who wants to marry her, and yet he proceeds to marry her fully aware at the time of contract that she is a prohibited degree. Some Hanafis maintain the distinction between regular and void marriages on the ground of the good faith or semblance (*shubha*) in the irregular marriage although both categories are not valid. Other Hanafi jurists, e.g. Kamalud-Din Ibn al-Hammam, treat both contracts alike, maintaining that marriage could be only either valid or invalid.

The Syrian Law mentions expressly one case of void marriage, namely the marriage of a Muslim woman to a non-Muslim (Art. 48/2). But the understanding is clear that any marriage that does not comply with the conditions of validity and conclusion is void.

The Jordanian legislator enumerates expressly three cases where the marriage shall be deemed void; namely:

(i) the marriage of a Muslim woman to a non-Muslim;
(ii) the marriage of a Muslim man to a non-Kitabi; and
(iii) the marriage of a man to a woman in a prohibited degree on grounds of kindred, affinity or fosterage (Art. 33).

The Kuwaiti legislator gives a succinct account of this classification in the following three Articles:

Article 43:
(i) There are two kinds of marriage: valid or non-valid.
(ii) Valid marriage is one which fulfils its essentials and all conditions for validity according to the provisions of this Act. Any other marriage is non-valid, which is either void or irregular.

Article 44:
A valid marriage is either effective and binding, effective and non binding, or not effective at all.

Article 45:
(i) An effective and binding marriage is one which is not subject to any other person's permission, nor is rescindable, according to the provisions of this Act.

(ii) An effective but non-binding marriage is one which can be rescinded on a ground allowable under this Act.
(iii) A non-effective marriage is one contracted subject to the approval thereof by a person having authority to approve it.

Further, Article 49 rules a marriage to be void in the following events:

(i) If such a defect in the formula or in the legal capacity of the contracting party occurs as to bar the conclusions of the contract.
(ii) If the wife is a prohibited degree on grounds of kindred, fosterage or affinity, or is a wife of another man or counting her iddat from him, or is a three-time divorcée of the husband, or is a case of unlawful conjunction or does not believe in divine religion.
(iii) If either spouse is apostate or if the husband is non-Muslim and the woman Muslim.

Provided, for paragraphs (ii) and (iii) that it is established that prohibition, and the grounds thereof, are known; no ignorance is a defence if it cannot reasonably be attributed to the sort of person who is alleging it. Every other invalid marriage, apart from these cases, shall be deemed irregular (Art. 50).

There seems to be no mention of void marriage in the other modern laws, presumably because it is not considered a marriage at all or is expressly prohibited by the competent authorized officers.

Manek in his handbook of Mahomedan Law (Muslim Personal Law) gives an easy-to-understand clue in order to distinguish between valid, fasid, (described here as irregular) and void marriages under the Sunni Law, based on the nature of the impediment to the marriage. If the impediment is an *absolute and permanent prohibition* the marriage is void. If it is only *relative or temporary or due to an accidental circumstance*, the marriage is invalid (irregular).[61]

The Shias and the Druzes alike do not recognize this distinction between void and irregular marriage, deeming every marriage in which the conditions for validity are not met to be utterly void. But this distinction is important for the Sunnis both under the Sharia and the modern laws. It makes it possible to retain some lawfulness of the marriage effects under an irregular contract before the discovery of the defect therein under certain conditions, and the correction thereof in certain cases. But nothing like that can be done for a void contract.

To start with, both irregular and invalid marriages prior to consummation shall have the same effect, that is to say no effect whatsoever, and the parties shall separate either on their own accord or by order of the court in a case for separation and annulment which it is the duty of every Muslim

61 Manek, *Mahomedan Law (Muslim Personal Law)* (Bombay, 1948), p. 43.

to institute. This is the Sharia Law adopted also expressly by the Jordanian legislator (Arts. 41, 42 and 43) and honoured by all the other countries where the Sharia provisions are applied in absence of any specific legal text.

If there was consummation under an irregular marriage contract, the Muslim Sunni jurists and the modern legislators are unanimous that it shall create the woman's entitlement to dower, her observation of the iddat, the lawful parentage of the offspring and a prohibited degree on grounds of affinity. The Jordanian Law excludes other effects such as mutual inheritance and maintenance before and after the dissolution without specifying the dower (Art. 42). Notwithstanding the above ruling of the necessity of separation between the parties under an irregular contract, no action in respect of any irregular marriage on grounds of minority shall be heard if the wife gives birth or is pregnant, or if the two parties at the time of the action possessed legal marriage capacity (Art. 43).

The Syrian Act is more specific. Under Article 51:

(i) An irregular marriage before consummation shall be deemed a void marriage.
(ii) Consummation shall bring about the following effects:
  (a) the wife shall receive the dower of the equal or the designated dower, whichever is less;
  (b) the parentage of the children is established under certain rules;
  (c) the creation of prohibited degrees on grounds of affinity;
  (d) the wife shall observe the iddat of divorce or death of the husband and shall receive the iddat maintenance but without any mutual rights of inheritance between the two spouses;
  (e) the wife shall be entitled to matrimonial maintenance for as long as she remains unaware of the irregularity of marriage.

The same provisions apply to suspended marriage before the approval (Art. 52). The offspring shall be considered the husband's if it is born after 180 days from the date of consummation, or if it is born between the minimum and maximum term of pregnancy, creating all the effects of parentage, including the prohibited degrees, rights of inheritance and kindred maintenance (Arts. 132 and 133).

The same provisions are set in Kuwaiti Articles 50 and 51.

Under the Moroccan Law, an irregular marriage on grounds of the contract *per se* shall be dissolved before consummation, but shall entitle the woman to a dower after consummation. If it is irregular on the grounds of the dower, it shall be dissolved prior to consummation without any dower and shall entitle the woman after consummation to the dower of the equal. Every marriage unanimously considered irregular, such as a prohibited degree on the grounds of affinity shall be dissolved without divorce prior to consummation and following it, but it shall create the necessity of iddat and the establishment of parentage, provided good faith is proved. A marriage where opinions differ on its irregularity shall be dissolved before and after consummation through divorce and shall create necessity for the observation of the iddat, the proven parentage and mutual inheritance prior to dissolution (Art. 37 [1] and [2]).

Under the Tunisian Law (Art. 22), the irregular marriage shall be deemed of necessity void without divorce; the mere fact of the contract shall not create any effect, but the fact of consummation shall only create the following effects:

(i) the entitlement of the woman to the dower agreed upon or a dower ordered by the judge;
(ii) the establishment of parentage;
(iii) the observation of iddat by the wife as from the date of separation;
(iv) a prohibited degree on grounds of affinity.

The Ithna-Asharis maintain that any marriage contract that lacks any condition of validity shall be invalid, and shall create no effects. The parties shall leave one another or shall be compelled to separate. It shall create no prohibited degrees on ground of affinity if separation takes place prior to consummation, the parties shall not inherit from each other and the dower of the equal shall be payable only after but not before consummation, even if another dower was agreed upon.

The void marriage, both with or without consummation, shall have no effect whatsoever, the relationship being deemed illegitimate, and any offspring shall be likewise deemed illegitimate. This is the Sharia Law retained expressly in the Jordanian Code (Art. 41), and in Kuwait (Art. 48). Only the Hanafis acknowledge one effect of consummation, which is the creation of the impediment of fornication which establishes, according to them, a prohibited degree on the grounds of affinity.

A valid and effective marriage contract shall create established legal effects in respect of the rights and duties for wife, husband and other rights and duties common to both of them (Moroccan, Art. 33). The Jordanian Code sums them up in dower and maintenance for the wife and mutual right of inheritance between them (Art. 35), adding certain conditions on the matrimonial home (Arts. 36, 37, 38 and 40). It also stresses the good treatment of the wife by the husband and her obedience to him in lawful matters (Art. 39). The Syrian law sums up the effects of valid and effective marriage as the dower and maintenance for the wife, her duty to follow her husband, the mutual rights of inheritance and family rights, such as the parentage of the offspring and the creation of prohibited degrees on the grounds of affinity (Art. 49).

In view of the importance of the dower and maintenance, they will be dealt with in separate chapters. Here we shall deal with the other effects of the valid and effective marriage, under the Sharia and the modern laws were applicable.

(1) Under the Sharia

The first duty of the spouses is faithfulness and chastity in that the man and the wife should not enter into any extra-marital relationship. Failure to observe this duty constitutes adultery which can constitute a ground for divorce. This is based on the Quranic verses: "And who guard their modesty – save from their wives or the (slaves) that their right hands possess, for then they are not blameworthy. But whoso craveth beyond that, such are transgressors."[62]

The Moroccan Law makes it a right of the husband that the wife shall guard her chastity (Art. 36/1).

(2) The common matrimonial home

It is the duty of the husband to provide and the right of the wife to have a suitable matrimonial home according to the Quranic verse: "Lodge them where ye dwell, according to your wealth, and harass them not so as to straiten life for them."[63]

The wife should follow the husband to the matrimonial home, provided that it complies with the Sharia requirements, that is, that it should be in accordance with the husband's financial standing, habitable, private and not occupied by others, even if they are the husband's kin, and provided that the husband is trustworthy towards her and her assets, and has paid her dower or the agreed prompt portion thereof. She shall not leave it without her husband's permission, but she can do so to perform a religious duty such as pilgrimage, accompanied by a member of kin of a prohibited degree. She may also visit a sick parent without the husband's permission, since the rights of parents, under the Sharia, are paramount to those of the husband. Otherwise her leaving it without his permission shall deprive her of her maintenance entitlement as she would then be rebellious (*nashiza*). This will be dealt with in the chapter on maintenance. This common life in a matrimonial home is stressed as a mutual right and a duty of the spouses under the Moroccan Decree, Article 34/1.

Matrimonial home is more elaborately dealt with in the Syrian law which makes it a duty of the husband to provide his wife with a home that is conventional for his equals (Art. 65) and makes it a duty of the wife to

62 Sura Muminun, XXIII, verses 5, 6, 7.
63 Sura Talaq, LXV, verse 6.

live with her husband after receiving the prompt instalment of her dower (Art. 66). The husband is not allowed to live with his wife and another wife at the same home without her consent (Art. 67). In the case of polygamy, the husband shall provide his wives with equal homes (Art. 68). The husband shall not bring any relatives of his to live with his wife (apart from his minor child under the age of discretion) if such relations maltreat her (Art. 69). The wife shall of necessity travel with her husband unless it is otherwise stipulated in the marriage contract, or unless the judge found an excuse for her not to travel (Art. 70).

According to the Jordanian Law, the husband shall provide a dwelling containing all the necessary appliances according to his means, and in the place where he lives and works (Art. 36). The wife, following the receipt of her prompt dower, shall obey and live in her husband's lawful home and shall, under pain of losing her right of maintenance, travel with him to any destination he wishes, even if it is abroad, provided her safety is secured and that the marriage contract does not stipulate otherwise (Art. 37). The husband shall not have his relatives or his child above the age of discretion (by another woman) live with him without the consent of his wife in the home he set up for her, except his poor disabled parents if he has no means to support them on their own, and has no alternative but to have them stay with him without their impeding matrimonial life together. Likewise, the wife shall not have her children by another husband or her relatives to live with her without the consent of the husband (Art. 38). The husband married to more than one wife shall be equally fair to them, and shall not have them live in the same home without their consent (Art. 40).

Similar provisions are laid down in the Kuwaiti Law. The husband must accommodate his wife in a home worthy of his equals (Art. 84/a); he shall not accommodate her, without her consent, with another wife of his (Art. 85); he shall not let anyone share their home, except his children under discretion and other children of his who need a home, and his parents, provided the wife will not be jeopardized thereby.

(3) The creation of prohibited degrees on the grounds of affinity

The respective ascendants and descendants of each spouse shall be prohibited degrees for either as explained in the impediments of marriage. Unlawful conjunction shall also apply.

(4) Proven parentage of the offspring

Marriage establishes the parentage of the offspring to the husband unless there is indisputable evidence to the contrary. The Hanafis maintain even that the very fact of the marriage contract, regardless of consummation, creates the parentage. Other jurists maintain that parentage is established on the ground of the contract with the possibility of consummation. We shall deal with this in more detail in the chapter on parentage.

(5) Mutual inheritance

Each spouse shall inherit from the other in the event of death while lawful matrimony exists in fact, or is deemed to be existing, unless there is an impediment to inheritance. This will be discussed in detail in the chapter on Inheritance. Except for the Shia, consummation of marriage is not a condition of inheritance: if either spouse dies after the valid contract and prior to consummation, the other shall inherit. For the Shia ruling, see the chapter on Inheritance.

Even though the muta marriage creates no mutual inheritance rights, a stipulation agreed upon by the two parties to that effect shall be lawful and effective.

(6) Decent treatment

It is the moral duty of each spouse to treat the other with respect and kindness and to live together in harmony and peace. This is a moral duty incumbent according to the Quranic verses: "And consort with them in kindness, for if ye hate them it may happen that ye hate a thing wherein Allah hath placed much good."[64] "And they (women) have rights similar to those (of men) over them in kindness."[65] "And of His signs in this: He created for you helpmeets from yourselves that ye might find rest in them, and He ordained between you love and mercy. Lo, herein indeed are portents for folk who reflect."[66]

The Moroccan Law makes "living together in harmony, mutual feelings of respect and kindness and concern for the welfare of the family" a mutual right and duty of the spouses (Art. 34/2).

The Jordanian Law provides that it is the duty of the husband to live decently with his wife and to treat her with kindness and a duty of the wife to obey her husband in lawful matters (Art. 39). This duty of the wife to obey her husband is also asserted under the Moroccan Law (Art. 36/2).

Further, the Moroccan Law adds to the above, two rights of the woman, namely, to be allowed to visit her relatives and to invite them to visit her in kindness and according to decent custom, and her complete freedom to dispose as she wishes of her property without any supervision or control by the husband who has no right of guardianship in respect of his wife's property (Art. 35/3 and 4). It also adds to the rights of the

64 Sura Nisaa, IV, verse 19.
65 Sura Baqara, II, verse 228.
66 Sura Rum, XXX, verse 21.

husband, that the wife shall suckle her offspring if she is able, shall supervise a household and put it in good shape, and shall honour her husband's parents and relatives in kindness and according to decent custom (Art. 36/3/4/5).

10. MIXED MARRIAGES

Several references have been made in the previous sections to the subject of mixed marriages, e.g. in the context of marriage impediments and formalities. Generally speaking, the same principles which govern valid marriage contracts in accordance with the Sharia and modern Islamic legislation apply to mixed marriages as well. However, in view of the importance of this subject with which the legal profession is confronted only too often in the daily practice, it behoves us to compile in a brief form the main rules which are dealt with in more detail in the previous sections in this chapter and in the following chapters of dower, maintenance, dissolution of marriage, the rights of children, inheritance and wills.

The same conditions on the legality of the marriage contract apply to mixed marriages. The most important condition relates to religion. Under the Sharia and all modern Islamic laws, both for the Sunni and Shia sects, a marriage of a Muslim woman to a non-Muslim man is null and void, even if it is validly solemnized according to the laws of any given non-Muslim state. For such a marriage to be valid the man must have converted to Islam at the time of the contract.

On the other hand, a Muslim man cannot enter into a valid marriage, under the Sharia and the Islamic modern laws, to a non-Muslim woman who is not Christian or a Jewess (or a magi according to the Shias). It must be stressed that that impediment is restricted to religion, without anything to do with nationality.

A non-Muslim woman validly married to a Muslim enjoys the same rights as a Muslim wife in respect of retaining sole control of her property. In fact this right is extended even to foreign women married to non-Muslims in Arab states.

Although under the Sharia, and in the overwhelming majority of modern Islamic states the Muslim man can have up to four wives at the same time, under certain conditions and restrictions, a non-Muslim wife can stipulate in her marriage contract that her Muslim husband shall not take another wife and can retain to herself the right to terminate the marriage on her own.

The dower is the legal right of the wife of a Muslim whether or not she is Muslim herself. During her marriage she has the inalienable right to be maintained by her husband regardless of any private means she may have. She is entitled also, under the laws of certain Arab states, to damages in the event of arbitrary divorce by her husband, over and above the maintenance due to her during her iddat which she must observe.

She has the right to custody of the male infant for the duration of suckling, according to the Shia, or until he reaches the age of discretion, according to the Sunnis, and of the female until she reaches puberty. In all cases she retains the right to access. The only restriction is that there should be no danger of her converting the child to a religion different from its father's.

A non-Muslim widow has no right to inheritance in the estate of her Muslim husband, since it is a condition for an heir to profess the same religion as the propositus. But she can be left a part of the estate, not exceeding one-third, by a will.

For details of these provisions, reference should be made to the relevant chapters.

Chapter 4

Dower

1. DEFINITION AND JURISTIC QUALIFICATION

The Dower (*Mahr*, *Sadaq* or *Oqr*, also referred to in the Quran as *Nehla*, *Ajr* and *Fareeda*-portion) is a sum of money or other property which becomes payable by the husband to the wife as an effect of marriage. The Quran ordains: "And give the women (on marriage) their dower as a free gift."[1] In another verse: "We know what We have appointed for them as to their wives."[2] It is an obligatory and fit gift by the man to win her heart and to honour marriage. The Moroccan legislator defines the dower as: "The property given by the husband to indicate his willingness to contract marriage, to establish a family and to lay the foundations for affection and companionship" (Art. 16).

Contrary to a widely held misconception in the West, dower is not a bride-price. In fact, it is expressly prohibited, under the Moroccan Law, Article 19, for the guardian, be he a father or not, to receive anything for himself from the suitor in consideration for the marriage of his daughter or ward to the suitor. The same prohibition is stressed under Jordanian Article 62, for the wife's parents or relatives to receive money or anything else from the husband in consideration of getting her to marry him, or giving her away to him. The husband shall recover whatever he has so given, or the value thereof. According to the Hanafi Jurist Al Kamal ibn ul Humam (died 861 AH), "Dower has been ordered to underline the prestige of the marriage contract and to stress its importance. . . . It has not been enjoined as a consideration like a price or a wage, otherwise it would have been set as a prior condition."[3] This is the reason why dower is neither an essential nor a condition for the validity, binding or

1 Sura Nissa, IV, verse 4.
2 Sura Ahzab, XXXIII, verse 50.
3 *Fat-hul Qadeer*, Vol. 3 (Cairo), pp. 143, 324. Al-Kassani, *Al-Badaia*, Vol. 4 (Cairo), p. 43.

effectiveness of the marriage contract. It is not mentioned as such in any modern Islamic legislation. A marriage contract is deemed valid without any mention of dower. The classical jurists cite the authority of the Quranic verse, "It is no sin for you if ye divorce women while yet ye have not touched them nor appointed unto them a portion (dower)."[4] The jurists infer that since no sin is committed by those who divorce their wives before marriage consummation or agreement on dower, and since divorce can only occur after a valid marriage, therefore this verse proves that a marriage contract can be valid without any mention of dower.

The qualification of dower as an effect or a consequence of the marriage contract rather than as an essential or a validity condition thereof, does not reduce or weaken in any way the wife's entitlement to it. In fact it is both an inalienable and imprescriptible right of the wife:

(i) It is *inalienable* in that it is taken for granted even if it is not expressly stated in the contract. The Shias maintain that if the husband makes a condition in the marriage contract that he shall pay no dower, this condition shall be null and void, but the contract shall remain valid.[5] Kuwaiti Article 52 provides that the dower shall be due to the wife by the very fact of a valid marriage contract. The Syrian Law adds to the same ruling that it shall be so, whether it is specified, not specified or ignored completely (Art. 53), and that the husband can only obtain discharge thereof by paying it to her (Art. 61). Dower of the equal shall apply in the event of failure to specify it or in an irregular specification thereof (Syrian, Art. 61/1; Iraqi, Art. 19). The Jordanian Law makes dower the property of the wife from which she cannot be compelled to buy furniture or domestic appliances (Art. 61). In Tunisia, it is the wife's exclusive property to dispose of in any way she likes (Art. 12). A similar provision to the last two applies under Moroccan Article 18.
(ii) It is *imprescriptible* in that the wife shall not lose her entitlement to it through prescription alone. This is a basic Sharia provision adopted expressly in the Syrian Law, "The deferred dower shall not be subject to prescription provisions even if a promissory note was made of it as long as the state of matrimony exists" (Art. 60/2). The same law also makes it "a privileged debt following immediately after the payable maintenance debt referred to under Article 1120 of the Civil Code" (Art. 54/3).[6]

The Moroccan and Tunisian Codes (Arts. 21 and 13, respectively)

4 Sura Baqara, II, verse 236.
5 Al-Hilli, *Jaafari Personal Status Provisions*, p. 6, Art. 12.
6. Art 1120, para. 1C of the Civil Code:
"The following claims are secured by a privilege over all the debtor's property, whether movable or immovable. (c) alimony due by the debtor to members of his family and his kin."

deny the husband any right to force the wife to connubial intercourse until he pays her her dower. However, if the wife allows consummation, she shall only retain the right to claim her dower as a debt due to her on her husband. His inability to repay it shall not be a valid ground for divorce.

2. QUALITY OF DOWER

According to Sunnis and Shias alike, the dower may consist of anything that can be valued in money, is useful and ritually clean. The Syrian and Moroccan Codes rule that "anything that can be the object of a lawfully valid obligation is a valid dower" (Articles 54/2 and 17-1, respectively). To this, Article 54 of the Kuwaiti Law adds: "be it a property, a service or a usufruct, provided it does not conflict with the husband's status of guardian". The Tunisian Law holds that "anything that is lawful and can be valued in money may be designated as a dower" (Art. 12).

Therefore, the dower may be immovable property, e.g. land and buildings, measurable movable property, e.g. cattle or crops, specific chattels or a usufruct with a pecuniary value. Wine and pigs are not valid dowers, being ritually unclean, even to a Kitabi wife. Nor is a non-pecuniary concession, such as not to take another wife or not to move the wife out of her town. The Explanatory Note to the Kuwaiti Law, in respect of the said Article 54, does not allow the husband becoming a servant to his wife as a dower, as it entails degradation of the husband, and runs against his being the guardian.

The property given as a dower must be reasonably specified for identification. The husband may designate a horse, a dress of certain material, or a weight of cotton, in which case he shall be bound to provide the article designated at an average value. But a vague dower, e.g. "an animal" or "a house" shall not be valid, without however invalidating the marriage contract itself, but the dower of the equal shall be due. According to an authentic tradition of the Prophet, respected by the Shias, teaching the Quran can be a valid dower.[7]

3. QUANTITY OF DOWER

Classical jurists and modern law makers set no ceiling for the dower (Arts. 54/1, Syrian; 17/2, Moroccan; 12, Tunisian; 53, Kuwaiti). Tradition has it that the Second Patriarchal Caliph, Umar ibn-ul-Khattab, tried to limit excessive dowers, but was stopped by a woman quoting the Quranic verses, "And if ye wish to exchange one wife for another and ye have given

7 Al-Hilli, *op. cit.* p. 19 and *Saheeh-ul-Bukhari* and *Saheeh-u-Muslim*, *Fiqh al-Sunna* by Sayyid Sabiq (Cairo), p. 136.

unto one of them a sum of money (however great) take nothing from it. Would ye take it by way of calumny and open wrong? How can ye take it (back) after one of you hath gone into the other and they have taken a strong pledge from you?"[8]

But there is no such unanimity on the minimal dower. The Shafiis, Hanbalis and Shias maintain that there is no such limit. On the authority of the Quranic ruling, ". . . so that you seek them with your property in honest wedlock, not debauching" (*ibid.* verse 24) they argue that any property, regardless of quantity, is acceptable as dower. This position is expressly held in Syria (Art. 54/1), Morocco (Art. 17/2) and Kuwait (Art. 53). It is also implied in Iraqi Article 19/1 and Jordanian Article 44, which both rule that the wife shall be entitled to the dower specified in the contract, with the Jordanian adding "however small or large".

The Malikis set a quarter dinar of gold or three dirhams of silver[9] as the minimal dower, by analogy with the statutory (Sharia) limit for punishable theft. The Hanafi doctrine, applied in Egypt and among the Lebanese Sunnis (Family Rights Act) maintain that the minimal dower shall be 10 dirhams, citing the authority of a tradition of the Prophet to that effect, a tradition whose authenticity is disputed by other schools.[10]

A similar position is held by the Tunisian legisaltor who rules that "dower shall not be insignificant (*tafih*) (Art. 12).

4. PROMPT AND DEFERRED DOWER

The dower, being a consequence of the marriage contract rather than an essential or a condition of it, shall be the right of the wife once the valid contract is made. However, it may not be paid in full at once, but may be split into two portions, prompt and deferred. This provision is retained from the Sharia in the modern Arab laws (Arts. 55, Syrian; 45, Jordanian; 20/1, Iraqi; 20/1, Moroccan; and 53/a, Kuwaiti). All these laws allow the whole or part of the dower to be deferred. However, Jordanian Law requires that any such agreement shall be recorded in writing, otherwise the whole dower shall be deemed prompt.

Iraqi, Syrian and Kuwaiti laws rule that if no such arrangement was written down, then custom prevailing shall be followed. That is also in general the Sharia provision applying the maxim that "a matter recognized by custom is regarded as though it was a contractual obligation." In

8 Sura Nisaa, IV, verses 20/21.
9 The Dirham is a silver coin weighing 2.97 grammes; see *Encyclopaedia of Islam*.
10 *Cf. Fat-hul Qadeer*, Vol. 3, pp. 185, 206.

Egypt, for example, the custom is to divide the dower into two equal shares.

The deferred dower shall become payable on the date agreed upon, otherwise it shall become payable immediately on the earlier of two events: divorce or death. The Iraqi Law makes any date for the payment of the deferred dower void in the event of divorce or death, when it becomes immediately payable (Art. 20/2). The Jordanian Law is more elaborate: under Article 46, if a date is set for the deferred dower, the wife shall not be entitled to claim it before the said date, even in the event of divorce. However, the Article continues, in the event of the death of the husband, that date will be void. Further, if the term is grossly indeterminate, like "till the time of affluence", or "on demand", or "at the time of wedding", the term shall be invalid, and all of the dower shall be deemed prompt. If no term was stipulated, the deferred dower shall be deemed payable on divorce or the death of either spouse.

5. SPECIFIED AND PROPER DOWER (DOWER OF THOSE EQUAL TO THE WIFE)

The dower may be specified (stipulated, designated, *musamma*) in the contract, in which case it shall be binding on the husband, provided that the contract is valid and subject to reservations by those who require a minimal value. If it is omitted, irregular, or if there is an invalid condition that no dower shall be payable, then the proper dower or the dower of the equal (*Mahr-ul-mithl*) shall apply (Arts. 54 Jordanian and 55b Kuwaiti). According to the Sunni and Shia jurists, the equal to be considered is a woman who is an agnate relative of the wife-to-be, e.g. her sister, paternal aunt or cousin. If there is no woman equal to the wife among her agnate relations, the equal may be a woman belonging to a family equivalent to her father's but not her mother's family.[11] The Shafiis differ, maintaining that in the absence of an agnate, the equal shall be a consanguine relative, otherwise the nearest woman in terms of age, education, wealth, beauty, pedigree and virginity or previous marriage.[12]

Jordanian Article 44, while retaining that the equal shall be an agnate woman relative, rules that in the absence of such relative the equal shall be considered among the wife's peers of her townfolk. Aspects of equality, according to the jurists, include beauty, youth, social status, e.g. being a

11 Al-Hilli, *op. cit.* p. 19; Abdullah, *Personal Status*, pp. 286, 287; Abu Zahra, *On Marriage*, p. 183.

12 *Al Umm*, Vol. 5, p. 64.

virgin, a divorcée or a widow, wealth, intelligence, piety, manners, being with or without children, etc.

The specified dower may be increased or reduced under certain conditions. The Sunnis and the Shias allow the husband, his father or grandfather if he lacks legal capacity, to add to the specified dower, on the authority of the Quranic verse "And there is no sin for you in what ye do by mutual agreement after a dower (*fareeda*) is prescribed."[13] Provided that the husband is sane, major and under no interdiction due to imbecility or prodigality, he may add to the basic specified dower. Such an addition shall be the right of the wife to claim, together with the basic dower, with the difference that it cannot be halved, unlike the basic dower in the event of divorce before consummation, but shall be dropped altogether.[14] The addition shall be binding on the husband on three conditions:

(i) That it is determinate. If a husband says to his wife, "I have added to your dower" without further specification, no addition shall be valid.
(ii) That it occurs while they are still actually or deemed to be linked by marriage, i.e. if they are not separated or during the iddat of a revocable divorce. Otherwise it is void.
(iii) That it is accepted, at the same sitting where it has been offered by the wife or her guardian if she lacks the legal capacity to accept. The idea is that such an increase is a gift whose essentials are offer by the donor and acceptance by the donee.

Likewise, a wife possessing full legal capacity may discharge her husband, subsequent to the marriage contract, of all or any part of her specified dower, it being exclusively hers to dispose of in any way she likes. The object of this discharge, which is tantamount to a reduction, is unidentifiable property, such as money, and measurable articles. It shall be valid if the husband accepts it or keeps silent, and shall be void if it is rejected. For identifiable property, e.g. a specific piece of land, or a given house, provided that it is free of any debt, the wife may make it a gift to the husband who has to accept it for it to be valid. Unlike increase, no father, grandfather or guardian of the minor wife has the power to reduce her specified dower.[15]

These Sharia provisions are included in the Jordanian Article 63 which reads: "The husband may increase the dower after the contract and the wife may reduce it provided that they possess full legal capacity of disposition. This shall be attached to the original contract if it is accepted

13 Sura Nisaa, IV, verse 24; Al-Hilli, *op. cit.* p. 20; Abdullah, *op. cit.* pp. 294–298.
14 Abdullah, *ibid.*
15 *Ibid.*

by the other party at the sitting where the increase or reduction has been offered." A similar ruling is incorporated in Article 58 of the Kuwaiti Law.

An identical text to the Jordanian Article constituted Article 57 of the Syrian Decree No. 59/1953, but it was amended under Article 5 of Act 34/1975 to read as follows: "No increase or reduction of the dower nor any discharge thereof during the state of matrimony or the iddat of divorce shall be considered, and it shall be deemed void unless it is made before the judge. Any such disposition made before the judge shall be attached to the original contract if it is accepted by the other party." The reason given in the explanatory memorandum to the said Act No. 34/1975 is to stop any duress, moral or otherwise, that either spouse may be subject to during marital life to accept any increase, reduction or discharge of the dower.

In another amendment destined to safeguard the interests of both spouses against complicity or excessive amounts of specified dower, the Syrian legislator, under Article 4 of Act No. 34/1975, added paragraph 4 to Article 54 of Act No. 59/1953 reading as follows: "Any person who alleges complicity or artificiality of the specified dower shall be required to duly prove such an allegation. On proving either, the judge shall order the dower of the equal unless a designated dower shall prove genuine."

6. ENTITLEMENT TO THE DOWER

Apart from a valid marriage contract which makes *per se* the dower an established right of the wife, consummation with the semblance of the right to have intercourse or under an irregular marriage contract shall also render the wife entitled to a dower. In the case of consummation with the semblance of the right, or under an irregular marriage contract, if the dower is validly specified, the lesser of the specified dower or the dower of the equal shall be due to the wife on separation. If the dower is irregularly specified the wife shall have the right to the dower of the equal.[16] While ignoring consummation with the semblance of the right to have intercourse, the modern Personal Status Laws of Iraq (Art. 22), Syria (Art. 63), Jordan (Art. 56), and Kuwait (Art. 50a), hold the previous Sharia provisions. Although the Shias treat an irregular marriage contract (*fasid*) as a void marriage to all intents and purposes, they maintain, nevertheless, that consummation under such a contract shall establish the woman's right, on separation, to the dower of the equal even if a specified dower has been agreed upon.[17]

16 Abu Zahra, *Personal Status*, p. 184.
17 Al-Hilli, *op. cit.* pp. 7 and 21.

Although the dower becomes an exclusive right of the wife under a valid marriage contract, the amount thereof due to her varies according to circumstances. She may be entitled to the whole dower, half of it, or may have no dower at all.

A. The Wife's Entitlement to the Whole Dower

It is unanimously agreed by the Sunnis that the whole dower shall become due to the wife on the occurrence of either of two events:

(i) the actual consummation of marriage;
(ii) the death of either spouse before consummation.

If it is the wife who dies, her heirs shall take the residue of her whole dower from the husband after deducting his share.[18] All the jurists agree that the whole dower shall be due to the wife in the event of the death of the husband, by natural causes, suicide or murder by a third party. It shall be also due on the husband killing his wife. Only Abu Hanifa and his two Companions rule that this right of the wife shall not be lost if she killed her husband, a ruling honoured in Egypt. But the three other Imams, Malik, Shafii and Ibn Hanbal and the Hanafi jurist Zufar maintain that the wife shall lose her entitlement to any dower if she killed her husband before consummation, on the grounds that crime shall not pay, by analogy to her being then deprived of the inheritance, therefore, *a fortiori*, of dower. The Kuwaiti legislator codifies this ruling in Article 62 which reads as follows: "If the wife kills her husband in a case of murder that bars her from inheritance, before consummation of marriage, she shall repay any part she received of the dower, and shall lose her right to any balance thereof. If the murder was committed after consummation, she shall have no right to any balance". The former Hanafi position is held in Egypt and adopted by the Moroccan Law, Article 20/3, and the Iraqi Law, Article 21, which rules that the wife shall be entitled to the whole *specified* dower on consummation or death of either spouse.

The Shias concur with this ruling, with the reservation that if the husband dies before consummation without having specified a dower nor set any portion for her in the contract, neither dower nor a *mutat* (a present, see B.) shall be due to the wife.[19]

Accepting these two grounds, the Hanafis add a third: the valid retirement between the two spouses which they deem as a consummation *de juro* if not *de facto*, relying on the authority of the Quranic verse, "How can ye take it (back) after one of you hath gone in unto the other and they

18 Al-Abiani, *Sharia Personal Status Provisions*, p. 81.
19 Al-Hilli, *op. cit.* p. 21.

have taken a strong pledge from you?" (Sura Nisaa, IV, verse 21), interpreting "one going in unto the other" as valid retirement. They also quote a tradition of the Prophet, "He who unveils his wife and looks to her shall be liable to pay her dower, whether there is intimacy or not."[20]

This rule is adopted in Egypt where the Hanafi doctrine prevails, and in the Lebanon by the Sunnis. It is also held in the Jordanian Law, "A dower specified under a valid contract shall be payable in full on the death of either spouse or on divorce after valid retirement . . ." (Art. 48).

The Shafiis and Malikis do not accept that valid retirement confirms the wife's right to the whole dower, invoking the authority of the Quranic verse: "If ye divorce them before ye have touched them and ye have appointed unto them a portion, then (pay the) half of that which ye appointed. . . ." (Sura Baqara, II, verse 237). However, the Malikis maintain that even without actual consummation, the whole dower shall be due to the wife if she moves into the matrimonial home to stay for a whole year.[21]

The Shias hold that valid retirement under a marriage contract shall not be a substitute for actual consummation, and shall not confirm the wife's right to the whole dower.[22]

On the other hand, the Hanbalis, whose doctrine under the Wahhabi version is strictly applied in the Kingdom of Saudi Arabia, concur with the three Hanafi grounds and add a fourth ground to confirm the entitlement of the wife to the whole dower; namely acts of undue familiarity (*al mulamasa al-fahisha*) by which is meant touching any part of a person of the opposite sex, even inadvertently, without there being any cloth or other substance between the parties of sufficient thickness to prevent warmth of body to be felt, or kissing or looking on his or her nakedness or lying together or embracing, provided:

(i) that neither of the parties is below age when the desire first arises; and
(ii) that the act is done with desire on the part of at least one of the parties, even if that occurs in the presence of other people.[23]

Valid retirement (*al-Khilwat-us-Sahiha*) is used to describe the event of the husband and the wife, under a valid marriage contract, being together by themselves in a place where they are secure from observation without anything in decency, law or health to prevent their having sexual intercourse. On grounds of decency there must be no third person with the spouses, whether awake or asleep, in possession of the power of sight or

20 Quoted by Abdullah, *op. cit.* p. 300.
21 Abu Zahra, *op. cit.* p. 193.
22 Al-Hilli, *op. cit.* p. 21.
23 *Fatawa Alamgiri*, Vol. 1 (Cairo, 131OH), p. 13. Neil B. E. Baillie, *Digest of Muhammadan Law*, Vol. II (London, 1869), p. 24.

blind, adult or a discerning child, except a little child without understanding. On grounds of law, neither spouse may be in a condition which prohibits intercourse, e.g. if either spouse is observing ordained fast, or performing the pilgrimage rite, or if the wife is during a menstrual cycle under the Quranic verse: "They ask thee concerning menstruation. Say: It is hurt and pollution (*atha*). So let women alone at such time and go not unto them till they are cleansed."[24] On grounds of health, neither party shall be too young or too ill to have sexual intercourse.

Apart from the confirmation of the whole dower, which is the opinion of the Hanafis and the Hanbalis, the valid retirement has the following effects in common with actual consummation according to the Sunnis:

(i) establishment of parentage, which is an effect really of the valid contract *per se* and not of valid retirement nor even of actual consummation under certain conditions as explained in more detail in the chapter on parentage;
(ii) the necessity for the wife to observe iddat after separation;
(iii) the unlawful conjunction (see temporary prohibited degrees) and the prohibition to take a fifth wife during the iddat;
(iv) the establishment of the wife's right to maintenance, accommodation and clothing during the iddat.

The last three effects relate to the observation of the iddat rather than valid retirement or actual consummation.

According to the Shias, the only effect of valid retirement is the establishment of the wife's right to maintenance and accommodation.[25]

The valid retirement differs from actual consummation in the following respects:

(i) Actual consummation establishes a prohibited degree between the husband and any descendant of the wife. Here valid retirement does not create such a prohibited degree under the Quranic verse: "... your step-daughters under your guardianship, born of your wives To whom ye have gone in ...";[26]
(ii) Coition with the wife revocably divorced during her iddat is deemed remarrying her, unlike valid retirement;
(iii) After consummation, divorce may be revocable or irrevocable, but after valid retirement, divorce can be only irrevocable even during the iddat.
(iv) Where a man has divorced his wife three times, it is lawful for him (except in Tunisia) to remarry her if there was actual consummation

24 Sura Baqara II, verse 222.
25 Al-Hilli, *op. cit.*
26 Sura Nisaa, IV, verse 21.

between her and her second husband from whom she is later lawfully separated through divorce or death. Valid retirement between her and her second husband shall not be enough to make it lawful for her after separation to remarry her first husband;

(v) Inheritance: No mutual inheritance shall be established between two spouses who were separated after valid retirement, should either die during the iddat. By contrast, there shall be mutual inheritance between spouses if a revocable divorce took place after actual consummation and either spouse died during the *iddat*.

B. Entitlement of the Wife to Half of the Dower and to the Mutat

The wife shall be entitled to half of the specified dower if the marriage is dissolved before consummation by any act on the part of the husband, under the Quranic verse: "If ye divorce them before ye have touched them and ye have appointed unto them a portion, then pay the half of that which ye appointed" (Sura Baqara, II, verse 237). On the basis of this ruling, Jurists deduce the following four conditions for half the dower to be due to the wife:

(i) that marriage is under a valid contract;
(ii) that the dower is validly specified in the contract;
(iii) that divorce occurs before consummation or valid retirement;
(iv) that divorce is due to an act on the part of the husband, other than his exercising the option of puberty or recovery from insanity since in this case the contract is deemed null and void.

The Syrian Law decrees that on divorce before consummation or valid retirement, half of the dower should go to the wife if a valid contract included a validly specified dower (Art. 58). Concurring, (Art. 63/a), the legislator adds that (b) the wife shall repay any excess she received of the half and (c) that if she made a gift to the husband of half or more of her dower, she shall repay nothing on divorce before consummation or valid retirement and shall repay the balance of the half if her gift to him was less than that. If there was no valid specification of the dower, the wife shall not be entitled to the half dower, but to the *mutat* or present, under the Quranic ruling: "It is no sin for you if ye divorce women while yet ye have not touched them, nor appointed unto them a portion. Provide for them, the rich according to his means, and the straitened according to his means, according to custom".[27] It is thus left to custom to determine the amount of the mutat. Under Hanafi Law, it consists of three articles of

27 Sura Baqara II, verse 236.

dress or of their value provided that the value shall not be less than 5 dirhams, being half the minimum dower according to the Hanafis, or more than half of the dower of the equal. The Sunnis in general hold that the mutat is regulated by the circumstances of both husband and wife. The Shias stick to the Quranic text and consider the circumstances and condition of the husband only.[28]

The mutat is expressly mentioned in the Jordanian Law (Art. 55) which specifies that the mutat, becoming due on divorce before the stipulation of dower and before consummation or valid retirement, shall be determined according to custom and the condition of the husband, provided that it shall not exceed half the dower of the equal.

The Syrian Law, followed by Kuwaiti Law (Art. 64), orders mutat for the wife (if there was no specified dower or if the stipulation thereof is irregular under a valid contract) on divorce before consummation or valid retirement (Art. 61/2). The Syrian legislator defines mutat as an article of dress worthy of the wife's equals to go out in, according to the condition of the husband, without exceeding the value of half of the dower of the equal (Art. 62).

The Moroccan Law stipulates that the wife shall be entitled to half of the dower if she is divorced before consummation by the husband of his own free will (Art. 22). The Jordanian legislator rules that if divorce occurred, under a valid marriage contract in which a dower was specified, before consummation or valid retirement, half of the specified dower shall be due (Art. 48). Iraqi Article 21 simply stipulates that the wife shall be entitled to half of the specified dower on divorce before consummation.

It must be stressed that the half due for the wife on separation before consummation (or valid retirement if applicable) is of the validly specified dower. Any addition thereto by the husband made after the contract shall not be halved, but shall be dropped altogether. However, if there is an inherent increase of the dower, involving, for example, an increase in the value of a garden or a mare, and if the increase occurs while the substance is still in the possession of the husband, such an increase shall be halved together with the specified dower on separation prior to consummation (or valid retirement if applicable). The same provision applies if the increase is connected with the dower, e.g. the building on a land given in dower or the rent of a house. If the increase occurs after the wife is in possession of the dower and *before the husband recovers his half by agreement or litigation*, the increase shall be the wife's, whether it is inherent in the dower or not, and whether it occurs before or after separation, unless it is added, like a building on a piece of land, in which case it belongs to the person who made it. If the increase occurs to the dower which the wife has

28 Al-Hilli, *op cit.* p. 23.

actually received *after the husband recovers his half by agreement or litigation*, the increase shall be halved between them, unless it is added to the dower, in which case it shall belong to the person who made it.[29]

C. The Loss by the Wife of the Whole Dower

No dower, whether specified or proper (dower of the equal) shall be due to the wife if the marriage is dissolved before it is confirmed in either of the two following events:

(i) If the marriage is dissolved by the husband before consummation (or valid retirement if applicable) through exercising his option of puberty or recovery from imbecility or insanity, in which case he is lawfully entitled to apply for the marriage to be annulled. For example, a guardian, other than the father or grandfather, may exercise his powers of compulsory guardianship to contract a marriage for his ward. However, on the removal of grounds for guardianship, when the ward attains puberty or recovers from his insanity or imbecility, he may exercise his option and apply to the Court for annulment of his marriage. Should the judge order annulment, the husband shall be released of the whole dower, since the very contract becomes null and void, and since there would be no point of the husband exercising his lawful option if he is ordered to pay half the dower.[30]

(ii) If the marriage is dissolved before actual consummation (or valid retirement where applicable) by an act by the wife whether it is lawful or unlawful. Examples of lawful acts by the wife are her exercising her own option of puberty or recovery from imbecility or insanity where she has the lawful right to apply for the annulment of marriage or if she were given the power to ask for a divorce, and she exercised it before consummation. Examples of unlawful acts are: apostasy, or, being a polytheist, her refusal to adopt Islam, or any kitabi religion after the conversion of her husband to Islam, or committing with an older relative or a descendant of the husband an act that creates a prohibited degree through affinity.[31]

These grounds for the loss of the whole dower are adopted in the Jordanian Law (Art. 52). It also rules, according to the Sharia provisions that no dower whatsoever shall be due

29 Abdullah, *op. cit.* pp. 311, 312
30 *Ibid.* p. 316.
31 *Loc. cit.*

(a) if separation occurred at the request of the wife on grounds of a deformity or a defect on the part of the husband or if her guardian applied for separation on grounds of inequality before consummation or valid retirement (Art. 49);
(b) if the contract is annulled before consummation or valid retirement, the husband shall recover any dower he may have paid (Art. 50);
(c) if the contract is annulled at the request of the husband on grounds of a deformity or defect on the part of the wife, before consummation, in which case the husband shall also recover any dower he may have paid (Art. 53).

The Moroccan Decree deprives the wife of the whole dower if the contract is annulled or rescinded by the husband on grounds of a defect of the wife or by the wife on grounds of a defect of the husband, before consummation (Art. 22).

According to the Syrian Law, the wife shall lose the whole dower if separation occurs by an act of the wife before consummation or valid retirement (Art. 59).

Kuwaiti Article 65 rules that the wife shall lose all her right to any dower or mutat if the divorce is due to a cause emanating from her, before consummation or valid retirement.

The husband shall also be released of the whole dower if the wife makes a gift of remission of it to him, the dower being her exclusive property of which she can dispose in any way she likes.[32]

7. LEGAL DISPUTES OVER THE DOWER

The most widespread legal suits over the dower are related to dispute over the stipulation of the dower, the amount of the contract dower and the receipt of the dower. These disputes may occur during the spouses' life, during the existence of matrimony or after separation. They may arise between a surviving spouse and the heirs of the other, or between their heirs if they are both deceased.

A. Dispute over the Stipulations of the Dower

If the spouses differ on whether the dower in the contract was stipulated or not, with one party claiming that a certain amount was specified and the other denying it, the court shall apply the general juristic maxim to the effect that "evidence is for him who affirms; the oath for him who denies".

32 *Ibid.*

If evidence is available, the judge shall order the specified dower accordingly. In the absence of evidence, the denying party shall be ordered to make an oath, failure of which will prove the claim of the other party. If an oath is made, the judge shall dismiss stipulation and order the dower of the equal, provided that it shall not exceed the amount claimed by the wife if she is the party who affirmed the stipulation, and shall not be less than what is claimed by the husband if he is the affirming party.[33]

This provision is held by the Jordanian Law, Article 57. It is also followed in general by Article 69 of the Kuwaiti Law which rules, however, that if the wife fails to provide evidence, the statement of the husband under oath shall be held, unless he claims a dower that does not benefit her according to custom, in which case, the judge shall order the dower of the equal, provided that it shall not be more than the amount claimed by the wife; this ruling to apply likewise in any dispute between a spouse and the heirs of the other, or between their respective heirs.

It must be stressed that such a ruling applies only in the case where the wife is entitled to the whole dower, whether during the continuation of the marriage or after separation, for whatever reason after the whole dower is confirmed to the wife. If the dispute occurs where only half of the dower is due to the wife, the judge shall order half the specified dower, if proven, or the mutat if the stipulation is dismissed.[34]

B. Dispute over the Amount of the Specified Dower

If both spouses agree on the fact of the stipulation of dower but differ on the amount thereof, the party who claims the higher amount shall be required to submit evidence, in the absence of which the other party shall have to make an oath. Notwithstanding this general rule, if it is the wife who claims the higher amount but could not prove her case, the judge shall order the dower of the equal if the amount claimed by the husband is not fit for the equal of the wife according to custom, or if the amount claimed by the wife is less than the equal's dower. The same provision applies if the dispute is between the surviving spouse and the heirs of the deceased, or between the heirs of both deceased spouses.[35]

This opinion of the Hanafi Jurist Abu Youssof is adopted in its entirety in Egypt (Act No. 25/1929, Art. 19), in Syria (Art. 54/4), in Kuwait (Art. 69) and in Jordan (Art. 58). However, the Jordanian Article 59 rules that no suit in respect of a dispute between the spouses over the dower of the contract shall be heard if it differs from the recognized contract document,

33 *Ibid.* pp. 336, 337; Al-Hilli, *op. cit.* p. 28.
34 Abdullah, *op. cit.* p. 338.
35 *Ibid.* p. 339.

unless a written proof is available of their agreement at the time of marriage on a dower other than that stated in the document.

C. Dispute over the Receipt of the Dower

The wife is lawfully entitled to refuse her husband connubial intercourse or to submit to her husband's authority till the payment of prompt dower agreed upon in the contract, or in accordance with the custom (Art. 21, Moroccan; Art. 13, Tunisian). In Syria, it must be paid to her in person if she possesses full legal capacity, unless she authorizes in the contract document an agent to receive it for her (Art. 60/1). In Jordan, the virgin, even if she is of full legal capacity, shall be deemed to have received the dower if it is paid to her guardian if he is her father, or agnate grandfather, unless she has prohibited the husband to pay it to her guardian (Art. 64).

By exercising this right, she shall not be deemed disobedient (*nashiza*) and, therefore, shall not lose her right to maintenance.

If the spouses dispute over the fact of payment of the whole or part of the prompt dower, with the husband alleging that he has paid the prompt dower to his wife and consequently she is disobedient if she refuses to submit to his authority and the wife denying it, she shall not be deemed disobedient. If the dispute occurs before consummation, the onus of the proof of payment shall be on the husband, since the dower, by the very fact of the valid marriage contract has become a debt on him from which he could only be discharged through actual payment. If he provides evidence to substantiate his claim, or if the wife refrains from making an oath if no evidence is available, the judge shall rule in his favour, otherwise his case shall be dismissed. The same rule applies if the dispute arises after consummation, unless the observed custom is that the wife would not submit herself to the husband until she receives her prompt dower, in which case the custom shall be sufficient proof of the payment. The same rules apply if the said dispute is between a surviving spouse and the heir of the deceased or between their respective heirs if they are both dead.[36]

There are three modern legal texts on this matter. The Moroccan Law rules, under Article 24, that in the event of the spouses disputing the payment of prompt dower, the claim of the wife shall prevail before consummation, while that of the husband shall apply after consummation. The Algerian Article 17 gives a similar ruling in the absence of any evidence, and applies it to the dispute over the fact of payment between the spouses or their heirs, provided that either claim be confirmed with an oath. The Kuwaiti Article 60 agrees with the Moroccan, adding the proviso: "in the absence of any contradicting evidence or custom".

36 *Ibid.* pp. 341–342.

Chapter 5

Maintenance

1. DEFINITION

Maintenance is the lawful right of the wife under a valid marriage contract on certain conditions. It is the right of the wife to be provided at the husband's expense, and at a scale suitable to his means, with food, clothing, housing, toilet necessities, medicine, doctors' and surgeons' fees, baths, and also the necessary servants where the wife is of a social position which does not permit her to dispense with such services, or when she is sick.

All the modern Arab Codes on personal status more or less repeat this general Sharia position with some slight modifications.

In Iraq, Jordan, Syria, Kuwait and Algeria, there is an identical provision that maintenance consists of food, clothing, housing and the amenities thereof, treatment fees according to custom, and servants for women whose equals have servants (Arts. 24/2, 66/a, 71/1, 75 and 78 respectively).

The Egyptian Law No. 100/1985 enumerates the components of matrimonial maintenance, by way of non-limitative illustration such as food, clothing, housing and medical expenses, adding "and any such other things as are dictated by the Sharia."

The Moroccan Decree simply states that it is the right of the wife to have lawful maintenance for food, clothing, medical treatment and housing (Art. 35/1).

The Lebanese Druze Personal Status Act No. 28/1948 rules under Article 28 that the maintenance shall include food, clothing, housing, medical treatment and servants for the wife on the grounds of her social position, infirmity or sickness. This maintenance is an obligation that must be met by agreement or by court order.

The Jordanian Law (Article 78) rules that the husband shall be liable for the fees of the mid-wife and the physician summoned for a birth, if need be, and the medicine and the cost of birth according to custom and to his means, whether or not the state of matrimony exists.

Maintenance by her husband is the lawful right of the wife, irrespective of her means or her religion. This position is virtually unanimously held by the Muslim Jurists and modern statutes. The only two exceptions are the Zahiris and the modern Tunisians. The Zahiri Andalusian Jurist Ibn Hazm holds that maintenance shall be the duty of the affluent wife if the husband is destitute, since she is a presumptive heir herself under the Quranic ruling "The duty of feeding and clothing nursing mothers according to decent custom is upon the father of the child. No-one should be charged beyond his capacity. A mother should not be made to suffer because of her child, nor should he to whom the child is born by his child. And on the father's heir is incumbent the like of that."[1] The modern Tunisian Personal Status Mejelle, which, while asserting that it is the husband's duty to provide for his wife and his children by her, according to his means, in all matters related to maintenance, rules that the wife shall contribute to the maintenance of the family if she has any means (Art. 23).

The entitlement of the wife to maintenance derives from the authority of the Quran, Prophet's Tradition and consensus. The above mentioned Quranic verse enshrines such a right.

For the divorced woman, the Quran commands "Lodge them where ye dwell, according to your wealth, and harass them not so as to straiten life for them."[2]

As for Tradition, the Prophet preached in his last sermon "Show piety to women, you have taken them in the trust of God and have had them made lawful for you to enjoy by the word of God, and it is your duty to provide for them and clothe them according to decent custom."

The maintenance of the wife is deemed a debt on the husband from the date of withholding it once it is due. Only payment or discharge shall settle this debt (Arts. 79, Syrian; 24/1, Iraqi; 78, Kuwaiti; 1, Egyptian Act No. 25/1920). In Syria, it has priority even over the privileged debt dower (Art. 54/3. See Chapter 4 Section 1).

2. ENTITLEMENT TO AND LOSS OF MAINTENANCE

Maintenance shall be due to the wife:

(a) under a valid marriage contract;

1 Sura Baqara, II, verse 233.
2 Sura Talaq, LXV, verse 6.

(b) if she places, or offers to place, herself in the husband's power so as to allow him free access to herself at all lawful times (the Arabic word is *Tamkeen*); and
(c) if she obeys all his lawful commands for the duration of marriage.[3]

This Sharia provision has been enacted in the modern laws of Egypt, Jordan, Iraq, Kuwait and Syria which make the wife's maintenance an obligation of the husband from the date of valid contract (Act No. 25/1920 Art. 1, and Arts. 67, 23, 74, and 72/1, respectively) even if they were of different religions (Jordan, Kuwait and Syria), if she submits or offers to submit herself to him (Egypt), and even if she is staying at her family's home unless the husband asks her to move with him and she refuses without a lawful excuse (same Jordanian, Iraqi and Syrian Arts.).

No maintenance, however, shall be due to the wife in the absence of any of the three conditions set out above.

A. The Non-Valid Contract

As explained in Chapter 3, a void, or, *before consummation*, an irregular, marriage contract is no contract at all and shall have no effect whatsoever. However, under an irregular marriage contract, *after consummation*, the wife shall not be entitled to maintenance, since the husband has no lawful right of access to her. They would be forbidden to live together as man and wife, and would be separated of their own free will or by a court order. If the marriage was, *prima facie*, regular, and the wife obtained a court order for maintenance before it transpired that the marriage was irregular (e.g. that the wife was a foster sister of the husband), he may claim back the money he spent on her maintenance. In the absence of such order, he has no such right to a refund.

The Jordanian Law expressly rules out any maintenance for the wife under an irregular contract, subsequent to consummation and before or after separation (Art. 42). The Iraqi Law confines any right of the wife under such circumstances to the lesser of the specified or proper (i.e. dower of the equal) dowers, or to the latter in the absence of any specification (Art. 22). Without really dissenting from this ruling, the Syrian Law grants the wife the right to matrimonial maintenance for as

3 Almost all the classical Sunni and Shia jurists add the condition that the wife, in order to be entitled to maintenance, shall not be too young to render conjugal rights to her husband. Only the Hanafi Jurist Abu Youssof holds that maintenance shall be due to a child-wife if her husband retains her in the matrimonial house for company. The Zahiris rule that maintenance is the right of the wife by the very act of the marriage contract "even if she is in the cradle". However, this whole issue is now of no relevance, since all modern Islamic laws of marriage prohibit child marriage. See Chap. 3.

long as she remains unaware of the irregularity of her marriage (Art. 51/3).

B. The Lack of Access

Since it is the tamkeen, i.e. the availability of the wife for her husband, and not the marriage contract itself, that makes maintenance the lawful right of the wife, this right shall be lost if the husband is denied access to the wife, even when, in certain cases, this denial is due to a cause not proceeding from the wife, subject to certain conditions:

(1) Imprisonment and abduction

No maintenance is due to a wife who is in jail, even if she is innocent, provided that the cause of her imprisonment proceeded from her, and that she had a choice. This provision is adopted by the Iraqi Law which deprives a wife jailed for a crime or a debt from maintenance (Art. 25/2). The Sunni jurists generally agree that the jailed wife is not entitled to maintenance if her imprisonment is before consummation. The general opinion is that she would lose her maintenance even if she were jailed after moving to the matrimonial home, and even if she could not avoid being in jail. Only Abu Youssof dissents, granting her maintenance on the grounds of a lawful excuse.[4]

The Shias restrict the loss of maintenance because of imprisonment to the event of the wife being jailed for a debt which she can afford to pay. She would keep her maintenance right if she is jailed for a debt she owes to the husband and if she cannot avoid the sentence.[5]

The same rule applies for an abducted wife, with Abu Youssof again dissenting on the ground that she has no choice.[6]

(2) The working wife

The majority of Islamic jurists, both Sunnis and Shias, rule that there shall be no maintenance for the wife who goes out to work without permission of her husband. The same attitude is adopted expressly in the Jordanian Law, Article 68, and the Syrian, Article 73. It is also implied in the Iraqi Article 25 which deprives the wife of her right to maintenance if she goes out of the matrimonial home without permission or lawful excuse (para. 1). The Iraqi lawyer Naji includes in this category the case of a wife

4 Abu Zahra, *On Marriage*, p. 238.
5 Al-Hilli, *Jaafari Personal Status Provisions*, p. 44.
6 Abu Zahra, *op. cit.*

who has a job or a profession and was forbidden to work by the husband but has not stopped.[7]

Following the opinion of more progressive Islamic jurists, notably Ibn-ul-Humam, The Egyptian Act No. 100/1985 adopts a more liberal approach, ruling that the wife shall not lose her right to maintenance if she goes out for a lawful job, without her husband's permission, provided that her exercise of that conditional right (to work) is not abused or in conflict with the family's interest and she was not forbidden by the husband. So it seems that while she does not need the husband's permission, she has to heed his prohibition.

In a similar view, Kuwaiti Article 89 does not consider it disobedience by the wife to go out for a lawful reason or a lawful employment unless it is not in the family interest.

(3) The disobedient or rebellious wife (nashiza)

The wife working against her husband's wishes denotes disobedience. But a special juristic term, *nashiza*, is reserved to the wife, defined in the Jordanian Act (Art. 69) and the Syrian Act (Art. 75) following the Sharia, as "the wife who leaves the matrimonial home without a lawful reason or denies her husband access to the home which she owns without first requesting him to accommodate her elsewhere." The Shias alone add another case of disobedience, *nushuz*, which is the woman denying her husband his conjugal rights while she is living with him.[8] The Shias also consider as nashiza, a wife who borrows money without an order by the judge or the husband.[9]

Among the lawful reasons for such disobedience, the Jordanian Law mentions the wife leaving home because of her husband beating or maltreating her (Art. 69). Other such reasons are:

(i) to have a co-wife living in the same house without the wife's consent (Arts. 67, Syrian; 26, Iraqi; 40, Jordanian);

(ii) to have the husband's kin living with the wife without her consent, except the husband's child below the age of discretion (Arts. 69, Syrian; 26, Iraqi).

The Jordanian Act also makes a further exception of the husband's incapacitated poor parents if he has no means to support them independently and they have no other place to live, provided that that will not interfere with the spouses' conjugal life (Art. 38);

In a similar ruling, Kuwaiti Article 85 adds to the husband's children below the age of discretion, his other children and his

7 Muhsin Naji, *Commentary on the Personal Status Act* (Baghdad, 1962), p. 231.
8 Al-Hilli, *op. cit.* p. 45.
9 *Ibid.* p. 44.

parents if need dictates that they should live with him provided that they shall cause no injury to the wife.

(iii) the wife shall not obey any command by the husband that conflicts with the Sharia and the judge shall order maintenance for her (Iraqi, 33);

(iv) if she has not received her prompt dower, or has not a decent home prepared for her (Syrian, 72/2; Iraqi, 23/2; and Jordanian, 67);

Kuwaiti Article 87 adds "or if he refused to give her maintenance and she could not enforce a maintenance court order against him because he apparently has no property".

(v) the Shias consider as a lawful excuse the wife going to visit her sick father who needs her to stay with him, having nobody else to look after him, even if he is not a Muslim, and even if the husband denied permission.[10]

The nashiza shall lose her right to maintenance for as long as she remains disobedient (Arts. 74, Syrian; 69, Jordanian; 11, *bis* 2, added to Egyptian Act No. 25/1929 under Act No. 100/1985). According to Kuwaiti Article 88, no obedience order obtained by the husband against her shall be implemented using force, the only penalty of non-compliance thereto being the loss of her maintenance (see the Explanatory Note to the said Article).

The disobedient wife's lost right to maintenance shall be revived on the removal of the cause.

(4) Travelling

The wife is bound to travel with her husband to wherever he wishes, provided that she is safe and unless otherwise stipulated in the marriage contract (Arts. 37, Jordanian; 2/3, Iraqi), or if the judge rules she has a lawful excuse (Syrian Art. 70; Kuwaiti Art. 90). Otherwise she would lose her entitlement to maintenance (Jordanian Art. 37).

On the other hand, the wife's maintenance right shall be suspended if she travels, unaccompanied by her husband, for as long as she is away from him, whether she travels on her own or in the company of a kin in a prohibited degree. Abu Youssof makes an exception of the wife who travels for the first time to perform the religious duty of pilgrimage if she is accompanied by a kin in a prohibited degree, after the consummation of marriage, in which case she is granted a "settlement" not a "travelling" maintenance.[11] Kuwaiti Article 91 enshrines this right of the wife. The Shias add to this the wife who travels for a desirable (*mandub*) or permissible (*mubah*) cause with the husband's permission.[12]

10 *Ibid.* p. 57.
11 Abu Zahra, *op. cit.* p. 240.
12 Al-Hilli, *op. cit.* p. 44.

(5) Apostasy

The Egyptian Legislator alone rules expressly that the wife shall lose her maintenance right if she apostasizes (Art. 1 Act No. 25/1920 amended under Art. 2 Act No. 100/1985). That the wife shall lose her maintenance right if she apostasizes can be inferred under the Sharia and other laws from the fact that apostasy renders the marriage contract void (see Chapter 3.B.(3)). Apostasy of the wife and its relevance to her right to maintenance is also dealt with by the Hanafis and Shias in the context of maintenance after divorce. The Hanafis rule that the irrevocably divorced wife shall not lose the right to maintenance (during iddat) except while she is in prison for apostasy. But the revocably divorced wife who apostasizes shall lose her right of maintenance, and shall not recover it on her subsequent return to Islam.[13]

Contrariwise, the Shias allow the divorced wife who apostasizes her right to maintenance if the divorce is revocable, but not if it is irrevocable. She also restores her right on reconversion.[14]

Tyabji suggests an explanation for this discrepancy between the Hanafis and the Shias. For the Hanafis, he takes the view that the reason is their disapproval of irrevocable divorces, some of which are even considered sinful, and therefore the husband is mulcted in maintenance in all circumstances after such divorces. On the other hand, the Shias do not permit the disapproved kinds of divorces and a considerable part of the iddat expires before any pronouncement of divorce can become irrevocable under the Shia Law. This Law considers divorces revocable and irrevocable on the same footing and a wife is more favoured during the period when the divorce is still revocable than after this has become irrevocable[15] (see Chapter 6).

(6) Loss of maintenance due to court procedure

Apart from the Sharia provisions in respect of the loss of the wife's right to maintenance, the Jordanian Law contains procedural provisions that would result in such a loss. Under Jordanian Law, Article 20, there shall be no maintenance for the period preceding agreement between the parties or application to the judge in respect of fixing an amount for maintenance. Under Article 17 of the Egyptian Act 25/1929, no iddat maintenance action shall be heard by the court for a previous period of more than a year from the date of the divorce. According to the Jordanian Act (Art. 80), if the divorcee was served with the document of divorce at

13 Alamgir, *Al Fatawa Alamgiriyya Almaarufa bil Fatawal Hindiyya*, Vol. 1, pp. 557/8.
14 Al-Hilli, *op. cit.* pp. 83, 84.
15 Tayabji, *Muhammadan Law* (Bombay, 1940), p. 323.

least a month before the completion of her iddat, she shall lose her right to maintenance if she fails to claim it before the expiry of the iddat.

C. Assessment of Maintenance

The ultimate sources which made maintenance the right of the wife on her husband, namely the Quran and the Prophet's Tradition, did not discuss it in detail, but simply ruled that the husband shall spend according to his means: "Let him who hath abundance spend of his abundance, and he whose provision is measured, let him spend of that which Allah hath given him. Allah asketh naught of any soul save that which He hath given it. Allah will vouchsafe, after hardship, ease."[16] It was left, therefore, to the jurists to assess the amount of maintenance which varies according to social environments, style of life and differences of persons, times and regions. The Hanafis rule that the matrimonial maintenance must be enough to satisfy the woman's needs, and therefore cannot be fixed *per se* and shall be assessed according to observed custom. The Shafiis dissent, ruling that maintenance is assessed under the Sharia, though they agree with the Hanafis that the condition of the husband must be taken into consideration whether he is affluent, impoverished or of average means. The Hanbalis assess the maintenance left unspecified in the Quran according to custom, considering again the conditions of the rich, the impoverished and the average.[17]

If the husband provides the wife with sufficient food, clothing and other basic needs and a decent home, there shall be no point in the wife requiring any maintenance from the court. This method of providing maintenance for the wife is called *tamkeen*, and is the normal way of living together as man and wife.

There is another method of maintenance for the wife which is the exceptional course of matrimonial life. Under this method called *tamleek*, (i.e. passing property) a certain amount shall be paid for the wife's maintenance whether by agreement or by court order. It can be either in kind such as food and clothing, or it may be an amount of money.

The judge, in assessment of the matrimonial maintenance, shall take into account the financial condition of the husband, regardless of the wife's condition, and the market prices. The judge's assessment may be revised upwards or downwards if this is requested by the interested spouse.

In assessing the house rent, the judge shall take into consideration the financial condition of the husband and the level of the rents. "Proper

16 Sura Talaq, LXV, verse 7.
17 Explanatory note to Egyptian Act No. 25/1929.

home" must fulfil four conditions:

(i) to be fit for the husband's condition, and comparable for the home of his equals according to custom;
(ii) to be solely for the use of the spouses without any third party even of their spouses' kin except the husband's child who has not reached the age of discretion;
(iii) all domestic appliances must be provided in accordance with the husband's means;
(iv) the home must be in a decent neighbourhood among good neighbours where the person and property of the wife are securely safe.[18]

These are the general Sharia provisions adopted in the modern laws of Egypt (Act 25/1929, Art. 16), Syria (Art. 76), Kuwait (Art. 76) and Jordan (Art. 70). The Iraqi legislator alone rules that the wife's maintenance shall be assessed against the husband according to the condition of both spouses (Art. 27).

Maintenance may be increased or decreased in accordance with the change of the husband's condition and the market prices, Syrian Law (Art. 77) implies the right to ask for increase or decrease in the court order of the amount of maintenance. The Jordan Law (Art. 71) follows the Syrian Law (Art. 77/2) in ruling that no application for such an increase or decrease shall be heard before the lapse of six months from the court order, save in exceptional emergencies, e.g. soaring prices. Kuwaiti Article 77 makes the time limit one year. The Iraqi and the Druze Codes (Arts. 28/1 and 29, respectively) allow such an amendment of the assessment of maintenance if there is any change in the condition of both spouses. Like the Jordanian and Syrian Acts, Iraqi Article 28/2 allows the consideration of increase or decrease of the ordered maintenance in the event of emergencies, without stipulating the time limit.

The judge shall order maintenance against the husband who fails to honour his obligation of maintenance as from the date of such failure (Arts. 78, Syrian; 30, Lebanon Druze Act; and 73, Jordanian).

The Algerian Article 78, provides that maintenance becomes due from the date of the commencement of court proceedings.

The Syrian Article paragraph 2 rules that no maintenance for more than four months prior to the legal action shall be ordered. The Jordanian Article empowers the Judge to order the payment of maintenance in advance. The Jordanian, Iraqi and Lebanese Acts deal with the absent husband who leaves his wife without maintenance or travels to a destination far or near, or is considered missing (Arts. 76, 29 and 32, respectively). In this case, the judge shall assess the wife's maintenance as

18 Abdullah, *Personal Status*, pp. 368/375.

from the date of application to the court on the strength of the evidence submitted by the wife of the existent state of matrimony. She must also make an oath that the husband has left her no maintenance and that she is neither disobedient nor divorced, having counted her iddat.

The Iraqi Article adds that the Judge may permit her if necessary to borrow on behalf of the husband.

If the wife is awarded against the husband a maintenance which cannot be collected from him, her maintenance shall be the obligation of any person whose duty it would have been to maintain her if she was not married, and he shall have the right to recover it from the husband (Arts. 80/1, Syrian; 75, Jordanian). If she borrowed maintenance from a stranger who is under no obligation to maintain her, the creditor has the choice to recover the loan from the husband or the wife (Arts. 80/2, Syrian; 33, Druze). The Jordanian and Kuwaiti laws remain silent on this point. The Iraqi Act adds that in the absence of any person willing to lend the money, with the wife incapable of earning a living, her maintenance shall be the duty of the state.

During the consideration of the court action, the judge may order a provisional maintenance of the wife against the husband. Such an order would be effective immediately (Arts. 82/2 and 2, Syrian; 31/1 Iraqi; 79a Kuwaiti; and Art. 16, Egyptian Act No. 25/1920).

Algerian Article 80 enacts that the Judge may order the payment of maintenance on the strength of evidence, for a period of one year prior to the commencement of court proceedings.

The accumulated sum of maintenance shall not be lost as a result of divorce or the death of either husband or wife.

Maintenance of the divorcee is an obligation on the husband and shall be ordered as from the date of counting the iddat (Arts. 83 & 84, Syrian; 80, Jordanian; and Art. 2, Egyptian Act No. 25/1920).

The maximum period of the maintenance during the iddat shall not exceed nine months in Syria, or one year in Jordan.

Jordanian Article 81 denies the divorced wife during her disobedience any maintenance during her iddat.

Iraqi Article 50 dissents, ordering maintenance during the iddat for the divorcee against her living husband even if she is disobedient, but rules out any maintenance during the iddat of death. The last ruling is upheld by Kuwaiti Article 164.

Chapter 6

Dissolution of Marriage

1. INTRODUCTION: METHODS OF DISSOLUTION

Under the Sharia Law, marriage may be dissolved, during the life-time of the parties thereto:

(i) by the act of the husband or wife (*talaq*);
(ii) by mutual agreement (*khula* or *mubaraat*); or
(iii) by a judicial order of separation in a suit by the husband or the wife (*tafriq*).[1]

1 These are the forms of dissolution of marriage that are recognized in the modern legislations on personal status. There are three more forms which are described by the classical jurists, but have little practical relevance now:
(a) Injurious Assimilation (*zihar*) in which the husband compares his wife to a relative within a prohibited degree, e.g. his mother. The Quran described this device and rules as follows:

> "God has indeed heard (and accepted) the statement of the woman who pleads with thee concerning her husband and carries her complaint (in prayer) to God: and God (always) hears the arguments between both sides among you: for God hears and sees (all things). If any men among you divorce their wives by Zihar (calling them mothers), they cannot be their mothers: None can be their mothers except those who gave them birth. And in fact they use words (both) iniquitous and false: but truly God is One that blots out (sins), and forgives (again and again). But those who divorce their wives by Zihar, then wish to go back on the words they uttered, – (it is ordained that such a one) should free a slave before they touch each other: this are ye admonished to perform: and God is well-acquainted with (all) that ye do. And if any has not (the wherewithal), he should fast for two months consecutively before they touch each other. But if any is unable to do so, he should feed sixty indigent ones."
> (Sura Mujadila, LVIII, verses 1–4)

(b) Vow of Continence (*ila*) when the husband makes an oath of abstention from the wife for four months or more. This device is regulated in the Quran: "For those who take an

The most common procedure has been the talaq, which is the right of the husband. However, modern personal status legislators show an increasing tendency to curb such a power of the man to the extent that, under some legislation, no divorce shall be effective, or even allowed, outside the court.

Dissolution of marriage is dealt with in separate chapters of the modern Personal Status Laws of Syria, Tunisia, Morocco, Iraq, Jordan, Algeria and Kuwait. Although no comprehensive personal status compendium has been promulgated in Egypt, various legal provisions have been decreed on the subject of dissolution of marriage under Act No. 25/1920 (on judicial separation on grounds of defects) and Act No. 25/1929 (on conditions of validity of divorce, further grounds for separation by court order, arbitration, the missing or jailed husband), both being amended by Act. No. 100/1985.

In the following sections, we shall deal with the various forms of dissolution of marriage in the order given above.

2. REPUDIATION – TALAQ

The definition of repudiation according to the Sharia is "the dissolution of a valid marriage contract forthwith or at a later date by the husband, his

---

oath for abstention from their wives, a waiting for four months is ordained. If then they return, God is oft-forgiving, Most Merciful" (Sura Baqara, II, verse 226). The Hanafis maintain that such a divorce shall be irrevocable after the lapse of the four months. The Malikis, Shafiis, Hanbalis and the Shias make the separation subject to a pronouncement of divorce by the husband or to a suit by the wife. It is then deemed revocable, although Malik makes return to the married status contingent to consummation. The Moroccan and Kuwaiti Laws deal with this form of divorce (Arts. 58 and 123/124 respectively), giving the wife the right to apply to the judge who shall give the husband a delay of four months, after which a revocable divorce decree is issued.

(c) Imprecation (lian) where the husband affirms under oath that the wife has committed adultery and that the child born of her is not his, and she affirms under oath the contrary, according to the Quran:

> "And for those who launch a charge against their spouses, and have (in support) no evidence but their own, their solitary evidence (can be received) if they bear witness four times (with an oath) by God that they are solemnly telling the truth. And the fifth (oath) (should be) that they solemnly invoke the curse of God on themselves if they tell a lie. But it would avert the punishment from the wife, if she bears witness four times (with an oath) by God, that (her husband) is telling a lie; and the fifth (oath) should be that she solemnly invokes the wrath of God on herself if (her accuser) is telling the truth."
> Sura Nur, XXIV, verses 6–9.

agent or his wife duly authorized by him to do so, using the word talaq, a derivative or a synonym thereof."

This definition is almost universally adopted by the modern Arab personal status codes (Arts. 87/2, Syria; 44, Morocco; 34, Iraq; and 87, Jordan, where a written document is required). There are, however, two exceptions where divorce can only be effected by the court, for the Druzes (of the Lebanon, Art. 37 and of Syria, Art. 307), and in Tunisia (Art. 30).

The definition quoted sums up all the conditions for repudiation to be valid, effective and binding. Analysing the definition in detail, these can be treated under the headings of: the valid marriage contract, the husband who pronounces the talaq, and the formula used.

A. The Existence of a Valid Marriage Contract

Repudiation is an effect of a valid marriage contract whereby the duties and rights emanating from the marital status are terminated either forthwith, in the irrevocable divorce, or after the lapse of the iddat in the revocable divorce.

The termination of a non-valid marriage contract is not a repudiation proper but an annulment, whether separation between the two parties is effected by them on their own accord or by an order of the court, and whether it occurs before or after consummation.

The modern laws expressly adopt this provision by ruling that the object in the repudiation is the wife under a valid marriage contract or counting her iddat of a revocable divorce. No repudiation of any other woman shall be valid even if it is suspended (Arts. 86, Syria; 45, Morocco; 103, Kuwait; and 84, Jordan). Therefore, the woman shall not be liable to repudiation in the following cases:

(a) if she is married under an invalid contract, since repudiation is by definition a dissolution of a valid marriage;
(b) if she is in her iddat of an irrevocable repudiation;
(c) if she is in her iddat as a result of a court order for separation on the grounds of the option of puberty or option of recovery from insanity or mental derangement or for the dower being less than that of the equal;
(d) if she has completed her iddat, even if it was of a revocable repudiation; and
(e) if she is a divorcée prior to consummation or valid retirement.

These provisions are unanimously accepted by the Sunnis and Shias.[2]

2 *Cf.* Abdullah, *Personal Status*, pp. 423–426; Abu Zahra, *On Marriage*, pp. 289–291; Al-Hilli, *Jaafari Personal Status Provisions*, p. 59.

B. The Husband

Apart from the legal texts governing the divorce of the Druzes and the Tunisians, repudiation is the right of the husband on fulfilling certain requirements, which are majority, sanity, and acting on his own free will, not under coercion. He must be aware of his utterances, regardless of his being of legal capacity or placed under interdiction on grounds of prodigality or imbecility. In the absence of any of these conditions, no repudiation shall be valid. It follows that the repudiation shall be void if uttered in any of the following cases:

(i) by the minor, even if he possesses discretion, and even if approved by his guardian, since it is the exclusive right of the husband;

(ii) by the insane or the mentally deranged;

(iii) by a person in a state of alcoholic intoxication.
This position of the Malikis, Shafiis and Hanbalis, as against the Hanafis, who allow repudiation by such persons, is adopted by the Egyptian legislator (Art. 1, Act 25/1929) and followed by the Laws of Syria (Art. 89/1), Morocco (Art. 49), Iraq (Art. 35/1), Jordan (Art. 88/a) and Kuwait (Art. 102). The Shias concur.[3]

(iv) by a person under coercion (the same Articles).
The Shias concur[4] but the Hanafis allow such a divorce on the ground that the husband would have a choice.

(v) a person in a state of rage to the extent of losing discretion (Arts. 89/1, Syria, 49, Morocco, 35/1, Iraq, 88/a, Jordan, 102, Kuwait). The Syrian and Jordanian legislators call a person under such a state "the stunned" "*al madhoosh*" who is defined as "a person who lost discretion because of rage or otherwise to the point of becoming unaware of his uttering" (Arts. 89/2 and 88/b, respectively). The same description occurs in Kuwaiti Article 102.

(vi) the fainting or sleeping person – Jordanian (Art. 88/a). A special case in this context is a person suffering from a terminal or mortal sickness (*marad al-maut*). Article 1595 of the Mejelle gives the following definition of such a sickness: "Mortal sickness is characterized by a strong likelihood of death. It renders the patient incapable of looking after his interest out-of-doors if he is a male or indoors if she is a female. The patient shall die within a year whether bed-ridden or not. . . ." The Iraqi legislators consider a repudiation by such a person void if he dies in that illness, and his wife shall inherit from him. The same ruling prevails if he was in a state where death is most likely (Art. 35/2). The Egyptian legislator (Inheritance

3 Al-Hilli, *op. cit.* pp. 58, 59.
4 *Ibid.*

Act No. 77/1943 Art. 11) and the Syrian legislator (Art. 116) provide that the wife shall inherit from the husband who repudiates her irrevocably (against her consent) during his mortal sickness or in a state where he is most likely to die and then dies because of that sickness, or in such a state while the wife is still counting her iddat provided that her entitlement to inheritance shall persist from the time of the irrevocable divorce until his death. But they do not follow the Iraqi legislator in ruling out such a repudiation altogether as void.

The husband who fulfils all the necessary requirements may pronounce repudiation either by himself or through an agent duly authorized by him who shall act on his behalf within the terms of his power of attorney. The husband may also authorize the wife to effect her repudiation either in the marriage contract or thereafter. However, the husband cannot stipulate on his own accord the wife's right to effect her repudiation. In such a case the marriage contract shall be valid and that stipulation shall be void. But if it is the wife who stipulated to be granted that power as a condition in the marriage contract, and the husband agrees, both the contract and the condition shall be valid and effective. The husband may authorize the wife to effect her repudiation at any time after the conclusion of the marriage contract in writing.

C. The Formula

The Iraqi legislator makes it a condition for the validity of repudiation that the legally appropriate formula be used (Art. 34). This formula is left unspecified and therefore recourse must be had to the Sharia regulations under Article 183 of the same Law. The formula used by the husband for the pronouncement of repudiation includes the medium of expression and the grammatical construction.

(1) The medium of expression

Repudiation by the husband can be through any medium denoting the termination of the marital relationship, by word of mouth, in writing, or by gesture for him who is incapable of either of them. This general Sharia provision is held in the Laws of Syria (Art. 87/1), Morocco (Art. 46), Jordan (Art. 86), and Kuwait (Art. 104).

The word used may be explicit (*sarih*) or implicit (*kinaya*). An explicit pronouncement of repudiation shall employ the word talaq or a derivative thereof and shall take effect regardless of the intention (*niyya*), according to all the Sunni schools and the modern laws of Syria and Jordan (Arts. 93 and 95, respectively).

The Shia Ithna-Ashari not only require a specific form: "You are repudiated" or "this" pointing to his wife, or "so and so" "is repudiated", but also stipulate the intention.[5] In other words, it must be specifically related to the wife concerned. They also reject the use of any metaphor to effect repudiation, even if the intention is proven, and even if there is circumstantial evidence to corroborate the intention.

On the other hand, the Sunni schools allow the use of metaphor for repudiation, provided that the intention can be established, a ruling followed in Egypt (Art. 4, Act 25/1929), the Sudan (Art. 4, Sharia Circular No. 41/1935), Syria (Art. 93), Jordan (Art. 95), and Kuwait (Art. 104).[6]

(2) Grammatical construction

The Sunnis allow the formula used in a divorce pronouncement by the husband to be either absolute, unconditional, with immediate effect (*munjaz*), or contingent (*muallaq*), subject to a condition, in the form of an oath, or relegated to some event in future.

The Shias differ again, recognizing only the absolute unconditional formula, although they allow the formal suspension, i.e. subject to a condition that actually exists, e.g. "You are repudiated if you are my wife".[7]

The absolute pronouncement of divorce shall be valid and take effect forthwith, provided that the husband and the wife comply with the conditions mentioned above, in countries where the husband has still the right to repudiate his wife without recourse to the court.

As for the contingent formula of a divorce pronouncement, the Sunni jurists, followed by the law-makers in Egypt, Syria, Morocco and Jordan, distinguish between three cases:

(i) A contingent pronouncement where the condition is meant to urge to do or abstain from doing something, as when a husband says to his wife, "If you leave home, you shall be divorced", or, "If I sell this article, my wife shall be divorced". This formula is construed as an oath. The classical jurists ruled that, as such, the husband shall have to choose, if the condition occurs, between a religious expiation (*kaffara*) or to effect

5 *Ibid.* p. 60.

6 There is another difference between the Shias who require witnesses, under the Quranic Verse: "And take for witness two persons from among you endued with justice and establish the evidence before God." (Sura Talaq, LXV, v. 2), and the Sunnis who allow divorce without witnesses on the ground that it is an established right of the husband which needs no evidence. However, this is rather academic, except in states where there is yet no modern personal status code, since all the other states require divorce to be formally recorded.

7 Al-Hilli, *op. cit.* pp. 65/66.

repudiation.[8] The Andalusian jurist Ibn-u-Hazm Al-Zahiri rules that this form shall be void without need to expiation. The modern laws maintain straightforwardly that this form of repudiation is null and void. The Egyptian Article 2 of Act 25/1929 stipulates "No contingent repudiation shall occur if it is meant to urge the doing of or abstention from any act." The same article is repeated in the Jordanian Article 89, and the Moroccan Article 52. The Syrian Article 90 adds the repudiation meant as an oath or for emphasis. Moroccan Article 50 is more specific: "No repudiation shall occur using an oath." Jordanian Article 92 is more restrictive: "No repudiation shall occur using an oath such as 'Repudiation befall me' or 'My wife is prohibited to me' unless the repudiation formula implies that the wife is addressed or meant."

(ii) A contingent pronouncement where the intention is that repudiation shall occur if a certain thing happens, as when a husband says to his wife "If you commit adultery you shall be repudiated", or "If you release me of your deferred dower you shall be repudiated." The Sunni jurists, again with the exception of Ibn-u-Hazm, rule that divorce shall duly occur if the condition happens. This ruling is maintained expressly in the Jordanian Law (Art. 96) and, by implication, in the Egyptian, Syrian and Moroccan Laws. Jordanian Article 96 reads, "It is valid to make repudiation subject to a condition and to defer it to the future. No refrain by the husband from suspended or deferred repudiation shall be admitted".

Both instances of contingent repudiations are dismissed in the Iraqi Article 36 which also rules out the third instance of non-absolute repudiation, following the Shia School.

(iii) A pronouncement deferred to the future is recognized as shown above in the Jordanian Article 96. The four major Sunni Schools agree that this is a valid repudiation, but differ on the time when it comes in force. For example, a husband says to his wife "You are repudiated in a year's time." The Hanafis and Malikis maintain that she shall be repudiated forthwith. The Shafiis and Hanbalis rule that divorce shall not occur until the end of the year. Ibn-u-Hazm, and the Shias, consider it a void repudiation.[9] Kuwaiti Article 105 stipulates that repudiation should be unconditional (munjaz).

D. Modes of Repudiation

A repudiation may be effected in two ways:

(i) *Sunna*, in the sense of the right way, not in the more common meaning of a tradition of the Prophet. It consists of one pronounce-

8 Ibnu Qayyim Aljouzia, *Alam-ul-Muwaqqeen*, Vol. 3, p. 71.
9 Al Hilli, *op. cit.* p. 66.

ment uttered during a *tuhr*, that is a period of menstrual purity during which no sexual intercourse occurs. The Sunna repudiation is again subdivided into *ahsan* (most approved) and *hasan* (good or approved):

(a) The *talaq ahsan* consists of a single pronouncement made during a period of menstrual purity and followed by abstinence from sexual intercourse for the period of iddat;

(b) The *talaq hasan* consists of three pronouncements made over three consecutive periods of menstrual purity during which no intercourse takes place. It becomes irrevocable on the third pronouncement.

(ii) *Biddat* (innovated or heretical) – any repudiation effected disregarding the above requirements. The four Sunni schools consider it valid, albeit a sin.

Only the Sunna repudiation is valid under the Shia Law which stipulates that the wife at the time of divorce must not be in menstrual or puerperal courses if the marriage has been consummated and the husband and wife co-habited. Nevertheless, the repudiation shall be valid if it is pronounced during a menstrual period if the marriage has not been consummated or while the husband is absent, having left his wife in a period of menstrual purity during which there was no intercourse, for a length of time during which another period of menstrual purity has occurred.[10]

This is not just a matter of piety. Without naming it, the modern legislators make it a legal provision. Moroccan Article 47 reads as follows: "If repudiation is pronounced while the woman is during menstruation, the Judge shall force the husband to revoke repudiation." Again, since the Sunna repudiation implies both the timing and the number of pronouncements, requiring the latter to be separate, the Laws of Egypt (Art. 3, Act No. 25/1929), the Sudan (Art. 3, Sharia Circular No. 41/1935), Syria (Art. 92), Morocco (Art. 51), Iraq (Art. 37/2), and Kuwait (Art. 109) include an identical provision: "A repudiation in which a number is implied whether verbally or by a gesture shall be counted as one pronouncement". The Jordanian Article 85 following the same trend rules "The husband is entitled to three separate pronouncements of repudiation at three sittings." This subject will be dealt with in more detail in the following section.

E. Revocable and Irrevocable Pronouncements of Repudiation

All forms of dissolution of marriage are either revocable – *raji*, or irrevocable – *bain*, in terms of their legal effects.

10 *Ibid.* p. 65.

(1) The revocable repudiation

The revocable repudiation, which is usually the rule, does not dissolve marriage until the period of iddat is completed. At any time during this period, the husband has the option to revoke the pronouncement either expressly by word of mouth or implicitly by resuming marital relations, without the necessity of a new contract or a new dower, and without even the consent of the wife.

This provision is based on the Quranic ruling: "And their husbands have the better right to take them back in that period if they wish for reconciliation" coming a few lines after "Repudiated women shall wait concerning themselves for three monthly periods."[11]

This Quranic ruling is adopted in all Islamic countries even though it is not mentioned expressly except in the Jordanian Article 97, which adds that the husband's right to take back his wife during the iddat cannot be relinquished. The Iraqi Article 38 requires the same proof for revocation of repudiation as for repudiation itself.

On the other hand, the marriage is dissolved forthwith on the utterance of an irrevocable pronouncement, apart from the Druzes, to whom every divorce is irrevocable for ever (Art. 38, Lebanese Act of 24/2/1948 and Syrian Art. 307/g). Usually every repudiation is deemed revocable except in certain cases listed by the Egyptian, Sudanese, Syrian and Kuwaiti legislators (Arts. 5, Egyptian Act No. 25/1929; 5, Sudanese Sharia Circular No. 41/1935; 94, Syrian and 110, Kuwaiti). These cases are:

(a) *A repudiation completing three divorces.* Under the Quaranic ruling "A divorce is only permissible twice: after that the parties should either hold together on equitable terms or separate with kindness."[12] The three repudiations must be separate, in three different sittings, divided by three iddats as explained in the Sunna repudiation. Three pronounements of repudiation or one pronouncement combined with a number denoted verbally or by a gesture shall be counted as one (Arts. 3, Egyptian Act No. 25/1929; 3, Sudanese Sharia Circular No. 41/1935; 92, Syrian; 51, Moroccan; 37/2, Iraqi; 85, Jordanian; 109, Kuwaiti) (See above D.).

(b) *A repudiation prior to consumation.* The marriage is dissolvced in this case immediately without any waiting period, under the Quranic verse: "O ye who believe! When ye marry believing women, and then repudiate them before ye have touched them, no period of Iddat have ye to count in respect of them; so give them a present, and set them free according to decent custom."[13]

11 Sura Baqara, II, verse 228.
12 *Ibid.* verse 229.
13 Sura Ahzab, XXXIII, verse 49.

These are the only two forms of irrevocable repudiation affected by the husband on his own, being the subject of this section. The other forms of irrevocable divorce are either effected through agreement between the two spouses (*khula* or *mubarat*) which shall be dealt with in Section 3 of this Chapter, or by the court, to be dealt with in Section 4.

(2) Types of irrevocable repudiation

The irrevocable repudiation is again subdivided into minor – *bain bainoona sughra* and major – *bain bainoona kubra*. In the minor irrevocable repudiation, the husband may remarry his repudiated wife under a new contract, for a new dower and subject to her consent. Such is the case after the lapse of iddat of the first and second repudiation by the husband. In the major irrevocable repudiation, occurring after the third pronouncement by the husband, the wife becomes temporarily prohibited for the husband to remarry. He can only remarry her after she has been duly married to another, genuine consummation has taken place, her second marriage has been duly dissolved, and she has counted her iddat, or the second husband has died. This general Sharia rule is observed throughout the Islamic world, even codified in the Jordanian Article 100. Only Tunisia, Article 19, prevents the husband for ever from remarrying the wife he has repudiated three times, following the Hanbalis who consider a marriage with a view to make the wife later lawful to her first husband void and religiously prohibited.

When the husband is allowed to remarry his wife whom he has previously repudiated and whose later marriage to another husband has since then been dissolved, the majority of jurists maintain that the former husband shall be entitled to three pronouncements anew. Indeed, Kuwaiti Article 108 rules that the former husband shall have such a right if his divorcée married another man and was later divorced from him.

On the repudiation becoming irrevocable, the wife shall be entitled to her deferred dower at once. Should either spouse die after an irrevocable repudiation, there shall be no inheritance by the surviving spouse on grounds of matrimony. The only exception is if the husband was on his deathbed and it could be proved that he was repudiating his wife with the malicious intention of depriving her of her inheritance rights. In this case, she would retain her inheritance rights, although he would not retain his, should she die before him.

To prove malicious intention, the following conditions must be fulfilled:

(i) that the irrevocable repudiation occurs against her will;
(ii) that the husband died after an illness during which the repudiation occurred and before her iddat was completed;
(iii) that the irrevocably repudiated woman shall be eligible at the time of

the repudiation to inherit; for example, that she was not then of another religion. If she was, and then converted to Islam after the repudiation, she shall not inherit from her Muslim husband.[14]

3. DISSOLUTION OF MARRIAGE BY AGREEMENT OF THE SPOUSES

Apart from the divorce effected by the husband, marriage may be dissolved by mutual consent by the wife giving the husband something for her freedom under the Quranic ruling, "And it is not lawful for you that ye take from women aught of that which ye have given them except in the case when both fear that they may not be able to keep within the limits imposed by God. And if ye fear that they may not be able to keep the limits of God, it is no sin for either of them if the woman ransom herself."[15]

This form is called khula, an Arabic word which means "To take off one's dress", relating to a metaphoric description of the spouses in the Quranic verse "They are raiment for you and ye are raiment for them".[16] As seen in the previous verse, it may be called "ransom". Some Jurists use also the word mubaraat (mutual discharge). One of these words, or a derivative thereof, must be used in this context, otherwise it shall be deemed a divorce for a pecuniary consideration (*talaq ala mal*), as when a husband says to his wife, "You are divorced for such and such sume of money" and she accepts. Both forms have in common that the dissolution takes effect forthwith, the consideration becomes due from the wife provided that she has the legal capacity thereto. They differ in that the divorce for a pecuniary consideration does not deprive the wife of her rights under the marriage contract, e.g. deferred dower and maintenance.[17]

Khula is dealt with in separate chapters in the Laws of Syria (Book II, Chapter II, Arts. 95–104, inclusive), Morocco (Book II, Chapter III, Arts. 61–65, inclusive), Iraq (Book IV, Chapter III, Art. 46), Jordan (Chapter II, Arts. 102–112, inclusive) and Kuwait (Part I, Book II, Chapter 1, Section 2, Arts. 111–119, inclusive). The Tunisian Article 31 allows divorce by the spouses' consent before the court, a provision required also by the Iraqi Article 46/1. Under Shia Law, the khula, like divorce, must be effected in the presence of two male Muslim witnesses of

14 Abu Zahra, *op. cit.* pp. 316–320; Abdullah *op. cit.* p. 470; Al-Hilli, *op. cit.* pp. 68–70.
15 Sura Baqara, II, verse 229.
16 *Ibid.* verse 187.
17 Abu Zahra, *op. cit.* pp. 327–338; Abdullah, *op. cit.* pp. 486–506.

approved probity, and it must not be conditional.[18] The Druzes combine the last two provisions, allowing dissolution of marriage by mutual consent to be declared in the presence of two witnesses before the judge who shall issue a divorce decree (Lebanese Druze Personal Status Act/1948, Art. 42).

For the khula to be valid, the husband must possess legal capacity to pronounce divorce and the woman must be a lawful object thereof (Arts. 95/1, Syrian; 46/1, Iraqi; 102/a, Jordanian; 112, Kuwaiti). A woman under the age of majority shall not be liable for the khula consideration without the consent of her guardian of property (Arts. 95/2, Syrian; 62, Moroccan; 106/b, Jordanian). The Moroccan and Kuwaiti legislators add as a condition for the husband's entitlement to the khula, consideration that the khula by the woman shall be of her own accord and free choice to leave the husband without coercion or harassment (Arts. 63 and 116 respectively).

The juristic qualification of khula differs in the case of the husband, when it is deemed an oath, from the case of the wife when it is considered to be compensation. Therefore, according to the Hanafis, the husband cannot withdraw from the khula and cannot retain the condition of option. On the other hand, the wife may withdraw her offer of khula before the husband gives his acceptance, or may leave the hearing before his consent is given, thus retaining the condition of option, during which she may accept or reject the khula offer. This Hanafi rule is dropped in the modern laws of Syria (Art. 96), Jordan (Art. 103), and Kuwait (Art. 113), which grant both parties the right to withdraw the khula offer before it is accepted by the other party, following thereby the Hanbali and Zaidi jurists.

The consideration for the khula may be pecuniary, advanced or deferred, or may be the nursing, maintenance and custody of their child. This provision is codified in an identical text reading "Everything that is a lawful object of obligation is suitable as a consideration for Khula" in the laws of Syria (Art. 97), Morocco (Art. 64), Jordan (Art. 104) and Kuwait (Art. 114). Following a general Sharia provision, the Jordanian legislator holds that if the consideration is unlawful, divorce shall be revocable, and the husband shall lose the consideration agreed upon (Art. 102/c).

The husband may receive from his wife in consideration for the khula an amount which is more or less than her dower (Iraqi Art. 46/3).

If the khula is for a pecuniary consideration other than the dower, it shall be payable and the two parties to the khula shall be discharged of all liabilities in respect of the dower and the wife maintenance (Arts. 98, Syrian; 105, Jordanian). The same provision shall apply if the two parties

18 Al-Hilli, *op. cit.* pp. 71–75.

fail to specify any consideration at the time of khula (Arts. 99, Syrian; 106, Jordanian). But the Algerian legislator empowers the judge, in the case of such a failure, to order a consideration not exceeding the dower of the equal at the time of judgment (Art. 54).

If the two parties to the khula declare that there is no consideration, the case shall be one not of khula, but of a simple revocable divorce (Arts. 100, Syrian; 107, Jordanian).

The iddat maintenance shall not be dropped, nor shall the husband be discharged therefrom unless the khula contract contains expressly such a stipulation (Arts. 101, Syrian; 108, Jordanian).

If it is stipulated in the khula contract that the husband shall be spared the fees for the fosterage or custody of the child, or that the wife shall keep the child, free of charge, for a given period or shall provide maintenance for it, and later she marries and leaves the child or dies, the husband shall be entitled to claim the equivalent of the fosterage and custody fees and the maintenance of the child for the rest of the period. But if the child dies, the father shall have no right for such a claim for the period following its death (Arts. 102/1, Syrian, 109, Jordanian).

The father shall be liable to the maintenance of the child if the mother is indigent at the time of khula or becomes so later; such a maintenance shall be a debt on the mother (Arts. 102/2, Syrian; 110, Jordanian).

A condition in the khula contract that the father shall keep the child for the period of custody shall be void while the contract remains valid, and the child's lawful custodian shall take it, and the father, if poor, shall be liable only for its maintenance, under the Jordanian Article 111 and also for its custody fees according to the Syrian Article 103 and Kuwaiti Article 1187.

No maintenance due to the child from the father may be set off against a debt to the father from the mother who has the custody of the child (Art. 104, Syrian). Moroccan Article 65 is even more sweeping "Nothing connected with the rights of children may be a consideration for khula, if the woman is destitute".

Of the modern statutes, only the Kuwaiti Personal Status Act, Art. 119, deals with a specific case: the khula by a wife who suffers from a fatal illness (*marad-ul-maut*) a case covered by the classical jurists whose provisions are applied by courts. They rule that khula in such a case shall be valid and the divorce shall be deemed irrevocable, as if the khula has taken place before her illness, and the consideration to be within one-third of her estate if the heirs do not consent to anymore, with the following reservations:

(i) In the event of the death of the wife while still in her iddat, the husband shall be entitled to the least valuable of three options: the khula consideration, his share of her estate or a third of her net estate, as if the Khula consideration was a bequest.

(ii) In the event of the wife's death during her illness but after completion of her iddat, the husband shall be entitled to the lesser amount of the khula consideration, or a third of her net estate. He shall no longer be entitled to a share of her estate as the marriage tie has been broken in all respects.

(iii) In the event of the wife's death after her recovery from the illness during which the khula occurred, the husband shall be entitled to the khula consideration.

In general, dissolution of marriage through mutual consent, khula, gives rise to the following effects:

(i) the dissolution shall be irrevocable;

(ii) the husband shall be entitled to the consideration subject to the previous reservations;

(iii) all acquired financial rights for each spouse at the time of khula, such as the deferred dower and maintenance dues shall be dropped. This does not apply to established rights of each spouse to the other on grounds other than the marriage so dissolved, e.g. ordinary debts or iddat maintenance unless otherwise specified.

4. DISSOLUTION OF MARRIAGE BY THE COURT

Although we have been discussing so far the dissolution of marriage by the husband or by mutual consent of the spouses without the intervention proper by the court, nevertheless, the court has not been entirely absent. It has already an active role both in Tunisia, and for the Druzes in Lebanon and Syria where divorce can only be effected before and by order of the judge. In some other countries, e.g. Iraq and Algeria, divorce even by the husband shall take effect from the time it is recorded with the court of jurisdiction of the locality if not before the judge.

Here we shall deal with the actual intervention by the court to effect dissolution of marriage. This is called "divorce proper".[19] In Arabic it is *tafriq*, a subject of controversy among jurists. The Shia Ithna-Ashari allow the tafriq only in the event of the husband's impotence, provided that the wife shall apply to the court for divorce, and that she has not known about it at the time of marriage, and that she applies for divorce immediately she

19 *Cf.* Black's *Law Dictionary* (5th ed., West Publishing Co., Paul Minn, 1979).

knows of her husband's impotence.[20] For the Lebanese Shias, divorce by the court does not apply.[21] The Hanafis maintain that dissolution of marriage is the exclusive right of the husband, with the court having the right to intervene only in the event of a serious genital defect of the husband such as impotence or castration. The Hanafi jurist Muhammad adds insanity and leprosy. The other three major Sunni Imams, Malik, ash-Shafii and ibn Hanbal grant the wife the right to apply to the court for divorce on specific grounds, the judge in such a case being asked to act on behalf of the husband to redress an injury. This more liberal interpretation has been adopted in the Ottoman Family Rights Act, which is the law applicable to the Sunni Muslims of the Lebanon, followed by the laws of Syria, Morocco, Iraq, Jordan and Algeria.

The Tunisian Mejelle, apart from investing the court with the exclusive power to effect divorce, rules that divorce shall be ordered:

(i) at the request of either spouse on grounds under the said Mejelle;
(ii) by mutual consent of the two spouses;
(iii) at the request of the husband to obtain divorce or the wife applying for it (Arts. 30 and 31).

However, it adds that the judge shall not order divorce except after doing his utmost to resolve the grounds of dissent between the two spouses and finding it impossible to reconcile them.

As for the other said laws, the grounds for applying to the court for divorce are five:

(a) injury or discord;
(b) a defect on the part of the husband;
(c) failure to pay maintenance;
(d) absence of the husband without an acceptable excuse;
(e) the imprisonment of the husband. We shall now deal with those grounds in the above order.

A. Injury or Discord

The two Imams Malik and Ahmad Ibn Hanbal maintain that the wife may ask the judge to order divorce if she claimed that the husband has caused her such an injury as to make the continuation of the marital life between the likes of them impossible. They cite the following examples; beating, insulting or forcing her to an outrage. Abu Hanifa and Ash Shafii dissent, holding that injury is no sound ground for divorce as it can be

20 Al-Hilli, *op. cit.* p. 76.
21 B. Baylani, *Lebanese Personal Status Acts* (Cairo, 1971), p. 134.

remedied through reprimanding the husband, or the wife's refusal to obey him. According to the first opinion, the judge must be convinced of the validity of the wife's claim either on the strength of her evidence or the admission of the husband. If the injury is such as to make their continued life together unbearable and the judge cannot reconcile them, then he shall order an irrevocable divorce. If the wife cannot prove her case, or the husband makes no confession, the case shall be dismissed. If she repeats her complaint and requests a divorce and the court cannot establish the validity of her claims, the judge shall appoint two arbitrators who are adult, of known propriety, well-acquainted with the spouses and capable of effecting a reconciliation. Preferably they shall be relatives of the spouses but otherwise they can be strangers. They shall investigate the causes of discord between the two spouses and attempt, as far as possible, to effect a reconciliation. Should they fail and the two spouses or the husband were to blame for the injury, or if the arbiters could not establish the facts, they shall decide on an irrevocable divorce. If the wife is to blame for the injury, they shall be separated through khula. Abu Hanifa, Ahmad and Ash Shafii make the arbiters' decision on divorce subject to being authorized thereto by the husband. Should the two arbiters fail to reach a consensus, the judge shall order them to make further investigations, and if they fail this time, he shall appoint two others, and their award shall be binding on him. This is all based on the Quranic verse: "And if ye fear a breach between them twain (the man and the wife), appoint an arbiter from his folk and an arbiter from her folk. If they desire amendment Allah will make them of one mind. . . ."[22] And on another Quranic verse "Divorce must be pronounced twice and then (a woman) must be retained in honour or released in kindness. . . ."[23]

The jurists argue that since retaining in honour is missed, release in kindness shall prevail. The jurists also quote the authentic tradition of the Prophet "There shall be no injury and no injury shall be remedied with another injury." The modern Islamic legislations have adopted these provisions (Egyptian Act No. 25/1929 as amended by Act No. 100/1985, Arts. 6, 7, 8, 9, 10 and 11; Syrian Arts. 112, 113, 114, 115; Tunisian Art. 32 as amended under Act No. 7/1981; Moroccan Art. 56; Iraqi Arts. 40, 41 and 42; Jordanian Art. 132 paras. a–i inclusive; Algerian Art. 53 paras. 6 and 7 and Art. 56; and Kuwaiti Arts. 126 to 135 inclusive) with various additions as follows:

(a) Syria. Either spouse may apply to the court for divorce on the ground of injury by the other, and the judge shall effect an irrevocable divorce between them if he failed to reconcile them, having been convinced of the

22 Sura Nisaa, IV, verse 35.
23 Sura Baqara, II, verse 22.

injury. If the injury is not proved, the judge shall adjourn the case for at least a month in the hope of a reconciliation being reached, failing which, with the applicant insisting on the dissolution of marriage, the judge shall appoint arbiters in the above manner, who shall swear on oath to accomplish their brief in fairness and honesty.

The arbiters shall hold a meeting under the auspices of the judge to be solely attended by the spouses and those invited by the arbiters.

The failure of either spouse to attend such a meeting, having been notified thereof, shall not affect the award. If the injury, or most of it, is on the part of the husband, the arbiters, having failed to reconcile the spouses, shall award an irrevocable divorce. If they find the injury or most of it, on the part of the wife, or equally due to both spouses, they shall award a divorce and order the full dower or a commensurate part thereof to the injury. The arbiters may also award the divorce without establishing the injury on either party, releasing the husband of a part of the wife's right subject to her consent. Should the arbiters disagree, the judge shall replace them, or add to them an umpire with a casting vote. The judge may accept the arbiters' award or reject it, in which case he shall appoint for the last time two other arbiters.

(b) Tunisia. The new Article 31 as amended under Act. No. 7/1981 rules that the injured spouse shall be granted damages for any material or moral injury inflicted as a result of divorce at the request of either party. The woman shall receive damages for any material injury in the form of a monthly allowance, to run after the expiry of the iddat, to secure for her the same standards of living she was accustomed to during her marriage. Such an allowance shall be liable to revision upwards or downwards as circumstances change, and shall continue for the lifetime of the divorcee or until she remarries and her social status changes or on acquiring such property as to enable her to do without such an allowance. It shall be a charge on the estate of the ex-husband on his death, to be settled through an agreement with the heirs or by court order for a lump sum to be determined with due consideration of her age at that date, unless she opts from the start for a lump sum in compensation for the material injury in a single payment.

Article 32 as amended under the same Act, provides that the court president, on failing to effect reconciliation between the two spouses, shall order all the necessary measures in respect of the matrimonial home, maintenance, custody of and access to the ward, unless the two parties agree expressly on leaving all or any such matters pending. His order shall be enforceable forthwith, and shall be liable for revision but not for appeal. The court shall rule in the first instance on divorce and all the matters related thereto, and determine the amount of the monthly allowance. Notwithstanding any appeal, the court orders in respect of custody, maintenance, monthly allowance, accommodation and access to the ward shall be enforceable forthwith.

(c) Iraq. Under Law No. 21/1978, amending some Articles of Law No. 188/1959, The Iraqui legislator, while granting both spouces leave to apply to the court for a divorce, distinguishes between the grounds of injury (Art. 40 – as amended) and of discord (Art. 41 – as amended).

Under injury, the Act lists the following grounds:

(i) marital infidelity by either spouse;
(ii) marrigae contract being solemnized, without the Judge's permission, before either spouse completes 18 years of age;
(iii) marriage being concluded outside the court through coercion, and consummation having occurred;
(iv) the husband taking another wife without the court's permission, without the wife having the right to set the criminal prosecution which shall be a public right.

Article 41 allows each spouse to apply to the court for a divorce in the event of any dispute between them, whether before or after consummation. The court shall then investigate the causes of discord, and, having found that it existed, shall appoint an arbiter related to the wife, and another related to the husband if possible, failing which the court shall order the spouses to elect two arbiters. If the spouses disagree, the court shall appoint the arbiters who shall try their utmost to reconcile them, failing which they shall report to the court on the responsibility for the injury. If they disagree, the court shall add an umpire with a casting vote. If the court is convinced of the continuation of dissension between the two spouses and fails to reconcile them, and the husband refuses to pronounce divorce, the court shall order a divorce. If divorce is ordered after consummation, the deferred dower shall be dropped if the injury is on the part of the wife, whether she is the applicant or the respondent, and she shall be ordered to repay an amount not exceeding half of the dower if she has received it in full. If both parties are responsible for injury, the deferred dower shall be divided in the proportion of their respective responsibility. If divorce is ordered before consummation and injury is proved on the part of the wife, she shall be ordered to repay the prompt dower she has received.

(d) Jordan. The Jordanian legislator (Art. 132), while allowing either spouse to apply to the court for divorce, distinguishes between the applicant being the wife or the husband. If it is the wife, and she can prove injury by the husband, the judge shall try his utmost to reconcile them, failing which he shall caution the husband to mend his ways, and shall

adjourn the case for at least a month, at the end of which the judge shall refer the case to two arbiters (Art. 132/a).

If the husband is the applicant for divorce, and would prove dissension and discord, the judge shall adjourn the case for at least a month, at the end of which, without the husband withdrawing his application or reconciliation being reached, the judge shall refer the case to two arbiters (Art. 132/b) who shall record their findings in a report, and if they fail to effect reconciliation, and find against the wife, they shall award divorce for a consideration they set, provided it shall not be less than the dower.

If they find against the husband, they shall award an irrevocable divorce, reserving all the wife's rights as if it was the husband himself who effected the divorce (Art. 132/e).

If they find against both spouses, they shall award a divorce between them in the proportion of their respective injury. If they cannot apportion the injury, they shall fix the consideration at their discretion (Art. 132/f). If any consideration is awarded against the wife who is the applicant for divorce, she shall secure the payment thereof before the arbiters award divorce, unless the husband accepts the deferment of such consideration, and the judge shall order the divorce. If the husband is the applicant for divorce and the arbiters award a consideration against the wife, the judge shall uphold the award of both divorce and the consideration (Art. 132/g).

If the arbiters fail to reach agreement, the judge shall replace them, or add an umpire with a casting vote, and the majority award shall prevail. The judge shall rule according to the agreed findings of the arbiters' report if it conforms with the provisions of this Article 132/a–i inclusive.

(e) Algeria. The arbiters shall be kinsmen of the spouses, and shall submit a report of their findings within two months of their being appointed to reconcile between the spouses among whom there is a severe dissension without proving the injury.

It is considered an injury entitling the wife to apply to the court for divorce that the husband should abstain from connubial intercourse for more than four months (Art. 53/3) or commit a flagrant outrage (*ibid.* para. 7).

(f) Kuwait. If the two arbiters fail to reach an award, the court shall appoint a third, with a casting vote, not being of either spouse and capable of repairing the rift (Art. 131/b). The three arbiters shall submit their unanimous or majority report to the court for decision. If they fail to agree or to report, the court shall proceed in the normal way (Art. 132/a and b). Injury shall be proven by the evidence of two men or a man and two women (Art. 133). Hearsay evidence, based on well-known facts about the life together of the two spouses, shall suffice to prove the occurrence, but not the absence, of injury (Art. 134). Evidence of the kin or a person

connected with the person in whose favour the evidence is given shall be admitted, provided that witnesses possess the capacity thereto (Art. 135).

B. A Defect on the Part of the Husband

Divorce on the ground of a defect in either spouse is a subject of some controversy among Islamic jurists. To start with, there are two extreme positions. The Zahiris bar any divorce on account of a physical defect on the part of either the husband or the wife. According to Ibn-u-Hazm "No marriage shall be nullified, once it is duly celebrated, by any leprosy, insanity, nor any other defect on the part of the wife, nor by impotence nor by a vaginal defect nor by any defect whatsoever."[24] On the other hand, the Hanbali jurist Ibn Qayyim maintains that every defect, whether on the part of the man or the wife, shall entitle the other spouse to petition for a divorce, since the contract was solemnized on the assumption of freedom from all defects, an implied condition based on custom, which ought to be fulfilled and was found to be lacking. He does not bother to enumerate such defects, but gives the widest description of them as any shortcoming that causes aversion to the other spouse.[25]

Between these two extremes, there is a wide spectrum of juristic opinion. The Shias maintain that a wife who finds her husband impotent without having known it at the time of marriage is entitled to petition for divorce if she did not consent to the continuation of the marriage. She shall have the same right if impotence occurs after the contract and before consummation, but she shall lose that right if she does not apply for divorce and she knows about the defect. The judge shall investigate and if the husband declares that he has not consummated the marriage, the judge shall grant him a delay of a whole lunar year including Ramadan, the wife's menstrual cycles and any absences or illnesses of either spouse, to start from the date of petition, unless the husband was young, in which case the delay should count from the day he reaches puberty. At the end of the delay, if the woman still complains, the judge shall order a divorce. The wife may annul the marriage at the expiry of this delay without recourse to the judge. If she finds the husband mutilated, castrated, or insane, without having known that at the time of the marriage, and therefore asks for a divorce, it shall be granted forthwith. She also has the right to annul the marriage on her own. If the husband denies impotence he shall be believed on taking an oath; if he refrains and the wife takes an oath before the adjournment described, he shall be given a delay of a year. After the expiry of this delay, she shall have the choice at the same

24 Ibn-u-Hazm, *Al-Muhalla*, Vol. 7, p. 109 (Cairo).
25 Ibn Qayyim Al Jouzia, *Zad-ul-Maad*, Vol. 4 (Cairo, 1369H), pp. 30–31.

hearing. If she opts for divorce, it shall be granted. If she opts for the continuation, or left the hearing before making a choice, she shall lose that right.[26]

Abu Hanifa and his disciples maintain that the judge has no power to order a divorce on the grounds of a defect on the part of the wife, as the husband possesses the right to repudiate her. They allow such a divorce to be ordered on the grounds of defects of the man. Abu Hanifa and Abu Youssof confine these defects to three genital ones: impotence, mutilation and castration, all being impediments of consummation and procreation, and constituting an injury to the wife. The judge, on the husband's refusal to repudiate, shall act on his behalf and order a divorce. A second disciple, Muhammad, adds the defects of insanity and leprosy. The three set three conditions for such a divorce:

(i) that the wife was not aware of the defect at the time of marriage;
(ii) that she petitions the court for a divorce and her case is proved;
(iii) that the judge shall order a divorce.

Mutilation shall entail a divorce forthwith. As for impotence and castration, the Judge shall adjourn the case for a whole (lunar) year, not counting periods of the husband's being away, after which, in the absence of any improvement, the wife insisting on her application and the husband refusing to repudiate, the judge shall order an irrevocable divorce with the woman entitled to the whole dower if valid retirement had taken place.[27]

The three other Sunni Imams, Malik, Ash-Shafii and Ahmad, allow a divorce by the court on the grounds of such defects on the part of either spouse. But Malik maintains it shall be an irrevocable repudiation, arguing that if it is not by the husband, it is by a cause emanating from him, and the injury could only be remedied if this is an irrevocable repudiation. The Malikis also enlarge the scope of such defects, giving the most general description without listing them definitively. They consider silence by the wife to be an implicit acceptance which deprives her of the right to apply to the court. In the case of insanity, they rule that a divorce should be adjourned for a year.

Ash-Shafii considers such a divorce a decree of annulment, since it is not effected by the husband personally and of his own free will. Ahmad concurs, but differs from Ash-Shafii in that he does not consider the wife's silence an acceptance of the defect, unless she knew about it and consented to consummation.

26 Al-Hilli, *op. cit.* pp. 76–77.
27 Al-Abiani, *Sharia Personal Status Provisions*, pp. 269–272; Abu Zahra, *op. cit.* pp. 354–359.

The modern Arab legislations in general adopt the position that the wife is entitled to sue for divorce on the grounds of a defect on the part of the husband, and retain many of the previous provisions.

(a) Egypt. The Hanafi doctrine on divorce for a defect on the part of the husband that renders him incapable of consummate marriage was followed in Egypt until the promulgation of Act No. 25/1920 which implicitly retained this provision and added further such defects which it described without naming them. Chapter 3, Articles 9, 10 and 11 of the said Act gives the wife the right to apply to the court for a divorce, stipulating three conditions:

(i) that the defect is of long standing and is incurable or only curable after a long time. If the husband can recover in a short time, the wife shall not be entitled to sue for a divorce;
(ii) that the continuation of marriage shall not be without an injury in view of such a defect such as insanity and leprosy, and that the injury shall affect her and her offspring. This condition shall be certified by medical experts;
(iii) that it is not proved that she consented having known of that defect. She shall not be entitled to sue for a divorce if the defect was existent at the time of the marriage, and she knew of it, and also, if, having not been aware of it at the time of the marriage, she did consent after acquiring that knowledge expressly or by implication. The same premise applies if the defect emerges later, and she consents to it. Such a divorce shall be irrevocable, at her request and by order of the court. Before the decree, there shall be no divorce, and all effects of marriage shall prevail.

(b) Syria. Divorce on grounds of the husband's defects is dealt with in Part III, Chapter I, Articles 105–108 inclusive. There are two specific cases when the wife is entitled to sue for a divorce:

(i) if the husband suffers from a defect that renders him incapable of consummating the marriage, provided that the wife is free from such a defect. With the exception of impotence, for which the right to apply for a divorce shall not lapse under any circumstances, the wife shall lose the right to petition for dissolution of the marriage by the court if she knew of the existence of the defect before the contract or if she consented to continue marriage thereafter;
(ii) if the husband becomes insane after the contract. The judge shall order a divorce forthwith if such a defect is incurable. If it is, the judge shall adjourn the case for a period not exceeding a year, at the end of which he shall order a divorce if no cure was found. Such a divorce shall be irrevocable.

(c) Morocco. The Moroccan legislator follows the Egyptian with some modifications. The wife may apply to the court for a divorce if she finds an incurable disease or one which it would take a long time to cure, during which time they cannot live together without great injury to her. Article 54/1 cites the examples of insanity, leprosy and tuberculosis. It is of no consequence that such a defect existed before marriage without her knowing about it or occurred after marriage, and she did not consent to stay with him. The judge shall adjourn the case for a year, at the end of which he shall order a divorce if no cure has occurred. This does not apply to incurable genital defects for which the judge shall order a divorce forthwith.

On the other hand, if the wife suffers from a defect such as insanity, leprosy, tuberculosis, or a genital disease which renders cohabitation impossible or unpleasurable, the husband, if he knew of such a defect before consummation, shall have the option to repudiate without incurring any liability, or to consummate marriage and pay the dower in full. If he knew it only after consummation, he may either retain her or repudiate her, and recover the balance of the least dower if it was the wife who misled him. If it was the guardian who misled him, then the guardian shall be liable for the monies paid by the husband. Recourse shall be made to medical experts to ascertain the defect. The divorce in this case is irrevocable.

(d) Iraq. Defects on the part of the husband are dealt with under paragraphs 4, 5 and 6 of Article 43, on the right of the wife to sue for a divorce by the court. She may apply to the judge if she finds her husband to be impotent or unable for any other defect to perform connubial intercourse due to organic or psychological causes, or if he becomes so defected after consummation, and a competent official medical committee certifies that such a defect is incurable. However, if the court finds that the cause is psychological, it shall adjourn divorce for a year, provided that the wife shall make herself available to her husband in the meantime. The wife shall also have the right to petition for dissolution if the husband is, or becomes, sterile after marriage without her having any surviving child by him. The same right shall prevail if she found after marriage that her husband was suffering from any such illness as to render living with him impossible for her without injury to herself. The examples cited are leprosy, tuberculosis, a venereal disease or insanity or the like, even if they occur later. However, should the court find, following a medical examination, that such a disease could be cured, it shall adjourn divorce until the actual cure; the wife meanwhile should avoid living with the husband. Nevertheless, the judge shall order an irrevocable (minor) divorce if there is no hope that the disease would be cured within a reasonable time and if the husband refuses to repudiate his wife.

(e) Jordan. Like the Syrian Law, the Jordanian legislator stipulates for the woman petitioning for a divorce on the grounds of the husband suffering from a condition she knows of rendering him incapable of consummation, such as mutilation, impotence or castration, that she herself should be free from any defect that makes connubial intercourse impossible. Except for impotence, she shall lose her right of option if she knew before the time of the marriage of such a defect on the part of the husband or if she consented to live on with him having known of that defect after the contract (Arts. 113 and 114).

The law then distinguishes between incurable and curable diseases. The judge shall order a divorce forthwith if the disease is incurable. If it is curable, the husband shall be granted a delay of a year from the day she makes herself available to him, or from the time the husband recovers from another illness. This delay shall not include any periods, long or short, during which either spouse is suffering from an illness preventing intercourse, or any absence by the wife, but shall include her menstrual periods during which the husband is away. If the defect is not removed by the end of the delay and the husband refuses to repudiate marriage, the judge shall order a divorce if the wife presses her petition. If the husband claims at the beginning or end of the proceedings that he has consummated marriage, the wife shall be examined, and if found not to be a virgin, the husband shall be believed on taking an oath; if found a virgin, she shall be believed without an oath (Art. 115).

As for other diseases such as leprosy, tuberculosis or venereal disease, which would make the continuation of matrimonial life an injury to the wife, she may apply to the judge for a divorce whether the diseases occurred before or after consummation. The judge shall order a divorce forthwith if competent experts certify that there is no hope of recovery. If there is such a hope, the divorce proceeding shall be adjourned for a year at the end of which the judge shall order a divorce if there is no recovery, the husband refuses to repudiate and the wife insists on her petition. However, such handicaps as blindness or lameness of the husband shall be no valid ground for a divorce (Art. 116).

The husband, on his part, is entitled to apply for the annulment of the marriage contract if he finds his wife to be suffering from a genital impediment to connubial intercourse or a repugnant disease that makes life with her impossible without injury to himself, provided that he did not know of it prior to the marriage contract and has not accepted it expressly or by implication (Art. 117); and provided that such defects on the part of the wife have not occurred after consummation (Art. 118).

A genital defect on the part of either spouse shall be proved by a report of a medical practitioner or a midwife who shall be called to give evidence (Art. 119).

Insanity of the husband after the celebration of marriage shall entitle the wife to sue for a divorce, in which case the judge shall adjourn proceedings for a year at the end of which, if the husband has not recovered and the woman insists on her petition, the judge shall order a divorce (Art. 120).

The Jordanian Law is unique in (i) giving the wife the right to defer the court action or to leave it in suspense for a time after the institution thereof (Art. 121); (ii) in depriving both parties from the right to sue for a divorce if they renewed the marriage contract under the previous provision after a divorce decree was issued (Art. 122).

(f) Algeria. The Algerian Article 53/2 simply grants the wife the right to apply for a divorce on the grounds of defects that impede the achievement of the objective of marriage.

(g) Kuwait. The Kuwaiti legislator gives each spouse the right to ask for the marriage to be rescinded on finding with the other an injurious or disgusting defect, or such as to render enjoyment impossible, whether it occurred before or after the contract, such right being waived if the defect was known before or expressly accepted after (Art. 139). But the wife shall not lose that right if the husband suffers from a defect which makes enjoyment impossible, e.g. impotence, inate or acquired, even if she expressly acquiesced (Art. 140). The court shall annul the marriage forthwith if the defect is incurable, otherwise it shall postpone trial for an appointed time at the end of which, if the defect is not cured and the applicant insists on rescission, the court shall issue a nullification decree (Art. 141).

C. Failure to pay maintenance

The Islamic jurists differ on deeming failure by the husband to pay maintenance as a valid ground for the wife to apply to the court for a divorce. The Hanafis are categorical that such a divorce is not permissible whether the reason for the failure to pay maintenance is insolvency of the husband, or just refusal. They quote the Quranic verse: "Let him who hath abundance spend of his abundance, and he whose provision is measured, let him spend of that which Allah hath given him."[28] This, according to the Hanafis, covers the case of the husband who fails to maintain his wife because he is indigent. As for the husband who inflicts injustice on his wife by refusing to maintain her although he could afford it, the Hanafis rule that this injustice could be redressed without recourse to the divorce which is the most detestable to God of all permissible things,

28 Sura Talaq, LXVI, verse 7.

e.g. he could have his property sold, or could be put in jail until he resumes paying maintenance.[29]

The Shias, as previously mentioned, restrict the right of the wife to apply for divorce to impotence of the husband. Failure to maintain would only give the wife the right to apply to the court for an order against the husband.

The other three Sunni Imams, especially Malik and Ahmad, allow a divorce by the judge at the request of the wife on the husband failing to maintain her, and if he has no known property. They agree that the Quran decrees: "(A woman) must be retained in honour or released in kindness. . . ."[30], and abstention from paying maintenance does not conform to retention with honour. They also agree that failure to maintain is a grievous injury to the wife which should be remedied by the court under the authentic Prophet's Tradition: "There shall be no injury, and no injury shall be remedied by another." They also agree that if the judge has the power to order a divorce on the ground of a defect on the part of the husband, a divorce for failure to maintain should be *a fortiori* allowable.[31]

The modern law-makers adopt the position of the three Imams, Malik, Ash-Shafii and Ahmad.

(a) Egypt. Act No. 25/1920, Article 4, reads as follows: "Should the husband abstain from maintenance of his wife, and has known property, a court order for maintenance shall be executed on his property. If he has no known property, and refuses to declare whether he has means or is insolvent while insisting on abstaining from maintenance, the judge shall order a divorce forthwith. If he proves his insolvency, the judge shall grant him a delay not exceeding one month after which if he still fails to pay maintenance, a divorce decree shall be issued."

Under Article 5, a husband who is away for a short period shall have a court order for maintenance executed on his property, if known. If not, the judge shall warn him, according to the normal procedure, fixing a time, at the end of which the judge shall order a divorce if the husband fails to send maintenance to the wife, or fails to return to support her. If the husband is away in a place where it is not easy to reach him, or is of unknown place of residence, and it is proved that he has no means from which the wife can get maintenance, the judge shall order a divorce forthwith. The same applies to the person who becomes insolvent and thus unable to pay maintenance.

29 Abu Zahra, *op. cit.* pp. 347–354. Abu Zahra concurs with the Hanafi doctrine on the ground that there is no express provision at all in the Quran, the Tradition or the Prophet's Companions, to allow divorce because of failure to pay maintenance.

30 Sura Baqara, II, verse 22.

31 Abu Zahra, *loc. cit.*

Such a divorce shall be revocable, that is, the husband may resume matrimony if he proves his solvency and is prepared to pay maintenance for the iddat. Otherwise the resumption of marriage shall not be valid (Art. 6).

(b) Syria. Articles 110 and 111 deal with divorce for failure of maintenance. The wife may apply for a divorce if the husband living with her refrains from maintenance, has no known means, and fails to prove his insolvency. Should he prove his insolvency, or be away, the judge shall grant him a delay not exceeding three months on the expiry of which, if the husband persists in refusing to pay maintenance, the judge shall order a divorce. Such a divorce shall be revocable, with the husband having the right to resume matrimony during the iddat on condition that he proves his solvency and is willing to pay maintenance.

(c) Morocco. The Moroccan legislator follows closely the Syrian Law, while making it expressly clear that the divorce by the court shall be issued forthwith if the husband has no known property and refuses to declare whether he has means or is insolvent, while insisting on refusal to pay maintenance (Art. 53/1 and 2).

(d) Iraq. Paragraphs 7, 8 and 9 of Article 43 state that the wife may sue for divorce on the following grounds:

(i) the abstention by the husband from paying maintenance without a lawful excuse after being given a notice to pay within 60 days;
(ii) the impossibility of collecting maintenance from the husband on account of his being away or in jail for more than two years;
(iii) if the husband refrains from paying the accumulated maintenance ordered against him by the court, having been given notice by the enforcement officer to pay within 60 days. Such a divorce shall be irrevocable.

(e) Jordan. Under Article 127, if a husband refuses to pay maintenance to his wife who has obtained a court order to that effect, maintenance shall be taken from his property, if any. If he has no property, and has not stated whether he is of means or impoverished, or stated that he has means but insists on refusing to pay maintenance, the judge shall order a divorce forthwith. If he claims to be insolvent he shall have to prove it, otherwise a divorce shall be ordered forthwith. If he proves it, he shall be given a delay of not less than a month, and not more than three months, after which, if he has failed to pay maintenance, the judge shall order a divorce. Under Article 128, if the husband is away for a short period, and he has property from which maintenance may be taken, a maintenance order shall be given and executed on his property. If he has no property, the judge shall

warn him and fix a time for him to pay. If the husband fails to send money for the maintenance of the wife, or has not come back himself to pay her maintenance, the judge shall order a divorce. If he is away and cannot be communicated with easily, or his whereabouts are unknown, and it is proved that he has no property from which the wife can get maintenance, the judge shall order a divorce without warning or fixing a time. The same provision applies to the person who cannot afford to pay maintenance.

Under Article 129, such a divorce shall be revocable if it occurs after consummation, and irrevocable if it is before consummation.

If the divorce is revocable, the husband may return to his wife during the iddat, if he can prove he has means through the payment of three months' maintenance out of the accumulated maintenance due to her from him, and showing his willingness to pay maintenance during the iddat, otherwise the resumption of matrimony shall not be valid.

(f) Kuwait. The Kuwaiti legislator is in general agreement with this provision, except that the judge shall issue an irrevocable divorce decree if the wife sues the husband more than twice for lack of maintenance and asks for a divorce on the grounds of injury (Art. 122).

(g) Algeria. Article 53, paragraph 1, grants the wife the right to sue for a divorce on account of the failure by the husband to pay maintenance after an order to that effect by the court, unless the woman knew of his insolvency at the time of the marriage.

D. Absence or Imprisonment of the Husband

The absence of the husband or his imprisonment are valid grounds for the wife to apply for a divorce according to Malik and Ahmad, although they differ in details. Both jurists agree that absence or imprisonment must cause actual, rather than anticipated injury to the wife, and would render her vulnerable to seduction. Absence or imprisonment must be for a long time, during which the wife suffers injury. Ahmad sets that time at six months according to a tradition of Omar, the Second Patriarchal Caliph. Malik is said to maintain the minimum of the duration of such an absence of one year or three years. Ahmad stipulates that the absence should be without an acceptable cause. As for imprisonment, the wife, according to Ahmad, may apply to the court for a divorce after one year of the husband staying in prison. All these periods are calculated according to the lunear year. Malik considers such a dissolution as an irrevocable divorce. Ahmad considers it an annulment. While accepting the two Imams' position in principle, the modern Islamic legislators take an eclective attitude.

(a) Egypt. Divorce by the court on account of the husband's absence or imprisonment is dealt with under Chapter 3, Articles 12, 13 and 14 of Act No. 25/1929. Under Article 12, if the husband is absent for a year or more without an acceptable excuse, his wife may ask the court for an irrevocable divorce should she suffer injury due to his absence, even though he has property from which she can get her maintenance.

Under Article 13, if it is possible to send messages to the absent husband, the judge shall fix a time for him with a warning that the wife would be granted a divorce by the court unless he returns to live with her, moves her to live with him, or divorces her. At the end of the delay, if the husband has not complied or submitted an acceptable excuse, the judge shall order an irrevocable divorce. Likewise, if no message could get to the absent husband, the judge shall grant the divorce without warning or setting a delay.

Under Article 14, the wife of the husband against whom a prison sentence of three years or more has been passed and become final may apply to the judge after one year of the husband's imprisonment for an irrevocable divorce on account of injury, even if the husband has property from which she could get maintenance.

The same provisions are ordered in Kuwaiti Articles 136, 137 and 138.

(b) Syria. Under Article 109, the wife whose husband has gone absent without an acceptable excuse, or who has received a prison sentence of more than three years, may apply to the court for divorce after one year of the absence or imprisonment, even if there is property of the husband from which she can get maintenance.

Such a divorce shall be revocable, with the released husband, on his return, having the right to get his wife back if she is still in her iddat.

(c) Morocco. Under Article 57, the wife may petition the court for an irrevocable divorce if the husband has been away at a known address for more than a year without an acceptable excuse, if she feels injured thereby, even if he has property from which she could get maintenance.

The provision of the Egyptian Article 13 is repeated in paragraph 2 of the same Moroccan Article.

(d) Iraq. Under Article 43, paragraph 1, the wife may apply for a divorce if the husband has received a prison sentence of three years or more, even if he has property from which she can get maintenance, or if the husband has deserted her for two years or more without lawful excuse, even if his address is known and he has property from which she can get maintenance.

(e) Jordan. Under Articles 128 and 130, the provisions of the Egyptian Articles 13 and 14 are adopted.

(f) Algeria. Under Article 53, paragraph 4, the wife may apply for a divorce if the husband has received a prison sentence of over a year for an offence that constitutes a disgrace to the family and renders the continuation of life together impossible. Under paragraph 5, she shall have the same right on his going absent for a year without an excuse or maintenance.

E. Other Grounds for Applying to the Court for Divorce

(a) The Syrian, Iraqi and Jordanian Acts (Articles 14/3, 6/4 and 9/1, respectively) grant the wife the right to apply to the court for a divorce if the husband fails to honour a stipulation agreed upon in the marriage contract. The Jordanian legislator adds that the wife may then claim all her matrimonial right. Jordanian Article 19/2 grants the same right to the husband who shall then be released of the wife's deferred dower, and the iddat maintenance.

(b) Under the Sunni Sharia, the nearest agnate guardian may apply to the court to nullify a marriage on the ground of non-equality between his minor ward and the husband. Dissolution of the marriage can be only by order of the judge, and until that order is issued, the state of matrimony shall hold and have full effect to the extent that should either spouse die during the court proceedings, the surviving spouse shall inherit. It shall constitute an annulment of the contract, so that the three pronouncements of repudiation to which the husband is entitled shall not decrease.

The Ottoman Family law which governs the personal status of the Sunnis in the Lebanon adopts this provision in Articles 45 and 47, under which marriage can be dissolved by the court in the following instances:

(i) if a major woman marries a husband who is not equal without the knowledge of her guardian;
(ii) if equality was stipulated in the contract and the husband was found out not to be equal;
(iii) if the husband alleged being equal before the contract and was believed by the wife and her guardian and was proved to be non-equal after the marriage.

The right to apply for annulment is the guardian's exclusively in the first case, and is equally shared by the wife and her guardian in the second and third instances.

These provisions are adopted in the Laws of Syria, Jordan and Kuwait: Articles 27, 29 and 32; 21 and 22; 34 and 38 respectively. Equality is to be considered at the time of the marriage only, and shall have no relevance if it ceases to exist thereafter (Art. 31, Syrian and 20, Jordanian). The right to apply for annulment on the grounds of non-equality shall cease on the wife becoming pregnant (Arts. 30, Syrian; 23, Jordanian). Kuwaiti Article 39 adds that this right shall also be lost on earlier consent or the expiry of one year after knowing of the marriage.

5. DISSOLUTION OF MARRIAGE BY OPERATION OF LAW

Only a valid marriage can be dissolved, as both irregular and void marriage contracts need no dissolution, and the parties thereto shall separate of themselves with the court only intervening to order them if they fail to do so.

Yet, a marriage contract that was valid to start with may become later invalidated to the extent that it is dissolved without any need for the husband to pronounce repudiation or for the court to order a divorce. This could happen in two ways:

A. Change of Religion

As previously explained in the Conditions of Marriage, no Muslim husband can take as a wife a non-Kitabi woman. Therefore, if after marriage a Muslim or a Kitabi woman become atheist or a non-Kitabi, the marriage shall be *ipso facto* dissolved. However, the Kuwaiti legislators' Article 145/b, following a prevailing Maliki opinion and some Hanabi jurists, rule that the Muslim wife's apostasy shall not dissolve the marriage.

If a Muslim husband apostasizes, or if a non-Muslim husband refuses to adopt Islam after his wife has done so, the marriage shall be automatically dissolved.

In more detail, the Kuwaiti law, under the heading "Annulment on the Grounds of Religious Difference", rules (Art. 143) that:

(a) If the two non-Muslim spouses together convert to Islam, their marriage shall stay.
(b) If the husband only adopts Islam, if his wife is a Kitabi, marriage shall sustain. If she is not, she shall be offered to convert to Islam. If she accepts or becomes a Kitabi, they shall remain married – otherwise marriage is nullified.
(c) If the wife only adopts Islam, the husband shall be invited to do the same; marriage shall remain if he consents and become nullified if he does not. If he lacks legal capacity, the marriage shall be dissolved forthwith if the wife has converted to Islam before consummation; if

the marriage has been consummated, then the iddat has to be observed.

In all cases, the court shall not investigate the sincerity of the convert to Islam, nor shall it enquire into the motives of such a conversion (Art. 144).

As contradistinct from the wife, marriage shall be dissolved on the husband apostasizing. Nevertheless, if apostasy occurs after consummation and the husband reverts to Islam during the iddat, marriage shall be resumed as if there were no nullification (Art. 145/a).

B. The Creation of a Prohibited Degree

According to the Sunnis, if either spouse commits with an ascendant or descendant of the other an act that creates a prohibited degree through affinity, the marriage shall likewise be dissolved *ipso facto*.

These universal Sharia provisions apply by operation of law of marriage even though modern legislators, apart from the Kuwaitis, keep silent on this issue, with the exception of the Egyptian Law (as explained under Apostasy, above) and Jordanian Law which decrees under Article 51 that a dissolution of marriage, *inter alia*, through the husband refusing to convert to Islam if his wife does so, or his committing an act that creates a prohibited degree through affinity, shall be liable to pay half the specified dower before actual or assumed consummation. On the other hand, under Article 52 of the same Law, the wife who apostasises, or refuses to follow her husband if he converts to Islam when she is non-Kitabi, or commits with an ascendant or a descendant of the husband and act that creats a prohibited degree through affinity, shall lose all dower, and shall have to refund any dower she may have received. The Shias concur that apostacy of either spouse renders the marriage void forthwith without any recourse to the court.[32] However, unlike the Sunnis they rule that the wife's adultery or misbehaviour with her step-son does not annul the marriage if it occurs during it.[33]

6. COMPENSATION OF THE WIFE IN THE CASE OF ARBITRARY REPUDIATION BY THE HUSBAND

The husband, under the strictest Sharia provisions, has the right to repudiate, without the divorcée having any financial rights other than

32 Al-Hilli, *op. cit.* p. 78.
33 *Ibid.* p. 69.

the whole dower if marriage was consummated, and the iddat maintenance. If such a repudiation occurred before consummation or valid retirement, the woman shall have no right to any dower if it was not validly specified, or was omitted altogether from the contract, and the only compensation for her in such a case is the mutat. The Quran left the amount of mutat to custom: "It is no sin for you if ye divorce women while yet ye have not touched them, nor appointed unto them a portion. Provide for them the rich according to his means and the straitened according to his means, a fair provision".[34]

The Hanafi jurists hold that the mutat is desirable for every divorcée after consummation, but that there is no mandatory or desirable mutat, prior to consummation, for a divorcée who is entitled to half the dower, nor for a widow.

This Quranic and Sharia ruling is adopted in Article 60 of the Moroccan Law: "Every husband shall have the obligation to provide Mutat for his divorcée if divorce proceeded from him, according to his affluence and her means, except the woman for whom a dower was specified and was divorced prior to consummation."

However, the modern Islamic personal status laws of Syria, Jordan and Egypt go much farther to safeguard the rights of the divorced wife.

All three Acts agree on the principles in general, namely that the wife shall be entitled, on repudiation by the husband after consummation of marriage, to the mutat compensation, but they differ on the amount thereof:

The Syrian Article 117 of the Decree No. 59/1953, as amended under Article 16 of Act No. 34/1975, reads as follows:

> "If a man repudiates his wife and the judge finds that the husband's pronouncement of repudiation has been arbitrary without any reasonable cause, and that the wife would suffer misery and hardship therefrom, the judge may order for her against her ex-husband, in proportion with his means and his arbitrariness, a compensation not in excess of the amount of maintenance of her equals for three years, over and above the iddat maintenance. The judge may order that such a compensation shall be paid in a lump sum or by monthly instalments as warranted by the circumstances."

In a similar vein, Article 134 of the Jordanian Provisional Law No. 61/1976 rules as follows:

> "If the husband repudiates his wife in an arbitrary manner. e.g. without a reasonable cause, and she applies to the judge for compensation, the judge shall order for her against her ex-husband

34 Sura Baqara, II, verse 236.

the compensation deemed by the judge to be fair, provided that it shall not be in excess of the equivalent of the maintenance due to her for a year. Such a compensation shall be paid either in a lump sum or by instalments as warranted by the circumstances while taking into consideration the conditions of the husband in respect to affluence or poverty. This shall not affect the other marital rights due to the repudiated wife, including the iddat maintenance."

The Egyptian legislator steers a middle course between the Syrian and Jordanian provisions in terms of the amount due. In another aspect, it is more generous towards the divorcée. Article 18 *bis* added to Act No. 25/1929 under Act No. 100/1985, rules:

"The wife with whom consummation occurred under a valid marriage contract, if she is repudiated by her husband without her consent nor for a cause proceeding from her, shall be entitled, over and above her iddat maintenance, to a mutat of no less than the maintenance of two years with due consideration given to the condition of the repudiating husband in terms of affluence or destitution, the circumstances of the repudiation and the duration of matrimony. The repudiating husband may be allowed to pay such a mutat by instalments."

The Tunisian legislators' position has been detailed under the Section of Injury or discord in A above.

The Kuwaiti Law, under the heading of "Compensation for Repudiation", sums up the general provisions in this matter in Article 165, as follows:

"A. If a valid marriage is disolved after consummation, the wife shall be entitled, over and above her iddat maintenance, to a mutat in an amount not in excess of a year's maintenance, according to the condition of the husband, which shall be paid to her in monthly instalments, on the completion of her iddat, unless the two parties agree otherwise in terms of the amount or method of payment.

B. The provisions of the previous paragraph shall not apply in the following events:

1. Divorce on the grounds of non-maintenance by the husband due to his insolvency.
2. Divorce on the grounds of injury if it proceeds from the wife.
3. Repudiation with the wife's consent.
4. Annulment of marriage at the behest of the wife.
5. Death of either spouse."

Chapter 7

The Iddat

1. INTRODUCTION: DEFINITION AND OBJECTS

The word "Iddat" is derived from the root "adda" meaning to count; in this case, it is the counting of days and months. By definition, the iddat is a waiting period, a period of abstinence, or a specified term during which the wife shall remain unmarried after the dissolution of marriage by divorce, death, or any other form of separation under certain conditions.

It constitutes for the woman a temporary prohibition to marry, to be lifted on the expiry of the term. Such a prohibition shall not apply to the man except if he is already married to four wives, including the divorcée in her iddat, and his aim is to avoid having more than four wives at one time, or to avoid unlawful conjunction (see Chap. 3 above) for the duration of the term.

There are three main objects of iddat:

(i) to ascertain whether the wife is pregnant, and if so, the paternity of the child;
(ii) to provide the husband with an opportunity to return to his wife if the divorce is revocable;
(iii) to mourn the dead husband, in the case of the widow.

These provisions of the Sharia are generally adopted in the modern codes for personal status. They are taken for granted in the Egyptian legislation, and mentioned explicitly in the laws of Syria, Tunisia, Morocco, Iraq, Jordan, Kuwait and Algeria. In the following sections we shall refer to the relevant articles, if any, of the general Sharia rules.

2. CONDITIONS FOR OBSERVING THE IDDAT

Under a valid marriage, the iddat shall be rigidly observed on divorce if consummation has actually occurred, or, according to the Sunnis, is deemed to have occurred, in conformity with the Quranic rulings: "Divorced women shall wait concerning themselves for three monthly periods."[1]

The Shias stipulate for the iddat to be observed that the marriage is actually consummated. Valid retirement without that requires no iddat.[2]

All schools maintain that no iddat shall be observed on divorce if the marriage has not been consummated, according to the Quranic ruling: "O ye who believe! When ye marry believing women, and then divorce them before ye have touched them, no period of iddat have ye to count in respect of them."[3]

The iddat shall nevertheless be observed, under a valid marriage, on the death of the husband even if there was no consummation or valid retirement. This is the main difference between a valid and a defective marriage when no iddat shall be observed. This provision is adopted in Articles 126 (Syria) and 79 (Morocco), which both make valid retirement equivalent to actual consummation, and in Articles 47 (Iraq) and 155/b Kuwait.

Although the Shia temporary (muta) marriage is not liable to divorce, expiring at the end of the term or making a gift of the remainder thereof to the wife (see Chap. 3), the temporary (muta) wife shall observe an iddat of two complete menstrual cycles, if she has not reached menopause, or of 45 days if she suffers from amenorrhoea, perhaps due to illness. If she is pregnant, she shall wait until her delivery or for 45 days, whichever term is the longer.[4]

3. DURATION OF THE IDDAT

The iddat shall be calculated by menstrual cycles (cycles of menstrual purity for the Shias), by months or until the delivery of the baby. Counting shall commence from the time of divorce under a valid marriage, from last cohabitation under a defective contract or from the death of the husband.

Some modern Arab legislations endorse expressly these provisions, e.g. Syrian Article 125 and Moroccan Article 78. Iraqi and Jordanian Articles 49 and 141 respectively add that the iddat shall start forthwith, even if the woman is not aware of the occurrence.

The Kuwaiti Article 156 succinctly sums up as follows:

"The iddat shall start:

(a) Under a valid contract, from the date of the repudiation or the husband's death.

1 Sura Baqara, II, verse 228.
2 Al-Hilli, *Jaafari Personal Status Provisions*, p. 79.
3 Sura Ahzab, XXXIII, verse 49.
4 Tayabji, *Muhammadan Law*, pp. 121–122.

(b) Under a defective contract, from the date of separation or the man's death.
(c) Under consumation with semblance of the right thereto, from the date of the last cohabitation.
(d) Under a court decree of divorce from the date it becomes final."

A. Iddat Calculated by Menstruation

In the case of a woman subject to menstruation, whose valid marriage has been dissolved after actual or presumed consummation, for a reason other than the death of her husband, and who was not pregnant at the time of dissolution, the iddat shall extend for three complete menses on the expiration of which the prohibition to remarry shall be lifted. This provision is based on the Quranic ruling: "Divorced women shall wait concerning themselves for three monthly courses."[5]

Schools differ on the interpretation of the prescribed three menses. Of the Sunnis, the Hanafis maintain that it means three menses between which two periods of menstrual purity intervene; the Shafiis and Malikis count three periods of menstrual purity. The latter is also the opinion of the Shias, who stipulate that divorce can only be pronounced when the wife is not menstruating or puerperal. The iddat for the Shias is terminated at the onset of the third menstruation. Nevertheless, according to the Sunni schools, if a wife is divorced while menstruating, that menstrual period shall not be counted for the purposes of the iddat.

The ambiguity of the term "monthly courses" (in Arabic, *quru*) in the Quranic text persists in Articles 48/1 (Iraqi), 135 (Jordanian) and 58 (Algerian). The Moroccan and Syrian Codes are more specific, counting three periods of purity (Art. 73) and three of menstruation (Art. 121/1) respectively. The Jordanian Article adds that the women's claim to have completed her iddat before three months shall not be accepted, and Article 136 goes on to rule that if the woman did not see blood at all or only once or twice during the said period, it shall have to be ascertained if she has reached menopause, in which case she shall observe an iddat of three months, otherwise she should complete a lunar year. The same provision is adopted in the Syrian Article 121/3, further dating the iddat from divorce or annulment. The Tunisian legislator does not calculate iddat by menstruation at all, but by months (Art. 35). The Kuwaiti legislator (Art. 57) combines both, ruling (c-1) that the iddat of the non-pregnant, otherwise than at the death of the husband, shall be three complete menstruations in a term not shorter than sixty days for those who menstruate.

5 Sura Baqara, II, verse 228.

B. Iddat Calculated by Months

The iddat shall be counted by months in two cases:

(i) For the woman who is not subject to menstruation, either because she has not reached puberty, or has reached menopause, under the Quranic ruling: "Such of your women as have passed the age of monthly courses, for them the prescribed period, if ye have any doubts, is three months, for those who have no course. . . ."[6]

To these two classes of women, the Shias add those who suffer from amenorrhoea because of a congenital defect, or from fostering (suckling a child) or some illness.[7]

Three lunar months shall be counted if divorce occurs at the start of the month calculated according to the Islamic calendar even if any month is less than 30 days, otherwise 90 days shall be counted.

These provisions are adopted in full in Kuwaiti Article 157.

Syrian Article 121/3 rules an iddat of three months for the woman in menopause, dropping the pre-adolescent girl who is not lawfully capable to marry under the Syrian law. The same provision is adopted under Algerian Article 58. Moroccan Article 73 counts three months for the woman in menopause, and the one who does not menstruate. The same iddat is stipulated for the woman who reached puberty and did not menstruate at all, under Iraqi Article 48/2. The Jordanian Article 137 follows the Syrian provision while further qualifying the women as having married under a valid contract, and were separated from their husbands after valid retirement, whether by divorce or annulment if they have reached menopause. The Tunisian Article 35 simply decrees that the divorced woman who is not pregnant shall count three complete months.

(ii) For the widow, under a valid marriage, if she is not pregnant. In this case, the iddat shall be four lunar months and 10 days as prescribed in the Quran. This shall be counted as one hundred and 30 days from the death of her husband.

This provision is adopted without any modification under Articles 123, 35, 74, 48/3, 143 and 59 of the Personal Status Codes of Syria, Tunisia, Morocco, Iraq, Jordan and Algeria, respectivley.

Kuwaiti Article 158 follows suit (para. a), adding two interesting rulings (b and c):

"(b) In the event of an irrevocable separation under repudiation or dissolution, if the man dies during the iddat, the woman shall

6 Sura Talaq, XLV, verse 4.
7 Al-Hilli, *op. cit.* pp. 79–80.

complete her iddat and shall not move to the iddat of the death of the husband, without prejudice to the provisions of case (5), paragraph (c) of the preceding article.

(c) The woman with whom cohabitation occurred with semblance of the right thereto, under a defective contract or without any contract, if the man dies on her, shall observe an iddat of separation, not of death."

Case (5), paragraph (c) of Article 157 referred to, provides that the woman shall observe the longer term of the iddat of repudiation or of death of the husband if she has been repudiated by the husband to trick her out of inheriting from him, should he die before she completes her iddat.

C. Termination of Iddat on the Delivery of a Baby

In the case of a woman who is pregnant at the time of dissolution of marriage, the iddat shall be observed until the delivery of the baby (or babies, in the case of multiple birth), under the general Quranic ruling: "And if they carry (life in their wombs), then spend (your substance) on them until they deliver their burden. . . ."[8]

The Sunnis observe this rule rigidly, regardless of the grounds for separation, whether under a valid, defective or even void marriage contract, or on the death of the husband, however short the period may be. The Shias maintain the same opinion generally, but differ in ruling that the pregnant widow shall observe the longer period of iddat, until the delivery of four months and ten days.[9]

All the modern Arab personal status laws agree that the iddat of the divorced woman who is pregnant shall be terminated on delivery of her child (Arts. 124, 35, 72, 48/3, 140, 60 and 157/b of the Laws of Syria, Tunisia, Morocco, Iraq, Jordan, Algeria and Kuwait respectively). However, a maximum term for pregnancy is set at one year (Arts. 35, Tunisian; 76, Moroccan and 160, Kuwaiti), or of 10 months (Art. 60, Algerian) calculated from the date of divorce or death of the husband.

Miscarriage shall terminate the iddat, provided that some organs of the embryo are identifiable (Arts. 124, Syrian; 140, Jordanian and 157/b, Kuwaiti).

Sunnis and Shias alike rule that an identifiable foetus must be taken from the mother in order to be absolutely sure that the delivery is complete. Otherwise, other methods of calculating the iddat are as follows.

8 Sura Talaq, XLV, verse 6.
9 Al-Hilli, *op. cit.* pp. 80–81.

D. Conversion from One Form of Calculating the Iddat to Another

The above-mentioned periods of iddat must not be combined, but it is possible to convert from one form of counting to another as follows:

(i) Conversion from iddat calculated by months to iddat calculated by menstruation: The woman whose iddat is calculated by months following the dissolution of marriage for a reason other than the death of her husband, and who menstruates before the expiration of the iddat calculated by months, shall start a fresh iddat of three complete menses. However, she shall not be required to do this if menstruation occurs after the expiry of the first iddat.

(ii) Conversion from iddat calculated by menstruation to iddat calculated by months: The iddat shall be counted afresh for three months if it started by counting menses, and these either become irregular, or are interrupted or terminated by the advent of menopause, provided that this change occurs before the expiry of the original three menses.

(iii) Conversion from the divorce to the death iddat: A woman who is revocably divorced and whose husband dies during her iddat shall interrupt the divorce iddat and start afresh, counting the death iddat of four months and ten days. This ruling does not apply to an irrevocably divorced woman, except that if the death occurred during the death illness of the husband, during her iddat, and if it can be proved that he fraudulently intended to deprive her of her inheritance, the irrevocably divorced woman shall observe the longer death iddat, although this will include the period already counted for the divorce iddat.

The conversion from the divorce to the death iddat as stipulated above is codified under Articles 127, 77, 48/4, 143 and 157/c-5 of the Laws of Syria, Morocco, Iraq, Jordan and Kuwait respectively. The Tunisian and Algerian Laws keep silent on this point. The Syrian Article 127, paragraph 2, adds that if the husband dies during an iddat of an irrevocable divorce, the woman shall observe the longer term of the death or the divorce iddat.

4. RIGHTS AND OBLIGATIONS OF THE SPOUSES DURING IDDAT

The iddat, being a transitional period between actual separation and final termination of marriage under a revocable pronouncement of repudiation, creates, while it lasts, certain obligations and rights for both spouses. These include a temporary legal bar to marry, the mutual entitlement to inheritance, maintenance and residence of the wife.

A. The Marriage Bar

During the iddat of a revocable divorce, the husband may resume the conjugal relationship with the wife without her consent. The wife is prohibited from marrying another man, and the husband is prohibited from marrying a fifth wife, or marrying a relative of the wife which would be in a prohibited degree to her had she been a man. A marriage contracted during the iddat shall be defective, under Sunni law, but shall be void under Shia law.

B. Parentage

A child born during the iddat shall be the husband's.

C. Mutual Rights of Inheritance

Under a revocable divorce, on the death of either spouse during the iddat, the surviving spouse shall inherit. Under an irrevocable divorce, the surviving partner shall only inherit if it is established that the partner who died during the iddat, as a result of a death-illness, intended fraudulently, by causing dissolution, to deprive the spouse from inheritance.

D. Maintenance

The right to maintenance of the woman during her iddat may be established, controversial, or may be lost altogether as detailed in the following paragraphs.

(i) Maintenance shall be the inalienable right of the woman during her iddat in the following two cases:
  (a) if the dissolution is under a valid marriage by way of a divorce pronounced by the husband or ordered by the judge for reasons proceeding from the husband; or
  (b) if separation was by way of annulment by the husband or by the wife, but through no fault of hers, e.g. if, on recovery from insanity, she exercises her option to terminate marriage which has been consummated.[10] The Shias dissent, ruling that the

10 Abu Zahra, *On Marriage*, p. 384.

wife shall lose her maintenance during the iddat of divorce due to using her option on reaching majority.[11]

Maintenance of the wife during her iddat shall also be imperative on the husband in cases of separation through a vow of continence (*ila*), imprecation (*lian*), refusal by the husband to profess Islam after his wife's conversion thereto, or his apostasy.[12]

(ii) While maintenance is unanimously held to be the right of a woman during her iddat of a revocable divorce, there is controversy over the right to maintenance during the iddat of an irrevocable divorce. However, it is unanimously agreed that in this case the woman shall be entitled to maintenance if she is pregnant, under the Quranic ruling: "And if they carry (life in their wombs), then spend (your substance) on them until they deliver their burden. . . ."[13]

Schools differ on the entitlement to maintenance during the iddat of an irrevocable divorce if the woman is not pregnant. The Shias[14] and the Sunni Shafiis rule that there shall be no maintenance in this case apart from lodging, under the Quranic imperative: "Let the women live (in iddat), in the same style as ye live, according to your means."[15] The Hanafis, whose opinion is upheld by the modern Islamic states' legislation in this respect, rule that maintenance shall be due, relying on the generality of the Quranic provision: "Let the man of means spend according to his means. . . ."[16] applying it to all divorced women whether revocably or irrevocably repudiated, without restriction. This generally is retained in Article 162.

(iii) The woman in her iddat shall not be entitled to any maintenance in three cases:

(a) if the iddat is subsequent to consummation under a void marriage contract, or to co-habitation under a semblance of legality;

(b) in the iddat of death, since maintenance is an obligation which shall not pass from the deceased husband to the heir;

(c) if the marriage was dissolved for some cause of a criminal nature originating from the woman, such as the wife's apostasy or her misbehaviour so as to establish a supervening prohibition. The Shia differ, making maintenance due for a wife in this case, since

11 Al-Hilli, *op. cit.* p. 83.
12 Al-Ghandour, *Divorce.*
13 Sura Talaq, LXV, verse 6.
14 Al-Hilli, *loc. cit.*
15 Sura Talaq, LXV, verse 6.
16 *Ibid.* verse 7.

misbehaviour does not render the marriage void if it occurred during but not before marriage.[17]

E. Residence

According to all schools, the iddat must be observed by a revocably divorced woman at the matrimonial home, under the Quranic ruling: "And turn them not out of their houses, nor shall they (themselves) leave, except in case they are guilty of some open lewdness."[18] This is both the woman's right and duty. Remaining in the husband's home is considered a continuation of the right of the husband to be obeyed, a right he retains until the completion of the iddat.

The Sunnis extend that duty to remain in the husband's residence to include the duration of the iddat following separation under a valid contract for whatever reason, including death and irrevocable divorce. The Shias restrict that duty to the duration of iddat of a revocable marriage and preferably the iddat of death.[19]

The Sunnis rule that should the woman leave the matrimonial home during her iddat without an acceptable excuse, she shall forfeit her right to maintenance until she returns. Among the acceptable excuses allowed by both the Sunnis and the Shias for leaving the matrimonial home during the iddat is fear of the house collapsing, its location in a remote area, fear of the woman for the safety of her person or property there, or forceful ejection by the landlord. A woman in her iddat of revocable divorce may then move to another home chosen by her husband, while a woman in the iddat of death may go wherever she chooses.[20]

Algerial Article 61 adopts the Quranic ruling above, and reads as follows: "Neither the divorced wife nor the widowed shall leave the matrimonial home during her iddat of divorce or death of the husband except in case she is guilty of some open lewdness. . . ."

Jordanian Article 146 is more detailed:

> "The woman observing an iddat of a revocable divorce or of death shall stay during her iddat at the home in which the spouses have lived together before separation. If she has been divorced or her husband has died while she was staying elsewhere, she shall return forthwith to her matrimonial home. The woman observing her iddat of divorce shall not leave her home except for a necessity; the woman

17 Al-Hilli, *loc. cit.*
18 Sura Talaq, LXV, verse 1.
19 Al-Hilli, *op. cit.* p. 82.
20 *Ibid.*

> in her iddat of the death of the husband shall only go out on some essential business, and shall not sleep in a place other than her home. If the spouses have to move elsewhere, the woman in an iddat of divorce shall move to wherever the husband chooses. If the woman in an iddat of the death of the husband is obliged to move, it shall be to the nearest location to her home."

Kuwaiti Article 161 confirms this ruling to a woman revocably divorced, moving, if necessity dictates, only to a home appointed by the Judge, and deems her nashiza if she left home without justification.

Chapter 8

Parentage

1. INTRODUCTION: THE CHILDREN'S RIGHTS

The child's first right is to establish parentage, a right both of the child and the father. This right may commence *in utero*, for example the baby may inherit from its father so long as the father's death occurred not more than 270 days before the baby's birth. The child's first right is followed by the right of upbringing – the right to maintenance by the father, and fosterage and custody by the mother, if these are assigned to her. After passing the age of custody, the minor shall have the right to care and guardianship by its agnates. If it has possession of property, it shall need administration and guardianship of its property, a need shared by those who lack legal capabilities.

In this chapter, we shall deal with the right of parentage. The following chapters will deal with the other rights of fosterage, custody, maintenance and guardianship, in that order.

2. GENERAL PROVISIONS OF PARENTAGE

Parentage of a child to its parents may be established through marriage, acknowledgment or evidence. One of the most important rights emanating from marriage is the establishment of parentage, i.e. maternity and paternity of the offspring of the spouses.

This legal relationship between parent and child gives rise to rights and obligations such as mutual rights of inheritance, guardianship and maintenance. It shall be the duty of the parent to ensure that such needs are satisfied with the interest of the child deemed paramount to any other consideration.

Parentage confers upon the child the status of legitimacy. Parentage is only established in the natural father and mother of a child. Adoption is not recognized in the Sharia, under the Quranic ruling: ". . . nor hath He made those whom ye claim (to be your sons) your sons. This is but a saying of your mouths. But God sayeth the truth and He showeth the way. Proclaim their real parentage. That will be more equitable in the sight of God. And if ye know not their fathers then (they are) your brethren in the faith and your clients."[1]

This principle, expressly codified in the Algerian Article 46, "Adoption shall be prohibited under the Sharia and the Law", and in Kuwaiti Article 167 "No parentage shall be established through adoption even of a child of unknown parentage", is unanimously adopted in Islamic states, with the exception of Tunisia where Act No. 27/1958 allows adoption under certain conditions and according to certain procedures which will be presented later in this chapter. Moroccan Article 83/3 rules adoption in the literal sense, null and void, while adoption for the purpose of rewarding or bequeathing, i.e. to accord a person the status of one's child, shall establish no parentage, and shall be deemed as a will.

Maternity is established only in the natural mother of a child, and it cannot be disclaimed whether birth occurred under a valid or invalid contract, or without any contract whatsoever. This Sharia provision is expressed in the Moroccan Article 83/2 "Illegitimate filiation is utterly void for the father, and shall have no effect whatsoever, but for the mother it shall be the same as the legitimate, because it is her child."

No paternity can be established for the illegitimate offspring. Apart from acknowledgment and evidence (see below) paternity can only be established for the offspring of wedlock, whether under a valid contract, an irregular contract, or under a semblance of the right to marital intercourse. Such cases are subject to the minimum and maximum terms of pregnancy.

The minimum term of pregnancy is unanimously reckoned to be six lunar months, under two Quranic verses: "And We have commended unto man kindness to his parents: in pain did his mother bear him, and in pain did she give him birth, and the bearing of him and the weaning of him is thirty months."[2] "And We have commended upon man concerning his parents: His mother beareth him in weakness upon weakness, and his weaning is in two years. . . ."[3]

By subtracting from 30 the 24 months for weaning, the pregnancy term was said to be six months. A child born in less than six months from the time of the marriage is deemed by all the four Sunni schools to be illegitimate. The Ithna-Asharis, while concurring in principle, allow a

1 Sura Ahzab, XXXIII, verses 4–5.
2 Sura Ahqaf, XLVI, verse 15.
3 Sura Lugman, xxxi, verse 14.

child born under a valid marriage contract less than six months after consummation to be acknowledged by its father if he declares that it was not an offspring of unlawful intercourse, and if he is not known to be telling a lie.[4] Some Sunni scholars agree.[5]

The maximum term of pregnancy used to be a matter of controversy among jurists, ranging from two to five years, but in practice it has been laid down as one lunar year. To the Shia Ithna Ashari, the maximum term for pregnancy is nine lunar months, with the same reservation mentioned above for a child born within less than the minimum term, for a child born more than nine months after consummation under a valid contract.[6]

The minimum term of six months for pregnancy is approved by all modern Arab personal status laws which are almost unanimous on a maximum term of one year, with the exception of Algeria, where this term is reduced to 10 months (Arts. 42 and 43). Under the Lebanese Druze Personal Status Act of 24/2/1948, Article 137, the minimum term for pregnancy is 180 days, and the maximum is 300 days. However, the Syrian Article 128 specifies a solar year, while the Jordanian Article 185 stresses that the year is a lunar one. Kuwaiti Article 166 defines the minimum and maximum term of pregnancy as six lunar months and three hundred and sixty-five days respectively. Moroccan Article 84 makes the two terms subject to the provisions of Article 76 which deals with cases of suspicion which should be referred by the court to medical experts to decide thereon. Iraqi Article 51 simply refers to the minimum term for pregnancy with the implication that the Sharia rule in this context shall prevail (Art. 1, paras. 2–3).

Apart from these general rules, provisions of paternity differ under a valid marriage, from those under an irregular marriage or consummation with a semblance of the right to marital intercourse.

3. PATERNITY UNDER A VALID MARRIAGE CONTRACT

Jurists are unanimous that the valid marriage contract is the ground for establishing the parentage of the father of a child born during its continuation. The Sunnis calculated the pregnancy term from the time of the contract, not of consummation. Some among them, namely the Hanafis, consider the contract in itself a sufficient ground for establishing parenthood by the husband regardless of consummation. The Hanbalis,

4 Al-Hilli, *Jaafari Personal Status Provisions*, p. 85.
5 Abu Zahra, *On Marriage*, p. 388.
6 Al-Hilli, *op. cit.* p. 85.

Malikis and Shafiis require the possibility of consummation, i.e. the husband having reached puberty and having access to his wife.[7]

The Shias stipulate that the marriage must be consummated, and count the pregnancy term from the time of consummation rather than of contract.[8]

The Syrian, Moroccan, Kuwaiti and Iraqi codes rule that the pregnancy term shall start from the date of the marriage contract and that the parentage of the child shall be established if meeting between spouses has been possible (Arts. 120/1a and b, 85, 169/a, and 51, respectively). The Syrian Article cites the two examples of the husband being in jail or away as proof of the impossibility of such meeting.

On the other hand, the Jordanian Article 148 rules that the six months (minimum term for pregnancy) shall be counted from the date of consummation or valid retirement.

Once a child is born under a valid marriage contract, within the specified limits of the pregnancy term and the consummation having been possible, its parentage is established and the husband can only deny his fatherhood through one of two devices:

(i) denial at the time of birth or during preparations for it if the husband is present, or at the time of his learning of it if he is absent;

(ii) The imprecation (*lian*) (see Chap. 6): *Lian* should be made before a judge who shall order the separation of the spouses. This separation is technically an annulment, not a divorce proper, and shall be irrevocable. The husband shall disclaim paternity of the child born to his wife provided that he has not previously acknowledged his paternity, or acquiesced in its being attributed to him, and his marriage was valid. There shall be no rights of inheritance between the two, or maintenance for the child, although prohibited degrees of relationship between the man and the child shall be created.

The Sunnis hold that the child may not give evidence against the husband,[9] but the Shias rule that the child may.[10]

Notwithstanding the above provisions, the Shia Ithna Ashari maintain that the denial of paternity shall not be effective if the husband or wife dies after the renunciation of the child before the lian or during it before they complete it.[11]

Those Sharia provisions are expressly asserted in the modern Codes of Syria and Kuwait. Syrian Article 129/3, reads, "If these two conditions

7 Abu Zahra, *op. cit.* p. 386.
8 Al-Hilli, *op. cit.* p. 85.
9 Abdullah, *Personal Status*, p. 577.
10 Al-Hilli, *op. cit.* p. 87.
11 *Ibid.*

(see above) are met the parentage of the child shall not be denied except through imprecation."

A whole section, 2, of Chapter 4, Book III, "Birth and Legal Effects Thereof", is devoted to the Denial of Parentage, which is the heading with the sub-title (Lian). It consists of Articles 176 to 180 inclusive. It repeats the general provisions for lian, specifying that a man may deny the parentage of a child within seven days of the birth, or the awareness thereof, provided that he has not acknowledged parentage whether expressly or by implication, in cases when the parentage of the child is established in the wedlock, under a valid marriage, existing or dissolved, or through consummation under a defective contract or with semblance of the right thereto. The lian suit procedure must be taken within fifteen days as from the time of birth or knowledge thereof. Once lian is effected between man and woman, the Judge shall declare the non-parentage of the child to the man who shall not be liable to any maintenance of the child, nor shall there be any mutual inheritance between them, and the child shall belong to its mother. If the man confesses to the effect that he was lying when he accused his wife and denied parentage of the child, that parentage shall be established even after the court's declaration of non-existence.

Although those general provisions on the denial of parentage are not asserted in other countries' codes, they are observed by the highest courts of Arab states, i.e. the Cassation Courts. It must also be stressed that the denial of parentage of a child can only be made through a final conclusive court decision. Moroccan Article 90 sums up the rule as follows: "Only a decision of the judge shall rule out a child's parentage or a wife's pregnancy by a certain man."

On the other hand, if the husband denies parentage of a child, no parentage suit shall be heard if it is proved

(a) that the wife has not met the husband from the time of the contract;
(b) in the case of a child born after a year from the husband's absence;
(c) for a child born to a divorcée or a widow after more than a year from the time of divorce or death of the husband (Arts. 15, Egyptian Act No. 25/1929; 147, Jordanian).

The Syrian legislator distinguishes between two cases of parentage under a valid marriage depending on whether the child is born during the continuation of marriage, in which case the above provisions prevail, or is born after separation or the death of the husband. Article 130 rules that if the divorcée or the widow has not declared that she has completed her iddat, the parentage of her child shall be proved if born within a year from the date of divorce or death. It shall not be proved if it is born after that, unless it is acknowledged by the husband or the heirs. Article 131 rules that a divorcée or a widow who declares having completed her iddat shall have a child's parentage proved if born within less than 180 days from the time of declaration, or less than a year from the time of divorce or death.

4. PATERNITY UNDER AN IRREGULAR CONTRACT OR WITH A SEMBLANCE OF THE RIGHT, OR AFTER SEPARATION

A. Under an Irregular Contract

According to all schools, the pregnancy term shall be counted from the time of consummation, not of contract, for an irregular contract. A child born to a woman between six months at least and nine months at most after that time shall be attributed to the husband under an irregular contract, before or after separation, and shall not be denied through *lian* which can only be made under a valid contract. No paternity shall be established if the child is born within six months of cohabitation, regardless of the date of contract.[12]

This provision is adopted in Articles 132 (Syrian, the term is 180 days), 86/1 (Moroccan), 172/a (Kuwaiti), and 148 (Jordanian, which makes valid retirement equivalent to consummation). If the child is born after separation, its parentage shall not be established unless the birth occurs within a year from separation (Arts. 132/2, Syrian; 86, Moroccan; 148, Jordanian, and 172/b, Kuwaiti), which makes the term three hundred and sixty-five days.

B. Consummation with a Semblance of the Right to have Lawful Sexual Intercourse

In the absence of any marriage contract, whether valid or irregular, i.e. in the case of consummation with a semblance of the right thereto (e.g. if the woman is thought by the husband to be his lawful wife, or not to be in a prohibited degree, without knowing that the contrary is the case), the child born within the above limits shall be attributed to the man on the strength of his acknowledgment, provided that he shall not declare it is an issue of adultery.[13]

This Sharia provision is observed throughout the Islamic countries and is mentioned expressly by the Syrian and Moroccan Laws which rule that:

12 Abdullah, *op. cit.* pp. 579–580.
13 *Ibid.* p. 581; Al-Hilli, *op. cit.* p. 88.

"The woman who is without a husband if she has had sexual intercourse with a semblance of the right thereto, if she gives birth to a child between the two limits of the pregnancy term shall have its parentge to her partner established," (Arts. 133/2 and 87, respectively). Algerian Article 40 also acknowledges the offspring of cohabitation with a semblance of the right thereto. It is dealt with in the same Kuwaiti Article dealing with parentage under an irregular marriage contract (172/a and b).

C. After Separation

A child born after separation, whether through revocable or irrevocable divorce, annulment or death, shall be attributed to the husband if the interval between separation and birth is one lunar year or less.[14] According to the Shias, no paternity shall be established for a child born after nine months from the death of the husband even if it is acknowledged by the heirs. Nevertheless, under Shia law, a husband may acknowledge a child born to his divorced wife after more than a year of separation, provided that he is not known to be lying.[15]

5. SETTLEMENT OF DISPUTES BETWEEN SPOUSES OVER THE FACT OF BIRTH AND THE IDENTITY OF THE CHILD

A. During the Continuation of a Valid Marriage

Any dispute between the husband and wife over the fact of birth or the identity of the newborn child shall be settled by the evidence of the midwife or the physician, according to the Hanafis, of two women, according to the Malikis, of four women according to the Shafiis, and of four women, two men, or a man and two women, according to the Shias. Jurists are unanimous that the witnesses must be known to be honest.[16]

B. After Separation

A dispute over the fact of birth between a woman in her iddat of revocable or irrevocable divorce and her husband, or between a woman in her iddat of death and the heirs, shall be settled, according to the Shias, by the same evidence as above, namely four women, or two men, or one man and two

14 Abdullah, *op. cit.* pp. 582–583.
15 Al-Hilli, *op. cit.* p. 88.
16 Abdullah, *op. cit.* pp. 583–586; Al-Hilli, *op. cit.* p. 90.

women, even if the husband or the heirs have acknowledged the fact of pregnancy.[17] The Sunnis require the evidence of two men or a man and two women to settle a dispute over the fact of birth, but rule that the evidence of the midwife shall suffice to establish birth if pregnancy has been acknowledged by the husband or the heirs, or if it was observed.[18]

6. PATERNITY THROUGH ACKNOWLEDGEMENT

Apart from marriage, whether valid, irregular or with a semblance of a right to marital intercourse, parentage can also be established through acknowledgement which could be by the father, by the mother, or by the child itself.

A. By the Father

A man may either expressly or implicitly acknowledge a child as lawfully his, upon which the paternity of that child shall be established in the man, provided the following conditions are met:

(i) that the child so acknowledged is not known to be the child of another man;
(ii) that the ages of the parties are such that they could be father and child;
(iii) that the acknowledgement is made in such a way that the father is indicating that the child is legitimate, and not the offspring of unlawful intercourse (*zina*);
(iv) that the child, if of discretion, confirms or acquiesces in the acknowledgement; such confirmation shall not be required if the child has not reached the age of discretion.[19] Kuwaiti Article 173 (a) adopts all these provisions. The Shias do not require such confirmation by the child, even when it is of discretion.[20]

B. By the Mother

A woman may declare her maternity of a child and her acknowledgement shall be valid on meeting the above requirements, if she was not married nor in her iddat at the time of the birth. This ruling is adopted in as many

17 Al-Hilli, *loc. cit.*
18 Abdullah, *loc. cit.*
19 *Ibid.* p. 588.
20 Al-Hilli, *loc. cit.*

words in Kuwaiti Article 174/a. If the mother is married, or in her iddat of a marriage, her acknowledgement shall not establish the paternity of the husband without his confirmation.[21]

Under the Shias, the mother of a child may claim after the death of a man that she was his wife, and that the child is his. Her claim shall be sustained if approved by the heirs, and shall be dismissed if they deny that she was a wife of the deceased, or if she was not Muslim at the time of his death.[22]

C. By the Child

A child may also acknowledge the parentage of a father or a mother. This acknowledgement shall be subject to the same conditions enumerated above, namely that the child is of unknown parentage, that it is not the issue of unlawful intercourse, that the age difference admits of such a relationship, and that the acknowledgement is confirmed by the parent. This ruling is the subject of Kuwaiti Articles 173/b and 174/b.

The other modern Arab status codes adopt the above rules in general, with some variations in details:

(a) Syria. Article 134/1 establishes the parentage of a child to a father who makes a declaration to that effect, even if during a fatal illness, provided that the child is of unknown parentage and the age gap warrants such a kinship. Under the same article, paragraph 2, a married woman or one in her iddat may make a declaration of her child being her husband's or ex-husband's without the parentage being established, unless the husband confirms it, or she provides evidence thereto. Under Article 135, the acknowledgement of a person of no known parentage of a father or a mother shall have such a parentage established if it is confirmed by the person acknowledged, provided that the age gap between them warrants such a relationship.

(b) Tunisia. Parentage may be established through the wedlock, the acknowledgement by the father, or through the evidence of two or more trustworthy people (Art. 68). If disputed, parentage shall not be established for a child born to a wife who definitely has not met her husband, or who gave birth a year after the husband's absence or death or the date of divorce (Art. 69). No acknowledgement shall be accepted if the contrary thereto is conclusively proved. An acknowledgement by a person of unknown parentage of a father or mother shall be established if it is confirmed by the person acknowledged whose age admits such a kinship,

21 Abdullah, *op. cit.* p. 587.
22 Al-Hilli, *op. cit.* pp. 90–91.

and who shall then have all the rights and duties of parents vis-à-vis the children. The paternity of a child born to the wife in six months or more from the date of a valid or irregular contract shall be established in the husband (Art. 71). Such a child's paternity, if disputed by the husband, shall only be denied by order of the judge (Art. 75), who shall then order the permanent separation of the two spouses as well (Art. 76).

(c) Morocco. Only the father has the right to acknowledge a child of unknown parentage. Such an acknowledgement shall be established, even when made during a death-illness provided that the deponent is a male, of sound mind and not belied "by sheer reason or custom" (Art. 92). Acknowledgement shall be proved beyond any doubt by an official certificate or in the deponent's own handwriting (Art. 95).

(d) Iraq. Parenthood acknowledgement, even during the death-illness, shall establish the parentage of the person acknowledged, who is of unknown parentage, if the like may be born to the like. Except that if the deponent is a woman, the parentage of the child to her husband shall only be established if it is confirmed by him, or if evidence is produced (Art. 52/1 and 2). The acknowledgement by a person of unknown parentage of any paternity or maternity shall be established if it is confirmed by the person acknowledged to whose like the like can be born (Art. 53).

(e) Jordan. The same above provisions apply albeit worded differently. Under Article 149 the deponent's acknowledgement of parentage even during a death-illness shall establish that parentage to a person of unknown parentage if the age gap warrants such a relationship and with the confirmation by the person acknowledged if the child has reached puberty. The acknowledgement of a person of unknown parentage of a father or mother shall establish parentage if confirmed by the person acknowledged and warranted by the age gap.

(f) Algeria. Parentage is established through valid marriage, acknowledgement, evidence, cohabitation with a semblance of a conjugal right thereto (Art. 40). Paternity of the child shall be established of the father, under a lawful marriage contract with the possibility of the spouses meeting, unless lawfully denied (Art. 41). Parentage shall be established by acknowledgement of the filiation, paternity or maternity, even if made during a death-illness, if it stands to reason or custom (Art. 44).

Apart from acknowledgement and wedlock, all degrees of kinship, e.g. of a father, mother, child or brother, etc., may be established through evidence by two men, or one man and two women according to the Sunnis, but only by two men according to the Shias. This general Sharia rule is codified under Articles 68 (Tunisia), 89 (Morocco) and 40 (Algeria). All that is required of the witnesses is to be trustworthy.

Apart from filiation, maternity and paternity, acknowledgement of any other kinship shall not affect any person other than the deponent unless it is confirmed by the person affected (Arts. 136, Syria; 93, Morocco; 54, Iraq; and 45, Algeria).

7. ADOPTION

Acknowledgement by a parent of a child of unknown parentage as his or hers naturally, differs from adoption, which is the taking a child of a known or unknown parentage, but known for sure not to be his or hers, as his or her own child. Adoption was widespread among the Arabs before Islam, and remained valid during the early days of Islam until it was prohibited under the Quranic edict ". . . Nor hath He made those whom ye claim to be your sons your sons. This is a saying of your mouth. . . . Proclaim their real parentage. That will be more equitable in the sight of God. And if ye know not their fathers, then (proclaim them) your brethren in faith and your clients."[23]

Adoption has since then been unacknowledgeable throughout the countries which apply the Sharia personal status provisions in spite of the fact that it has been expressly prohibited only in three instances:

(i) under the Moroccan Article 83, paragraph 3, "Adoption as understood customarily is void and shall produce no legal effect. Adoption for the purpose of rewarding or bequeathing, known as according a person the status of one's child, shall not establish a parentage, and shall be subject to the provisions of the will";
(ii) under Article 46 of the Algerian Act No. 84/1984, "Adoption shall be forbidden, under the Sharia and the law".
(iii) under article 167 of the Kuwaiti Personal Status Law "No parentage shall be established through adoption even if the adoptee is of unknown parentage".

However, there is only one exception to this virtual unanimity – Tunisia. On 4/3/1958, Act No. 27 in respect of Public Guardianship, Taking into Care and Adoption, was promulgated in an obvious attempt to find a remedy for the growing numbers of foundlings and children of refugees, according to the Explanatory Note issued by the Ministry of Justice. The Act tried to steer a middle course between the social and the Sharia exigencies. On the one hand, it granted the right to adopt to every adult, whether male or female, on complying with the conditions of being married, possessing civil rights, being of sound character, mind and body,

23 Sura Ahzab, XXXIII, verses 4–5.

and capable of looking after the adoptee. Other conditions are attached concerning the adoptee and third parties. The difference in age between the adopting parent and the adoptee shall be a minimum of 15 years, except when the adoptee is a child of the adopter's spouse; the adoptee needs not be Tunisian (Art. 10). In all cases, the adopter's spouse's consent must be obtained (Art. 11). The adoptee itself must be a minor, whether male or female (Art. 12). The district court shall issue the adoption order after ascertaining compliance with the requirements and confirmation of all those concerned and present, including the natural parents or the representative of the relevant administrative authority, the adopter and spouse; the adoption order shall then be final (Art. 13). The child shall bear the name of the adoptive parent, and shall enjoy all rights and liabilities of real children, of maintenance, custody and inheritance (Arts. 14 and 15).

On the other hand, honouring the Sharia rule, all the prohibited degrees for marriage purposes shall remain observable by the child if his relatives are known (Art. 15).

8. LEGAL EFFECTS OF PARENTAGE

The establishment of a child's parentage creates forthwith certain rights and duties, the most important of which are fosterage, custody, maintenance and guardianship, which shall be dealt with in the following chapters.

We shall here deal with those rights connected with mutual inheritance which will not be dealt with in the chapter on Inheritance.

A direct acknowledgement of parentage as explained above shall establish forthwith the reciprocal rights of inheritance between the parties concerned, subject to the provisions stated.

An indirect declaration of parentage which affects a third party shall be binding only on the person who makes it, and shall require that further evidence as to the kinship of the beneficiary be provided by the maker of the declaration. For instance, if an orphan acknowledges a man of unknown parentage to be his brother, his acknowledgement shall be effective only on him, and not on the other heirs if they dispute the claim. The acknowledged brother shall receive half the deponent's share, according to the Sunnis,[24] or the balance between that share and what the deponent deserves under his acknowledgement according to the Shias. An illustration: A man dies leaving two sons: A who acknowledges the brotherhood of C, and B who disputes this kinship. B shall receive half the

24 Abdullah, *op. cit.* p. 589.

estate, A shall get one third and C shall inherit one sixth. Obviously, if A is the only heir, he shall get a half, and C shall get the other half.[25]

If the deponent dies leaving no heir, his estate shall devolve on the acknowledged person if

(i) the person is of unknown parentage;
(ii) the person is not proven to have a different parentage;
(iii) the deponent has not withdrawn acknowledgement;
(iv) there is no impediment to inheritance (Art. 41, Egyptian Inheritance Act No. 77/1943).

9. THE FOUNDLING

A foundling is a newborn baby, abandoned by its parents on grounds of poverty or shame, and so unable to fend for itself. Care of a foundling is a religious duty if there is any risk that the baby might otherwise die. Once found and taken into care, a foundling must never again be abandoned. The baby's finder has sole right to its guardianship unless he is unfit or is non-Muslim and a Muslim disputes that right, in which case, the Muslim shall be the guardian; if they are of the same religion, the judge should decide who shall be the guardian.[26]

A foundling is considered under Sunni law to be a Muslim if found in a Muslim locality, or a Christian or a Jew if found by such a person in his own locality.[27] Under Shia law, a foundling shall be deemed a Muslim regardless of the religion of its finder, or the place where the baby is found.[28]

If any money is found on a foundling, it shall be the foundling's. Its guardian shall use the money for its upbringing on authorization by the court. If the guardian spends his own money on the foundling, he shall be entitled to recover his expenses either from public funds, or from the foundling when it comes of age and can afford it. The guardian has the right to educate the foundling, or to provide for its learning a trade.

If any man claims paternity of the foundling, such a claim shall be valid subject to the previously mentioned conditions of acknowledgement, but the foundling shall remain a Muslim regardless of the religion of the putative parent.[29]

Under Shia law, a married woman may claim a foundling as her child. The claim shall be accepted if supported by her husband who shall then be

25 Al-Hilli, *op. cit.* p. 91.
26 Abu Zahra, *op. cit.* p. 400.
27 *Ibid.*
28 Al-Hilli, *op. cit.* p. 92.
29 Abu Zahra, *loc. cit.*

acknowledged as the father, or if the woman proves giving birth to it. If she is unmarried, cannot prove the birth, or is not supported by her husband, the custody of the foundling shall be given solely to her.[30]

If a baby who is proved to be a foundling has no money, remains unclaimed and its guardian refuses to provide for it, its maintenance shall be a charge on public funds to provide for its needs in respect of food and clothing.[31]

Only the Tunisian Law includes provisions on the foundlings, adopting many of the above rulings. Anyone who pledges to provide maintenance for a foundling and obtains permission of the judge thereto shall be under the obligation of maintenance until the foundling is capable of earning a living, unless it has means of its own (Art. 77). The finder shall have the custody of the foundling unless its father appears, claims it, and the judge grants him custody (Art. 78). Whatever property is found on the foundling shall remain its own (Art. 79). If the foundling dies leaving no heir, its earnings shall revert to the treasury, but the finder may claim back from the state his expenditure by way of maintenance of the foundling within the limits of earnings thereof (Art. 80).

30 Al-Hilli, *op. cit.* p. 94.
31 Abu Zahra, *loc. cit.*; Al-Hilli, *loc. cit.*

Chapter 9

Child's Rights during Infancy Fosterage and Custody

1. FOSTERAGE

Parentage is a right for the child and the father. Once established, it is followed by the child's right to be brought up, a right which imposes a duty on the father, namely maintenance, and another on the mother, namely fosterage and custody until the end of infancy.

Fosterage has already been discussed in the context of giving rise to a prohibited degree for marriage purposes. As a right of the child, it creates an obligation on both parents and raises the question of wages.

A. Fosterage as a Duty of the Mother

During the first stage of its life, the infant needs feeding through suckling. It is the mother's duty, in the first instance, to feed her baby, under the Quranic ruling "The mothers shall suckle their offspring for two whole years for those who wish to complete the suckling."[1] Although the verse is in the indicative mood, all Muslim jurists agree that it is imperative, setting a religious duty on the mother to feed the baby, whether she is married to its father or divorced and has completed her iddat.

However, they differ on whether she should be ordered by the court to suckle the infant. The Hanafis maintain that the mother may be compelled by the father to nurse her infant child if no suitable nurse other than the mother is available, if neither the father nor the infant has any property, or if the infant refuses any other breast but the mother's.[2]

1 Sura Baqara II, verse 233.
2 Al-Abiani, *A Brief Commentary on Personal Status Sharia Provisions*, p. 318.

This Hanafi position is adopted under the Jordanian Article 150, and is very similar to the Shia's, with the sole addition that the mother may be exempted if a third woman agrees to hire, at her expense, a wet nurse for the infant.[3]

The Malikis hold that the mother shall be under the legal and religious obligation to feed her baby free if she is married to its father or revocably divorced from him, unless it is not the custom of her class to suckle their babies. They make an exception in the latter case if the baby refuses any other breast, when she is entitled to a wage like a divorced mother.[4]

The Hanbalis maintain that it is the duty of the father alone to provide for the feeding of the baby.[5]

Some Zahiris rule that the mother shall be compelled to suckle her baby whether she or her husband like it or not, unless she is divorced, has no milk, or her milk is not wholesome to the baby.[6]

Iraqi Article 55 makes it the duty of the mother to suckle her baby unless pathological states prevent her from so doing.

Kuwaiti Article 186, ruling that the mother shall be obliged to suckle her baby if it cannot be fed on anything except her milk, steers a compromise between the protection of the baby from disease or death and the respect of the mother's will.

B. The Father's Duty in Respect of Fosterage

If the mother does not have to suckle the baby and refuses to do so, or if she is dead and no woman volunteered to feed it, the father shall hire a wet nurse for the baby. The nurse will not have to stay at the custodian's (*hadina*) home to suckle the baby unless expressly stipulated in the contract.[7]

In the absence of any agreement on a specific arrangement for suckling, e.g. that the baby be taken to the nurse's home for feeding and brought back to the custodian's, the baby shall be suckled at the mother's or other custodian's home, since the two rights of fosterage and custody are distinct, and the mother's refusal to feed the baby does not deprive her of the right of custody.[8]

This generally held Sunni position is not followed by the Shia Jaafaris who maintain that if the mother refuses to suckle her baby when she is not under any obligation to do so, she shall lose her right to custody, and the

3 Al-Hilli, *Jaafari Personal Status Provisions*, p. 95.
4 Badran, *Children's Rights*, pp. 50–51.
5 *Ibid.*
6 *Ibid.* p. 52.
7 Abdullah, *Sharia Personal Status Provisions*, p. 595.
8 *Ibid.*

father shall hire a wet nurse who shall not have to feed the infant at the mother's home.[9]

If the hire duration expires before the baby can do without suckling, the wet nurse shall be compelled to extend the period if the baby refuses any other breast until weaning.[10]

In all cases it is the father who shall be liable for the wages for feeding the baby whether they are to the mother or to the wet nurse, unless the infant itself has property. If the father is destitute, unable to earn a livelihood or dead, the wages for suckling the baby shall be payable by the person whose duty it is to provide maintenance for the baby (Arts. 152/1, Syrian, adding "whether it is natural or artificial feeding"; 112, Moroccan; 56, Iraqi).

C. Wages for Fostering

Only the Shia Ithna Asharis rule that the mother is entitled to receive payment for nursing her own infant during the continuation of marriage, during or after the iddat of a revocable or irrevocable divorce – and the husband may hire her for fostering.[11]

The Sunni Schools and the modern laws (Arts. 152/2, Syrian; 113, Moroccan; 152, Jordanian; and 189/a, Kuwaiti) rule, on the contrary, that no wages for fostering shall be paid to the wife during the continuation of marriage or in the iddat of a revocable divorce.

However, such wages shall be payable after the expiry of the iddat under the Quranic ruling on the divorced woman ". . . and if they give suck for you give them their due payment".[12] The mother shall then receive the wages for the equal, which shall be commensurate with the condition of the person whose duty it is to pay (Art. 153, Jordanian).

Since suckling the infant is not only the mother's duty but also her right, she shall have priority thereto unless a wet nurse is available who offers to nurse the baby free of charge or for less wages than the mother, under the Quranic verse "No mother shall be treated unfairly on account of her child, nor father on account of his child" (Sura Baqara, II, verse 233), the father being held responsible for the cost of nursing. This ruling is unanimously held, with the Shias adding that the mother shall then lose her right to custody, but could retain her right to access,[13] while the Sunnis again distinguish between the two rights. Articles 153 (Syrian) and 114 (Moroccan) stress that suckling even free of charge by a wet nurse

9 Al-Hilli, *op. cit.* p. 95.
10 *Ibid.* p. 96.
11 *Ibid.*
12 Sura Talaq, LXV, verse 6.
13 Al-Hilli, *op. cit.* p. 96.

shall take place at the mother's home, if the mother asks for wages and the father is destitute.

According to the Sunnis and Shias alike, pursuant to the Quranic ruling "The mothers shall suckle their offspring for two whole years for those who wish to complete the suckling",[14] the fosterage wages shall be payable for a maximum of two years (Art. 153, Jordanian, and 188/b, Kuwaiti).

Nursing wages shall be a valid debt on the father under the Sharia to be settled only through payment or discharge (Kuwaiti Art. 187) and shall be a charge on the estate in the event of the death of the father.

2. CUSTODY

Custody is an established right for the baby from the time of its birth. It is one form of guardianship of the child which the jurists divide into three categories:

(i) guardianship of the infant (*hadhana* or *hidhana* in Arabic) during the early years of life, when the infant needs women to look after it;
(ii) guardianship of education (*wilayat at-Tarbiyya*) believed under the Sharia to be the duty of men rather than women;
(iii) guardianship of property (*al wilayatu alal maal*) if the child has any property, a task again worthier of men than of women.

In this section we treat custody in the first stage, leaving the two other forms of guardianship to later chapters.

Custody under the Sharia is defined as the caring for the infant during the period when it cannot do without the women in a prohibited degree who have the lawful right to bring it up. There are similar definitions enshrined in three modern North African laws: ". . . the caring for the child at its home and looking after its upbringing" (Art. 54, Tunisian); ". . . the protection of the child as far as possible from any potential cause of injury thereto and the provision for its upbringing and safeguarding of its interest" (Art. 97, Moroccan); ". . . the catering for a child, its upbringing and education in the religious faith of its father, and provision for its protection, health and righteousness" (Art. 62, Algerian).

A. The Persons Entitled to Custody

All Schools, Sunni and Shia alike, hold that the mother, whether she is separated or living with her husband, has the first claim to the custody of

14 Sura Baqara II, verse 233.

her infant, but she cannot be compelled to undertake it, due to her inability to do so, unless there is no-one else to undertake it.

If she is dead or disqualified (see next section), Schools differ widely on the person to whom the custody of the child should pass. These differences are reflected in the modern and Personal Status Legislations.

(1) The Hanafis

The second claim to the custody of the child, if the mother is not available or eligible, goes to the following persons in the given order:

(a) the maternal grandmother, how-high-soever;
(b) the paternal grandmother, how-high-soever;
(c) the full, uterine and consanguine sister, in that order;
(d) the maternal aunts, in the same order;
(e) the paternal aunts, in the same order.[15]

The general rule is that since the mother has prior right, the relations through her are given preference over those on the father's side, and among the latter the order is from the full to the uterine to the consanguine relation. (A full brother is, for example, a brother by both parents; a uterine brother is only from the mother's side, and a consanguine brother is from the father's side.)

If there is no woman either from the paternal or maternal side, then the right of upbringing is in the agnates in the same order of priority as the inheritance beginning with

(a) the father;
(b) paternal grandfather, how-high-soever;
(c) full brother;
(d) consanguine brother (N.B. a uterine brother is not an agnate);
(e) sons of the full brother;
(f) sons of the consanguine brother;
(g) their descendants how-low-soever;
(h) paternal uncle;
(i) paternal uncle's son, provided always that no agnate male shall be entrusted with the custody of a female minor whom he is not prohibited to marry.[16]

The above order is held by the Lebanese Druze Personal Act 1948, Article 57, the Syrian Act No. 59/1953 as amended by Act No. 34/1975, Article 139. The Jordanian Provisional Act No. 61/1976, Article 154

15 Badran, *op. cit.* pp. 64–65.
16 *Ibid.* pp. 66–67.

follows closely, "The real mother has prior right to the custody of her child, and to bring it up for the duration of marriage and after separation, such right passing from the mother to the woman next to her in the order set by Imam Abu Hanifa." This is the order cited above, except that, unique in that respect, the Jordanian Law seems to confine the right of the custody of the infant solely to women.

(2) The Malikis

Failing the mother, custody shall go to her mother, how-high-soever, then the full uterine maternal aunt, then the mother's maternal and then the mother's paternal aunt, then the father's mother, then his mother's mother, then his father's mother; the nearer excludes the further, and those related through the mother shall have precedence over those through the father. Failing these, custody should go to the father, then the sister, then the father's sister, then the father's paternal then maternal aunt, then the daughter of the full, then uterine then consanguine brother, then the daughter of the sister in the same order. Failing these, custody shall go to the guardian, male or female, then the brother, then his son (failing a maternal grandfather), then the paternal uncle, then his son, the nearer preferred to the further.

This order is followed in Morocco and in Kuwait. Article 99 of the Moroccan Personal Status Decree reads:

> "Custody is a duty of the parents as long as they live together in matrimony; on the dissolution of marriage, the mother shall have the first claim to the custody of her child, then her mother, then her mother's mother, then the mother's full sister, then her uterine sister, then her consanguine sister, then the father's mother, then the father's maternal or paternal grandmother how-high-soever, then the sister, then the paternal aunt, then the father's paternal aunt, then the father's maternal aunt, then the sister's daughter, then the brother, then the paternal grandfather, then the brother's son, then the paternal uncle, then his son. In all cases, the full relation shall have precedence over the uterine, who is followed by the consanguine."

Article 100 reads:

> "The guardian shall take precedence over all other agnates for the male ward and the female ward while she is a minor, and in the event of her majority if he is in a marriage prohibited degree to her, or if he is married and trustworthy." "This order shall be observed if the first is eligible or available then to the next."

Article 189 of the Kuwaiti Law No. 51/1984 repeats the Maliki order of eligibility for custody, and adds, in paragraph c, that in the event of equal claims for eligible custodianship, the Judge shall select the best among them for the ward.

(3) The Shafiis

The eligible custodians may be a group of men and women, solely females or solely males.

In the first case, the mother shall have priority over the father, followed by the mother's mother, how-high-soever, provided she is a presumptive heiress, failing which the father, then his mother, then her mother, how-high-soever, provided she is a presumtive heiress – failing which the nearest of kin of female, then the nearest male kin.

In the second case, i.e. of only female relatives, priority goes to the mother, then her mother, then the father's mother, then the sister, then the maternal aunt, then the daughter of the sister, then of the brother, then the paternal aunt, then the daughters of the maternal aunt, the paternal aunt, the paternal uncle and the maternal uncle, in that order.

In the third case, when only male kin are available, priority goes to the father, then the grandfather, then the germane, then the consanguine, then the uterine brother, then the son of the germane or consanguine brother, then the full then the consanguine paternal uncle, then his son, who "not being a prohibited degree, shall appoint a trustworthy person, e.g. his own daughter, to take care of the female minor".[17]

(4) The Hanbalis

Priority goes to the mother, then her mother, then her mother's mother, and so on, then the father, then his mother, how-high-soever, then the grandfather, then his mother, then the sister, the maternal then the paternal aunt, then the father's maternal then paternal aunt, in all these categories the order going from the germane to the uterine to the consanguine, the same order being followed with nieces and cousins.[18]

(5) The Ithna Asharis

The Shia Ithna Asharis grant the mother the prior right to custody of the male infant until it is weaned at two, and of the girl until she is seven; the right passes then, if the mother is dead or disqualified, to the father, failing which to the father's father, then to grandparents, consanguine sisters,

17 Al-Jazeeri, *Jurisprudence According to the Four Doctrines*, Vol. IV, pp. 595–596.
18 *Ibid.*

then to the nephews and nieces in the same order, then to the maternal aunts and uncles, then the paternal aunts and uncles, then to the children of paternal and maternal uncles, then to the mother's maternal aunt, the father's maternal aunt, and so on. In the event of a tie, a lot shall decide. If no kin of a prohibited degree for marriage is available or eligible, the infant shall be looked after by a non-prohibited agnate such as the daughters of paternal or maternal uncles or aunts, failing which the judge shall appoint an honest, trustworthy woman.[19]

(6) Other, more eclectic, modern Arab legislations

(a) Tunisia. Tunisian Article 57 rules that custody of the children is the right of their parents as long as the marital condition stands. Article 64 rules that any person entitled to the custody of the children may relinquish his right thereto, whereupon the judge shall appoint a different guardian. In the event of the termination of marriage due to death, the custody shall be given to the surviving parent. If marriage is dissolved while the spouses are alive, custody shall be granted to either of them or to a third person. The judge shall take into account the welfare of the ward in making any decision (Art. 67).

(b) Algeria. Algerian Article 64 gives the mother the priority, followed by her mother, then the maternal aunt, then the father, then the father's mother, then the next nearest of kin, provided that the ward's interest shall be observed in all cases.

(c) Iraq. The Iraqi Act No. 188/1959 as amended under Act No. 21/1978 moves nearer to the Shia position. The persons entitled to the custody of the infant are described under Articles 57, the relevant parts of which read as follows:

> "(1) The mother has prior right to the custody and upbringing of the infant, both for the duration of marriage and after separation, unless the ward suffers injury thereby. . . . (7) In the event of the mother becoming disqualified or of her death, custody shall pass to the father, unless the infant's interest dictates otherwise, in which case custody shall pass to whomever the court shall choose, with the best interest of the child being the paramount consideration. . . . (8) If neither parent is eligible for custody, the court shall entrust the custody of the child to a trustworthy person, female or male, and may likewise order the child to be brought up in a state-run nursery is available. (9) In the event of the father's death or disqualification, the child shall remain with its mother for as long as she remains

19 Al-Hilli, *op. cit.* p. 100.

qualified, with any of its female or male kin having the right to challenge her right thereto until it reaches the age of majority."

B. Eligibility for Guardianship

The right to the custody of the infant is subject to certain conditions, some of which are common to females and males, others are for females and a third group for males.

(1) Common conditions for custody

According to Sharia, both women and men have to comply with the following conditions to be eligible for custody.

(a) Majority, sanity and freedom. The minor, the insane and the imbecile, and the slave, need themselves to be looked after by another; *a fortiori*, they cannot look after an infant.[20]

These conditions, save for freedom, are adopted in the modern legislations (Arts. 137, Syrian; 55, Lebanese Druze Act; 58, Tunisia; 98, Morocco; 57 (2) Iraq; 155 Jordan; and 190/a, Kuwait.

(b) Ability to bring up the ward, look after its interests and protect it both physically and morally. Kuwaiti Article 190/a incorporates this phrase to the letter. Therefore, no person shall be entrusted to the custody of a child if he or she is incapacitated due to a handicap, old age, disease or occupation, or moral corruption. Moroccan Article 98/5 and Tunisian Article 58 both specify the condition of freedom from any infectious disease. The Sudanese legislative circular of 16/2/1927 adds that even living with a patient suffering from an infectious disease shall debar a person from being entrusted with the custody of a child. Syrian Article 139 (2) rules that a female shall not lose the right to custody of her children because of her work, provided that she secures their care in an acceptable way, a ruling generally held by the Egptian courts.[21] However, the ability of the working person to care for the infant shall be left to the discretion of the court.

(2) Conditions for the female custodian (hadina)

In addition to those common conditions, a female custodian (*hadina*) shall also fulfil the following requirements:

(a) Marriage restrictions. She shall not be married to a stranger or to a kin

20 Badran, *op. cit.* p. 68.
21 *Ibid.* p. 69.

who is not in a prohibited degree to the infant. This condition is based on a tradition of the Prophet when he granted a divorced wife the custody of her son, saying "You have the first right to look after him unless you marry." Although the tradition would imply that the mother, and, *a fortiori*, any other female custodian, would lose the right to custody of the child once she's married, regardless of the husband's relation to the infant if he is not its father, it is not always interpreted so sweepingly. The Hanafis and Malikis restrict the marriage that deprives the woman of her right to custody to that with a stranger or a relation who is not prohibited to marry the infant. A woman who marries, say, a cousin of the infant shall lose that right, but shall retain it if she marries its uncle, in which event, loving care for the infant may be assumed, even if the wife's attention to the child may compromise part of her services to her husband.[22]

This ruling is held in Articles 137 (Syrian) and 156 (Jordanian). Kuwaiti Article 191/a concurs, adding the condition "if the marriage is consummated". Iraqi Article 57 (2) stipulates, that the woman shall not be married to a stranger. Moroccan Article 105 deprives a woman of the right to custody on marrying a stranger not in a prohibited degree to, or a guardian of the ward, unless she herself was a guardian or a foster mother other than whose breast the baby rejects. However, in Article 106, the next person in line for the custody of the child shall lose that right on keeping silent for a year after knowing of consummation of marriage. A similar ruling is stipulated in Tunisian Article 58: a female shall be entitled to the custody of the infant provided that she has no husband with whom marriage has been consummated unless the husband is in a prohibited degree to or guardian of the infant, . . . or the next in line to the right of custody shall remain silent for a year after knowing of consummation of marriage without claiming that right, . . . or the woman is a wet nurse, or both a mother and a guardian of the ward. However, the same Articles give the court discretion to allow the woman to keep the child, even if she is married, if the welfare of the ward so requires. Again, Article 191/b of the Kuwaiti law deprives the next in line for custody of that right on keeping silent for a year without any excuse, after learning of the consummation of marriage and adds that ignorance of this provision is no excuse.

On the other hand, the Jaafaris maintain that any marriage with a man, even in a marriage-prohibited degree to the infant shall deprive the woman of the right to custody if the infant's father is alive and eligible, such right passing then to the father. In the absence of a father, the mother shall retain that right after her marriage, taking precedence over the grandfather.[23]

22 Abdullah, *op. cit.* p. 604.
23 Al-Hilli, *op. cit.* p. 99.

Should that impediment to custody be removed on the dissolution of marriage, the woman shall recover her right to custody according to the Jaafaris, Hanafis, Shafiis, and Hanbalis, and Articles 141 (Syrian), 110 (Moroccan), 158 (Jordanian) and 193 (Kuwaiti), all of which apply to all cases of temporarily losing that right. The Malikis rule out any such recovery.

(b) Relationship to ward. The woman shall be a relation in a prohibited degree to the ward. A stranger, even in a prohibited degree on fosterage grounds, shall not be eligible.

(c) Residence. She shall not live with the ward at a home where it is not liked. This provision is expressly stated in the Jordanian Article 155.

(d) Religion. Only the Jaafaris and Shafiis require that no non-Muslim woman is qualified for the custody of a Muslim child born to a Muslim father, although a Kitabi shall have the custody of a Kitabi infant.[24] The Hanafis, followed by the Jordanian legislator (Art. 155) consider apostasy a sufficient reason to deny a woman her right to custody.

Generally speaking, other Sunni jurists and legislators do not insist on the identity of religion between the female and her ward, provided that it shall be brought up in the faith of its father (Algerian Art. 62). However, the Sunnis rule that if there are reasonable grounds to think that the hadina would influence the infant's religious beliefs, e.g. her teaching it the articles of her faith, performing her religious rites in front of it, accompanying it to her church, making it eat pork or drink wine, the ward shall be taken away from her. The Zahiri Ibn Hazm maintains that identity of religion is not a condition during fosterage, but it becomes necessary thereafter.[25]

The Kuwaiti Article 192 of the Personal Status Law reads as follows:

> "The non-Muslim hadina of a Muslim child shall be entitled to its custody until it starts to understand about religions, or until it is feared that it may become familiar with a faith other than Islam, even if it does not understand about religions." "In all cases, such a child shall not remain with such a hadina after it has reached five years of age."

Articles 59 (Tunisian) and 108 (Moroccan) deal, in almost identical terms, with the case of a female eligible for the custody of a child and professing a faith other than the father's. Again, she loses her right to custody on the ward completing its fifth year of age, unless she is the

24 *Ibid.*
25 Ibn Hazm, *Al Muhalla*, Vol. 10, p. 323.

mother and there is no fear of her bringing it up according to a religion different from the father's.

(e) The disobedient wife. Article 145 of the Syrian Personal Act rules that if the wife becomes disobedient and the children are over five years of age, the judge may, at his discretion, grant their custody to either spouse provided that due care shall be taken of the children's interest on reasonable grounds.

(3) Conditions for the male custodian (hadin)

In addition to the general conditions of eligibility, the male (*hadin*) shall comply with the following two requirements:

(i) To be a relative within a prohibited degree to the female ward. Therefore, a cousin shall not be eligible for the custody of his female cousin.

This general rule is held under Tunisian Article 58 and Kuwaiti Article 190/b in which both add the condition that such a relative shall have living with him a woman capable to look after the child. Article 99 (2) of the Moroccan Personal Decree grants the guardian, without any qualification, the right to custody of a female minor.

(ii) To profess the same religion as the ward, if the hadin is a male agnate. The reason is that his right to custody is based on his right to inheritance, a condition of which is the identity of religion. If the non-Muslim infant has two full brothers, a Muslim and a non-Muslim, its custody shall pass to the non-Muslim.

However, a non-agnate relative is not required to be of the same faith as the ward, since the right to custody here is based on a kinship within a prohibited degree, not on the right to inheritance. This case has no room in the Shia law which requires identity of religion even for a hadina.[26]

C. Wages for Custody

The hadina may be the mother or not. The mother, according to the Hanafis, shall not be entitled to custody wages during the continuation of marriage or the iddat of a revocable divorce, since in both cases she receives matrimonial or iddat maintenance. But the mother who receives no such maintenance, e.g. if she is in an iddat of the death of the husband, or has been divorced on a discharge or has completed her iddat, shall be entitled to custody wages. She shall have that right also if she has ceased to

26 Al-Hilli, *op. cit.* p. 99.

receive her iddat maintenance on the expiry of one year after her being divorced.[27]

This Hanafi ruling is held in the modern Arab personal laws, Articles 104 (Moroccan), 57 (3) Iraqi) and 160 (Jordanian). Syrian Article 143 rules that the mother shall not be entitled to custody wages for the duration of matrimony or during the iddat of divorce, without qualifying it as revocable. The same ruling is adopted under Kuwaiti Article 199/a, which extends it to the duration of a mutat ordered by the court for the hadina against the ward's father. Paragraph b provides that the hadina must receive wages until the boy reaches seven and the girl nine years of age.

The Hadina who is not the mother shall receive wages for custody unless she offers it free. This is accepted by all schools. The Shafiis and Hanbalis rule that even the mother may ask for wages for custody. The Jaafaris maintain that such wages are not imperative. But the mother is not compelled to give it free, but may ask for wages. The father then shall have the choice between paying her such wages or taking the infant away from her. If custody is not incumbent on the father, and no person volunteered for it free of charge, the mother may be granted the wages she demands unless she asks for more than the wages of the equal.[28]

Wages for custody shall be payable from the time of agreement or court's order or from the time the mother undertakes it without any need for agreement or court's order.

The infant shall be liable for the custody wages if it has property, under the Sunni and Shia laws. If it has no property, such wages shall be due from and according to the means of the person who is liable for the maintenance of the infant (Arts. 143, Syrian; and 159, Jordanian). Moroccan Article 103 adds that such wages are distinct from maintenance and suckling wages. Tunisian Article 65 specifies the wages for custody as confined to the cost of serving the ward, preparing meals and laundry according to custom. Algerian Article 72 orders that the father shall provide or rent a home for the infant who has no property to provide maintenance and dwelling for itself.

Under the Sunni law, if the female entitled to the custody of the child refuses to take it without wages, and a woman offers to accept custody free of charge, the volunteer, if she is a relative in a prohibited degree and the infant has property, shall have precedence over the female entitled to custody, whether the father has or has no property, as this would save any cost incurred by the infant and obtain loving care for it.[29]

27 Al-Abiani, *op. cit.* p. 336.
28 Al-Hilli, *op. cit.* p. 100.
29 Abdullah, *op. cit.* pp. 620–621.

The volunteer shall also be preferred to the mother if in a prohibited degree and neither the infant nor its father has property, pursuant to the Quranic verse "A mother should not be made to suffer because of her child nor a father on account of his child".[30] The father in this case would suffer hardship to pay the mother wages.

It is evident, therefore, that a stranger who volunteers for fosterage is preferable to a mother who demands wages if the stranger is offering free suckling or wages lower than those asked for by the mother, whether or not the infant or the father has property.

Under the Jaafari law, however, if the infant's mother refuses to look after it free of charge, and a volunteer fit for custody, even if she is a stranger, can be found, or if the father is able to provide custody, even with the help of others, such as a servant or his own wife, the mother shall be given the choice between free custody or handing the infant over to the volunteer or to the father, without prejudice to the mother's right to access.[31]

D. Place for Custody

(1) When the mother is the hadina

The infant shall stay normally with its mother at the matrimonial home during the continuation of marriage. The mother then shall not move to a different place, with or without the infant, until it can do without her and custody is terminated, without the husband's permission.[32] This provision is held under the Syrian Article 148/1.

If the mother is divorced, she shall keep the infant with her at the place where she spends her iddat, which she cannot leave or be made to leave, under the Quranic verse, "Expel them not from their houses nor let them go forth unless they commit open immorality." (Sura Talaq, LXV, verse 1). Since staying on in the matrimonial home is a duty to honour both the right of the husband and the right of the Sharia, she shall not leave it with her child, even with the husband's permission.[33]

Having completed her iddat, she may move with the child to a city so near to her previous home as to allow the father to travel to see his child and return to his original place to spend the night there.[34] Tunisian and Moroccan Articles 61 and 107 rule that the hadina shall lose her right to

30 Sura Baqara II, verse 233.
31 Al-Hilli, *op. cit.* p. 101.
32 Abdullah, *op. cit.* pp. 611–615.
33 *Ibid.*
34 *Ibid.*

custody if she moves to or settles in a different town where it would be difficult for the father or guardian to look after the interests of the child.

She can move to a remote town on two conditions: that it is her town of origin, and the place where she married the father. Otherwise she shall have to obtain the father's consent. This provision is held under Syrian Article 148 (2), (3) and (4), which allows both the mother and her mother to move after the completion of the iddat, without the guardian's permission, to her original town where her marriage was solemnized, and to travel with the child within the territory to the town where she lives or works for a public authority, provided a relative in a prohibited degree to her lives there. Jordanian Article 164 makes the travelling of the guardian or the hadina with the minor to a town within the Kingdom subject to its not unfairly prejudicing the child's attitude in his or her favour, otherwise the child shall be taken away by the other party: Article 166 allows the hadina to leave the Kingdom with the ward, only with the consent of the guardian and after ascertaining that its interest is secured. Kuwaiti Article 195/a prevents a hadina from travelling to another state to stay there without permission by the guardian, and b forbids the guardian, whether he is the father or not, from travelling with the ward for a stay without permission by its hadina.

(2) If the hadina is not the mother

The hadina who is not the mother shall remain in the town where the father lives. She cannot travel with the infant anywhere without the father's or the guardian's permission. This provision, held expressly under the Lebanese Druze Personal Act, Article 66, and the Syrian Article 149, is observed both by the Sunnis and the Shias, who confine the right to give permission to the father, although they allow the mother to travel with the child even to a place remote from the father's residence during her hidanat (period of female custody) provided no injury to either parent ensues, since custody is at the time exclusively hers and not shared with the father.[35]

Under Algerian Article 69, a custodian who wishes to reside abroad shall refer to the judge to confirm or cancel custody, taking the ward's interest into consideration.

It transpires from the above rules that in the hidanat a balance should be struck between the ward's interest and the right of both parents, combining the hidanat by the mother or female relatives and the supervision and guardianship by the father.

In the same vein, no father may travel with the infant without

35 Al-Hilli, *op. cit.* p. 102.

permission of its mother during her custodianship.[36] This Hanafi provision is expressly held under Syrian Article 150 and Tunisian Article 62 which adds "unless the ward's interest requires otherwise". The Shia Jaafaris concur, adding that if the father takes the child away from the mother who has lost her right to custody because of marriage, he may travel with it until the mother recovers the said right.[37] This provision is also held under Article 65 of the Lebanese Druze Personal Act.

The Malikis, Shafiis and Hanbalis rule that the father has the right to travel with the ward in both cases.[38]

E. Access

Under the Sharia, no hadina, mother or no mother, may prevent the father from seeing his child in her custody. Nor shall she be compelled to send it to his home, but shall be ordered to bring the child to a place where the father can see it.[39]

Nor can the father to whom the child has been handed bar the mother who has lost her right or has terminated its custody, from seeing it but, again, he shall not be compelled to send it to her residence, but shall be ordered to bring it to a place where she could meet it.[40]

The classic juristic texts do not define the frequency of such access for each parent. But by analogy with the wife's right to see her parents, each parent of the child shall see it once a week.

Like the mother, the female relatives, such as the maternal aunt or the sister, have the right of access to the child, but less frequently, usually once a month.[41]

The Shia Ithna-Asharis maintain that the mother shall retain her right to access to the child even if she does not suckle it[42] or loses her right to its custody.[43] The right of access is secured for both parents under the following articles:

Art. 148 (5) Syrian:

> "Each parent shall have the right to see children entrusted to the custody of the other periodically at the place where the ward lives, and if this is disputed, the judge shall order such right to be secured

36 Al-Abiani, *op. cit.* p. 339.
37 Al-Hilli, *op. cit.* p. 102.
38 Badran, *op. cit.* p. 82.
39 *Ibid.* p. 85.
40 *Ibid.*
41 *Ibid.* p. 86.
42 Al-Hilli, *op. cit.* p. 96.
43 *Ibid.* p. 101.

and the method to put it into effect forthwith without any need to an order by the trying judge. Any person who objects to access or the method thereof shall refer to the court. Any non-compliance with the judge's order shall render the offender liable to the sanctions of Article 482 of the Penal Code."[44]

Art. 66 Tunisian:

"If the child is under the care of one parent, the other parent shall not be prevented from visiting and supervising it. The said other parent shall incur the expenses of the child travelling to visit her or him if she or he asks for such a visit."

Art. 111 Moroccan:

"If the child is in the custody of one parent, the other shall not be prevented from seeing it and following its conditions. If the other parent asks for the child to be taken to visit him or her, this request shall be granted for once a week at least unless the judge rules otherwise in the interests of the child."

Under Article 20 of the Egyptian Act No. 25/1920 as amended by Act No. 100/1985, both parents, and, in their absence, grandparents have the right of access to the minor. If it is difficult to reach an amicable arrangement, the judge shall arrange for access, provided that it shall be at such a place as to spare the child any psychological stress.

The access order shall not be executed forcibly, but should the person entrusted with the custody of the minor refuse to carry out the order without a reasonable excuse, he (she) shall first be warned by the judge, and, on repeating the offence, the judge may issue an enforceable order of passing custody provisionally to the next in line for the right thereto, for a period set by the court.

Article 196 of the Kuwaiti Personal Status Law rules as follows:

(a) The right of access is confined exclusively to the parents and grandparents.
(b) The hadina shall not stop any such person from seeing the ward.
(c) In the event of such stopping, and on one party refusing to go to see the child at the other's place, the court shall order a regular time and a suitable place of access to the child where the rest of its kin may see it.

44 Article 482 of the Syrian Penal Code reads as follows: "The father, mother, or any other person who does not comply with a judge's order, by refusing or delaying to bring in a minor under 18 years of age, shall be liable to imprisonment for three months to two years and a fine of S.£100.00."

F. Duration of Custody

As previously stated, the Jaafaris rule that the mother's custody of the child shall continue for the duration of suckling for the male, and for the female till the age of seven, although some jurists make the duration of custody seven years for the boy and nine for the girl.[45] The latter view is held under Article 64 of the Lebanese Druze Personal Act.

However, these terms are made by the Jaafaris subject to no injury being suffered by the child as a result of being taken away from the mother. The father shall be compelled to take the child into his care if the mother refuses to keep it on or if its staying on with her is detrimental to it.[46]

The four Sunni schools differ on the ages when the female custody of the children should come to an end.

The Hanbalis do not distinguish between the boy and the girl. They hold that the duration of female custody for both of them shall run from birth till the seventh year of age at which the child shall be given the choice between either parent and its choice shall be respected.[47]

The Shafiis do not distinguish, to start with, between the boy and the girl during the female custody period, to which they set no definite term. It shall continue until the infant reaches discretion and is assumed capable of making a choice, which shall be observed, between the two parents. On reaching this stage, boy and girl part ways. If the boy chooses his mother, he shall stay with her for the night and spend the day time with his father, who shall then undertake his education. The girl who opts for her mother shall live with her day and night. Lots shall be drawn between the parents if the child opts for both. If it remains silent, it shall stay on with its mother.[48]

The Malikis rule that female custody for the boy shall continue from birth till he reaches puberty, and for the female until she gets married.[49] This ruling is enshrined in Article 102 of the Moroccan Personal Decree, which, under Article 109, while granting the father and other guardians of the ward the right to look after its education and guidance, rules that the ward shall spend the night with its hadina, and nowhere else, unless the judge orders otherwise in the interest of the ward. The same provision is repeated in the Tunisian Article 60. Kuwaiti Article 194, following the same trend, rules that female custody for the boy ends of his reaching puberty, and for the female, on her marriage and its consummation.

45 Al-Hilli, *op. cit.* p. 101.
46 *Ibid.*
47 Badran, *op. cit.* p. 87.
48 *Ibid.*
49 *Ibid.*

According to the Hanafis, female custody for both boys and girls alike starts from birth. It comes to an end on the boy reaching an age where he can achieve a degree of independence, becoming able to feed, clothe and cleanse himself. This age is set by some at seven, by others at nine years of age. However, the prevailing Hanafi opinion is that custody for the boy ends at seven years, whether or not the hadina is the mother.[50]

According to Muhammal bin Al Hassan, whether the hadina is the mother or grandmother or any other female, the custody for the girl ends with her reaching puberty, an age set by the Hanafis at 11 or 9 years which is the prevailing opinion. Other Hanafi jurists hold that the girl may stay in the custody of her mother or grandmother until the age of womanhood; but until the age of puberty if the hadina is another female.[51]

The relevant Articles in the modern Arab Personal Law are set out below in chronological order of their promulgation:

Syria.

Art. 146: "Custody shall come to an end for the boy on completing nine and for the girl on completing eleven years of age."

Tunisia.

Art. 67: "The ward shall live with the hadina until the age of seven years for the boy and nine for the girl, after which age the ward shall be handed over to its father if he so requests, unless the judge shall rule it fittest to keep the ward with the hadina."

Iraq.

Art. 57: ". . . (4) The father may supervise the conditions of living and education of the minor until it reaches the age of 10. The court may extend the custody of the minor until it completes 15, if the interest of the minor so requires on the strength of evidence submitted by specialised medical and grass-root committees, provided that the minor shall spend the night with its hadina. (5) On the ward completing 15 years of age, it shall the right to live with either parent it chooses, or with a relative, until it reaches 18 years of age, if the court finds such a choice sensible . . . (9) If the minor's father dies or loses his eligibility, the minor shall remain with his mother, if she still remains eligible, without any female or male relatives thereof having the right to dispute her custody until it reaches the age of majority."

Jordan.

Art. 161: "Custody entrusted to a female other than the mother shall end on the boy completing 9 and the girl 11 years of age."

50 Qadi Khan, *Al Fatawa Al Khaniyya*, Vol. I, pp. 423–424.
51 *Ibid.*

Art. 162: "Custody by the mother who devotes herself entirely to the care and education of her children shall run until they reach puberty."

Egypt.

Art. 20 of Act No. 25/1929 as amended by Act No. 100/1985: "The female's right to custody of the child shall come to an end on the boy reaching the age of 10 and the girl reaching the age of 12 years. The judge may grant females the custody of the boy who has reached 7 years of age until he is 9, and of the girl who has reached 9 years of age until she is 11, should their interests so require."

Algeria.

Art. 65: "Custody for the boy shall end on his reaching 10 years and for the girl on reaching marriage age. The judge may extend custody for the boy until he is 16 years old if the hadina is a mother and has not remarried. Provided always that decision on the termination of custody shall be subject to the ward's interests."

With the termination of female custody, a new phase begins: the guardianship of the person of the minor, which is its right and a duty of the guardian and cannot be renounced, subject to certain conditions which will be discussed in detail in a later chapter.

Chapter 10

Maintenance for Descendants, Ascendants and Collaterals

1. GENERAL

The general Sharia and legal rule is that, with the exception of the wife, whose maintenance is the duty of the husband regardless of her or his means, no person is capable of being maintained by another (Art. 154, Syria; 58, Iraqi; and 167, Jordanian). Even the minor shall only be entitled to maintenance by its father if it has no property (Egyptian Art. 18 *bis*, secondly, Act No. 25/1929 as amended by Act No. 100/1985).

We have already discussed in Chapter 5, maintenance as a lawful right of the wife under a valid contract, during the continuation and after the dissolution of marriage. In this chapter, we are going to deal with maintenance as the right of children, the fourth such right due to established parentage, and of other poor relations who are classified into two categories of kinship:

(a) Lineal kinship (Al Qaraba al-Amoudia) between ascendants and descendants, whether immediate, between the child and its parents, or intermediate, i.e. grandparents and grandchildren. Such kins are always within the prohibited degrees of marriage.

(b) Collateral kinship (Qarabat-ul-Hawashi), which may be within the prohibited degrees, like siblings and their descendants, uncles and aunts, or not within the prohibited degrees, like cousins.

Maintenance includes basically food, raiment and lodging. Tunisian Article 50 and Moroccan Article 127 add education and whatever is considered necessary according to custom. Jordanian Article 170 includes treatment fees. It shall be assessed according to the means of the maintainer (Art. 52, Tunisian), and after achieving self-sufficiency (Art. 128, Moroccan), and taking into account the cost of living (Art. 79, Algerian).

Maintenance of descendants and ascendants, unlike that of collaterals, shall be due without a court order. It shall run, for collaterals, from the date of legal action (Arts. 161, Syrian; 130, Moroccan, only for parents; 63, Iraqi; 175, Jordanian; and 80, Algerian). The Algerian Article allows the judge to order maintenance with retrospective effect not exceeding a year. For the children, the same Syrian Article 161 empowers the judge to order maintenance against the father as from four months at most prior to the legal action.

2. RELATIVES ELIGIBLE FOR MAINTENANCE

Islamic jurists and modern Arab personal laws are unanimous that maintenance is a right of the minors who have no property on their father and a right for the poor parents on their children who have means to provide it. However, they differ on the extent of this lineal kinship which establishes the right of maintenance. They differ even more on the entitlement to maintenance in respect of other, collateral relatives.

(a) The Malikis confine maintenance exclusively to immediate parents and children, quoting the Quranic verses "But if they (parents) strive with thee to make thee ascribe unto Me as partner that of which thou hast no knowledge, then obey them not. Consort with them kindly."[1] "Mothers shall suckle their children for two whole years for those who wish to complete the suckling. The duty of feeding and clothing nursing mothers in a seemly manner is upon the father of the child. No-one should be charged beyond his capacity."[2] and ". . . And (show) kindness to parents."[3] The Malikis argue that these Quranic texts must be taken at their face value to mean just the father, mother and child. They also cite the Prophet's Tradition, "Thou and thy property are thy father's", extending it to the mother by analogy.[4]

This Maliki doctrine is adopted by the Moroccan Law, Article 128, although it makes it a duty upon the prosperous to provide subsistence for the needy (Art. 132). Moreover, Article 131 rules that whoever makes a covenant to maintain another person, whether a minor or a major for a

1 Sura Luqman, XXXI, verse 15.
2 Sura Baqara, II, verse 233.
3 Sura Israa, XVII, verse 23.
4 Abu Zahra, *Personal Status*, p. 414.

specific period, shall be bound by his covenant, the judge determining according to custom the unspecified period.

(b) The Shafiis follow the Malikis in ruling the entitlement to maintenance solely of children and parents, quoting the same authorities. But they extend the denotation to include all the lineal kins, grandchildren, how-low-soever and grandparents how-high-soever on the grounds that they share the same inheritance provisions. They argue that two Quranic verses on inheritance apply equally to children and grandchildren "Allah chargeth you concerning your children: to the male the equivalent of the portion of two females" and to parents and grandparents "And to his parents a sixth of the inheritance if he has a son".[5]

This Shafii doctrine[6] is adopted in Tunisia and Algeria. Under the Tunisian Article 43, "Those entitled to maintenance on grounds of kinship are of two categories: the parents and the father's parents how-high-soever and the lineal children, how-low-soever." Algerian Article 77 reads as follows, "The maintenance of the ascendants shall be incumbent on the descendants and vice versa, according to means, needs and the degree of kinship in inheritance." Kuwaiti Article 200 reads "There shall be no maintenance to any relatives apart from ascendants, how-high-soever and descendants how-low-soever."

(c) The Hanbalis, adopting the enlarged Shafii denotation of ascendants and descendants, add to those entitled to maintenance, and those on whom it is incumbent, the presumptive heirs. These are the relations who would inherit from the person to whom or from whom maintenance is claimed if he were immediately to die, whether or not they are within a prohibited degree. They derive their position from the Quranic ruling ". . . And on the heir is incumbent the like of that"[7] following provisions on maintenance and from the general juristic rule, "Disadvantage is an obligation accompanying enjoyment." Since the entitlement to maintenance according to the Hanbalis is derived from the right to inheritance rather than to the kinship within a prohibited degree, they make it conditional on adherence to the same faith, which is an essential condition for inheritance.[8]

The modern laws of Syria, Iraq and Jordan follow this Hanbali doctrine, except that they do not stipulate the common faith in respect of ascendants or descendants, following the Hanafis instead.

(d) The Hanafis derive the right to maintenance for relations other than

5 Sura Nisaa, IV, verse 11.
6 Ash-Shafii, *AL UMM*, Vol. 5, p. 89.
7 Sura Baqara, II, verse 233.
8 Ibn ul Qayyim, *Zad ul Maad*, Vol. 3, p. 164.

ascendants how-low-soever and descendants how-high-soever from a prohibited degree of kinship, rather than from the right to inheritance as the Hanbalis do. They base their position on the Quranic verse "(Show) kindness unto parents and unto near kindred".[9] They interpret "near kindred" as those within a prohibited degree being the strongest blood kinship. They also quote a reading by Abdullah ibn Masud of the above cited verse of the Quran, ". . . And on the heir, *who is a cognate within a prohibited degree*, is incumbent the like of that" to which they accord a Tradition status, having been heard from the Prophet. Therefore, no son of a paternal uncle shall be eligible for maintenance although his right to inheritance is prior to that of a maternal uncle who can claim maintenance.[10]

This Hanafi interpretation is observed by the Egyptian courts, in the absence of any codified text on this subject.

Ibn Hazm Al-Zahiri holds that maintenance by the relatives shall be due for ascendants, descendants, brothers, sisters and wives in the first place, being all equal in terms of entitlement, followed by the cognates within a prohibited degree, and those from whom the would-be maintainer would inherit, if they are in need and earn no living.[11]

The Shia Ithna Asharis grant the right to maintenance to descendants, ascendants, and poor cognates who are presumptive heirs whether or not they are within a prohibited degree, provided that they adhere to a common faith except for the wife, ascendants and descendants.[12] This ruling is held under Article 80 of the Lebanese Druze Personal Act.

3. MAINTENANCE OF DESCENDANTS

Islamic jurists are unanimous that a child who has no property of its own is entitled to receive maintenance, in the first instance from his father, under the two authorities of the Quran "The duty of their feeding and clothing according to seemly custom is upon the father of the child"[13], and the Tradition of the Prophet who told a woman complaining to him of the parsimony of her husband, "Take of his property what suffices for you and your child according to fair custom."

However, this right is subject to two conditions:

A. that the child is in need, i.e. indigent and unable to earn a living; and
B. that the father has the means to provide maintenance from capital or

9 Sura Nisaa, IV, verse 36.
10 Badran, *Children's Rights*, pp. 104–105.
11 Ibn Hazm, *Al-Muhalla*, Vol. 11.
12 Al-Hilli, *Jaafari Personal Status Provisions*, p. 108.
13 Sura Baqara, II, verse 233.

income. These two conditions shall be dealt with more fully in the following paragraphs.

A. The Child in Need

Inability to earn a living can be a matter of age, and physical or mental condition.

According to Sunni and Shia Sharia, a boy with no property of his own shall lose his right to maintenance by his father on reaching the age at which he can earn a living, even before puberty, but shall retain that right if he cannot work due to an illness or handicap.

However, according to the Sunnis, the maintenance of a student shall continue after that stage, provided that the course of studies he pursues is religiously acceptable.[14]

The son who has reached majority shall also be entitled to maintenance by his father if the son is incapable of earning a living because of a chronic disease, a mental or a physical handicap and has no private means, or, according to both Sunni and Shia jurists, is of such a social status as to render it impossible to be employed to do a menial job.[15]

As for the daughter who has no property, the condition of her being in need is fulfilled by the very fact of her sex, even though she may have the ability to earn her own living, e.g. through sewing at home, which she cannot be obliged to do. The duty to maintain her shall pass to her husband once she marries.[16] However, if she later ceases to be maintained, for example, on divorce or beause of disobedience to her husband, her father shall be bound, once more, to maintain her.[17]

Here are the relevant Articles of the modern Arab Personal Law on this subject in chronological order:

Arts 67 and 68 Lebanese Druze Personal Act – 67:

> "Maintenance in its three categories shall be incumbent upon the father for his poor minor child, whether male or female, until the male reaches the age for earning a living and is capable thereto, and

14 A contemporary Arab jurist, Dr. A. R. As-Sabouni, commenting on Art. 221 of the UAE draft Personal Code, remarks that it makes the pursuit of a given course of studies subject to its suitability for the like of a student in order to qualify him for continued maintenance by his father. He argues that it needs further elucidation, as such a student may have a talent for singing or dancing, hardly a course apt for the building-up of a developing nation. (A. R. As-Sabouni, *Nizamul Usra* (Cairo, 9th ed.), pp. 233–234).

15 Abu Zahra, *On Marriage*, p. 415.

16 Abdullah, *Sharia Personal Status Provisions*, p. 630; Al-Hilli, *op. cit.* pp. 102–103.

17 Al-Abiani, *Commentary*, p. 349; Al-Hilli, *op. cit.* p. 104.

until the female marries": 68: "It is the duty of the father to provide maintenance for his poor adult son who is incapable of earning a living due to an incapacitating handicap and for his poor adult daughter unless she marries."

Art. 155 (Syria):

1. "If the child has no property, its maintenance shall be the duty of its father unless he is indigent, incapable of providing maintenance or earning a living due to a physical or mental handicap.
2. The children's maintenance shall continue until the female marries and until the boy reaches the age at which his likes earn a living."

Art. 46 (Tunisia):

"It is the duty of the father, how-high-soever, to provide maintenance for his minor children and those who are incapable of earning a living, how-low-soever. Maintenance of the female shall run until it becomes a duty on her husband, and for the male until he reaches 16 years of age and becomes capable of earning a living."

Art. 126 (Morocco):

"1. It is the duty of the father to provide maintenance for his minor children and those who are incapable of earning a living.
2. Maintenance for the female shall continue until it becomes a duty of her husband, and for the male until he reaches puberty and becomes of sound mind and capable of earning a living.
3. Unless he is a student following a course of studies, in which case his maintenance shall continue until he completes his course or reaches the age of twenty-one."

Art. 59 (Iraq):

"1. If the child has no property, its maintenance shall be incumbent upon its father unless he is indigent, incapable of providing maintenance or earning a living.
2. Children's maintenance shall continue until the female marries and the boy reaches the age at which his like earn a living, unless he is a student.
3. The adult son who is incapable of earning a living shall be deemed similar to the minor."

Art. 168 (Jordan):

"(a) If the child has no property, its maintenance shall be incumbent solely upon the father unless he is indigent and incapable of earning a living because of a physical or mental handicap.
(b) Children's maintenance shall continue until the female who is

not self-sufficient through her work or earnings marries and until the boy reaches the age at which his like can earn a living unless he is a student."

Art. 169:
"The father who has means and has to maintain his children shall also have to provide the costs for their education throughout their learning stages until the child obtains its first university degree, provided that the child shall be successful and be possessed of the capability to learn, due consideration being taken in all cases of the financial condition of the father and provided that maintenance shall be within sufficiency limits."

Art. 18 *bis*, (Egyptian Act No. 25/1929 as amended by Act 100/1985):
"If the minor has no property, its maintenance shall be incumbent on its father. The children's maintenance by the father shall continue until the girl marries or earns what is sufficient for her maintenance and until the son completes fifteen years of age and is capable of earning a suitable income. If he reaches that age while he is incapable of earning due to a a physical or mental handicap, or because of his pursuing a course of learning that is fit for his like and for his aptitude, or because of such an earning not being available, his maintenance by his father shall continue. The father is under the obligation to provide his children with a decent accommodation according to his means, and at a level that befits their like. The maintenance of the children by the father shall be due from the date he refuses to provide for them."

Art. 202 (Kuwait):
"The father who has means, how-high-soever, shall provide maintenance for his indigent child incapable of earning a living, how-low-soever, until it can do without it."

Art. 75 (Algeria):
"The maintenance of the child shall be a duty incumbent on the father, unless it has means. For the males it shall run until the age of majority and for the females until they marry. Maintenance shall go on if the child is incapable because of a mental or physical defect, or is a student and shall lapse once it becomes possible to earn a living."

A special case in this context is the daughter-in-law: According to both Sunni and Shia jurists, the father is under no obligation to provide maintenance for the wife of his impoverished son unless he guarantees it. However, he may be ordered to maintain her and all expenses he incurs shall be a debt to be repaid by his son when his condition improves.

This provision is enshrined in Article 74 of the Lebanese Druze Personal Act and Article 157 of the Syrian Personal Law.

B. Capability to the Father to Provide Maintenance

This is the second condition for the children to be entitled to maintenance by the father. As previously stated the father who is possessed of sufficient means or is capable of earning a living shall be solely liable for the maintenance of his needy children.

If the father is impoverished, but can earn a living, he shall be ordered to do so, under pain of imprisonment if he refuses. If he cannot earn enough for himself and his children, or if no livelihood is available, the obligation of the children's maintenance shall pass to the person next to the father. Here Shias and Sunnis part ways.

The Shias hold that this liability shall be upon the father's father, failing which, upon the latter's father and so on how-high-soever, then to the children's mother, then to her father and mother and so on. All maintenance so paid cannot be claimed back from the father when his financial conditions improve.[18]

According to the Sunnis, this obligation passes to the mother if she has means, otherwise to the father's father whose duty it is to provide maintenance to his son, and likewise to his grandchildren. In both cases, the maintenance so paid shall be a debt repayable by the father when he can afford it.[19]

But if the father is incapable of earning a living due to a chronic illness, paralysis or a handicap, he shall be released from the obligation to maintain his children as if he were dead. The children's maintenance shall then be incumbent upon the nearest relatives without being a repayable debt.[20] The Shias rule that the order of maintaining relatives shall be the same as in the case of the impoverished father.[21]

The Sunnis set a different order for the obligation to maintain the children whose father is dead. Relatives are either ascendants, how-high-soever, or collateral. They also may or may not be presumptive heirs. There are three possible contingencies: (i) that all the relatives are ancestors; (ii) that some are ascendants and others are collateral; (iii) that they are all collateral.

(i) In the first contingency, four cases are possible: (a) that some are and some are not presumptive heirs, but they are all equal in nearness. Here it is upon the presumptive heir that maintenance shall be incumbent, e.g. the father's father rather than the mother's father; (b) the same case but not equal in nearness: here maintenance shall

18 Al-Hilli, *op. cit.* p. 103.
19 Al-Albiani, *op. cit.* p. 344.
20 *Ibid.*
21 Al-Hilli, *loc. cit.*

be incumbent upon the nearest regardless of the right to inheritance, e.g. upon the mother rather than her father, and upon the mother's father, who does not inherit rather than the father's father who does: (c) and (d) that they are all presumptive heirs but vary in the degree of nearness: here maintenance for the children shall be shared in proportion to the presumptive inheritance, e.g. a mother's mother and a father's mother shall bear maintenance equally as they are equal in nearness and in inheritance share; a mother shall contribute one third and a father's father two thirds of the maintenance according to their shares, although they are different in nearness to the child.

(ii) In the second contingency, two cases are possible: (a) that some are presumptive heirs and others are not; here maintenance shall be incumbent upon the ascendants regardless of the right to inheritance, e.g. a father's father shall be liable for maintenance rather than a full brother, and a mother's father, who does not inherit rather than a full brother who does; (b) that both ascendants and collateral relatives are presumptive heirs; here they shall be liable for the maintenance of the child according to their inheritance shares, e.g. a mother shall be liable for one third and a full brother for two thirds.

(iii) In the third contingency, all the collaterals shall contribute to the maintenance in the proportion of their inheritance shares.[22]

Here are the relevant clauses in the modern legislations:

The Lebanese Druze Personal Act

"69. The maintenance of the child shall be the duty of the father exclusively, unless he is insolvent and unable to earn a living, in which case he shall be deemed like the dead and the obligation shall pass on to the person upon whom the maintenance of the child is incumbent in the event of the non-existence of the father.

"70. The obligation of the maintenance of the child in the event of the father being insolvent shall pass to the mother before any other relative. If both parents are insolvent and have children who are entitled to maintenance, it shall be ordered against the nearest relative if he has means and shall be compelled to render it. Maintenance paid by a relative shall be a debt repayable by the father once his condition improves, whether the maintainer is a mother, a grandfather or any other.

"71. If the minor's father is deceased and it has ascendants who have means, if some of them are (presumptive) heirs and others are not, but are all equal in nearness, the (presumptive) heir shall be

22 Al-Abiani, *op. cit.* pp. 345–347.

committed to the maintenance of the minor; if they vary in nearness, the nearest shall be ordered to provide maintenance; if all the ascendants are (presumptive) heirs, they shall share the obligation to maintain the minor in the proportion of their inheritance rights.

"72. If some of the relatives of the poor child whose father is dead are ascendants and others are collateral and if one category are (presumptive) heirs and the others are not, the ascendant rather than the collateral shall be ordered to pay maintenance whether or not he is a (presumptive) heir; but if both ascendants and collaterals are (presumptive) heirs, maintenance shall be ordered against them in the proportion of their inheritance rights."

Syria Art. 156:

"(1) If the father is unable to provide maintenance and not incapable of earning a living the maintenance of the child shall be ordered against the person upon whom it is incumbent in the event of the non-existence of the father.

(2) Such a maintenance shall be a debt for the maintainer on the father to be repaid by him when his condition improves."

Tunisia Art. 47:

"In the event of the father's indigency, the mother's obligation shall precede that of the grandfather to maintain her children."

Morocco Art. 129:

"If the father is incapable of providing maintenance for his children and the mother has means, their maintenance shall be incumbent upon her."

Iraq Art. 60:

"(1) If the father is unable to provide maintenance the maintenance of the child shall be ordered against the person upon whom it is incumbent in the event of the non-existence of the father.

(2) Such a maintenance shall be a debt for the maintainer to be repaid by the father if his condition improves."

Jordan Art. 170:

"(2) If the father is indigent and unable to provide the physician's fees, treatment or the cost of education and the mother has means and can afford all that, she shall be compelled to pay such expenses which shall be a debt she can claim back from the father at better times. The same applies if the husband is away and no maintenance can be received from him.

(3) If both father and mother are indigent the person upon whom maintenance is incumbent if the father were not existent shall be

liable for the maintenance for treatment or education, to be repaid by the father to the maintainer at better times."

Art. 171:

"If the father is indigent, capable of earning a living and his earnings just suffice for his needs, or if he cannot find a job, the obligation to maintain the child shall pass to the person upon whom maintenance would be incumbent if the father were not existent, such maintenance being a debt for the maintainer on the father to be repaid in better times."

Algeria Art. 76:

"In the event of the father being incapable (of providing maintenance) the children's maintenance shall be incumbent upon the mother if she has means to provide it."

Kuwait Art. 202:

"The father who has means, how-high-soever, shall provide maintenance for his destitute child who is incapable of earning a living, how-low-soever, until it can do without it."

Art. 203:

"(a) If the father is insolvent and the mother has means, the maintenance of her child shall be incumbent upon her, and shall be a debt on the father repayable if his circumstances improve; the same applies if the husband is absent and no maintenance can be exacted from him.

(b) If both father and mother are indigent, the maintenance shall be incumbent on the one whose duty it would be to provide maintenance had it not been for the parents, and shall be a debt on the father to be claimed back from him when his circumstances improve."

4. MAINTENANCE OF THE ASCENDANTS

Sunni and Shia jurists are unanimous that it shall be a duty on the child who has means, whether a minor or a major and whether a male or a female to provide maintenance for his poor parents, grandfathers or grandmothers, whether they are Muslim or Kitabi and whether they are capable or incapable of earning a living, this being its duty unshared by anybody else.

If the father suffers from a handicap or is afflicted by a severe illness that makes him in need of a wife to look after him or to a servant to help him, maintenance of such a wife or a servant shall be incumbent on the child who has means. However, the child shall be responsible for the maintenance of only one step-mother if there are more than one.[23]

The maintenance of a needy woman married to a person other than the child's father shall be incumbent upon her husband not upon the child, who shall nevertheless be ordered, if it has means, to maintain her, such a maintenance being deemed a debt against her husband who is indigent or absent, to be repaid on the improvement of his condition or on his return.[24]

A poor son shall not be liable for the maintenance of his poor father unless the son is earning and the father is handicapped and cannot earn a living. In the latter case, the father shall share the son's livelihood as a matter of religious piety. The needy mother shall be deemed like the handicapped father, even if she suffers no handicap. The poor son who supports dependants shall make his needy parents join them and support the whole lot without being obliged to support his parents separately.[25]

The above provisions are adopted, almost verbatim, in Articles 75, 76 and 77 of the Lebanese Druze Personal Law 1948. Here are the relevant Articles from the other modern legislations:

Syria Art. 158:

> "It is the duty of the child who has means, whether male or female, a minor or a major, to provide maintenance for its poor parents, even if they are able to earn a living, unless the father shows himself as insisting on a preference for unemployment over any job that is worthy of his likes, out of sluggishness or obstinacy."

Tunisia Art 44:

> "It is the duty of the child or children who have means to provide maintenance for the poor father and mother and paternal grandfathers and grandmothers."

Art. 45:

> "If there are many children, the obligation of maintenance (of the parents) shall be shared in the proportion of their means, not according to their number nor to their inheritance rights."

Morocco Art. 125:

> "Maintenance of parents by the children, if they are more than one, shall be shared according to the children's means, not their inheritance rights."

23 *Ibid.* p. 352; Al-Hilli, *op. cit.* p. 106.
24 Al-Hilli, *loc. cit.*; Al-Abiani, *op. cit.* p. 353.
25 Al-Abiani, *op. cit.* pp. 353–354; Al-Hilli, *op. cit.* pp. 106–107.

Art. 128:

"No man shall be liable to provide maintenance for his parents and children until he has secured sufficient maintenance for himself."

Iraq Art. 61:

"It is the duty of a child who has means, whether a minor or a major, to provide maintenance for his two poor parents even if they are able to earn a living, unless the father shows his insistence to opt for unemployment."

Jordan Art. 172:

"(a) It is the duty of the child who has means, be it a male or a female, a minor or a major, to provide maintenance for his two poor parents, even if they are able to earn a living;
(b) If the son is poor but can earn a living, he shall be compelled to provide maintenance for his two poor parents."

Algeria Art. 77:

"The maintenance of the ascendants shall be incumbent on the descendants and vice versa according to means, need and degree of kinship in inheritance."

Kuwait Art. 201:

"The child who has means, be it male or female, shall have incumbent on it the maintenance of its poor parents, grandfathers and grandmothers, even if they profess a different faith or can earn a living. If there are many children, they shall contribute in proportion to their means."

5. MAINTENANCE OF OTHER RELATIVES

In Section 2 above, we discussed the various opinions of Sharia Schools on the relatives, other than ascendants and descendants, that are eligible for maintenance by their relatives. In Section 4 we discussed the maintenance obligation of collateral relatives for children whose father is incapacitated or dead.

Before quoting the relevant provisions in modern Arab Personal Laws, it must be pointed out again that the Laws of Tunisia and Algeria, adopting the Shafii doctrine, enlarge the mutual rights of maintenance to encompass ascendants and descendants how-high or how-low-soever. The Moroccan Law, following the Maliki school, limits such mutual rights to the immediate parents and children. However, it rules under Article 131 that: "Whoever undertakes to provide maintenance for another person, who may be a minor or an adult for a limited period shall have to honour his commitment. If the period is not limited, the judge shall rely on custom to define it." In a similar vein, Tunisian Article 49 reads as follows: "Whoever undertakes to provide maintenance from another person whether a major or a minor for a limited period shall be bound by his commitment. If the period is not limited *per se* his word for it shall be accepted."

Moroccan Article 132 also rules "The sustenance of the needy is a duty upon him who has excess."

The Articles dealing with the maintenance of collateral relations in other Arab modern personal laws are now quoted:

The Lebanese Druze Personal Act
Art. 80:

"The maintenance of every poor cognate in a prohibited degree shall be the duty of every presumptive heir among his relations who have means even if they are minor, in the proportion of their inheritance rights from him."

Syria Art. 159:

"The maintenance of every indigent relative who is unable to earn a living because of a physical or mental handicap shall be the duty of the presumptive heirs among his relatives who have means according to their respective inheritance shares."

Art. 160:

"No maintenance shall be due in the event of difference of religion except for ascendants and descendants."

Art. 161:

"The maintenance for relatives shall be ordered from the date of the court action. The judge may order maintenance for the children against their father to cover a period prior to the legal action provided that it shall not exceed four months."

Iraq Art. 62:

"The maintenance of every indigent relative who is unable to earn a living shall be the duty of the presumptive heirs among his relatives who have means according to their respective inheritance shares."

Art. 63:

"The maintenance for relatives shall be ordered by the court from the date of the court application."

Jordan Art. 173:

"The maintenance of the indigent minors and of every indigent adult who is unable to earn a living because of a physical or mental handicap shall be the duty of the presumptive heirs among their relatives who have means according to their inheritance shares. If the presumptive heir is indigent, maintenance duty shall pass to the next in the order of inheritance to be repaid by the first presumptive heir when he has means."

Art. 174:

"In the event of a dispute over the state of having or not having means, the evidence of means shall prevail except in the case of purported contingent destitution, when the evidence of the purporting person shall prevail."

Art. 175: same as Iraqi Art. 63.

It is obvious from the above that according to Shia and modern legislations there are the following differences between the maintenance for the wife, the lineal and the collateral relatives:

(i) Only the wife is entitled to maintenance by the husband, regardless of her means or his financial conditions. Every other kin, whether lineal or collateral, shall not have the right to maintenance unless he (or she) is needy and the maintainer has means and earns more than his immediate needs.

(ii) Adherence to a common faith is not a condition of eligibility for maintenance in the case of the wife, ascendants or descendants, but is an essential condition for the collaterals' right to maintenance, as it is based on possible inheritance which cannot occur between persons of different religions.

(iii) The wife shall be entitled to maintenance by her husband from the date of the valid marriage subject to the conditions set out above in the relevent chapter. For ascendants and descendants it may start with retrospective effect before the date of a court application. For collaterals it begins from the date of the legal action.

Chapter 11

Guardianship

1. DEFINITION

Djurdjani in his *Tarifat* gives the following definition of Guardianship (*wilaya* or *walaya*): "The carrying through of a decision affecting a third person whether the latter wishes or not."[1]

Guardianship may be of persons or property. The guardian of a person may or may not be the same as the guardian of property. It is mainly a duty incumbent on a person on the grounds of kinship, by testament or by court order towards another person of imperfect or no legal capacity. There are three grounds under the Sharia for being placed under guardianship: minority, insanity, and, within limits, the state of being female.

A special form, namely marriage guardianship, has been dealt with in Chapter 3, 3.C. The earliest form of guardianship of the person, custody of the child, forms the subject matter of Chapter 9, 2.B. This present chapter deals in more detail with the remaining provisions of guardianship of the person and the whole subject of guardianship of property.

Apart from the classical references of Islamic jurisprudence, guardianship of the person and of property is treated in the Personal Status Acts of the Lebanese Druzes, Syria, Tunisia, Morocco and Algeria. The Kuwaiti Personal Status Law devotes a chapter (Articles 208 to 212 inclusive) to the Guardianship of the Person, connecting it with the child custody. Guardianship of the Property is left out, and therefore the authoritative Maliki opinion shall prevail (Art. 343). The Jordanian Personal Status Law does not mention guardianship of property, and deals with guardianship of the person only in the context of the custody of the child. Therefore recourse must be had to the authoritative Hanafi opinion on this subject pursuant to the general Article 183 of the said Act.

1 Djurdjani, *Tarifat*, p. 275.

In Egypt, Decree No. 118/1952 rules on grounds for the dismissal of the guardian of the person, while Decree No. 11/1952 deals fully with the guardianship of property. Articles quoted in the following paragraphs refer to the said Acts.

2. CATEGORIES OF GUARDIANS

Guardians fall into three main categories according to the grounds of their guardianship and their relationship to the ward:

A. The Natural Guardian (*al waley*)

Under the Moroccan Law (Art. 148), and the Lebanese Druze Law (Art. 81), the father is the natural guardian of the child. Tunisian Article 154, as amended under Act No. 7/1981 rules that the minor's natural guardian is the father, or mother in the event of the father's death or loss of legal capacity. A testamentary guardian appointed by the father does not take over unless the mother has died or lost her legal capacity. On the death or loss of legal capacity of both parents, without the minor having any testamentary guardian, the judge shall appoint a guardian. Under Article 155, amended likewise, those guardians shall not lose their guardianship without court order on legal grounds. Shia doctrine rules that the natural guardian is the father and the grandfather jointly and severally.[2] Under the Sharia, and Article 1 of the Egyptian Act No. 119/1952, it is the father, then the valid grandfather. In all these cases, the natural guardian is of the person and the property of the minor. The Syrian Article 170 distinguishes between the two: under paragraph 1, the father, then the agnate valid grandfather, shall have the obligation of the guardianship of both the person and the property of the minor; under paragraph 2, other relatives in the order of inheritance shall have guardianship of the minor's person, but not its property. Kuwaiti Article 211 simply requires of the waley to be trustworthy and capable to look after the minor's interests, and professing the same faith (paragraph a); on losing any such requirement he shall lose his guardianship (paragraph b).

The waley shall be removed if he is deemed missing, or is jailed on being convicted of a criminal offence for more than a year (Art. 21, Egyptian Act 119/1952). The Syrian Article 174 adds as further grounds for the removal of the waley the attachment of his property, and makes disqualification because of imprisonment subject to the condition that as such it would be detrimental to the minor's interests. Under Article 175, the court shall

2 Al-Hilli, *Jaafari Personal Status Provisions*, pp. 109–111.

appoint a special guardian should any conflict arise between the interest of the minor and the guardian. Kuwaiti Article 209, along similar lines, is more elaborate: (a) Guardianship of the person shall go to the father, then the agnate grandfather, then to an agnate by himself in the order of inheritance provided he is in a prohibited degree; (b) the court shall choose the fittest if there are various eligible candidates for guardianship; (c) in the absence of any eligible candidate, the court shall appoint a suitable guardian.

B. The Testamentary Guardian (*al wasey al-mukhtar*)

The father may appoint in a testament a guardian to look after his children, including those born after his death (and he may also revoke such an appointment). Immediately on the father's death, such a guardianship shall be submitted to the court for confirmation (Art. 151 of Moroccan Law). Article 28 of the Egyptian Act 119/1952 requires in addition that the appointment shall be confirmed in a formal deed or in an informal document with the authentication of the father's or al wasey al mukhtar's signature, or written in the father's handwriting and signed by him.

Articles 178 (Syrian), 27 (Egyptian) and 153 (Moroccan) set out the qualifications for a wasey who must be of good character (*adl*), fit to carry out his task, of full legal capacity and of the same religion as the minor. The same Egyptian and Syrian Articles and the Moroccan Article 154 exclude expressly as unfit to be a wasey the following categories:

(i) any person convicted of an immoral or dishonest offence;
(ii) any person declared bankrupt by the court until he is rehabilitated;
(iii) any person (or, in Syria and Egypt, any person or any ascendant, descendant, or spouse of that person) who is involved in either a legal dispute with the minor or indeed any family conflict which may endanger the minor's interest. The Egyptian and Syrian Articles add any person whom the father before his death, on the strength of a written document, barred from being appointed as a wasey.

C. The Curator (*al-qayyim*, or in Northern African Law, *al muqaddam*)

A guardian appointed by the court for the minor, born or conceived, who has no wasey (Moroccan Arts. 148 and 152) or for the insane, the idiots, the imbeciles or the prodigals (Syrian Art. 163). The same qualifications for the wasey shall apply to the curator.

Article 68 of the Egyptian Act 119/1952 sets the order to be followed for the eligibility of the curator as the adult son, failing which the father, failing which the grandfather, failing which, another person appointed by the court.

Both the Syrian Law, Articles 163/2 and 3) and 202–206 inclusive, and the Egyptian Act, Articles 74 to 79 inclusive, add another category of guardianship, namely the Judicial Agent (*al wakeel al qadaiee*), to be appointed by the court for the missing person to look after the property of a person who has gone missing without anyone knowing whether he is alive or dead.

In the following sections, we shall deal with guardianship of the person, legal capacity and interdiction, guardianship of property, and the provisions in respect of the missing person, in that order.

3. GUARDIANSHIP OF THE PERSON

Guardianship of the person of the infant has been dealt with in the Section on "Custody" (Chapter 9.2). The father, failing which the agnate grandfather, takes over from the mother or other hadina when the child reaches a certain age. In fact, their guardianship can be exercised even during the female's hadana. It is defined under Article 170/3 of the Syrian Act No. 59/1953 as amended by Act No. 34/1975 to include "the authority to discipline, to provide medical care, to educate, to direct to a craft for a living, to give consent to marriage and all other matters related to the care of the person of the minor." Paragraph 4 of the same Article deems the failure by the guardian to see to the completion of the minor's education till the end of the compulsory stage as a sufficient reason for depriving him of the guardianship just as the hadina who objects to or shows negligence in her guardianship may be so deprived. The tasks of the guardian of the person, under Kuwaiti Article 210, include looking after the interests of the ward and seeing to his protection, education and suitable preparation for life's duties, without prejudice to the provisions of hadana.

The guardianship of the person of the minor ends on the boy reaching puberty unless he is insane, when it will continue by the same guardian even if he is not the guardian of property or the maintainer.

The guardianship of the person of the girl is either in respect of marriage, which has been dealt with in Chapter 3, 3.C. or in respect of care and protection. This latter guardianship comes to an end on the girl reaching the age at which she can fend for herself and is no longer in need of anybody to protect her from dangers that threaten her dignity and honour, or reaches a station in her life of education or career at which she can safeguard her interests without recourse to her guardian for help.

Such a guardianship is also deemed to terminate on marriage, with the husband providing the care and protection under the marriage relationship, rather than by way of guardianship of the person.[3]

However, guardianship of the person shall be resumed on the occurrence of any mental defect that renders the person in question of no or of defective legal capacity.

4. LEGAL CAPACITY (*al-ahliyyat*)

The ultimate ground for guardianship of whatever form is the state of inadequacy of the wards, being of partial or nil legal capacity, to care for their persons or manage their properties. Only full legal capacity can qualify a person to act independently of any guardian.

The Sharia recognizes two types of legal capacity: capacity of obligation (*ahliyyatul wujub*) which is the capacity to acquire rights and duties, and the capacity of execution (*ahhliyyatul adaa*), i.e. the capacity to contract, dispose and validly fulfil one's obligations.[4]

The capacity of obligation is established for every human being from the time of being an embryo, before actual birth, to the time of death and after, until the estate is divided and debts are repaid.[5] It covers, therefore, a longer span than the legal personality which, according to Arab modern codes of civil law, commences from the time a child is born alive and ends at death (Arts. 29/1, Egyptian; 31/1, Syrian; 34/1, Iraqi; 29/1, Libyan; 25, Algerian; and 30/1, Jordanian). However, the same Articles under paragraph 2, rule that the Law [of Personal Status] determines the right of a child *en ventre de sa mere*, i.e. part of the capacity of obligation.

It is the capacity of execution that constitutes the full legal capacity to enjoy civil rights and it is the inalienable right for every person who attains majority, being in possession of mental faculties and not under any legal disabilities (Arts. of the Civil Codes 44/1, Egyptian; 46/1, Syrian; 46/1, Iraqi; 44/1, Libyan; 40, Algerian; 43/1, Jordanian).

Although they all agree on the age of majority being an essential requirement to acquire legal capacity, they differ on that age. In Lebanon, Syria, Iraq and Jordan, it is 18 complete solar years; in Algeria, 19 years; in Tunisia, 20 years (Arts. 153 of Personal Status Mejelle); in Egypt, Libya, Kuwait and Morocco (Art. 137 of the Personal Status Decree) "21 years completed in accordance with the Gregorian Calendar."

The Sharia jurists did not set any specific age of majority, although they

3 Abu Zahra, *Guardianship of the Person*, pp. 46–67.
4 Abu Zahra, *Theory of Contract*, p. 272.
5 *Ibid.* p. 273.

set an age for puberty ranging from 15 years for the boy and the girl according to the bulk of jurists, 17 years maximum according to Malik, to 17 for the girl and 18 for the boy according to Abu Hanifa.[6] The Shias date puberty from the appearance of the signs, otherwise at the age of 15 years for the boy and 9 for the girl, again distinguishing between puberty and majority.[7]

The opposite of full legal capacity is nil legal capacity, which is the case of the person devoid of discretion owing to youth, feeble mindedness or insanity (Civil Code, Arts. 45/1, Egyptian; 47/1, Syrian; 96 and 108, Iraqi; 45/1, Libyan; 42, Algerian; 44/1, Jordanian; Personal Code, Arts. 156 and 163, Tunisian; 134, Morocco). Again, Arab legislators vary on the age of discretion, making it from seven (Egypt, Syria, Iraq, Libya, Kuwait and Jordan), under 12 (Morocco), under 13 (Tunisia) to under 16 (Algeria) all in Gregorian calendar years.

A half-way house between the nil and full legal capacity is partial legal capacity. This is the status of the person who has reached the age of discretion but has not attained majority, as well as a person who has attained his majority but is a wastrel or an imbecile. The age of discretion under the Sharia and the law is 7 years.

Persons of nil or partial legal capacity are governed, as the case may be, by the rules of the natural or legal guardianship or curatorship subject to the conditions and in accordance with the rules laid down by the Law (Civil Code, Arts. 47, Egypt; 49, Syria; 46/2, Iraq; 46, Jordan; 44, Algeria; Moroccan Personal Status Code, Art. 136). These provisions follow the Hanafi doctrine.[8]

Such persons shall have their dispositions in the matter of their property restricted in the following manner:

(i) A person who is devoid of legal capacity, i.e. a minor devoid of discretion and the insane shall have all his legal dispositions deemed void (Civil Code, Arts. 110, Egypt; 111, Syria; 96, Iraq; 110, Libya; 117, Jordan; 87, Kuwait; Personal Status Code, Arts. 156 and 163, Tunisia; 139 and 146, Morocco; 82 and 85, Algeria).

(ii) A person of partial legal capacity, i.e. a minor possessing discretion, an imbecile or a wastrel, shall have his dispositions of property deemed valid if they are wholly to his advantage and void when wholly to his disadvantage.

His dispositions of property which may be, at the same time, profitable and detrimental, may be annulled if this is in his interests or ratified by the

6 *Ibid.* pp. 283–284.

7 Al-Hilli, *op. cit.* pp. 124–125.

8 Abu Zahra, *Theory of Contract*, pp. 300–301.

guardian of his property (Civil Code Arts. 111, Egypt; 112, Syria; 97, Iraq; 111, Libya; 118, Jordan; 99, Kuwait).

It follows that the person of partial legal capacity may accept gifts, being wholly advantageous, but cannot make donations, being wholly detrimental. As for other dispositions such as sale, purchase, bartering, letting, etc., which may be partly advantageous and partly detrimental to such a person, they shall be left to the guardian or curator at his discretion.

5. INTERDICTION (Hajr)

Interdiction denotes both the status and act of imposing legal restrictions on the capacity to dispose of property in such a way as to render the acts of the person placed under interdiction legally null and void. Its object is the verbal utterances of the interdicted person who shall therefore be liable for his unlawful deeds and responsible for making good, out of his own property, any damage he causes.

The persons that are liable to interdiction are those described in the previous Section (4) as possessing nil or only partial legal capacity. However, in addition thereto, Shia and some Sunni jurists urge the authorities to pronounce interdiction against the irresponsible Mufti who teaches the public reprehensible tricks, the ignorant physician who is a danger to his patients, and the bankrupt transport contractor who receives his payment in advance and deprives people of the performance of their *haj* or the like.[9]

The Sharia, followed by modern personal laws, distinguishes between several types of mental defectiveness: insanity, mental derangement, prodigality and imbecility.

The insane (*majnoon*) is afflicted with a mental illness which renders him incapable of sound judgment or rational behaviour, usually accompanied by a state of confusion and excitement. Insanity may be intrinsic when a person reaches puberty in the state of being insane, or transient if insanity occurs after puberty. It may be permanent or interim; under Islamic jurisprudence, insanity in general shall render the person afflicted interdicted without requiring a court ruling to that effect, and all his acts shall be without effect, even if authorized by the guardian. On restoration of sanity, the interdiction shall be removed without necessitating a court ruling, and all his acts shall be valid and effective.[10]

The mentally deranged (*maatooh*) by definition is a person suffering

9 Al-Hilli, *op. cit.* p. 123; Al-Zailaie, *Tabyeen*, Vol. 5, p. 193.
10 Abdullah, *Sharia Personal Status Provision*, pp. 660–661.

from a mental handicap which makes him mix sane and insane utterances.[11] Such a person may be either in possession or devoid of discretion, and his acts shall be treated in the same way as those of the minor possessing or lacking discretion respectively.

It must be stressed that the above Sharia provision is followed by the Civil Code of Iraq (Art. 94), Jordan (Art. 127/1), and Kuwait (Art. 85), whereby the minor, the insane and the mentally deranged may all be placed under interdiction without requiring a court decision. Nevertheless, under the Civil Codes of Egypt (Art. 113), Libya (Art. 113), Syria (Art. 114), and Tunisia (Personal Code Art. 161), Morocco (Personal Code Art. 145), the courts shall pronounce or lift interdictions on all persons suffering from insanity, mental derangement or imbecility and on prodigals in accordance with the rules and procedures prescribed by the law.

Under the latter Civil Codes, an act entered into by a person suffering from insanity or mental derangement after the registration of the sentence of interdiction is null. Before such a registration, such an act is null only if the state of insanity or derangement was a matter of common notoriety at the time the contract was entered into or if the other party had knowledge thereof (Arts. 114, Egyptian; 115, Syrian; 114, Libyan). Tunisian Personal Status Article 163 rules that the acts of the insane are unconditionally null, while the acts of the feebleminded are voidable before interdiction if his feeblemindedness was known before the act. According to Moroccan Personal Status Article 146, the acts of both the insane and the prodigal are null if they are entered into during the state of insanity or prodigality.

The prodigal (*safeeh*), such as the spendthrift, is a person who is unnecessarily wasteful or lavish, and lacks sound judgment while being of sound mind (Personal Status Art. 164, Tunisian; and 144, Moroccan). The Hanafis refuse to place the prodigal under interdiction which they consider de-humanizing, but the majority of jurists rule that he should be placed under interdiction in order to protect him and his interests. If the act or contract is liable to rescission, it can either be binding, in which case it can only be rescinded by mutual agreement, or non-binding, being subject to an option, in which case the prodigal may rescind it unilaterally.[12]

The imbecile (*dhul ghafla*) is a person who can easily be defrauded in property transactions due to his naiveté. The provisions in respect of the prodigal's acts shall apply in this case.[13] The Moroccan and Tunisian Personal Status Laws use the same word (safeeh) to denote both the prodigal and imbecile (Arts. 144 and 164, respectively).

11 Djurdjani, *op. cit.*
12 Abdullah, *op. cit.* pp. 666–667.
13 *Ibid.* p. 673.

The prodigal and the imbecile, under the Sharia, can only be placed under interdiction by an order of the court which shall also lift it. A legal disposition by them after the registration of the order shall be tantamount to that of a minor possessing discretion: before registration it shall only be void or voidable if unfair advantage has been taken of them or if there has been fraudulent collusion (Civil Code, Arts. 115, Egyptian; 116, Syrian; 109, Iraqi; 115, Libyan; 129, Jordan; 85, 99 and 101, Kuwait).

More explicitly, the Tunisian Personal Status, Art. 165 maintains that all acts entered into by the prodigal before the sentence of interdiction are valid, effective and irrevocable; after the sentence, their validity shall be subject to the ratification thereof by the guardian. Article 166 adds that the prodigal's declarations on financial matters shall be void.

However, the constitution of a waqf, or the execution of a will by a person placed under interdiction for prodigality or imbecility is valid if the interdicted person has been duly authorized by the court. Acts of management carried out by a person under interdiction for prodigality or imbecility, who has been authorized to take possession of his property, are valid within the limits provided by the law (Civil Code, Arts. 116, Egypt; 117, Syria; 116, Libya; 130, Jordan; 102/104, Kuwait). The law referred to is the series of Sharia provisions in respect of guardianship by the Waley, Wasey and Qayyim, codified, with some modification, in Book Four (Legal Capacity and Agentship) of the Syrian Personal Status Act, and in the Egyptian Decree No. 119/1952 on Guardianship of Property and in the Kuwaiti Civil Code Articles 85 to 109 inclusive.

6. GUARDIANSHIP OF PROPERTY

In addition to those persons interdicted due to their nil or partial legal capacity, guardianship of property is imposed upon the absent and missing persons whose exercise of their full legal capacities is virtually impossible. The powers of the guardians of property vary with their categories under the provisions of the Sharia and the law.

A. The Natural Guardians

The father's powers to administer the property of his child depend on his character. If he is known to be reliable, of sound business judgment, or even if nothing is known of him to his disadvantage, he shall have full capacity to dispose of his ward's property as if it was his own, save making a gift for no consideration as this constitutes a disposition that is wholly to the disadvantage of the ward.

A father who is not a spendthrift nor unreliable but is not endowed with sound business judgment shall have his disposition of the ward's property restricted subject to the condition of being to the ward's advantage.

But a father who is known to be unreliable, spendthrift and of poor business judgment shall exercise no guardianship of his ward's property. Indeed, he shall be himself subject to guardianship of his own property.

A general Sharia and Civil Code provision rules that no-one may contract with himself, in the name of the person he represents, either for his own benefit or that of a third party without the authority of his principal who, nevertheless, may ratify the contract. The Hanafis make an exception from this general provision for the father who may buy the minor's property for himself or sell his property to the minor, it being taken for granted that the reliable wise father shall have his ward's best interests at heart.

The valid (or agnate) grandfather is the equal to the father in all dispositions of the ward's property, according to the Shias and Muhammad Ash-Shaibani. Abu Hanifa and Abu Youssof confine the grandfather's powers over the property of the minor to those of the testamentary guardian.

These are the general Sharia rules on the natural guardian of the property of the minor. There are a number of modifications thereto in the modern Arab Laws.

The Tunisian and the Moroccan Personal Laws, Articles 155 and 149, respectively, make the natural guardianship of the minor's property the legal duty of the father solely. Algerian Article 87 makes it the legal duty of the father and on his death, of the mother. Moroccan Article 150 adds that the judge shall prevent the destitute father from taking possession of his child's property and to safeguard it shall appoint a supervisor to watch over the acts of the father.

Algerian Article 88 rules that the natural guardian shall carefully dispose of the minor's property and shall be liable therefore in accordance with the requirements of the public law. He shall have to obtain the court's authorization for:

(i) the sale, division, mortgage or a compromise arrangement of the real property;
(ii) the sale of movables of a particular interest;
(iii) the investment of the minor's property by way of giving or receiving loans, or buying a company's shares;
(iv) the letting of the minor's property for more than three years or for more than one year after the minor reaches the age of majority.

Syrian Article 172 makes guardianship of the minor's property the sole right and duty of the father and the agnate grandfather, from whom it shall not be withdrawn unless their dishonesty or poor management is proven. Neither of them may make a gift of any of the minor's property or usufructs, nor sell or mortgage its real property, without permission of the judge who must be convinced of the sound grounds thereto.

Article 110 (1) of the Kuwaiti Civil Code gives guardianship of the property of the minor to its father, then the testamentary guardian chosen by the father, then the paternal grandfather, then to the guardian appointed by the court with due observance of the provisions of Article 112. Under paragraph (2), the father and his father are forbidden to withdraw from guardianship without an acceptable excuse. Under Article 112 (1), a Kuwaiti minor whose guardianship of the property is not established in his father, testamentary guardian or grandfather, shall have that guardianship undertaken by the Administration of Minors' Interests, according to the law, unless the Government appoints another guardian (2). The court may, from time to time and at the request of any interested party, appoint another guardian instead of the Administration of Minors' Interests, if the minor benefits therefrom.

Articles 103 and 124 of the Iraqi and Jordanian Civil Codes respectively allow as valid, a disposition by the father or agnate grandfather of the minor's property if it is of the same value or only slightly less. If, however, they are known to be of poor management sense, the judge may restrict or cancel the guardianship.

The Egyptian Act No. 119/1952 introduces further restrictions and amendments to the Sharia provisions on guardianship of the property:

To start with, it drops the distinctions between the spendthrift, reliable and unreliable father, requiring only of the natural guardian (who is the father then the valid grandfather in the absence of a testamentary guardian, see Art. 1) that he should possess legal capacity to administer his own property (Art. 2). It excludes from the guardianship any gift made to the minor if stipulated by the donor (Art. 3). The natural guardians cannot, without the court's permission and in order to discharge a humanitarian or family duty, make a gift of any of the minor's property (Art. 5), dispose of the minor's immovables to his advantage or to that of his wife or their kin to the fourth degree (Art. 6), dispose of the immovables, goodwill or security of a value in excess of £E300 (Art. 7), give or receive loans on the minor's behalf, carry on with a business transferred to the minor (Art. 10), or accept a gift or a legacy to the minor encumbered with certain obligations (Art. 12). He cannot without permission and the supervision of the court, dispose of any inheritance to the minor if the propositus has so specified (Art. 8). He cannot mortgage the minor's immovables as a security for a debt on him (Art. 6). Nevertheless, these restrictions do not apply to any property given to the minor by way of gift, whether express or implicit, by the father (Art. 13).

Following the Hanafi rule, the father may enter into a contract on the minor's behalf to his or to a third party's advantage, unless otherwise provided by the law (Art. 14).

The Egyptian legislator adopts Muhammad Ash-Shaibani's opinion treating the valid grandfather in the same way as the father, save for the provision that the grandfather cannot, without the court's permission, dispose of the minor's property, conclude an arrangement with the creditors thereon, or forego or reduce security (Art. 15). Again, while the father is only liable for a gross mistake, the grandfather shall be liable in the same way as the testamentary guardian (Art. 24).

The waley shall compile a list of all the minor's property, failing which the court may rule that the said property is jeopardized (Art. 16), in which case the court may dismiss or reduce the powers of the waley (Art. 20).

The waley may receive maintenance for himself from the property of the minor if it is due on the latter and may give maintenance in the same way to those who are entitled thereto (Art. 17).

B. The Testamentary Guardian and the Curator

Generally speaking the testamentary guardian (al wasey) and the curator (qayyim) enjoy fewer powers than the waley.

Under the Sharia and the modern laws of Syria (Art. 176) and Algeria (Art. 92) the father or the grandfather may appoint a testamentary guardian. This right is confined to the father solely under the laws of Morocco (Art. 149). Egyptian Art. 28 gives that right to the father or a donor who bars the father from disposing of the gift.

Over and above the restrictions imposed on the father in respect of the property of his ward, the testamentary guardian and the curator cannot, without the court's permission, undertake the following: any act that involves a transfer or creates a real right; invest; liquidate or borrow the minor's property; let a real property of the minor for more than three years or for a period extending to a year after the minor reaches the age of majority; give maintenance to whom it is due from the minor's property without a conclusive court decision; meet obligations incumbent upon the estate or the minor without a final court decision; institute court actions unless there is a risk of an injury to or a loss of a right of the minor; withdraw court actions or waste the right to appeal against court decisions; or, spend money in respect of the marriage or education of the minor (Arts. 39, Egypt; 182, Syria; 158, Morocco).

The tasks to be performed by the wasey or the qayyim include depositing with the treasury or a bank appointed by the court, in the name of the minor, all the monies received and all valuable possessions such as securities and jewellery, from which nothing can be withdrawn without the court's permission. He shall submit an annual account duly documented of all dealings on behalf of the minor.

Jurists differ on the entitlement of such a guardian to fees, under the Quranic verse "Whoso is rich, let him abstain generously; and whoso is poor, let him take thereof according to decent custom" (Sura An-Nisa, IV, verse 6). Egyptian Article 46 rules that such guardianship shall be for no consideration unless the court, at the request of the guardian, orders fees for him or grants him some remuneration for a specific task. Syrian Article 187 follows suit adding that no fees may be ordered for a period prior to the application. Moroccan Article 157 (3) allows fees according to decent custom if the guardian applies therefor. Kuwaiti Article 144 (Civil Code) follows suit.

Guardianship both of the person and of property comes to an end on the ward reaching the age of majority unless the court orders the continuation thereof thereafter if the ward is insane or feeble-minded (Arts. 18, 47, Egyptian; 189/b, Syrian).

For the guardian, it ends on his resignation, loss of legal capacity, being dismissed or going missing (Arts. 47, Egyptian; 189/a–h inclusive, Syrian; 164, Moroccan; 82, Iraqi).

Guardianship of the property of a missing or absent person is invested in a general agent left by such a person to be confirmed by the court, or in a legal deputy appointed by the court (Arts. 74 and 75, Egyptian; 204, Syrian). In both cases, the agent shall exercise the same power as a wasey. The missing person is one about whose life or death there is uncertainty, or who is known to be alive without knowing his whereabouts (Art. 202, Syrian). An absent person is one who has been away from home for over a year (Art. 203, Syrian). "Missing" shall end on the return of the missing person, or his death in fact or *de juro* on reaching 80 years (according to Art. 205, Syrian). Absence, under Egyptian Article 76 comes to an end on the cause thereof being removed, on the death of the absentee or on a judgment being issued by the competent Personal Status Court declaring him dead.

Chapter 12

Inheritance

1. HISTORICAL BACKGROUND AND GENERAL RULES

Succession to the estate of the deceased "propositus" is governed by compulsory rules laid down in the Quran. These rules constitute the doctrine of *Faraiid*, that is, the Prescribed Portions, described by the Prophet as a major part of the discipline of law.[1] The power to make a legacy is limited to one third of the estate, the remaining two thirds to be distributed among heirs according to the rules of Faraiid.

Although the whole set of rules may seem to fit in admirably, no principle appears to the system and the rules have to be memorized without any guide or clue unless they are approached historically and related to their formation in their pre-Islamic customs. For instance, the first, and, in some respect, the most important, group of heirs, the sharers (*As-hab-ul-Furud*) includes, among others, the spouses, parents and uterine siblings, but the son is conspicuously excluded therefrom. This can only be understood against the background of the customary law of succession in the pre-Islamic society, the main characteristics of which could be summed up as follows:

(i) Females and cognates were excluded from inheritance. In certain cases women even constituted part of the estate. A stepson or brother took possession of a dead man's widow or widows along with his goods and chattels.[2] The Quran forbade this custom: "O ye who believe! It is not lawful for you forcibly to inherit women."[3]

Similarly, male minors who were unable to carry arms were deprived of any share in the estate. The tradition has it that some

1 Al-Bardisi, *Islamic Law of Inheritance and Wills*, p. 13.
2 Al-Ghandour, *Inheritance under Islam and the Law*, p. 3.
3 Sura Nisaa, IV, verse 19.

people disputed as much the Prophet's ruling to give a girl half of the estate of her father while she did not ride a horse or fight against the enemy as his ruling to give a boy a share of the inheritance while he was of no avail in wars.[4]

(ii) The nearest adult male agnate or agnates succeeded to the entire estate of the deceased. Male agnates who were equally distant to the propositus shared together the estate *per capita*.[5]

(iii) Descendants were preferred to ascendants, who in turn were preferred to collaterals.

(iv) The adopted son, even if his real father was known, had the same right to the estate as the real sons if he was able to carry arms.

(v) Mutual inheritance between two men was recognized through a contract of alliance. The famous formula was for one of them to say to the other: "My blood is your blood, my destruction is your destruction, you inherit me and I inherit you, you pursue my blood feud and I pursue yours."[6]

The Islamic law of inheritance has not entirely abolished the customary pre-Islamic law, but rather introduced radical changes to it. The doctrine of shares then becomes understandable once it is realized that the sharers consist of those who were not entitled to succeed under the customary law, in the circumstances in which they are granted the right to take their respective shares. Tyabji expresses succinctly the spirit of the Islamic innovations in the formula: "Unto her that hath not and unto the relations of her shall be given; and from him that hath, shall be taken a little (or may be the whole) of what he seemeth to retain."[7] It is almost the reverse of the famous verse of Luke: "For whosoever hath, to him shall be given; and whosoever hath not, from him shall be taken even that which he seemeth to have."[8]

These innovations were not promulgated at once but in stages and in answer to specific questions.

Tradition has it that the widow of Saad ibn-ur-Rabie came to the Prophet with her two daughters saying: "O Apostle of God, these are the two daughters of Saad ibn-ur-Rabie who was killed under your banner as a martyr in Uhud, and their agnate uncle has taken all their money, leaving them nothing. Nobody will marry them without money." To which the Prophet answered that God would decide. The verse of the sharers referred to below (An-Nisa, IV, verses 11–12) was revealed to the

4 Al-Ghandour, *op. cit.* p. 5.
5 *Ibid.* p. 3.
6 Madkoor, *Succession under the Islamic Jurisprudence*, p. 16.
7 F. B. Tyabji, *Muhammadan Law* (Bombay, 1940), pp. 826–827.
8 Luke, VII, 18.

Prophet who then instructed the uncle: "Give Saad's daughters two-thirds (of the estate), their mother one-eighth and the residue shall be yours."[9]

To start with, fraternization between the *Muhajireen* (migrants from Mecca) and the *Ansar* (the citizens of Medina) entitled each to inherit from the other. This provision was abrogated after the conquest of Mecca under the two Quranic verses: "And those who accept faith subsequently and left their homes and strove along with you, they are of you; but kindred by blood have prior rights against each other in the ordinance of God."[10]; and "Blood relations among each other have closer ties in the ordinance of God than (other) believers and Muhajireen."[11] Earlier, bonds of brotherhood were temporarily approved to establish the right of inheritance, under the Quranic ruling: "And unto each we have appointed heirs of that which parents and near kindred leave; and as for those with whom your right hands have made a covenant, give them their due."[12]

Later, inheritance through adoption was abrogated, as an inevitable consequence of the abolition of the whole institution of adoption, under the Quranic verses: "Nor hath he made those whom ye claim (to be your sons) your sons. This is but a saying of your mouths. But God sayeth the truth and showeth the way. Proclaim their real parentage. That will be more equitable in the sight of God. And if ye know not their fathers, then (call them) your brethren in the faith and your clients."[13]

The right of inheritance for the kindred was first established through the will, in the following Quranic verses: "It is prescribed for you, when one of you approacheth death, if he leave wealth, that he will bequeath unto parents and near relatives according to decent custom. This is due from God-fearing. And whoso changeth the bequest after hearing it, the sin thereof is only upon those who change it."[14] This ruling was the first parting from the customary law which denied women and children the right to inherit, as parents include both father and mother and near relatives comprise both children and adults.

The stage was now set for the final phase of legislation on inheritance, in the famous verses of Sura Nisaa. The principle covering females and males is laid down in verse 7: "Unto the men belongeth a share of that which parents and near kindred leave and unto the women a share of that which parents and near kindred leave, whether it be little or much – a

9 Abdul Latif, *Inheritance under the Islamic Sharia*, p. 22.
10 Sura Anfal, VIII, verse 75.
11 Sura Ahzab, XXXIII, verse 6.
12 Sura Nisaa, IV, verse 33.
13 Sura Ahzab, XXXIII, verses 4 and 5.
14 Sura Baqara, II, verses 180–181.

legal determinate share." Three verses later, the detailed distribution of the shares:

> "Allah chargeth you concerning (the provision for) your children: to the male the equivalent of the portion of two females, and if there be women more than two, then theirs is two-thirds of the inheritance, and if there be one (only) then the half. And to his parents a sixth share of the inheritance to each if he left children; and if he left no children and his parents are his heirs, then to his mother appertaineth the third; and if he have brethren, then to his mother appertaineth the sixth, after (the payment of) any legacy he may have bequeathed, or debt. Your parents or your children: Ye know not which of them is nearer unto you in usefulness. It is an injunction from Allah. Lo! Allah is All-Knowing, All-Wise.
>
> And unto you belongeth a half of that which your wives leave, if they have no child; but if they have a child then unto you the fourth of that which they leave, after (any payment of) any legacy they may have bequeathed, or debt. And unto them belongeth the fourth of that which ye leave if ye have no child, but if ye have a child then the eighth of that which ye leave (the payment of) after any legacy ye may have bequeathed, or debt. And if a man or a woman leave neither parent nor child, and he (or she) have a brother or a sister then to each of them twain the sixth, and if they be more than two, then they shall be sharers in the third, after (the payment of) any legacy that may have been bequeathed or debt not injuring. A commandment from Allah. Allah is All-Knowing, Most Forbearing."[15]

At the end of the same Sura, there is a provision on the collaterals:

> "They ask thee for a pronouncement. Say: God hath pronounced for you concerning those who leave no descendants or ascendants. If a man die childless and he have a sister, hers is half the heritage, and he would have inherited from her had she died childless. And if there be two sisters, then theirs are two-thirds of the heritage, and if they be brethren, men and women, unto the male is the equivalent of the share of two females."[16]

Tyabji explains the different Sunni and Shia interpretations of the Quranic enunciations on inheritance in the following manner: although

15 Sura Nisaa, IV, verses 11–12. The Quranic statement is so concise that it is necessary to add words between brackets, which are not part of the text, in order to make the meaning clear.

16 *Ibid.* verse 176.

the existence of a few common principles underlying the Quranic amendments to the pre-Islamic customary law is recognized by all, there has been much divergence of opinion as to what those principles were and what was implied in them. Taking the Hanafis to represent the Sunnis and the Ithna Ashari the Shia, he sums up the main differences between the two sects as follows:

> "I. The Hanafis allow the frame-work or principles of the pre-Islamic customs to stand: they develop or alter those rules in the specific manner mentioned in the Quran, and by the Prophet.
> II. The Shias deduce certain principles, which they hold to underlie the amendments expressed in the Quran, and fuse the principles so deduced with the principles underlying the pre-existing customary law, and thus raise up a completely altered set of principles and rules derived from them."[17]

In more detail, he enumerates the following general principles of the Hanafi distribution of the estate:

"(a) The nearest male agnate (or customary heir) is not disinherited, but his rights are liable to be affected by the rights (or interests in the estate) created in favour of the heirs newly entitled by Islam which are referred to below. The newly entitled heir is never remoter than the customary heir. He (or she) may therefore:
(i) either be related to the deceased in exactly the same mode as the customary heir in which case the newly entitled heir takes by way of inheritance half as much as the customary heir. (As the newly entitled heirs are generally females, in most instances the males take twice as much as females.)
(ii) or the newly entitled heir may be nearer than the customary heir, – in which case the estate is divided equally between the customary and the newly entitled heir.
(b) as regards the rights of the newly entitled heirs amongst themselves, – if the newly entitled heirs of the same class differ from each other in their sexes they take equally: the males do not take more than the females."[18]

The Shia interpretation of the law does away entirely with the priority of the agnates over the cognates and makes the estate devolve (subject to the rights of the husband or wife) upon the nearest blood relations, who divide

17 F. B. Tyabji, *op. cit.* pp. 825–826.
18 *Ibid.* pp. 827–28.

it amongst themselves *per stirpes*, allotting to females half the share allotted to males in each grade.[19]

2. LEGAL SOURCES

The Quranic enunciations quoted in the previous section are complemented by the Tradition of the Prophet, the consensus of the Prophet's Companions and the reasoned opinion of the early jurists. Some modern Arab states have promulgated laws of inheritance, based on the established Sharia rules without sticking to any one particular doctrine.

A. The Tradition of the Prophet

This deals with details of particular cases. The main rules:

(i) The Quran says: "after (the payment of) any legacy he (the deceased) may have bequeathed or debt." In a tradition narrated by Caliph Ali, the Prophet rules that debt should be paid before any legacy is considered, and that uterine kindred should have prior right to inherit over the consanguine.
(ii) "No Muslim shall inherit from a non-Muslim." More generally "No inheritance between two people of different religions." The Shias differ, allowing a Muslim to inherit from a non-Muslim.[20]
(iii) "No murderer shall inherit from his victim."
(iv) "Once a newly-born cries, it shall have the right to inherit."
(v) Zaid bin Thabet narrated that the Prophet ruled that of an estate left by a woman survived by a husband and a full sister, the husband should be given a half.
(vi) "A grandmother shall get one-sixth of the estate if there is no mother."
(vii) "The maternal uncle inherits from him who leaves no other heir."
(viii) "The offspring of fornication with a free woman or slave is deemed illegitimate and shall not inherit nor shall be inherited from."
(ix) "The son of imprecation (lian) shall be inherited from by his mother and her heirs thereafter."

B. The Consensus of the Prophet's Companions

This has been adopted in respect of the entitlement of the agnate grandfather in the absence of the father, the share of the son's daughter

19 *Ibid.* p. 829.
20 Al-Hilli, *Jaafari Provisions*, p. 145.

how-low-soever, of the son's son how-low-soever and of the consanguine sister.

C. The Reasoned Opinion of the Early Jurists

This has been observed in matters of the inheritance of the cognates, proportionate abatement (*aul*) return (*radd*), and on some questions of exclusion from inheritance (*hajb*).

D. Modern Arab Legislation in Chronological Order

Egypt. The Hanafi doctrine remained the inheritance law of the land until 1943 when Act No. 77/1943 was promulgated. This is mostly derived from the Hanafi School with some amendments from other schools, the most important of which are the return, under certain conditions, to the surviving spouse of the residue of the estate, the non-exclusion by the grandfather of brothers and sisters from inheritance, the order of priority among heirs and the sharing of the full brothers and sisters with the uterine in the estate.

Syria. The Syrian Legislative Decree No. 59/1953 on Personal Status includes Book 6 on Inheritance, in 8 Chapters and 42 Articles (260–301 inclusive) and is based on the Egyptian Law with some amendments.

Tunisia. The Personal Status Mejelle of 1956 contains Book 9 on Inheritance, in 8 Chapters and 68 Articles (85–152 inclusive), based mainly on the Maliki doctrine.

Morocco. Personal Status Degree No. 1-58-112 contains Book 6 on Succession in 9 Chapters and 73 Articles (225–297 inclusive) based on the Maliki doctrine.

Iraq. Until 1959, succession was governed by the respective Sunni and Jaafari Sharia Laws. An attempt was made to unify the succession provisions in the Personal Status Act No. 188/1959 which dealt with the will and inheritance under the same Chapter 8. Article 74 rules that the heirs and their shares would be subject to the provisions of Articles 1187–1199 of the Civil Code, in respect of the succession to the rights of disposition of state land. These provisions were derived from the Ottoman Laws and incorporate many of the Sharia rules on inheritance, but differed on two main themes:

(i) the grandchildren were given the right to inherit the share of their dead father in their paternal grandfather's estate to the exclusion of the great uncles, which is a Shia ruling;

(ii) males and females were given equal shares.

However, this Article was abrogated under Article 3 of Act No. 11/1963 which further added a whole new Chapter, 9, dealing exclusively with inheritance. Article 90 restores the Sharia provisions in respect of the distribution of shares as applied prior to the promulgation of Act No. 188/1959.

Jordan. The Personal Status (provisional) Act No. 61/1976 includes two detailed Articles (180 and 181) on the sharing of full and uterine siblings and on return. For all other issues on inheritance, the General Article 183 refers to the authoritative Hanafi opinion.

Algeria. The Family Act No. 84/1984 devotes a whole Book, III, to Inheritance, in 10 Chapters and 58 Articles (126–183 inclusive).

Kuwait. Act No. 51/1984 in the Matter of Personal Status, devotes a whole part, III, in 7 Books and 54 Articles (288–341 inclusive) to inheritance, adopting an eclectic approach.

3. COMPONENTS OF THE ESTATE

The Jurists of all Muslim Schools are unanimous that the inheritable estate comprises:

(i) real and movable property, whether in the deceased's actual acquisition or not, e.g. in the hands of a leaseholder or a usurper;

(ii) monies due to the deceased but left uncollected by him at the time of death, e.g. debts owing, revenues from pious foundations (waqf), blood-money, etc.;

(iii) rights *in rem*, not being monies *per se*, but apt to be assessed in or related to monies such as water rights, rights of way and rights of mortgage;

(iv) certain rights of rescission, i.e. in the case of a defect, the right of the buyer to cancel the sale contract (*khiyaru-l-ayb*), and the right of the buyer to choose from among several objects (*khiyarush-shart*).

There is no distinction in the Islamic law of inheritance between movable and immovable property in their being inheritable, except that under the Shia Law a childless widow shall not take any share in her deceased husband's land, but shall receive her share in the value of the trees and buildings standing on the land.[21] There is, however, controversy over the inheritability of a usufruct (*manfaa*) as contradistinct from the thing or dubstance (*ayn*), *res in commercio* (*mal*).

The Hanafis rule that a usufruct, not being a tangible, assessable substance, cannot be inherited, but the general consensus of the jurists other than the Hanafis is that usufruct is inheritable.[22] The Egyptian Civil Code on ownership rules that this object is a right as contradistinct from the thing, which is the subject of rights. Therefore the inheritance is established of usufruct, lease, patent rights, etc., all of which fulfil the essential elements of property, namely utility, assessability, and acquirability. Some purely personal rights are considered by the Hanafis not to be inheritable, but in some Islamic countries, such as Egypt and Tunisia, such rights are inheritable. One example is the right of acceptance of a will. Should the lagatee die after the testator, but before accepting the legacy, then the right of acceptance passes to his heirs. A further example is the right of pre-emption (*Shufaa*) i.e. the right of the nearest neighbour to acquire by compulsory purchase, in certain cases, immovable property in preference to all other persons.

4. CHARGES ON THE ESTATE

The Hanbalis, some Hanafis and the Shias maintain that the estate of the deceased should be applied successively in payment of:

(i) the funeral costs, including the death-bed charges and the burial expenses according to decent custom;[23]
(ii) the debts of the deceased, payable from the gross estate;
(iii) valid and effective legacies within one-third of the remainder;
(iv) the shares of the heirs from what is left. If there are no heirs, the net estate shall devolve on the Treasury.

This order is followed in Egypt (Art. 4), Syria (Art. 262/1), Iraq (Art. 87), Algeria (Art. 180), Iran (Art. 869), Kuwait (Art. 291) and Jordan (Art. 1093 of the Civil Code).[24]

On the other hand, the Malikis, Shafiis, Zahiris and the authoritative Hanafi opinion put the payment of the deceased's debts before the funeral

21 *Ibid.* p. 149.
22 Abdul Latif, *op. cit.* pp. 32–33.
23 The Egyptian legislator in fact goes beyond the Hanbalis and extends the funeral costs chargeable on the estate even to those whose maintenance was incumbent on him, if they had died shortly before him (Art. 4 of the Inheritance Act).
24 Under the legacy laws of Egypt, Syria, Morocco, Tunisia, Iraq, Jordan and Kuwait, the mandatory will takes precedence over the voluntary will. See Chap. 13 on Wills.

and interment expenses. This opinion is observed in the Sudan and in both Tunisia and Morocco, where Articles 87 and 218 respectively apply, being the Hanafi distinction between debts secured by a charge on the estate, and uncontested debts on the deceased, which are payable after the funeral costs.

A. Debts Equal to or Exceeding Assets of the Estate

In this case the assets are distributed among the creditors in proportion to their claims. Consequently, the creditors have the right to nullify any transactions such as sales, purchases or gifts, which were concluded by the deceased during his death-illness[25] if such transactions affect the value of the debts.

The executor and/or guardian appointed by the deceased before his death, or by the judge, should the deceased fail to nominate an executor or guardian, shall dispose of the estate to repay the debts and deal with the creditors.

The executor and/or guardian shall discharge the debts of the estate with funds derived from claims recovered, cash in hand, proceeds of the sale of movables, and, if the funds so obtained are insufficient, with the proceeds of the sale of immovable property of the estate (Civil Code, Arts. 893, Egypt; 854, Syria; 1104, Jordan).

B. Assets of Estate Exceeding Debts

If the estate exceeds the value of the debts the executor nominated by the deceased shall also act as a guardian and as an agent of such heirs as are minors or absent. He shall repay the debts in cash if available from the assets, or else shall sell any such part of the estate as is sufficient to repay the debts, even if there are majors among the heirs. He shall not sell any real property apart from what is absolutely necessary to repay the debts on the estate.

Should the deceased have failed to appoint an executor, the judge shall appoint an executor to administer the estate for the benefit of the minors

25 Death-illness (*marad-ul-maut*) is one which it is highly probable will end in death. Art. 1595 of the Mejelle which codifies the Hanafi Jurisprudence gives the following definition: "Death-illness is one where there is preponderance of apprehension of death, and which renders the patient incapable of attending to ordinary avocations, out-of-doors for the male and in-doors for the female. The patient would die in this state of affairs within a year. Should the illness linger on for a year, unchanged, the patient shall be deemed like a healthy person unless his condition gets worse and death follows before the lapse of one year, in which case the condition from the time of worsening to death shall be deemed a death-illness."

and pay the debts. This need will not arise should all the heirs be adults, in which case they themselves will settle with the creditors.

C. When there are no Debts

In this case the heirs shall be fully entitled to deal with the estate. An executor appointed by the deceased shall have more restricted powers with regard to a major than with regard to a minor. He shall collect the debts due to the estate, proceed to the partition of the inheritance, sell the movables for the absent major heirs to avoid the loss or destruction thereof, and execute the will if there is one. No judge in this case shall have the power to appoint an additional executor. Should any dispute arise between partners, they shall have recourse to the court to settle the dispute.

D. Order of Payment of Debts

The first debts due for payment are charges on the property or the purchase price of anything bought and unpaid for before death. These are followed by debts incurred while the deceased was suffering from the death-illness. Last come the debt arising from an acknowledgement made during the death-illness which is not considered a legacy and therefore is not restricted to one third of the estate. Valid legacies are deducted from the remaining assets within this limit.

The remainder shall be distributed among the heirs. It should be pointed out that the heirs have no right on the estate until all debts have been paid. But heirs can, if they so wish, pay all the debts due on the estate and thereby acquire the whole estate for themselves. In such a case, neither the creditors nor the judge can refuse to allow such a procedure. After the payment of debts and legacies, which may not exceed one third of the net estate, the heirs for their part may nullify any transactions as may affect their prescribed shares. Such transactions are usually unilaterally disadvantageous, e.g. a donation or a sale for less than the value, as they are regarded as a legacy if they are made during the death-illness and therefore are subject to nullification or approval by the heirs should they exceed the prescribed one third.

5. GROUNDS FOR INHERITANCE

Under the Sharia, there are three grounds for inheritance: marriage, consanguinity and clientage. Clientage (a form of protection) is of two categories; clientage of manumission (*Wala-ul-Itq*), i.e. the personal relationship between the patron and the client or the slave freed by him, both being called *mawla*, and clientage of oath of brotherhood (*Wala-ul-Muwalat*). The first category is held to be entitled to inherit by Maliki, Shafii and Hanbali jurists on the strength of the Prophet's Tradition: "There can be only clientage for him who manumits." In this case, only the patron, and, after him, his agnates, would inherit from his former slave. The Hanafis and the Shia Ithna-Ashari acknowledge the right of the second category to inheritance, quoting the Quranic verse: "And unto each We have appointed heirs of that which parents and near kindred leave; and as for those with whom your right hands have made a covenant, give them their due."[26] Other jurists dissent, arguing that this ruling has been abrogated by a later verse: "And blood-relations among each other have closer personal ties."[27] In practice both forms of clientage have little effect, although the first category is acknowledged in Article 7 of the Egyptian Inheritance Act. The (Shia) Irani Law omits all forms of clientage, even that of the absent Imam who is considered by the Ithna-Ashari the heir to him who leaves none.

The modern Personal Laws of Syria (Art. 263-1), Tunisia (Arts. 89, 90), Morocco (Art. 225), Iraq (Art. 86-b), and Algeria (Art. 126) confine grounds for inheritance to consanguinity and (valid) marriage.

Marriage under a valid contract is a ground for inheritance between spouses. The right of the wife to inherit cannot be frustrated by irrevocable divorce during the death-illness of the husband if he dies during the iddat. Conversely, the husband inherits if the wife has caused the dissolution of the marriage during her death-illness, and dies during the iddat. This rule is entwined in the Algerian Personal Act which orders mutual inheritance between spouses even if there was no consummation of marriage (Art. 130), no inheritance under a void marriage contract (Art. 131), and the inheritance by the survivor should either spouse die before the divorce decree is issued or death occur during the iddat of divorce (Art. 132).

Consanguinity is the blood relationship between the deceased and the heirs, including descendants, ascendants, siblings, uncles and aunts, etc. Their shares vary according to their closeness to the deceased and whether they are of the patriarchal or matriarchal lineage.

26 Sura Nisaa, IV, verse 33.
27 Sura Ahzab, XXXIII, verse 6.

6. CONDITIONS OF AND IMPEDIMENTS TO INHERITANCE

For the succession to the estate to take effect, two conditions should be fulfilled:

(i) Death of the succeeded propositus, whether in fact or by court decision in the case of the missing person of whom it is not known for sure whether he is alive or dead. The judge may base his decision on circumstantial, not necessarily conclusive, evidence. Islamic law does not recognize any interest expectant on the death of another; and until that death occurs, which gives birth to the right as heir of the person entitled thereto under the rules of succession, he possesses no right at all (Arts. 1, Egyptian; 260/1, Syrian; 85, Tunisian; 86-c/1, Iraqi; 127, Algerian; and 288, Kuwaiti).

(ii) The certainty that the heir has survived the deceased (Arts. 2, Egyptian; 260/2, Syrian; 85, Tunisian; 220, Moroccan; 86-c/2, Iraqi; 128, Algerian; and 289a, Kuwaiti). It follows:

(a) The missing person shall not inherit forthwith. But his share shall be set aside for him to collect if he is found to be alive. If he is deemed dead under a court ruling, that share shall be redistributed among the other heirs. The inheritance of the missing person will be dealt with in more detail in a separate Section of this chapter.

(b) If a man dies, leaving a pregnant wife, the life of the child in her womb is not established at the time of the death of the propositus, and therefore it shall not inherit immediately. But in view of the probability of its being born alive later, a provisional share for it shall be reserved until it is born and its exact share is known. If it is still-born, there shall be no inheritance. The inheritance of the unborn child is the subject of a separate Section of this chapter.

(c) If two or more persons who are competent to inherit from each other die without it being known for certain which has died first, they shall not inherit from each other. For the purpose of this provision, it is irrelevant whether they died simultaneously or at different times, in the same accident or not. Their respective estates shall be divided among their heirs who survive them at the time of the death of the propositus. This general Sharia provision is adopted in Article 3 (Egypt), 261 (Syria), 86 (Tunisia), 224 (Morocco), 129 (Algeria) and 290 (Kuwait).

Apart from the two conditions set out above, i.e. the actual or presumed death of the propositus and the sure survival of the heir, a third condition is the non-existence of any impediment to inheritance. The three conditions are summed up in the two Algerian Articles 127 and 128.

There are three main grounds for exclusion from succession: homicide; difference of religion; difference of domicile.

A. Homicide

Anyone who has caused the death of the deceased shall be excluded from succession, be he a murderer or an accomplice, or should he, by perjury, cause a death sentence to be passed and executed. (Complicity in murder shall include those pointing out the victim and those keeping watch during the murder.)

For homicide to be an impediment to inheritance, four conditions should be fulfilled:

(i) That it is deliberate. Therefore, homicide committed in retaliation or as a punishment laid down by the Quran (*hadd*) shall not exclude the murderer from inheritance.
(ii) That the murderer is criminally responsible. Therefore a minor under 15, an insane person, an imbecile or a person in a state of trance due, for example, to drugs, shall not be barred.
(iii) That the homicide is not an act of legitimate defence of life or property.
(iv) That there is no justification for homicide, e.g. in the case of a husband surprising his wife and her lover in the act of adultery and killing both or either of them.

While accidental homicide shall not bar the killer from inheritance, it shall, under Shia Law, exclude him from any share in the blood-money (i.e. an indemnity which may be claimed for the death) (*diya*), but not from the rest of the estate.[28] The same provision applies in the case of the minor and the insane, and is adopted in the Algerian Article 137. These provisions are held under Articles 5 (Egypt), 264-a (referring to 223) (Syria), 88 (Tunisia), 229 (Morocco), 292 (Kuwait), and Algerian Article 135/1 and 2 with paragraph 3 adding the person who has had prior knowledge of the murder or the planning thereof without reporting it to the competent authorities. Article 136 goes on to rule that any such person debarred from inheritance shall not exclude any other heir.

28 Al-Hilli, *op. cit.* p. 145.

B. Difference of Religion

Among Muslims: under Sunni Law, there shall be no inheritance by a non-Muslim of a Muslim and vice versa (Arts. 6, Egypt; 264, Syria; 228, Morocco; 293/a and b, Kuwait). Kuwaiti Article 294 rules that: (a) the apostate shall not inherit from anyone; (b) his property before and after apostasy shall devolve on his Muslim heirs on his death, otherwise on the public treasury; (c) an apostate who adopts the nationality of a non-Muslim State shall be deemed dead and the estate goes to Muslim heirs; (d) if he returns to Islam after adopting a non-Muslim State as his domicile, he shall recover the balance held by his heirs or the treasury. Algerian Article 138 rules that lian and apostasy debar from inheritance. Under Shia Law, a Muslim may inherit from a non-Muslim, or an apostate.[29]

Among non-Muslims: non-Muslims may inherit from one another even if they differ in religion (Kuwait, 293/b).

C. Difference of Domicile

Under the Sharia, difference of domicile does not bar inheritance among Muslims or among subjects of Muslim states, even if they are non-Muslims. But it shall bar inheritance between non-Muslims if one of them is subject to the laws of a non-Muslim state. Therefore, if a Christian dies in Egypt and has heirs living in England or in America, they shall not inherit from him because of the difference of domicile. However, the Egyptian Law of Inheritance, Article 6, restricts this impediment to one condition, namely that the law of the non-Muslim state bars foreigners from inheritance; otherwise, this impediment shall not apply. Therefore, if, for example, a member of the Jewish faith dies in Egypt, and his heirs are subjects of a foreign state which does not bar foreigners from inheritance, they will inherit from their Egyptian kin. The same provision is held in Article 264-c of the Syrian Personal Status Act, and Article 293/d of the Kuwaiti law.

So far the Sunnis and Shias follow fundamentally the same rules, except for some slight differences which have been pointed out. They part ways when it comes to the distribution of the estate among heirs. They differ so much over those who should inherit and, once they are specified, over what portions are due to each, that it will be best to consider them separately in the remaining Sections.

29 *Ibid.*

7. THE SUNNI LAW OF INHERITANCE

A. Introduction and General

There are three classes of heirs: sharers, residuaries, and distant kindred.

(i) Sharers are those who are entitled to a fixed share (*fard*) of the inheritance.
(ii) Residuaries are those who take no fixed share but succeed to the residue after the claims of the sharers are satisfied. If there are no sharers, the residuaries will succeed to the whole estate.
(iii) Distant kindred are those relations by blood who are neither sharers nor residuaries. If there are no sharers nor residuaries, the estate will be divided among such of the distant kindred as are entitled to succeed thereto.[30]

There are certain cases in which heirs are excluded, or have their shares reduced due to the existence of other heirs who themselves take no share, because they are excluded by nearer heirs. The following example may demonstrate the point at issue. A man dies leaving behind him his father, mother and two sisters. In this case the father will exclude the two sisters. The two sisters, though themselves excluded, will reduce the share of the mother from one-third to one-sixth, and the rest, being five-sixths, will go to the father as residuary. The same will be the result if there are two brothers, or one brother and one sister, instead of two sisters.

Total exclusion debars a person absolutely from succeeding to the estate. It arises, for example, where the heirs are the father's mother, mother's maternal grandmother and father. In such a case, the father's mother, being the nearer true grandmother, would completely exclude the mother's maternal grandmother, and the father's mother herself is excluded by the father. Thus the father will take the whole as residuary.

As to the doctrine of proportionate abatement (*aul*), if, on assigning their shares to the sharers, it is discovered that the total of shares exceeds the unity, the share of each sharer is to be proportionately reduced by diminishing the fractional shares to a common denominator, and increasing the denominator in order to make it equal to the sum of the numerators.

30 The Egyptian Law (Arts. 39, 40), following the Sharia, includes the manumitter, in the absence of distant kindred, followed by his agnates. Since this is only of academic interest, in view of the abolition of slavery, it has been left out altogether. The Tunisian Law drops the distant kindred, making the Treasury the heir of a deceased who leaves no sharers or residuaries (Art. 144).

Return (*rudd*) is the converse of proportionate abatement. In the case of return, the total of the shares is less than unity. In the rudd case, the shares undergo what may be called a rateable increase, while in the aul, it is a rateable decrease.

The doctrine of return applies if there is a residue left after satisfying the claims of sharers. In the absence of a residuary, the residue reverts to the sharers, apart from the spouses, in proportion to their shares.

B. Sharers

Sharers are those heirs who are entitled to a fixed share of the inheritance, and whose specific shares should be given in the first instance after payment of funeral charges, debts and legacies, before distributing the inheritance among the second class of heirs, i.e. residuaries. The sharers are 12 in number: husband, wife, father, mother, true grandfather how-high-soever,[31] true grandmother how-high-soever,[32] daughter, son's daughter how-low-soever, full sister, consanguine sister, uterine brother and uterine sister.

The sharers constitute the first and the most important group of heirs. Conspicuous by their absence from this group are the sons. The reason, as explained above, is that sharers consist entirely of those who were not entitled to succeed under pre-Islamic customary law, which excluded females and cognates, gave the nearest male agnates the entire estate of the deceased, and preferred descendants to ascendants, and the latter to collaterals.

We shall now deal with each of the 12 sharers who are entitled to a fixed share.

(i) The husband shall inherit half when there is no child or child of a son how-low-soever, and a quarter if there is.

(ii) The wife inherits a quarter when there is no child or child of a son how-low-soever, and one-eigth if there is. Two or more wives collectively inherit a quarter or one-eighth, which shall be divided equally among them.

The husband and wife cannot be utterly excluded from succession, although their share may be reduced as above. However, no spouse shall have a return if there is a residue, unless there is no residuary or a distant kindred.[33] The Hanafis and Hanbalis rule out any return to the spouse.[34]

31 A male ancestor between whom and the deceased no female intervenes.

32 A female ancestor between whom and the deceased no false grandfather intervenes. "False grandfather" means a male ancestor, between whom and the deceased a female intervenes.

33 Arts. 30, Egyptian; 288/2, Syrian; 167, Algerian; 318, Kuwaiti.

34 Abu Zahra, *On Estates and Inheritance*, pp. 202–203.

However, for the inheritance by either spouse to take effect, two conditions must be fulfilled:

(a) That the marriage contract is valid because there shall be no reciprocal inheritance under an irregular marriage contract.
(b) That the marriage stands *de facto* or is deemed so to stand on the death of a spouse, while the wife is still in her iddat of a revocable repudiation. Under Hanafi and Maliki (but not Shafii) Law, the wife is entitled to inherit if the irrevocable repudiation is made during the husband's death-illness, and the wife has not expressly or implicitly consented to the repudiation (talaq). This rule is adopted in the Egyptian, Syrian and Kuwaiti Laws of Personal Status.

Similarly, if the marriage is dissolved by an act proceeding from the wife during her death-illness, and then she dies during the iddat, the husband is entitled to inherit.

(iii) The father shall inherit, as a sharer, one-sixth when there is a child or child of a son how-low-soever. When there is no child or child of a son how-low-soever, the father inherits as a residuary. He inherits both as a sharer and a residuary when there are only daughters or son's daughters how-low-soever.

(iv) The mother shall inherit one-sixth (a) when there is a child or child of a son how-low-soever; or (b) when there are two or more brothers or sisters, or even one brother and one sister, whether full, consanguine or uterine. She shall inherit one-third when no child or child of a son how-low-soever exists, and no more than one brother or sister (if any); but if there is also a wife or husband and the father, then only one-third of what remains after deducting the wife's or husband's share.

(v) The true grandfather shall be excluded by the father and a nearer true grandfather. If there are no full or consanguine brothers or sisters, he shall inherit one-sixth as a sharer with a son or a son's son how-low-soever. He shall receive one-sixth as a sharer and again as a co-residuary with the daughter and a daughter of a son how-low-soever. He shall inherit solely as a residuary if there is no other heir.

When the deceased leaves full or consanguine brothers or sister, the Imam Abu Hanifa, following the opinion of some eminent Companions of the Prophet, including Abu Bakr, the first Patriarchal Caliph, rules that the true grandfather excludes the siblings. All the other three Imams and the two Hanafi Companions, following the opinion of Ali ibn Abi Talib, maintain that the siblings are not excluded, but again differ on the share of the true grandfather with them.

The Imam Malik, whose doctrine is followed in Tunisia, Morocco, Algeria and Kuwait, rules that the grandfather shall take the more advantageous to him of one-third of the estate, or as a co-residuary with the siblings if there is no sharer; if there is, then the better part of his entitlement as a co-residuary, one-sixth, or one-third of the residue. In the famous Akdari case, the total of his and the sister's shares are divided between them in the proportion of two to one. This provision of Tunisian Article 146 is further illustrated in the Moroccan and Algerian Articles 258 and 175 respectively: A woman dies leaving a husband, a mother, a full or consanguine sister and a true grandfather. The shares of the grandfather and the sister shall be added together, and then divided with the male taking twice as much as the female. With proportionate rebatement, the whole estate shall be divided by 27, the husband receiving nine, the mother six, the sister four and the grandfather eight parts.

Under the Egyptian Law (Art. 22), the true grandfather shall receive the more advantageous to him of the share of a brother as a co-residuary as a sharer (one-sixth) if there are brothers and sisters. If there are sisters who inherit as sharers, he shall get the more advantageous to him as a sharer (one-sixth) or as a co-residuary. This provision is also adopted under Syrian Article 279.

(vi) The true grandmother whether maternal or paternal is excluded by the mother according to all Islamic jurists, followed by all the modern legislators. They are almost unanimous, except the Hanbalis, that the paternal grandmother is excluded by the father or the grandfather through whom she is related to the deceased, a provision enshrined in Articles 25 (Egyptian), 283/1,2 (Syrian), 141 (Tunisian), 255 (Moroccan), 161 (Algerian), and 313/c (Kuwaiti). A nearer true grandmother shall exclude a further one. In the absence of any such exclusion the true grandmother shall inherit one-sixth, and two of the same degree shall share it.

(vii) The daughter shall inherit half if there is no son. If there are two or more daughters and no son, they shall together inherit two-thirds of the estate. If there is a son (or sons), the daughter (or daughters) become a co-residuary – taking half a son's share, after deduction of the portion of other sharers.

(viii) The son's daughter, how-low-soever, is excluded by a male descendant nearer to the deceased and by two daughters or daughters of a son nearer to the deceased unless she is made co-residuary with a son's son of the same or lower degree of nearness if she cannot inherit otherwise, in which case she shall get half of the share of a male. With one daughter or son's daughter nearer to the deceased, she gets one-sixth, to be shared if there are two or more in the same degree. If there is no daughter or son's daughter nearer to the deceased, one son's daughter shall receive one-half of the estate, two or more shall receive two-thirds.

(ix) The full sister is excluded from inheritance by a child, a child of a son how-low-soever, and the father. In the absence of a male residuary, one full sister shall get one-half, two or more shall share two-thirds. With the full brother she takes as a residuary, the brother taking a double portion. In default of a full brother and the other residuaries, the full sister shall take, and two or more shall share the residue after the shares taken by a daughter or daughters or a son's daughter or daughters how-low-soever.

(x) The consanguine sister shall be excluded from inheritance by the father, the son, the son's son how-low-soever, the full brother and the full sister if co-residuary with daughters, whether with or without a consanguine brother. She shall also be excluded by two full sisters unless there is a consanguine brother with whom she becomes a residuary. She gets, on her own, one half; with another like sister or more, they all share two-thirds. She shall take or share with like sister/s one-sixth if there is a full sister and no consanguine brother. With a consanguine brother or brothers with whom she becomes a residuary, they shall share the residue left of the estate after the other sharers receive their dues with the brother taking twice as much as the sister.

(xi) The uterine brother is excluded by any descending heir whether as a sharer or residuary, and any male ascendant entitled to inherit. If not so excluded, he gets one-sixth on his own, and shares one-third with brother/s or sister/s.

(xii) The uterine sister follows as for the uterine brother above.

The following table describes the sharers, their normal shares, the conditions under which these are inherited, and their variations.

C. Residuaries

The residuaries shall inherit the residue of the estate after the sharers take their allotted shares or shall inherit the whole estate if there are no sharers after payment of funeral expenses, debts and legacies. There are three groups of such relatives in the following order:

(1) The residuaries in their own right (*asaba bil nafs*)

These are all the male relatives between whom and the deceased no female intervenes. There are four categories of such relatives in the following order of priority:

(i) The son and the son's son how-low-soever.
(ii) The male ascendants of the deceased, that is, the father and the true grandfather, how-high-soever.

TABLE OF SHARERS – Sunni Law

Sharers	Normal share of: One	Normal share of: Two or more divided equally	Conditions for inheritance of normal share	Share as varied by special circumstances
Father	1/6		When there is a son or son of a son h.l.s.	The father inherits as a sharer and a residuary with a female descending heir and as a residuary in the absence of any descendant.
True Grandfather	1/6		When there is a son or son of a son h.l.s. and no father or nearer true grandfather.	With no father, the same as for father above. With full or consanguine brothers or sisters (a) according to Malik, the more advantageous of 1/3 or a brother's share in the absence of sharers, with a sharer the more advantageous of a brother's share, 1/6 or 1/3 of the residue, taking twice a full sister's share out of their shares total (b) Egyptian Law – the more advantageous of a brother's share of 1/6 or as a residuary with sisters inheriting as sharers.
Husband	1/4		As for father above.	1/2 when there is no child or child of a son h.l.s.
Wife (or Wives)	1/8	1/8	As for father above.	1/4 when there is no child or child of a son h.l.s.
Mother	1/6		As for father above, OR when there are two or more brothers or sisters, or one brother and one sister, whether full, consanguine or uterine.	1/3 when no child or child of a son h.l.s. and no more than one brother or sister (if any). When there is also a wife or husband as well as the father, only 1/3 of remainder after deducting the husband's or wife's share.
True Grandmother	1/6	1/6	When no mother and no nearer true grandmother either paternal or maternal.	Paternal true grandmother is entirely excluded by the father and a grandfather through whom she is related to the deceased.

Daughter	½	⅔	When there is no son.	She becomes a residuary with a son, taking half his share.
Son's Daughter h.l.s.	½	⅔	When there is no son, daughter, higher son's son, higher son's daughter or equal son's son.	No share at all with a higher son's son. No share with two daughters or two higher son's daughters, unless she becomes a residuary with an equal or inferior son's son when she gets half his share. ⅙ on her own share with like son's daughter, when there is one daughter or higher son's daughter if there is no male co-residuary.
Uterine Brother or Sister	⅙	⅓	When no child, child of a son h.l.s., father or true grandfather.	A male receives the same share as a female.
Full Sister	½	⅔	When no son, son of a son h.l.s., father or full brother.	No share at all with a male descendant h.l.s., or a father. Only the Hanafis make a true grandfather exclude her as well. She becomes a residuary with a full brother taking half the share of a male, sharing one third with uterine siblings, and a residuary by a female descendant, e.g. daughter or son's daughter h.l.s. if there is no full brother.
Consanguine Sister	½	⅔	When no son, son of a son h.l.s., father, full brother or sister or consanguine brother.	No share at all with the father, an inheriting male descendant h.l.s., a full brother or a full sister becoming residuary with daughters. No share when there are two full sisters unless there is a consanguine brother with whom she becomes a residuary and takes ½ his share. ⅙ as a sharer on her own or sharing it with like sister/s when there is one full sister and no consanguine brother. As a residuary with an inheriting female descendant.

(iii) The descendants of the father of the deceased, that is, full or consanguine brothers and their sons, how-low-soever.

(iv) The descendants of true grandfathers, how-high-soever, e.g. the deceased's full or consanguine paternal uncles and grand-uncles and their sons and grandsons. Only the Malikis, among the Sunnis, differ on the priority of the true grandfather over the full or consanguine brothers, making them of the same right to succession to the estate, after the father and before the male descendants of said brother. The Hanafis alone rule that the true grandfather excludes the full or consanguine brothers from inheritance in the same way as he unanimously excludes the uterine. But all modern Arab legislators, following the Malikis, treat him as equal to the agnate brothers, provided his share shall not be less than one-sixth.[35]

The above order of priority is followed in that each category shall exclude any other below. Within the same category, the nearest, i.e. with fewer links to the deceased, excluded the more distant. If they are equal in the category and nearness, the stronger relative, i.e. related to the deceased through both father and mother, e.g. a full brother, shall take precedence over the consanguine. If they are equal in all these aspects, they shall receive equal shares.

(2) The residuaries through another (*asaba bil ghayr*)

These are all female sharers who need a residuary in his own right to share with. There are four such female sharers: the daughter with the son; the son's daughter, how-low-soever, with an equal or lower son's son; the full sister with the full brother; and the consanguine sister with the consanguine brother, whether of the same or different mother. They shall share the residue after the sharers, with the male receiving twice the portion of a female. In the previous Section on the sharers, those females usually receive one half if on her own, and share two-thirds if many.

(3) The residuaries with another (*asaba maa al ghayr*)

There are only two females in this class, the full and the consanguine sisters, who are both sharers, but, in the absence of a male agnate, they become residuaries with the daughter/s or the son's daughter/s how-low-soever or even one daughter and one or more son's daughters. A residuary with another differs from a residuary through another in that she does not share with her co-residuary, but inherits the residue left after the sharers take their share.

35 Arts. 22, Egyptian; 279, Syrian; 158, Algerian; 297–309, Kuwaiti.

Notes on the distribution among sharers and residuaries. There are five heirs (referred to as "Primary Heirs") that are always entitled to a share of the inheritance and are never excluded entirely, although their share could be reduced. They are the child (son or daughter), father, mother, husband and wife. The child of a son, how-low-soever, true grandfather, how-high-soever, and true grandmother, how-high-soever are considered as substitutes of the primary heirs who exclude them if they exist.

Near male relatives can be excluded in some cases. For example, if a woman leaves a husband (share one-half), the mother (share one-sixth) and a uterine brother (share one-third), the inheritance is exhausted, and nothing is left over for full brothers.

D. Distant Kindred

Distant kindred are those relations by blood of the deceased who are neither sharers nor residuaries. They consist of males or females related to the deceased through one or more female links. They are called in Arabic *dhawu-l-arham* or *ulu-l-arham* (relatives by virtue of the womb), and are entitled to inherit only on failure of any heir who belongs to the class either of the sharers (except a spouse) or residuaries. Distant kindred are divided into four classes in the following order of priority:

(1) Descendants of the deceased through a female link

(i) daughters's children how-low-soever;
(ii) children of son's daughters how-low-soever.

When there is only one, he/she shall inherit the whole estate in the absence of sharers and residuaries, and shall inherit the residue when there is a surviving spouse after his/her share is deducted. If there is more than one in this category of different degrees of kinship, the closest shall exclude the others.

If they are equal in degree of kinship, a child of a sharer shall exclude the others.

If they are equal in degree without any being the child of the sharer, or if all are children of a sharer, they shall inherit collectively (Arts. 32, Egyptian; 291, Syrian; 168, Algerian; 321, Kuwaiti).

Nevertheless, their exclusion from inheritance is subject to the provisions of the modern Arab laws on the mandatory will, as explained in the next chapter on Wills. Algerian Articles 169/172 inclusive enact the same provision as a rule on inheritance, where the grandchildren take the place of their ascendant as an heir.

(2) Ascendants of the deceased through a female link

These are the false grandfather or false grandmother, how-high-soever. The closest to the deceased shall exclude the others. If they are equal in degree, the ascendant of a sharer shall exclude the others.

If they are equal in degree and ascendants of sharers, or none of them is an ascendant of a sharer, the father's cognates shall inherit two-thirds and the mother's one-third, with the male within each group taking a double portion to the female. This ruling is held under Articles 33 (Egypt), 292 (Syria), and 322 (Kuwait).

(3) Descendants of the deceased's parents who are neither sharers nor residuaries

(i) male or female children of full, consanguine or uterine sisters;
(ii) daughters or son's daughters of full, consanguine or uterine brothers, how-low-soever;
(iii) sons of uterine brothers and their children how-low-soever.

The closest in kinship, even a female, shall exclude the others. If they are equal in degree, the descendant of a residuary shall exclude that of a distant kindred, otherwise they shall be treated as if they were residuaries among themselves, the descendant of the two parents excluding a consanguine descendant who shall exclude a uterine one. If they are equal in both aspects, they shall equally share (Arts. 34, Egyptian; 293, Syria and 323, Kuwait).

(4) Descendants of the deceased's immediate grandparents (true or false)

These are in brief all paternal aunts (*ammat*), all maternal aunts and uncles (*khalat wa akhwal*) and uterine paternal uncles (*aamam li umm*) – in the following detail:

(i) Uterine paternal uncles of the deceased and full or half maternal uncles or aunts.
(ii) The children of (i) above, how-low-soever, and daughters or son's daughters of full or consanguine paternal uncles, how-low-soever, and the children of said females, how-low-soever.
(iii) The deceased's father's uterine paternal uncles, full or half paternal aunts, full or half maternal aunts or uncles; the deceased's mother full or half paternal or maternal aunts or uncles.
(iv) The children of (iii) above how-low-soever, the daughters and son's daughters of the deceased's father full or consanguine paternal

uncles how-low-soever and the children of said daughters how-low-soever.

(v) The deceased's father's paternal aunts or uncles, and their full or half maternal aunts or uncles, and the deceased's mother's mother's or father's mother's full or half paternal or maternal aunts or uncles.

(vi) The children of (v) above how-low-soever and the daughters and son's daughters of the deceased's father's father's full or consanguine paternal uncles how-low-soever and the children of said females how-low-soever.[36]

For class (i) above, if the group consists solely of paternal relations or maternal relations, those related to the deceased through both parents shall exclude the consanguine who shall have priority over the uterine. If they are equal, they shall share. If the class combines both paternal and maternal relations, those of the father's side shall receive two-thirds and on the mother's side one-third, with distribution running on the above lines. These provisions shall also apply to classes (iii) and (v) above.

For class (ii) above, the nearer kin shall exclude the more distant regardless of the side. On being equal in distance and of the same side, the stronger kinship shall have priority if they are children of a residuary or a cognate, and the paternal side shall exclude the maternal, with the distribution running in the afore-mentioned fashion.

These provisions shall also apply to classes (iv) and (vi) above (Arts. 35 and 36, Egyptian; 295 and 296, Syrian; 324 and 325, Kuwaiti).

For all distant kindred, the male shall receive the share of two females (Arts. 297, Syrian and 327, Kuwaiti).

E. Miscellaneous

(1) The acknowledged person

If the deceased has acknowledged as a kin a person of unknown parentage, the acknowledged person shall be entitled to the deceased's estate, provided that its parentage to a third person is not established, that the deceased has not revoked his acknowledgement, that there is no impediment for the acknowledged person to inherit, and that he/she is alive at the time of the actual or death of the deponent (Arts. 41, Egyptian; 298, Syrian; 328, Kuwaiti).

(2) The unborn child

The Sunni jurists are unanimous that an unborn child who is a prospective heir shall inherit if it already exists, as an embryo, at the time of the

36 Al-Bardisi, *op. cit.* p. 76.

death of the propositus, and if it is later born alive. Its existence as an embryo then can be inferred from the time span between the death of the propositus and its actual birth, namely within the maximum and minimum duration of pregnancy.

The jurists agree that an unborn child of the propositus who has died while the marriage was standing shall inherit if it is born within the minimum limit of pregnancy, i.e. within six months according to the majority of jurists, and nine months according to the Hanbalis, after the death of the father. If the death occurred while the wife was counting her iddat of an irrevocable marriage, the child shall inherit if born within the maximum duration of pregnancy, over which they differ, from two years according to the Hanafis and one lunar year (354 days) according to the Maliki jurist Muhammad ibn-ul-Hakam.[37]

The Egyptian legislator (Art. 43) rules that if a man dies leaving his wife or divorcée during her iddat, her unborn baby shall inherit from him if born alive within 365 days at most from the date of death or separation. The Tunisian and Kuwaiti legislators (Arts. 150 and 330 respectively) follows suit. The Algerian legislator (Art. 43) holds that the child's parentage shall be established if it is born within 10 months from the date of separation or death. Syrian Article 300 reads as follows: "If a man dies leaving his wife or divorcée during her iddat, her unborn child shall not inherit from him unless it is born alive with proven parentage to him in the manner shown under this law", namely if it is born less than 180 days after the declaration of the termination of the iddat and less than one year after separation or death (Art. 131).

If the propositus is not the father of the unborn child, e.g. if he is a brother or grandfather, the unborn child shall not inherit from him unless:

(i) if it is born alive within 365 days at most after the death or separation, if its mother is counting her iddat of death or separation and the propositus died during the iddat; or
(ii) if it is born alive within 270 days at most from the date of the death of the propositus, if marriage was standing at the time of death (Arts. 43, Egyptian; 150, Tunisian and 330, Kuwaiti). This way, the existence of the embryo at the time of the propositus' death is certain.

On complying with these conditions, the unborn child shall have set aside for it from the deceased's estate the larger share of a male or female (Art. 42, Egyptian; 299, Syrian; 329, Kuwaiti). Concurring to this provision the Tunisian (Art. 147) and Algerian (Art. 173) legislators add that if it excludes entirely all other prospective heirs, no shares shall be given and the whole estate shall stay undivided

37 Abdul Latif, *op. cit.* p. 151.

until the child is born. After the birth, the share set aside shall be adjusted upwards or downwards (Arts. 44, Egyptian; 301, Syrian; and 321, Kuwaiti).

(3) The hermaphrodite or person of non-determined sex

Such a person shall take whichever portion is less, whether that of the male or female (Arts. 46, Egyptian and 334, Kuwaiti).

(4) The illegitimate child

The illegitimate child or child whose paternity was solemnly contested (*lian*) shall not inherit from the wife's husband, but is eligible to inherit from and be inherited from by the mother and her kindred (Arts. 47, Egyptian; 303, Syrian; and 152, Tunisian). Kuwaiti Article 335 concurs, adding that the time span under Article 330 shall be observed, i.e. to be born alive within 365 days maximum from the date of death or separation.

(5) The missing person

If a person dies, and among his heirs is a missing person, the estate shall be divided on the basis that that missing person is present until it is known for sure whether he is alive or dead. If he is discovered to be alive, he shall take his share of the inheritance. If it is duly proved that he died after the deceased, his share shall go to his heirs. If his death is duly confirmed before that of the propositus, the missing person shall not be entitled to any share. If he is found to be alive after his death has been declared by a court, he shall receive his share that has been given to the other heirs (Arts. 45, Egyptian; 302, Syrian; 151, Tunisian; and 115, Algerian). Under Articles 332 and 333 of the Kuwaiti law, the missing person appearing after his being declared dead by the court shall take back what is left of his original share with the other heirs.

8. THE SHIA LAW OF INHERITANCE

A. Introduction and General

The main difference between the Sunni and Shia Laws of inheritance is that the Sunni distinguish between the agnates, the *asaba*, i.e. the persons related to the deceased without the intervention of female links, and the cognates, *dhawu-l-arham*, related to the deceased through one or more female links, while the Shias do not acknowledge such a distinction. Consequently the Sunnis, as explained in the previous section, hold three grounds for inheritance: a prescribed share (*fard*), a kinship through males (asaba) and distant kindred. The Shias acknowledge only two grounds of inheritance: a prescribed share and kinship, whether through males or females. Therefore the heirs are classified into three groups:

(i) those who are solely sharers – they are inclusively the spouses and the mother;
(ii) those who are sharers and can also be residuaries, e.g. daughters and full or half-sisters; and
(iii) those who are always residuaries, e.g. the sons.

The Iranian Law sums up this classification in Articles 893–98 inclusive which read as follows:

> "Article 893 – An heir maybe either a sharer, both a sharer and a residuary, or a residuary.
> Article 894 – The sharers are those heirs who have a prescribed portion in the estate, such a portion being called a share.
> Article 895 – Shares are one-half, a quarter, one-eighth, two-thirds, one-third and one-sixth of the estate.
> Article 896 – The sharers are the mother and the surviving spouse.
> Article 897 – The heirs who are both sharers and residuaries are the father, the daughter or daughters, the full or consanguine sister or sisters, and the uterine sisters and brothers.
> Article 898 – All heirs who are not specified in the previous two articles are residuaries."[38]

The Shias further distinguish between two categories of heirs: the first through kinship and the second through marriage.

The heirs through kinship are divided into three classes:

(1) Heirs of the first class

There are (a) parents, and (b) children and other lineal descendants how-low-soever. Under this class, there is no difference between a male and a female. The only criterion for priority is proximity to the deceased. The sharer shall get his or her due first, together with a return if there is no other heir.

(2) Heirs of the second class

These are (a) grandparents how-high-soever (true as well as false), and (b) brothers and sisters and their descendants how-low-soever. Equally,

38 Quoted by Abu Zahra, *Inheritance According to the Jaafaris*, pp. 82–83. We owe a great deal to this valuable reference in the section on the Shia Law of inheritance. All references to Abu Zahra in the notes below are made to this book.

in this class there is no difference between agnates and cognates. The sharer shall have priority over the residuary or shall have the right to a return if there is no other kin in the same class. Priority among the grandparents and the parents' descendants shall be according to proximity to the deceased. Those related through the mother shall have one-third and those through the father two-thirds.

(3) Heirs of the third class

These are paternal and maternal uncles and aunts of the deceased, and of the deceased's parents and grandparents how-high-soever, and their descendants how-low-soever. Again proximity to the deceased shall determine priority, e.g. a maternal uncle shall exclude the son of a paternal uncle. The relations through the mother who are as near to the deceased as those through the father shall get one-third, leaving to the others two-thirds.

B. The Spouses

It must be noted that in all classes, the sharer, if any, shall have priority, and that residuaries come after the sharers. Since the spouses are always sharers, and therefore shall have priority over other sharers, and since they are the only sharers who are not necessarily blood relations, and notwithstanding the above order, we shall begin with them, following the Iranian law, although the Shia jurists begin otherwise.[39]

Both the Sunnis and the Shias give the widower half the estate of the deceased wife if she has left no child, and a quarter if she has; the widow shall receive one-quarter or one-eighth respectively. Both schools rely on the authority of the Quranic verse:

> "And unto you belongeth a half of that which your wives leave, if they have no child; but if they have a child then unto you the fourth of that which they leave, after any legacy they may have bequeathed or debt. And unto them belongeth the fourth of that which ye leave if ye have no child, but if ye have a child then the eighth of that which ye leave, after any legacy ye may have bequeathed or debt."[40]

However, the two sects differ on the meaning of the child which reduces the share of the widower and widow from a half to a fourth, and from a quarter to an eighth respectively.

The Sunnis maintain that such a child is any descendant whose relation

39 Abu Zahra, *op. cit.* p. 84.
40 Sura Nisaa, IV, verse 12.

to the deceased can be traced without the intervention of female links, e.g. a son's son or daughter. Under that definition a daughter's son is no descendant of the deceased and therefore shall not reduce the share of the surviving spouse.

The Shias consider that every descendant of the deceased, whether related through male or female links, is a child which shall reduce the share of the surviving spouse. Therefore, with a daughter's son or daughter, the widow shall receive one-eighth and the widower one-quarter of the net estate. The Shias quote the authority of a tradition ascribed to the two Imams, Jaafar us-Sadiq and Muhammad ul Baqir to that effect. They also use the term "posterity" (*dhurriyya*) to denote all descendants however they are related to the deceased.[41]

If there is no posterity, in this general sense of the term, and there were no other sharers or blood relations, the widower shall receive the residue by way of "return" (*radd*). The widow, according to the most authoritative Ithna-Ashari opinion, is not entitled to any such return.[42] The Iranian Law adopts this ruling in Article 905 which reads as follows:

> "Every sharer shall receive his portion of the estate. The remnant shall devolve upon the blood relations. If there are no blood relations of the same class as the sharers to participate with them in the residue of the estate, such residue shall be added to the shares of the sharers as an additional right of inheritance except for the surviving spouse. Nevertheless the husband who is the sole heir to his deceased wife shall receive the residual part of the estate as an additional portion"[43] (that is, by way of return).

Like the Sunnis, the spouses can mutually inherit if the marriage stands *de facto* or is deemed to stand on the death of a spouse while the wife is still in her iddat of a revocable repudiation whether or not there was consummation. This does not apply, however, in the event of marriage during a death-illness where the Shias differ from the Sunnis and distinguish between the husband and wife: the wife shall not inherit from a husband who married her during his death-illness and died before consummation which renders the marriage void.[44] Contrariwise, the husband shall inherit from a wife who married during her death-illness and died before consummation as her death then does not render the marriage void.[45]

41 Abu Zahra, *op. cit.* p. 85.
42 Al-Hilli, *op. cit.* p. 144.
43 Quoted by Abu Zahra, *op. cit.* p. 86.
44 *Ibid.* p. 88. It is noteworthy that the Malikis, of all Sunni schools, concur with the Shias in this ruling.
45 *Ibid.* p. 89.

Another difference between the husband and wife in terms of inheritance is that the husband shall inherit the half or the quarter of all the estate left by the wife without distinction between real and movable property. As for the wife the most authoritative Imami opinion is that a widow with a child by the deceased shall receive her share of both real and movable assets of the estate, but a childless widow shall receive nothing from the land left by the deceased and shall only take her share of the value of machinery, buildings and trees.[46] A different Imami opinion does not distinguish between widows who have a child by the deceased and those who do not. This opinion rules that a widow shall not inherit any real property but only the value of the buildings and the household effects. It is this latter ruling that the Iranian Law has adopted in Articles 946, 947 and 948 as follows:

> "Article 946 – The Sharia share of the husband in the estate of his wife shall be calculated in all the property left by her. However, the wife's Sharia share in her husband's estate shall be taken from his following assets only:
> (i) All his movable possessions of whatever kind.
> (ii) Buildings and household effects.
> Article 947 – The wife shall take her share of the value of the buildings and household effects but shall take no part of the substance of said buildings and household effects. The value thereof shall be assessed on the basis that such buildings and household effects shall remain on the land without the owner of the land being entitled to any consideration therefor.
> Article 948 – In the case described in the previous Article, if the heirs refuse to pay the value of the buildings and household effects, the surviving wife may demand her share in substance."[47]

C. Blood Relation Heirs of the First Class

These include the immediate parents and the descendants. They are considered by the Shia to be of the first class: any member whereof surviving shall exclude all other relatives, be they brothers, sisters, uncles or aunts. The reason is that the shares of children and parents are defined in the same Quranic text with the omission of all others:

> "God chargeth you concerning your children, to the male the equivalent of the portion of two females, and if there be women more than two, then theirs is two-thirds of the inheritance and if there be

46 Al-Hilli, *op. cit.* p. 149.
47 Quoted by Abu Zahra, *op. cit.* p. 90.

only one then the half. And to his parents a sixth of the inheritance, if he left children. If he left no children and his parents are his heirs, then to his mother appertaineth the third, and if he have brethren, then to his mother appertaineth the sixth, after any legacy he may have bequeathed, or debt. Your parents or your children: You know not which of them is nearest unto you in benefit. It is an injunction from God. Lo! God is All-Knowing, All-Wise."[48]

Moreover, according to the Shia, the inheritance by brothers and sisters is subject to the non-existence of ascendants and descendants, under the Quranic verse:

> "And if a man or a woman have a distant heir, having left neither ascendants nor descendants (kalalat), and have a brother or a sister, then to each of them twain the sixth, and if they be more than two, then they shall be sharers in the third."[49]

The inheritance by brothers or sisters is also described in the Quran as kalalat:

> "They ask thee for a pronouncement say: God hath pronounced for you concerning those who leave no ascendants or descendants as heirs (kalalat). If a man die childless and he have a sister, hers is half the heritage and he would have inherited from her had she died childless. And if there be two sisters then theirs are two-thirds of the heritage. And if they be brethren, men and women, unto the male is the equivalent of the share of two females."[50]

Unlike the Sunnis, children are interpreted by the Shia, strictly following the Quranic texts without reference to any exegesis, to include all descendants of the deceased, through male or female links, while parents are restricted to the immediate father and mother.

(1) The shares of mother and father

The mother on her own, without a spouse or a member of the first class or a group of brothers or sisters, shall receive the whole estate: one-third as a sharer and the residue by way of return. If she inherits with a husband, he shall take his share of one-half. A wife shall take a quarter, and the mother in both cases shall receive what is left: one-third as a sharer and the residue by way of return.

Likewise if the father is on his own as an heir, he shall inherit the whole estate. With a spouse he shall receive the rest after the spouse's share.

48 Sura Nisaa, IV, verse 11.
49 *Ibid.* verse 12.
50 Sura Nisaa, IV, verse 176.

With both parents surviving, the mother shall get one-third and the father the residue. Both with one spouse, the mother shall receive one-third of the whole estate, the spouse his or her share and the father what is left thereafter.

With a number of brothers and/or sisters, the mother's share is reduced to one-sixth on five conditions:

(i) The number should be two brothers, or four sisters or one brother and two sisters. Less than that, the mother's share shall not be reduced.
(ii) Siblings should be on both sides or on the side of the father. Uterine siblings shall not reduce the mother's share, since she is the link through which they are related to the deceased.
(iii) The father must be alive, in which case the father shall receive what is left over after the siblings take their share and the mother her sixth.
(iv) They must not be debarred from inheritance through any impediment as a debarred person shall not exclude or reduce the share of any other heir.
(v) They must be actually existent. A sibling unborn at the time of the death of the deceased shall not be counted in the quorum and shall not reduce the mother's share to one-sixth.

A School of Shia does not accept this condition which has also been dropped from Article 892 of the Iranian Law which reads as follows:

> "If the propositus has left a number of brothers and/or sisters, the mother's share shall be reduced to one-sixth of the estate on the following conditions: 1. That the propositus leaves two brothers, or one brother and two sisters or four sisters. 2. That their father is alive. 3. That they are not debarred from inheritance. 4. That they are full or consanguine brothers and/or sisters."[51]

(2) The parents with one female descendant as heir

A parent with a female descendant shall take her/his share of one-sixth and the descendant her share of a half, the residue being further divided between them in the proportion of their share, with the parent getting a quarter and the daughter three-quarters of the residue. For example, with the deceased leaving a wife, a mother and a daughter, the wife shall receive one-eighth, the mother one-sixth and the daughter one-half, the residue being then distributed between the mother (one-quarter) and the daughter (three-quarters).

If the deceased has left a father, a mother and a female descendant,

51 Quoted by Abu Zahra, *op. cit.* p. 108.

without brothers to reduce the share of the mother, each parent shall receive one-sixth, and the female descendant her share (one-half). The residue shall be shared between them, one-fifth to each parent and three fifths to the daughter.

If there are brothers, they shall reduce the mother's share to one-sixth and exclude her from return, although they themselves inherit nothing. Therefore, in the previous case adding brothers, the mother shall get only one-sixth, the father one-sixth and the daughter one-half. The residue shall be shared between the father (one-quarter) and the daughter (three-quarters). Only Mueen-ud-Deen Al Misri dissents, ruling two-fifths of the residue to the father and three-fifths to the daughter, on the ground that the father should get the mother's one-fifth of the residue which she has lost due to the existence of the brothers.[52]

Article 908 of the Iranian Law deals with this case as follows:

> "If the propositus has left a mother and/or a father and an only daughter, each of the surviving parents shall take one-sixth, the daughter a half and the residue shall devolve by way of return to all heirs in the proportions of their Sharia shares. However, if the mother is partially excluded, she shall take no part of the return."[53]

(3) The parents with more than one female descendant

With two or more daughters, each parent shall take one-sixth, and the daughters shall take two-thirds. If it is only one parent with the daughters, he/she shall receive one-sixth, the daughters two-thirds and the residue shall be divided in the proportions of one-fifth for the parent and four-fifths to be shared by the daughters.

With a surviving spouse, both parents and more than one daughter, the spouse shall take his/her share, each parent one-sixth, and the residue, being less than two-thirds, shall be shared by the daughters. Here we find a distinctive difference from the Sunnis, as the Shias do not allow aul (proportional increase). If the sum total of the fractions of shares exceeds unity, the deficit is borne solely by the females whose share is reduced if there is a male.

This case is covered by Article 909 of the Iranian Law:

> "With one or both parents surviving with more than one daughter, all the daughters shall equally share two-thirds of the estate and each surviving parent shall take one-sixth of the estate, the residue, if any, to be distributed among all heirs in the proportion of their Sharia

52 *Ibid.* p. 109.
53 *Ibid.*

ORDER NUMBER

PO NYAATP08

BOOK NUMBER

5839212

BAY NUMBER

9015-13

AUTHOR	Nasir, Jamal
TITLE	The Islamic Law of Personal Status (Arab and Islamic Laws Series)

DESCRIPTION

This is an ex-library book and may have the usual library/used-book markings inside.This book has soft covers. Book contains pencil markings. In fair condition, suitable as a study copy.

share. However, if the mother is partly excluded, she shall have no part of the return."[54]

(4) The parents with children as heirs

If there is a male among the children surviving the deceased, inheriting with one or both parents, the parents shall take their share, and the residue shall be divided among the children, the male receiving the share of two females under the Quranic verse: "God chargeth you concerning your children: to the male the equivalent of the portion of two females."[55] Therefore there is no return in this case. The children, male and female, shall take whatever is left after the sharers receive their portions. If a man leaves his wife, a father and mother, son and daughter; the wife shall take one-eighth, the father one-sixth, the mother one-sixth and the rest shall be divided between the son (two-thirds) and the daughter (one-third). Here, the Imamis concur with the Sunnis, both applying a clear Quranic ruling.

(5) The children's shares

An only child of the deceased shall take the whole estate if on its own: a son through kinship, and a daughter as a sharer (one-half) and by way of return (one-half). On the same grounds, an only child with a spouse of the deceased, shall take the whole residue after deducting the spouse's share. More than one child, males and females, shall share the whole estate if there is no sharer, and the residue if there is a sharer, the male taking twice the portion of the female. If they are all males or females they shall equally share such a residue. These rules are adopted under Iranian Article 907 which reads as follows:

> "If the propositus has left a child or several children, without leaving a father or a mother, the estate shall be divided in the following manner:
> 1. If there is only one child, male or female, it shall succeed to the whole estate.
> 2. If there are a number of children, all being males or females, they shall share the whole estate equally.
> 3. If there are both males and females, the male shall receive twice as much as the female."[56]

The eldest son, provided that he is not a prodigal nor an adherent to an unorthodox doctrine (that is other than Imami) shall get his dead father's

54 *Ibid.* p. 110.
55 Sura Nisaa, IV, verse 11.
56 Abu Zahra, *op. cit.* p. 112.

Quran, sword, seal and robes as a prior charge before even the legatees. This is not a matter of inheritance, but an act of favouritism dictated by the legislator in return for the said son performing on behalf of his dead father what the latter missed in respect of the rites of prayers and fasting.[57]

(6) The grandchildren's shares

Every grandchild shall be excluded by a direct child of the deceased, under the general Shia rule that within the same class of blood relations, the nearest excludes the more remote. A daughter's daughter shall be excluded by a daughter or a son, a son's son shall not inherit if there is a son or a daughter, and so forth. But grandchildren may inherit with the parents, being of different categories (descendants and ascendants) albeit of the same class. This ruling is enshrined in Article 901 of the Iranian Law: "If the propositus leave any child, even an only child, the grandchildren shall not inherit anything."[58]

The entitlement of grandchildren to the estate is governed by three basic rules:

(i) The higher descendant shall exclude the lower on whatever side, e.g. the daughter's son shall exclude the son's son's son.

(ii) A descendant shall inherit the share of its ascendants, whether male or female. Suppose a deceased left a son's daughter and a daughter's son; they shall get respectively the shares of the son and the daughter had they been alive. This is known as the principle of representation which is rejected by the Sunnis.[59]

(iii) If a dead child of the deceased has left several children, they shall share their parent's portion, had he been alive, with the male taking twice as much as the female. As an example, the deceased left a son and a daughter of his daughter, and a son and a daughter of his son. The daughter's son shall take two-thirds, and her daughter one-third of their mother's share, had she been alive. The son's daughter shall take one-third and his son two-thirds of their father's share.

Iranian Articles 911 and 912 sum up these provisions as follows:

"Article 911 – if the propositus has left no children, their children's children shall take their place under the right of representation, and shall as such be considered heirs of the first class and shall share the estate with the surviving parent or parents of the deceased. As for distribution among grandchildren it shall apply by stirps, that is to

57 *Ibid.* p. 113.
58 *Ibid.* p. 114.
59 Except in the special case of the mandatory will in modern Arab laws, cf. Chap. 13.

> say, the heirs of each descendant shall inherit the share of their ascendant whom they represent and who forms their link with the propositus. For example, the share to be inherited by the children of the propositus' son shall be twice that devolved upon the propositus' daughter.
> Article 912 – The descendants of the deceased, how-low-soever, shall inherit in accordance with the previous article."[60]

The children's children shall inherit in the same manner as their ascendants, vis-à-vis other sharers. A daughter's children shall share in the return in the same way as their mother would have done. The son's children shall take, on the ground of blood relation the residue after the parents' and the spouse's shares. A spouse inheriting with grandchildren shall take only his/her share and nothing by way of return, exactly as if their parents had been alive.

Parents do not exclude children's descendants and shall inherit with them as if those descendants' ascendants were alive.

Representation applies only to descendants, not to parents or grandparents.

D. Blood Relation Heirs of the Second Class

Brothers and sisters and their descendants share the same class of blood relations, the second, with the grandparents because both categories relate to the deceased via a parent. To make a grandfather or a grandmother equal to a brother or a sister respectively is a rule maintained also by the bulk of Sunni jurists. However, Sunnis and Imamis (Shias) differ in three important issues:

(i) While the Sunnis accord a grandparent the status of a sibling, they stipulate a minimum for his share, one-sixth or one-third according to different jurists. The Shias do not rule any such minimum.

(ii) The grandfather considered by the Sunnis as an equal to the brother is a "true grandfather", i.e. an ascendant between whom and the deceased no female link intervenes. The Imamis make any grandfather in the same status for inheritance as siblings, and their descendants, whether there was or not a female link intervening between him and the deceased. Likewise, they consider a grandmother as an equal for inheritance purposes to a sister, regardless of the way she is linked to the deceased.

(iii) The true grandfather, under the Sunni doctrine, excludes the children of brothers and sisters. Contrariwise, he does not exclude

60 Abu Zahra, *op. cit.* p. 115.

them according to the Shias. Grandparents shall share with the descendants of brothers and sisters, be they full, consanguine or uterine.

The members of the second class shall only inherit if there is no member whatsoever of the first class of blood relations, i.e. immediate parents and descendants, how-low-soever.

There are three possible eventualities for the inheritance by the second class: no grandparents and only brothers or sisters or their children; grandparents on their own; and grandparents sharing with brothers or sisters or their children.

(1) No grandparents, but only brothers and/or sisters

The brothers and sisters shall inherit with the surviving spouse, if any, taking his/her prescribed share, the uterine sister or brother her/his share, the residue devolving on the full or consanguine brothers and sisters.

The uterine brothers and sisters are not excluded by the full brothers and sisters, but shall take their share with them. Contrariwise, consanguine brothers or sisters are utterly excluded by full siblings, whether the latter inherit as sharers or residuaries. Here the Imamis differ from the Sunnis who rule that the consanguine brothers and sisters shall inherit with a full sister who shall only exclude the consanguine if she is residuary with the daughter.

Uterine sisters shall share equally with uterine brothers in absolute conformity with the Sunnis ruling under the Quranic verse: ". . . but if more than two, they share in a third;".[61] But a male shall receive twice as much as a female if there are full or consanguine sisters with full or consanguine brothers, again in conformity with the Sunnis, under the Quranic verse: "If there are brothers and sisters the male shall have twice the share of the female."[62]

Uterine brothers and sisters shall not take part of any return if there are full brothers or sisters who shall share the return.

Full brothers or sisters of the deceased shall take the whole estate, the male taking twice as much as the female if there is no sharer. If there is a sharer, e.g. a spouse or uterine brothers or sisters, the full siblings shall get the residue.

If the deceased left only consanguine brothers and sisters, they shall receive the shares that would have been for full brothers and sisters: one sister shall receive one-half, two or more shall receive two-thirds and the brothers shall equally share the residue.

61 Sura Nisaa, IV, v. 12.
62 *Ibid.* IV, v. 176.

The Iranian Law Articles 918, 919, 920, 921, 922 and 927 cover the inheritance of brothers and sisters as follows:

918. If the propositus left full brothers or sisters they shall utterly exclude the consanguine but not the uterine brothers and sisters.
919. If the propositus left only full or consanguine brothers or only full or consanguine sisters they equally share the estate.
920. If the heirs are full brothers and sisters or consanguine brothers and sisters, the male shall receive twice the share of a female.
921. If the heirs are the deceased's uterine brothers and/or sisters they shall equally share the estate.
922. If the estate is shared by full brothers and sisters with uterine or consanguine brothers and sisters, the devolution shall be in the following manner:

If there is only one uterine brother or sister, she/he shall receive one-sixth of the estate and the residue shall devolve on full brothers and sisters. If there is no uterine brother or sister, the sixth shall be taken by the consanguine brothers and/or sisters under the rules set above. If there are several uterine brothers and/or sisters, they shall share one-third equally between them, with the full brothers and/or sisters receiving the residue which shall be divided according to the rules set above.
927. In all cases treated in this section, the surviving spouse shall first of all receive his/her Sharia share, being half the estate for the widower and a quarter for the widow. The prescribed share shall also go to the relations of the deceased on the mother's side, be they ascendants or brothers and sisters. If the sum total of shares exceeds the estate due to the survival of a spouse of the deceased, the shares of the full brothers or consanguine brothers and/or sisters or of ascendants shall be reduced accordingly."[63]

(2) Nephews and nieces

If the deceased left no brothers or sisters, the estate shall devolve on their children, if any. No child of a brother or sister shall receive any part of the estate with any brother or sister surviving. If the deceased left a uterine brother and a son of a full brother, the latter will receive nothing of the estate which shall be entirely taken by the uterine brother, in accordance with the fundamental Imamis rule that the proximity overrides any other consideration within the same class of blood relations. Applying the same rule the nearest in degree of kinship among the children of brothers and sisters shall exclude the more remote. The son of a uterine sister shall

63 Abu Zahra, *op. cit.* pp. 122–123.

succeed to the whole estate excluding the grandson of a full brother and so on.

Again, applying the principle of representation, distribution of shares among the members of the same class with the same degree of proximity to the deceased proceeds by stirps, not per capital. The children of several brothers or sisters of the deceased shall take, between them, the share their father or mother would have taken had he/she survived the deceased, e.g. the deceased left a son of a uterine brother, a son of a full sister and a son of a consanguine brother. The first shall take one-sixth, the second shall take one-half as a sharer, and by way of return, the two portions being those of the uterine brother and the full sister. Like his father, the son of a consanguine brother shall be excluded by the full sister or her son who represents her in this case.

The children of a full brother or sister shall share their father's/mother's prescribed portion with the male taking twice the portion of a female. Those of a uterine brother or sister shall share equally their father's/mother's share, according to the rules outlined above.

The distribution of the estate among the nephew and nieces is canonized in Article 925 of the Iranian law as follows:

> "In all cases treated in the previous Articles, if the deceased left no brothers or sisters, the children of brothers and sisters shall succeed to the estate by the right of representation and shall share with the surviving ascendants of the deceased, the distribution being by stirps, i.e. the heirs of each collateral shall succeed to their ascendant's share through whom they are related to the deceased and shall take the prescribed portion to which the said ascendant would have been entitled had she/he survived the deceased. Therefore, the children of the full uterine or consanguine brother or sister shall take the portion of the full, uterine or consanguine brother or sister. In dividing the estate among the members of the same class, the male shall take twice the share of a female if the heirs are children of full or consanguine brothers or sisters. But if they are children of uterine brothers or sisters, they shall share their ascendant's share equally."[64]

(3) Grandparents on their own

Grandparents how-high-soever are considered in the same degree of kinship to the deceased as brothers and sisters and their descendants how-low-soever, having the same links with one deceased, namely a parent of whatever sex.

64 *Ibid.* pp. 125–126.

A grandfather or a grandmother on his/her own shall succeed to the whole estate after the surviving spouse receives his/her share.

The nearest grandparent to the deceased, whether maternal or paternal, male or female, shall exclude a more distant grandparent. A maternal grandfather shall exclude a paternal great-grandmother and shall succeed to the whole estate and so on.

If several grandparents survive the deceased and are equally near, there are three possibilities:

(i) That they both be on the father's side, for example the father's father and mother. Here the grandfather shall receive two-thirds and the grandmother one-third, the male taking twice the share of a female as in the case of full or consanguine brothers and sisters.
(ii) That they both be on the mother's side, e.g. the deceased's maternal grandfather and grandmother. The link is the mother and therefore each grandparent shall receive one-half of the estate, as in the case of uterine brothers and sisters.
(iii) That they be on the mother's and the father's side, e.g. the deceased's maternal and paternal grandparents. In this case, the maternal grandparents shall take one-third and the paternal shall take the residue. The maternal grandmother shall share the third equally with the maternal grandfather. Of the residue, the paternal grandfather shall take two-thirds and the maternal grandmother one-third.

If grandparents are heirs with a spouse, a sole grandparent shall take the residue after the spouse's share. If more than one in the same degree, the maternal grandparents shall share the residue equally and a paternal grandfather shall take two-thirds of the residue leaving one-third for the paternal grandmother.

If paternal and maternal grandparents succeed to the estate with a surviving spouse, the maternal grandparents shall equally share one-third of the whole estate, the spouse shall get his/her prescribed share and the residue shall go to the paternal grandparents, with the male taking twice the share of the female, as in the case of surviving father and mother of the deceased. The mother would have taken one-third of the whole estate, the spouse his/her share and the father the residue.

These provisions are adopted in the Iranian Article 923 which reads as follows:

> "If the sole heirs of the deceased are grandfathers or grandmothers, the estate shall be divided among them in the following manner:
> If it is solely the grandparent, whether on the mother's or father's side of the deceased, she/he shall succeed to the whole estate.

If there are several grandparents, the estate shall be distributed among them on the basis that the male shall receive twice the share of the female on the paternal side, while the maternal grandparents shall receive equal shares.

If the paternal grandparent inherits with the maternal grandparent, one-third of the estate shall be equally shared among the maternal grandparents and the remaining two-thirds shall devolve on the paternal ascendants, with the male receiving twice the share of a female."[65]

(4) Grandparents with brothers and/or sisters

Grandparents do not exclude brothers or sisters nor even their descendants. They shall inherit together, the grandfather as a brother and the grandmother as a sister sharing the estate with brothers and sisters or their children.

Maternal grandparents shall share with uterine brothers and/or sisters or their descendants, taking one-third of the estate to be shared equally between male and female, e.g. the deceased's mother's father and mother shall equally share one-third with the uterine brothers and/or sisters. They shall succeed to the whole estate as sharers, and by return if there are no paternal grandparents or full or consanguine brothers/sisters. If there are paternal grandparents, they shall share with full and/or consanguine brothers/sisters with the male taking the portion of two females.

Again, according to the principle of proximity, the nearest grandparent to the deceased shall exclude the more distant, and share with brothers/sisters. The mother's mother of the deceased shall exclude the mother of the father's father. Likewise, the nearest nephews and nieces of the deceased shall exclude the more remote, and share with grandparents.

A few examples illustrate these general rules:

(i) A deceased left a father's mother, a uterine brother, a uterine sister, a full brother, a full sister, a consanguine brother and a consanguine sister. The uterine brother and sister shall equally share one-third. The consanguine brother and sister shall be excluded by the brother and sister. From the residue, the father's mother shall receive the same as the full sister who shall get half of the full brother's share.

(ii) A deceased left a mother's mother, a father's mother and a uterine brother. The brother shares the third equally with the mother's mother, while the father's mother, replacing a full sister, shall succeed to the whole residue as a sharer and by return.

65 *Ibid.*

(iii) A deceased is survived by a father's father, a full brother's son, a full sister's daughter, a uterine brother's son and a uterine sister's daughter. The relations on the mother's side shall share equally one-third, i.e. the uterine sister and brother's children shall get the share of their respective parent. The residue shall devolve on the grandfather, the full sister's daughter (representing her mother) and the full brother's son (representing his father), with the male taking twice the share of a female.

Articles 924 of the Iranian Law rules as follows on the inheritance of grandparents with brothers and sisters.

> "If the ascendants of the deceased inherit with the uterine brothers/sisters, two-thirds of the estate shall go to the deceased's relations on the father's side, with the male getting twice the share of a female and the remaining one-third to the relations on the mother's side, to be shared equally between them.
>
> However, if the deceased leaves only a uterine brother or sister the share that devolves to either of them shall not exceed one-sixth."[66]

Although the immediate parents, being of the first class, exclude the grandparents who belong to the second class of relations the Imamis strongly recommend that the father or mother who receives more than one-sixth should give the excess, up to one-sixth, to his or her surviving ascendant. However, they restrict this voluntary recommended grant to the immediate grandparent and not any further.[67]

E. Blood Relation Heirs of the Third Class

This class includes the descendants of grandparents both maternal and paternal. They come after the grandparents and brothers and sisters because they relate to the deceased through the grandmother or grandfather and are therefore more remote. For the same principle of proximity, the descendants of the first grandparent have priority over, and exclude, those of the second grandparent, and so forth. The son of an uncle excludes the brother of a grandparent. In general, the cousins, how-low-soever, have priority over the descendants of the second grandparent.

The whole estate shall devolve on any such relative if he/she is the only surviving heir. With a surviving spouse, he/she shall take the residue after deducting the spouse's share.

To the general rule of proximity, there is one major exception: the son of a full brother to the father shall have precedence over and exclude the

66 *Ibid.* p. 131.
67 *Ibid.* p. 132.

consanguine brother of the father. This exception, on the authority of a tradition of the Imam Ali ibn Ali Talib, is confirmed in this case. A maternal uncle or a spouse shall exclude such a cousin.[68]

When equal in the degree of proximity to the deceased, those relations on the mother's side shall succeed to one-sixth of the estate if only one and shall equally share one-third if several, as if they were uterine brothers/sisters. Those relations on the father's side shall share the residue, with the male taking twice the share of a female. This distribution shall follow the share of a spouse, if any.

The relations on the side of both mother and father shall exclude those solely on the father's side, but not on the mother's side.

Iranian Articles 928–38 inclusive deal with the inheritance of uncles and aunts and their descendants in the following manner:

> "928 – If the deceased left no relatives of the second class, the estate shall devolve on heirs of the third class.
> 929 – A sole relation of the third class shall succeed to the whole estate. Among several such relations, the distribution of the estate shall proceed according to the following provisions:
> 930 – If the deceased left full or consanguine paternal aunts/uncles or maternal full or consanguine aunts/uncles, the maternal and paternal aunts/uncles who are the consanguine sisters/brothers of the deceased's mother/father shall be excluded by their full siblings, but shall replace them if there are not any.
> 931 – If the deceased left only paternal aunts/uncles, they shall equally share the estate if they are uterine brothers/sisters of the deceased's father. If they are full or consanguine brothers/sisters of the deceased's father, they shall share the estate with the male taking twice the portion of a female.
> 932 – If the deceased left paternal aunts/uncles who are uterine sisters/brothers of the deceased's father, together with paternal aunts/uncles who are full or consanguine sisters/brothers of the deceased's father, the aunt or uncle who are the uterine sister/brother of the deceased's father shall take one-sixth if on his/her own and one-third to share equally if more. The residue shall devolve on the deceased's aunts and uncles who are full or consanguine sisters/brothers of the deceased's father with the male taking twice the share of the female.
> 933 – If the deceased left solely maternal aunts/uncles, they shall share the estate equally, whether they are the deceased's mother's full, uterine or consanguine sisters/brothers.

68 Al-Hilli, *op. cit.* p. 155. This provision enables the Shias to assert the priority of Ali's claim to the Imamat over Al-Abbas, who was a consanguine uncle to the Prophet, while Ali's father, Abu Talib, was a full brother of Abdullah, the Prophet's father.

934 – If the deceased left maternal full or consanguine aunts and uncles together with uterine maternal aunts and uncles, one-sixth of the estate shall go to the uterine maternal aunt or uncle if alone; if they are several, they shall equally share one-third. The residue of the estate shall go to the aunts and uncles who are full or consanguine sisters and brothers of the deceased's mother to be shared equally between them.

935 – If the deceased left one or more paternal uncles and aunts with one or more maternal uncles and aunts, one-third of the estate shall go to the maternal uncles and aunts, and two-thirds to the paternal uncles and aunts.

Maternal uncles and aunts shall share equally. However, if there is among them a uterine brother or sister of the deceased's mother, he/she shall take one-sixth of the total share of maternal uncles and aunts. If there are several maternal uncles and aunts who are uterine brothers/sisters of the deceased's mother, they shall share equally one-third of the said total share. As for the two-thirds which go to the paternal uncles and aunts, it shall be divided on the basis that the male shall take twice the portion of a female. However, if there is among the paternal uncles and aunts of the deceased a uterine brother/sister of the deceased's father, he/she shall get one-sixth of the total share of paternal uncles and aunts; if there are several, they shall equally share one-third of the said total. The remaining five-sixths or two-thirds of the rest of the paternal uncles and aunts shall be divided, as the case may be, between full paternal uncles and aunts, or those who are consanguine brothers/sisters of the deceased's father, according to the rule that the male shall take twice the portion of a female.

936 – Paternal and maternal uncles and aunts shall exclude paternal and maternal cousins. However, if the deceased left a paternal cousin who is the son of a full brother of the deceased's father and paternal uncle who is a consanguine brother of the deceased's father, the full paternal cousin shall exclude the consanguine paternal uncle.

937 – If the deceased left with the full paternal cousin a maternal uncle or aunt or several paternal uncles and aunts, the full paternal cousin shall be excluded from inheritance, even if the paternal uncles and aunts are consanguine brothers/sisters of the deceased's father.

938 – In all cases provided for in this section, there shall be first taken from the estate the share of the surviving spouse, which is half the estate for the widower and a quarter for the widow then the share of blood relations on the deceased's mother side. The residue shall be divided among his relations on the father's side."[69]

69 Abu Zahra, *op. cit.* pp. 137–140.

Chapter 13

Wills

1. LEGAL INTERPRETATION

The topic of the will is dealt with in the Egyptian Act No. 71/1946, and in separate chapters of the Personal Status Acts of the Lebanese Druze, Syria, Tunisia, Morocco, Iraq, Algeria and Kuwait. It is referred to in the context of priority of charges on a deceased's estate, coming after the confirmed debts and before inheritance. The only reference thereto in the Jordanian Personal Act concerns the Mandatory Will (Art. 182). Where there are no specific legal texts on wills in the Arab states, recourse is made to the teachings of a specific school of Islamic jurisprudence, e.g. the Hanafi in Jordan (Art. 183).

2. DEFINITION AND GENERAL PROVISIONS

Islamic jurists give various definitions of the will, the most common of which is "A transfer of ownership for no consideration to take effect after death".[1] Others define it as "A gift made by a person to another of a substance, a debt or a usufruct, in such a way that the beneficiary shall take possession of the gift after the death of the testator."[2] The first definition is adopted in the Lebanese Druze Article 145 and Algerian Article 184, and by the Shias.[3] Moroccan Article 173 reads: "The Will is an act by which the author thereof creates on the third of his property a right which becomes exigible on his death."

The Egyptian Article 1, followed by the Syrian Article 207 and Kuwaiti Article 213, defines the will as "A disposition of the estate to take effect after death", with the Iraqi Article 64 adding, "implying transfer of

1 Al-Abiani, *A Short Commentary*, pp. 440–441.
2 Sabiq, *Sunna Jurisprudence*, Vol. 3, p. 414.
3 Al-Hilli, *Jaafari Provisions on Personal Status*, p. 132.

ownership for no consideration." Tunisian Article 171 adds further "whether the property bequeathed is a substance or a usufruct." According to the Explanatory Memorandum to the Egyptian Article, this definition is the most comprehensive, as it includes a discharge of a debt, or a right linked to property, like the deferment of a debt falling due. By "estate" is meant everything left by the deceased to devolve on heirs, including property, usufruct or any other right related to property.

According to some Arab legislators, a will can be made by word of mouth, in writing or by an intelligible gesture for a mute or an illiterate. To this Hanafi opinion, the Egyptian and Kuwaiti legislators add the Maliki opinion that certification is a condition for the validity of contracts for no consideration, requiring a written document for any suit to confirm a will if it is disputed; the Kuwaiti allowing, if needs be, the evidence of two right witnesses to prove a verbal will (Arts. 2, Egyptian; 208, Syrian; 214, Kuwaiti).[4]

It is a condition for the validity of a will that it shall not contravene the Sharia (Syrian Art. 209, according to Islam or the religion of the non-Muslim testator; Egyptian Art. 3). An example is a bequest for a mistress.[5] Moroccan Article 174 requires for the validity of a will that it shall not contain any contradictory, ambiguous or illegal stipulations. Kuwaiti Article 215 stipulates for the validity of a will that it shall not be for a sin, or the motive thereof shall not contravene the intentions of the legislators; non-Muslim testators can make a valid will unless it is prohibited under the Islamic Sharia.

A will may be subject to a valid condition, i.e. a condition to the welfare of the testator, the beneficiary or others, not contravening the Sharia (Arts. 4, Egyptian; 201/1, 2, 3, Syrian). An invalid condition shall be void without invalidating the will (Arts. 210/4E, Syrian; 172, Tunisian). Kuwaiti Article 216, paragraphs a/b/d, concurs, while ruling (paragraph c) that a will suspended on a non-valid condition shall be void.

3. THE TESTATOR

The testator must possess the legal capacity to make a disposition for no consideration (Arts. 5, Egyptian; 211/1, Syrian). The Iraqi legislator adds (Art. 67): "and be the owner of what he bequests". The Algerian Article 186 spells it more clearly, requiring the testator to be of sound mind, not under 19 years of age, i.e. the Algerian age of majority. The Shias explain

4 Hanafi, *The Wills Act*, pp. 2–3.
5 *Ibid.* p. 6.

it more fully: the testator must be "free, adult, of sound mind and acting on his own free-will".[6]

Nevertheless, the Syrian Law (Article 211/2) makes the will by a person put under interdiction on grounds of prodigality or naivité valid, subject to a court order. Egyptian Article 5 adds to the same ruling a person who has reached 18 calendar years of age, i.e. 3 years under the Egyptian age of majority. This ruling, adopted also by Kuwaiti Article 217, follows the Shafii opinion, but is more restricting than that of the Hanafis, Malikis and Hanbalis, who allow a will by a prodigal and is adopted under Tunisian Article 178 provided that such a will is passed by the court.[7] The Shias allow a will by a boy of 10 and a prodigal under interdiction if it is for charity.[8] Exceptionally the Hanafis allow a bequest by a boy possessing discretion for his funeral expenses.[9]

As for insanity, the Hanafis rule that a will shall be void if the testator becomes incessantly insane until death, setting for such madness a duration of a year (Muhammad) or a month (Abu Youssof). The Malikis and Hanbalis dissent.

The Egyptian (Art. 14) and Syrian (Art. 220/a) legislators steer a middle course, ruling that the will shall be void if the testator became incessantly insane until death. The Iraqi legislator (Art. 72/2) rules that the will shall become void on the testator losing his legal capacity until his death.

According to the Sunni and Shia jurists, no will by a testator whose estate is exhausted with debts shall be effective unless the creditors allow it, debts having priority over any will.[10]

This provision is adopted in Articles 38 (Egyptian) and 238/3 (Syrian).
Kuwaiti Article 217/d makes an apostate's will valid on return to Islam.

4. THE BENEFICIARY

The beneficiary of a will may be an individual or individuals, a more or less defined group of persons, or an organization, or the proceeds of a bequest may be used for some purpose. In the event of many beneficiaries, under the Hanafis the whole bequest shall be taken by the surviving beneficiaries if one or more die before the testator, unless each beneficiary was allotted a definite part of the bequest, with each having such a part of

6 Al-Hilli, *op. cit.* p. 132.
7 Abu Zahra, *On the Wills Act*, pp. 65–66.
8 Al-Hilli, *op. cit.* p. 132.
9 Al-Abiani, *op. cit.* p. 442.
10 Abu Zahra, *op. cit.* p. 67; Al-Hilli, *loc. cit.*

the bequest as he would have taken if all the beneficiaries had survived the testator.[11] For the Shias, a bequest to a person who predeceased the testator shall pass to his/her heirs.[12]

According to the Sharia, the beneficiary must be identifiable, in existence at the time of the making of the will, and not a belligerent nor murderer or accomplice to the murder of the testator; and not an heir.

Identification of the beneficiary may be by recognized name, such as "A, the son of B" or a named mosque or institute; by demonstration, such as "this woman" or "the embryo in this woman's womb" or by description, such as "the poor of my village". No will shall be valid if the beneficiary is unidentifiable or not clearly identified. A will shall be unanimously deemed void if it is made to "a person" without identification. A will made to "either of these two men" is held by Abu Hanifa to be void because it is not clear which of them is meant.[13] Egyptian and Syrian Laws require the beneficiary to be known (Arts. 6/1, 212/a, and 218 respectively).

The beneficiary must be existent at the time of the making of the will. This is imperative if the beneficiary is identified by name or demonstration. If the beneficiary is identified by description such as "the children of A", the majority of Sunni jurists, except the Malikis, stipulate that while the beneficiary may not have existed at the time of the making of the will, it must exist at the time of the testator's death; consequently, children born more than six months after the death shall not be entitled to any part of the bequest.[14] The Malikis, followed by Moroccan Article 178, allow the entitlement of the embryo born after the testator's death.[15] The Shias allow up to nine months, provided that it is possible through the symptoms of pregnancy, to presume its existence at the time of the making of the will.[16] The Egyptian Law (Art. 6/2) adopts the Maliki opinion, as does the Algerian Article 187. Iraqi Article 68/1 follows the Hanafi position. Tunisian Article 184 stipulates that the embryo must exist at the time of making the will, and that it is born alive.

Under Shia law, it is irrelevant whether the pregnant woman is married or in her iddat of divorce or death.[17] The Hanafis distinguish between two cases: where the testator acknowledges and where he fails to acknowledge the existence of the embryo beneficiary at the time of making the will. In the first case, the will shall be valid if the child is born within two years of

11 Badran, *Inheritance, Wills and Gift*, p. 133.
12 Al-Hilli, *op. cit.* p. 136.
13 Madkoor, *Inheritance and Wills*, p. 330.
14 Al-Abiani, *op. cit.* pp. 448–449.
15 Hanafi, *op. cit.* p. 11.
16 Al-Hilli, p. 133.
17 *Ibid.*

the making of the will, whether the mother is married or in her iddat of divorce or death. In the second case, there is a further distinction between two contingencies: if the mother-to-be is actually or deemed to be married, e.g. in her iddat of a revocable divorce, when the will shall be valid only if the child is born less than six months after the making of the will, but if she is in her iddat of an irrevocable divorce or of death, the will shall be valid if the child is born within two years.[18] This Hanafi doctrine was adopted in Egypt until the promulgation of the Will Act 71/1946 which made the minimum and maximum terms of pregnancy for the purposes of the will nine months (270 days) and one solar year (365 days) respectively, while maintaining the basic Hanafi provisions (Art. 35).

In the event of multiple births, the babies born alive shall share the bequest equally. Similarly, Algerian Law, Article 187, Egyptian Will Law, Article 36, Syrian, Article 237.

Apart from individuals, the beneficiary may be a juristic person of a charitable object, in which case it is not required to be in existence at the time the bequest is made. The same ruling is defined in the following modern legislation, Syrian Article 213/1/2, Egyptian Will Law, Articles 52, 53, 57.

It is a condition for the will to remain valid at the time of the death of a testator that the beneficiary shall not be a belligerent, according to the Sunnis, Hanafis and the Shia Ithna-Ashari.[19] Difference of religion on its own, does not invalidate a will, unlike inheritance. Nevertheless, the modern Egyptian, Syrian, Tunisian and Kuwaiti Will Acts stipulate only the principle of reciprocity in so far as a national of a foreign country is concerned (Egyptian Will Law, Art. 9 and Syrian Art. 215/1/2; Tunisian Arts. 174, 175 and Kuwaiti Art. 221).

The Hanafis rule that no will is valid for a beneficiary who causes the death of the testator, whether the will is made before or after the act causing death. The Shafiis and some Hanbalis and Malikis consider the will a form of gift and therefore do not deem homicide of whatever kind to render a will void. The authoritative Maliki opinion and some Hanbalis hold that a will shall become void if the beneficiary murdered the testator after the making of the will. But if the cause of death preceded the making of the will, it shall be valid in deference to the wish of the testator who decided to benefit his murderer whom he knows.[20] This ruling is adopted in Moroccan Article 179.

Under the Iraqi Law, Article 68/2, a murderer of the testator shall be disqualified as a beneficiary. The Algerian Article 188 disqualifies a

18 Al-Abiani, *loc. cit.*
19 Madkoor, *op. cit.* p. 335
20 *Ibid.* p. 338.

beneficiary who murders the testator with intent. Egyptian and Syrian Articles 17 and 223 respectively set as a ground for the disentitlement to mandatory or voluntary will, the murder of the testator with intent, whether the murderer is a principal agent, an accomplice or a perjurer whose false evidence resulted in a death sentence against the testator being passed and executed, if the killing was for no just cause or reasonable excuse, and the murderer was of sound mind and not under 15 years of age. The Egyptian Article adds that using excess force in self-defence is a reasonable excuse. Kuwaiti Article 227 concurs in full.

A great controversy surrounds the last requirement of a beneficiary, namely not to be an heir. At one extreme, the Zahiris and some Malikis, Shafiis and Hanbalis rule that a will to an heir is utterly void, on the authority of a Tradition of the Prophet to that effect. They deem it as an act of injustice against the other heirs who may allow it, in which case it shall not be a bequest but a gift.[21] This ruling is repeated twice (Arts. 176 and 179/d "the beneficiary shall not be a presumptive heir at the time of the death of the testator") by the Moroccan legislator. On the other extreme, the Shia Ithna-Asharis and Zaidis accept as valid a will to an heir within one-third of the net estate without requiring the consent of the other heirs.[22] A middle course is steered by the Hanafis, the Hanbalis, the Shafiis and the majority Malikis, who hold that a will to an heir is valid subject to the consent of the other heirs, adding to the cited tradition of the Prophet "except if allowed by the heirs".[23]

Article 37 of the Egyptian Will Act equates an heir with a non-heir as a valid beneficiary of a will without requiring the consent of the heirs, following the Ithna-Ashari opinion. The Syrian Article 238/2 and Tunisian Article 179 makes such a will to an heir subject to such an approval. Article 70 (Iraqi) simply rules that the bequest shall be within one-third of the estate, and any excess shall be subject to the heirs allowing it, without specifying that the beneficiary must be an heir. Algerian Article 189, following the Hanafis, rules that no will is valid for an heir unless approved by the heirs after the death of the testator.

5. THE BEQUEST

A bequest may be real or movable property, monies, rights *in rem*, all of which are inheritable, or it may be a usufruct (whether for life or for a definite period), or anything that is capable of being transferred. The

21 *Ibid.* pp. 341–342.
22 Al-Hilli, *op. cit.* p. 133.
23 Madkoor, *op. cit.* p. 343.

bequest need not be in existence at the time of making the will, but must exist at the time of the testator's death. It must be capable of being inherited or transferred, owned by the testator and in existence at the time of his death; and it is limited to within one-third of the estate.

Like the inheritable estate, a bequest must be capable of being assessed, acquired and used, such as property, both movable and immovable, rights and usufructs, apart from the personal non-pecuniary rights and uses. No testator can create by will an estate repugnant to law. Things that are outside the ambit of trade and cannot be the object of property and the sale of which is void, e.g. animals not ritually slaughtered (mayta), blood and pigs, cannot be valid subjects of a Muslim's will. The same applies to things in which there is no ownership (*mal mubah*), such as air and water, rivers and public roads.[24]

This leads to the second condition of a bequest, that it shall be in existence and owned by the testator. This condition applies to property as contradistinct from usufruct. A will shall be void if the bequest, being a defined property *per se* or part of a defined whole, is not existing *at the time when the will is made*, since no person has the right to dispose of property he does not own. Such a will shall remain void even if the testator subsequently becomes the owner of the subject of the bequest, unless a new will is then made. Nevertheless, if the subject of the bequest is part of the whole property or class of property, e.g. a quarter of one-third of the estate or of books or animals, the will shall be valid provided that such property exists *at the time of the death of the testator*. A bequest need not be in the actual acquisition of the testator at the time of his death, but may be in the hands of a third party, e.g. a trust with a lien or a debt with a debtor, or even in the possession of a usurper.[25]

That the bequest shall not exceed one-third of the estate is a condition for a valid will to take effect. A Muslim who leaves heirs cannot dispose by will of more than one-third of what remains of his estate after payment of funeral expenses and debts. The remaining two-thirds of the estate is distributed according to the inheritance law among his heirs. A bequest in a will in excess of the legal one-third may be validated by the consent of the heirs, expressly or by implication, after the death of the testator, although the Shias allow such a consent to be given before the death of the testator, in which case the heirs cannot withdraw it after his death.[26] Where some and not all of the heirs consent to the bequest, it shall be payable to the beneficiary from the shares of the consenting heirs alone.[27]

24 *Ibid.* pp. 368–369.
25 *Ibid.* pp. 370–372.
26 Al-Hilli, *op. cit.* p. 133.
27 Madkoor, *op. cit.* p. 374.

Some Shia and Abadi jurists,[28] followed by Druzes (Lebanese Art. 148 and Syrian Art. 307/h) allow a bequest of the whole or any part of the estate to an heir or non-heir.

The dispositions regarding the bequests are summed up in the Egyptian Article 10 as follows: "The bequest is stipulated to be (1) an object that can be inherited or may be an object for a contract during the life of the testator: (2) a valuable asset in the possession of the testator if it is a property: (3) owned by the testator, if it was definite *per se*, at the time of the will." The whole Article is adopted in Kuwaiti Article 222 with the addition of "with due observance of paragraph (a) of Article 216" which allows a will to take effect in the future, and to make it subject to a valid condition. The valid condition of the Egyptian Article is repeated under paragraph (b) of the Syrian Article 216 of which paragraph (a) rules that the ownership of the bequest must be transferable on the death of the testator, and a valuable asset according to his religious law. Iraqi Article 69 simply requires the transferability of the ownership of the bequest after the death of the testator. Algerian Article 190 allows the testator to make a bequest of the property which he owns or is going to own before his death, be it a substance or a usufruct. Moroccan Article 188 simply rules that the bequest must be capable of being taken possession of.

6. THE MANDATORY WILL

According to the Explanatory Note to the Egyptian Will Act No. 71/1946, this is a disposition created as a remedy to a growing source of complaints, namely the position of the grandchildren whose parents die during the lifetime of their father or mother, or die, or are deemed to die with them, e.g. as a result of a sinking ship, building collapse, or fire. Such grandchildren rarely inherit on the death of their grandparent, as they are often excluded from inheritance, even though their dead parents might have contributed to the growth of the grandparent's wealth. Indeed, on the death of their father, they might have been supported and maintained by their grandfather who would have left them part of his property but died too soon for that, or was prevented from so doing through some temporary events.

On these grounds, Article 76 rules that if the deceased has left no will for the descendants of a child of his who died before, or is deemed to have died with him, bequeathing to such grandchildren the share of the estate that would have devolved on the child had he been alive, there shall be a

28 *Loc. cit.*

mandatory will in the amount of such share within the limits of one-third of the estate, provided that the said descendant is not an heir, and that the deceased has not given thereto, for no consideration, by another disposition, the amount due thereto. If the gift is less than the said amount, the will shall be for the balance. Such a will shall be to the benefit of the first class of the descendants of the lineal daughters or sons, how-low-soever, with every ascendant excluding the respective but not any other's descendant. The share of every ascendant shall be divided among the descendants thereof according to the rules of inheritance as if the ancestor(s) through whom they are related to the deceased had died after him. Under Article 77, if the beneficiary who is qualified to benefit of a mandatory will has been left in a will by the deceased a bequest in excess of what is due thereto, the excess shall be deemed a voluntary will. If the deceased left a will for only some of those qualified for a mandatory will, the rest shall be entitled to their due. Under Article 78, the mandatory will shall take precedence over all voluntary wills.

In the Explanatory Note, the Legislator derives the doctrine of the Mandatory Will for the non-heirs among relatives from a multitude of Followers, Jurists, and the Authorities of Jurisprudence and Tradition, among whom are Saieed ibn ul Musayyab, Al Hassan al-Bisri, Tawoos, Imam Ahmad, Dawood Al-Tibri and Ibn Hazm. The ultimate authority is the Quranic ruling: "It is prescribed for you, when one of you approacheth death, if he leave wealth, that be bequeath unto parents and near relatives in kindness. This is a duty for all those who ward off evil."[29]

While Abu Zahra praises this doctrine as asserting a just and equitable principle,[30] some other Egyptian jurists criticize it. Shaikh Sanhouri objects that it is based on the premise that the orphaned grandchildren are entitled to compensation for the lost share of their dead parent. But that parent would not have been entitled to any share if it differed in religion from the propositus, and therefore there would be no room for compensation, an opinion shared by his disciple Professor Madkur.[31]

However, the whole doctrine of the Mandatory Will with all the provisions related to in the Egyptian Law has been adopted by the Syrian legislator (Chapter 5, Art. 257, paras. 1/a, b and c and 2) and the Jordanian legislator under Art. 182, which is the only text therein dealing with the will. The Iraqi legislator added the doctrine of Mandatory Will under Article 74, paragraphs 1 and 2 of Law No. 188/1959 as amended by Law No. 72/1979. The Tunisian legislator added the whole doctrine under the heading of "Mandatory Will" in Articles 191 and 192, as per

29 Sura Baqara II, verse 180.
30 Abu Zahra, *op. cit.* p. 198.
31 Madkoor, *op. cit.* pp. 449–450.

Law No. 77/1959 dated 19 June 1959. There is no mention of the Mandatory Will in the Algerian Law No. 84-11/1984 under that name, but identical provisions are enacted under the heading "Tanzeel", i.e. according a grandchild the status of a child for the purposes of inheritance (Book Three: On Inheritance, Chapter Seven, "Tanzeel". Arts. 169–172, inclusive). The same expression with similar provisions is used in Article 83, paragraph 3 of the Moroccan Law. Again it constitutes the object of a whole chapter (VII) of the fifth Book (on Wills), Articles 212 to 215 inclusive, but tanzeel here could apply to any person, not necessarily a grandchild, whom the testator wishes to be treated as an heir of his but who is in fact a beneficiary of a will. In the sixth Book (on Succession) the Moroccan legislator devotes a whole chapter (VII), Articles 266 to 269 inclusive to the Mandatory Will, incorporating all provisions of the Egyptian doctrine.

The Kuwaiti legislator mentions the mandatory will twice:

(i) Art. 227 on the voidability of voluntary or mandatory wills;
(ii) Art. 291 which sets the mandatory will third in priority of charges on the estate, following funeral expenses and debts of the deceased and preceding voluntary wills and distribution of heirs' shares.

Chapter 14

Waqf

1. DEFINITION

The term waqf (*habs*) literally means to prevent, restrain. In legal terms it means "to protect a thing, to prevent it from becoming the property of a third person (*tamlik*)".[1]

According to Islamic jurists, waqf is the permanent dedication by a Muslim of any property, in such a way that the appropriator's right is extinguished, for charity or for religious objects or purposes, or for the founder of the waqf during his lifetime and after his death, for his descendants, and on their extinction, to a purpose defined by the founder.[2] It follows that there are two categories of waqf – a charity waqf and a "family endowment".

According to Abu Hanifa:

> "It signifies the appropriation of any particular thing in such a way that the appropriator's right in it shall continue, and the advantage of it shall go to some charitable objects; or it is the detention of a specific thing in the ownership of the Waqif or appropriator, and the devoting or appropriating of its profits or usufruct in charity, or the poor, or other good objects. . . ."[3]

According to the two disciples of Abu Hanifa, whose opinion is accepted by the Hanafi school: "Waqf signifies the appropriation of a particular article in such a manner as subjects it to the rules of divine property, whence the appropriator's right in it is extinguished, and it becomes the property of God by the advantage of it resulting to his creatures."[4] Shia text book "*Sharaiul Islam*" considers waqf as a contract,

1 Sarakhsi, *Mabsut*, XII, p. 27.
2 Yakan, *Waqf*, p. 7.
3 Neil B. E. Baillie, *Digest of Mohammadan Law Part I* (1st edn 1865), pp. 459 (557).
4 *Minhaj* Book, p. 232.

the fruit or effect of which is to tie up the original and to leave its usufruct free.

Algerian Law Article 213 states that "Waqf is the detention of property. . . ."

Islamic jurists hold the view that waqf is an imperfect form of ownership in which ownership and utility are never combined at the same time by the same person.[5] The waqf is considered a juristic person to be represented by the administrator thereof (*al mutawali*) who is merely a manager of the waqf. Under the Sharia, when waqf is created, all rights of property pass out of the waqif and rest in God Almighty. The founder of a waqf may constitute himself the first mutawali. A mutawali may be a female, or even a non-Muslim. Equally, a body of persons in the form of a committee may be entrusted with the administration of the waqf, but no minor or a person of unsound mind can be appointed a mutawali. Muslim law does not recognize any right of inheritance to the office of mutawali. If the founder and his executor are both dead, and there is no provision in the waqfiya document for the succession to the office, the mutawali at the time may appoint a successor on his death bed.[6]

According to the Sunni Law, the essentials of a valid waqf are:

(i) a permanent dedication of property;
(ii) the dedicator (*waqif*) should be a person professing the Muslim faith, of sound mind, and of age[7] and must have full right of disposal over his property;
(iii) the dedication should be for a purpose recognized by Islamic Law as religious, pious or charitable.

The essentials of a valid waqf under the Shia Law are as follows:

(a) it must be perpetual;
(b) it must be absolute and unconditional;
(c) possession must be given of the item dedicated;
(d) it must be taken out of the dedicator. That is, he should not retain any interest.

Under Shia Law, a waqf is not completed unless either possession of the waqf property is delivered to the first beneficiaries, or they are authorized to administer the waqf property, or where the waqf created is for the

5 Abu Zahra, *On Waqf*, p. 89.
6 *Ibid.* pp. 303–313.
7 Minority under Muslim law terminates on completion of the 15th year. A Muslim who had attained the age of 15 is competent to make a will disposing of his property (Amir Ali, 4th edn, Vol. I, pp. 212–213).

benefit of a body of persons, a mutawali is appointed, and possession is delivered to him.[8]

A dedication by way of waqf may be either oral or in writing.

2. THE OBJECT OF THE WAQF

Under the Sharia, waqf may be made for any purpose whatever which is recognized by Islam. Thus a Muslim cannot create a waqf for a church or synagogue. A waqf, being a form of *sadaqa* (the object being to acquire merit in the sight of God and a reward (*thawab*) in the next world)[9] cannot be used for purposes unpleasing to God.

The purposes recognized by Islam are the following:

(i) The man's duty to his family: The Quran approves of righteousness of him who spends "of his substance, out of love for Him, on kin, orphans, the needy, the wayfarer, those who ask and on the ransom of slaves . . .",[10]

Waqf, in all systems, may be created for the support of the founder's own immediate descendants, and for collaterals with the remainder to go to the poor. It is to be noted that in Abadi Law if a man leaves property as waqf for his descendants, whether for one or two generations, or in perpetuity, his immediate children can either confirm the waqf or reject it, and deal with the property as their own property.[11]

(ii) The maintenance of mosques dedicated to God for worship according to the teachings of Islam.

(iii) Charities such as hospitals, schools, universities, pensions and other works of public utility.

3. THE PROPERTY CAPABLE OF BEING GIVEN AS WAQF

The following items may be created as waqf:

(i) *Al-Mal al-Mutaqawwim* – i.e. capable of legal ownership and legal transfer.

8 Abu Zahra, *op. cit.* pp. 53–54.
9 *Minhaj loc. cit.* p. 234.
10 Sura Baqara, II, Verse 177.
11 Anderson, *Islamic Law in Africa* (London, 1954), p. 77.

(ii) *Mulk* – i.e. in actual ownership – It must be in existence at the time of creation of the waqf and must be capable of immediate delivery.[12]

4. THE FORM OF CREATING A WAQF

This takes the following methods:

(i) Divesting of ownership: The founder of the waqf must strip himself of all title in the property settled. According to all systems, a waqf that is recoverable is not valid.
(ii) Formalities of waqf: A waqf, as explained above, may be made either verbally or in writing.
(iii) The formalities by a will: A waqf in death-illness is subject to the same restrictions as, and does not have any priority over, other gifts or legacies.
(iv) It must not be subject to a condition that is not in existence at the time of the constitution of the waqf.
(v) It shall not be timed to commence after death, otherwise it will be tantamount to a will.
(vi) It shall not be subject to an option.
(vii) It shall not be subject to a condition that is inconsistent with the essence of the waqf.
(viii) It must indicate either explicitly or implicitly, the permanence of the waqf, and cannot be revoked after its dedication has been completed.[13]

5. PRIVATE WAQFS

(i) The dedicator may assure the permanence of his family from generation to generation. This type of waqf is one for the settler's own family, and his descendants, and is called waqf *ala al-awlad* and is in favour of unborn descendants.[14]
(ii) The dedicator may avoid the strict requirements of the law of inheritance. In the case of waqf in favour of descendants, the succession is contrary to the rule of the Hanafi Law of Inheritance. Males and females, in the absence of a contrary provision in the deed of waqf, take equal shares.

12 Sabiq, *Sunna Jurisprudence*, p. 382.
13 *Ibid.* pp. 381–382.
14 *Ibid.*

6. POWER OF THE FOUNDER (WAQIF)

The founder has an unlimited power of laying down the succession of beneficiaries. However, Algerian courts hold, according to Algerian Law, that the founder shall not have the power to exclude from the waqf his own son and his own daughter from taking a benefit on his estate.[15]

In the absence of any specific direction by the founder, the following principles shall be followed:

(a) male and female have the same share;
(b) agnate and cognate share alike;
(c) children of deceased beneficiaries represent their parents even during the lifetime of those beneficiaries nearer in degree.

But as explained elsewhere, the founder has unrestricted power, and if he so wishes, may take steps that any or all of these rules be barred by specific direction.

(d) The founder may, during his lifetime, appoint, remove and control the mutawali, define the amount of remuneration and appoint a new mutawali.[16]

7. THE ADMINISTRATOR (MUTAWALI)

The administration of the waqf is in the hands of a person known as the mutawali or kaiyim, who is merely a manager of the waqf. The first administrator is usually appointed by the founder and receives a salary for his services. Frequently, the first administrator is the founder himself, and he shall be deemed the mutawali if he does not appoint another person to act in that capacity. He may appoint one or more mutawali during his lifetime, or provide for this to take place after his death. He may repeatedly dismiss any mutawali he has appointed on any grounds. On the death of the founder, the mutawali shall be dismissed unless otherwise stated. In the absence of a mutawali appointed by the founder after his death, the judge may apoint a mutawali who shall preferably be a descendant or a relative of the founder, provided the appointee shall possess legal capability. Otherwise, the judge may appoint a person not a blood relation, until a member of the founder's family becomes eligible. The mutawali must be sane, adult, honest and capable of the administra-

15 *Cf.* Art. 218 "The conditions laid down by the founder shall be fulfilled unless they contravene the Sharia requirements of the waqf in which case the condition shall be void and the waqf remain valid."

16 Abu Zahra, *op. cit.* pp. 130–153.

tion of the waqf. The mutawali may be non-Muslim, blind, mute, male or female. In the event that two mutawalis are appointed by the founder to administer the waqf after his death, neither of them may act severally without the other's permission. If only one of them has accepted the administration, and the other has declined, the judge may appoint a second person to administer jointly the waqf or may empower the one mutawali to adminster the waqf if he is capable on his own. The judge cannot dismiss a mutawali appointed by the founder, nor can the founder dismiss a mutawali appointed by the judge unless the mutawali ceases to be capable of performing his duties as a result of inability or betrayal of trust.

The mutawali represents the waqf in all legal actions related thereto, whether as a claimant or a defendant. He acts on behalf of the beneficiaries. Like inheritance, entitlement to the proceeds of a waqf cannot be disclaimed by the beneficiary.[17]

8. THE CONDITIONS OF WAQF CONTRACT

The waqf is a Sharia contract to be formed by the founder's will, and the offer is subject to acceptance if it is temporary, or to a particular person. The founder must be in possession of legal capacity that is to say, he must be sane, adult and not placed under interdiction for prodigality, imbecility or insolvency. If a debtor under no interdiction constitutes a waqf in his death-illness, and his debts exhaust his assets, the creditors shall be entitled to apply for the declaration of the waqf as void. If a debtor under no interdiction constitutes a waqf while in a state of health, the waqf shall be valid and effective, and creditors shall have no right to dispute it, even if the waqf was founded in order to escape debts. A Muslim may constitute a waqf for the non-Muslim poor, and vice versa.[18]

9. COMPARISON BETWEEN TRUST AND WAQF

(i) The waqf requires a religious, pious, or charitable purpose.

(ii) The founder of a trust may be a beneficiary under such a trust. With the exception of Hanafi Law, the founder may not reserve to himself any benefit from such a waqf.

17 *Ibid.* pp. 303–339.
18 *Ibid.* pp. 48–61.

(iii) A trust may be made for any lawful object, but a waqf may only be created for a charitable, religious or pious motive, though as explained above, its object may be a family settlement to assure the permanence of his family.

(iv) Any transferable property may be the subject of a trust.

(v) The mutawali, as explained, has fewer powers than the trustee.

(vi) The waqf is perpetual.

(vii) The waqf property is inalienable.

(viii) In the case of a trust, if it is incapable of execution, it results for the benefit of its founder.

Chapter 15

Gifts

The gift as a legal disposition has been treated extensively in the Sharia Law and in the modern Arab Civil Laws of Egypt, Jordan, Syria, Iraq, Kuwait, Libya and the Lebanon (the Law of Obligations and Contracts). The Tunisian and Algerian legislators deal with gifts in the Personal Status Law.

In the sections below, we shall start with the general Sharia provisions on gifts, followed by those of the corresponding modern Arab legislations to show where they agree or differ.

1. DEFINTION

According to the Sharia, a gift is a contract by which a person (the donor), disposes, without consideration, of property belonging to him during his lifetime to another person.[1] This definition is adopted in the modern Arab Civil Codes (Arts. 486/1, Egyptian; 475/1, Libyan; 200, Tunisian; 202, Algerian; 454/1, Syrian; 601/1, Iraqi; and 524, Kuwait. Jordanian Article 557 adds "the disposition of a property right."

All these Articles, except the Iraqi, add in a second paragraph that a donor, without being diverted of the intention of making a gift, may impose upon the donee the performance of a specific obligation. Iraqi Article 601/2 adds that a charity, that is a property given out of religious piety, is considered as a gift unless otherwise provided.

The disposition of a property distinguishes gift from *Aariya*, i.e. a loan for use which is a contract whereby the lender hands over to the borrower without consideration, a non-consumable thing for his use during a specific time, or for a specific purpose, to be returned after use.

The stipulation of making the gift during the lifetime of the donor

1 Sabiq, *Sunna Jurisprudence*, p. 388.

distinguishes the gift from a bequest which takes effect after the death of the testator. By the "no consideration" component, the gift differs from sale.

According to the Sharia Law, neither the offer nor acceptance of a gift need be made in writing, whether the subject of the gift is movable or immovable, although delivery of the gift is a condition of validity.[2] Modern Arab legislation, however, makes a distinction. Egyptian Article 488/1 rules that: "The gift must be made by an authentic document under pain of nullity, unless it is made in the form of some other contract."

A gift of movables, however, may be completed by delivery to the donee, without an official instrument being necessary (same Art., para. 2). Similar provisions are to be found in Syrian Article 456, Libyan Article 477, Iraqi Article 602–603, Jordanian Article 566, Algerian Article 206 and the Lebanese Law of Obligations and Contrasts, Article 509–510. Kuwaiti Article 525/1 provides that a gift may be completed either by taking possession, or by an authentic document.

However, the Egyptian Law, Article 20, while ruling that contracts between persons are governed as regards their form by the law of the country in which the contracts are concluded, allow such contracts also to be governed by the law regulating basic provisions of a contract, by the law of domicile of the parties, or by their common national law.

2. ESSENTIALS

It would seem that the gift, like any other contract, requires the two essentials of offer and acceptance. However, Islamic jurists differ here. Of the Hanafis, the Imam Abu Hanifa and the two Companions Muhammad and Abu Youssof, maintain that offer alone is the essential of a gift, since it is a contract for no consideration, acceptance being only a condition for confirmation of transferred ownership. Another Hanafi, Zufar, requires acceptance as well, even receipt, as further essentials of a gift. The Shias, Hanbalis, Shafiis and Malikis also insist on both offer and acceptance, on the ground that no ownership of property can be transferred to and become binding on another person without the latter's acceptance.[3]

Under the Sharia, offer and acceptance of the gift may be by word of mouth, in writing, by deed, and, according to the Malikis, by a gesture, even if the donor/donee is capable of speaking.[4]

2 Badran, *Inheritance, Wills and Gift*, p. 222; Al-Hilli, *Jaafari Provisions*, p. 126.
3 Sanhouri, *Sources of Right*, pp. 42–43; Al-Hilli, *loc. cit.*; see also Abul Naja, *Summary of Hanbali Jurisprudence*, p. 51.
4 Al-Aqil, *The Gift Contract*, pp. 47–48.

Tunisian Article 204 does not acknowledge the validity of a gift unless it is made in a formal document, although movables can be the valid object of a gift through delivery.

Most modern Arab laws on gift stipulate that no gift shall be complete until it is accepted by the donee or by his representative (Arts. 487/1, Egyptian; 445/1, Syrian; 476/1, Libyan; 507, Lebanese; 558/1, Jordanian; and 206, Algerian).

Under the second paragraph of the same Articles, the representative of the donee is the natural or legal guardian of the donee if the latter is a minor.

Apart from that, offer and acceptance in respect of the gift are governed by the same Civil Code Rules for other contracts.

Tunisian Article 201 rules that a gift shall not be effected without the delivery of the object. A gift is void if the donor or donee dies before delivery, even if the donee tried hard to have the gift delivered. However, the donee may claim the gift if the delivery thereof is not affected (Art. 203).

3. CONDITIONS OF THE GIFT

The Islamic jurists set conditions for the validity of the gift in respect of the two parties, the object and the form.

The gift being a disposition of property for no consideration, the donor must possess legal capacity to that effect, i.e. he must be a major, of sound mind, acting on his own free will, and not subject to interdiction, and the owner of the object of the gift. No minor or insane person can make a valid gift, because it is a disposition of property wholly to his disadvantage. No father can make a gift of a property of his minor child for no consideration as this is an injury to the child.[5]

The majority of Islamic jurists rule that a healthy wife of age has the right to make a gift of all or any part of her property to whomsoever she chooses without her husband's permission. Only the Malikis set a limit of one third of her property.[6]

The Shias subscribe to these conditions, but add that a person who is not a prodigal may make a gift of his whole property if that does not render him needy. Some Shias allow a voluntary agent (*foudouli*) to make a gift of a property which is not his.[7] The Hanafis make such a gift subject to the approval of the owner.[8]

5 *Ibid.* pp. 53–54.
6 Badran, *op. cit.* p. 228.
7 Al-Hilli, *op. cit.* p. 126.
8 Sanhouri, *Commentary on the Civil Code*, Vol. 5, p. 120.

The draft Egyptian Civil Code included Article 665 to the effect that it would be a condition for the validity of the gift that the donor be the owner of the given property, and enjoy the legal capacity to make a gift. However, during the committee stage, this Article was omitted on the grounds that the general rules of the contract were sufficient. Instead, Article 491 of the Egyptian Civil Code rules that if a definite and specific thing does not belong to the donor, the rules of the sale of a thing belonging to another shall apply, namely that the purchaser may demand the annulment of the sale or the owner may ratify the sale and the gift.

This provision, which differs from the Sharia, is adopted in Articles 459, Syrian; 480, Libyan; 559, Jordanian; and 530, Kuwaiti. But the Sharia rule is maintained in Iraq, where Article 609 (1) requires that the gift be owned by the donor, and in the Lebanon where Article 513 prohibits making a gift of a property which the donor does not own at the time of the contract. The same provision is also implied in Algerian Personal Status Article 205 which allows the donor to make a gift of all or any part of the property, whether it is a thing, a usufruct or a debt on a third party.

The bulk of Islamic jurists rule that the donee must be actually existent at the time of the gift. Only the Malikis allow a gift to an unborn child provided that it is born alive, otherwise it shall remain in the ownership of the donor. If it died after birth, the gift shall devolve on its heirs. However, if the donee is a minor or insane, his legal or natural guardian or his tutor may accept possession of the object or gift on his behalf.

Modern legislations concur (Arts. 487, Egyptian; 455, Syrian; 476, Libyan; 558 (2), Jordanian; and 604, Iraqi). However, Article 12 of the Egyptian Act No. 119/1952 on guardianship of property forbids a guardian from accepting a gift or a bequest for a minor, creating certain obligations, without the court's permission. Algerian Article 209 enacts that a gift may be made to an unborn child provided it is born alive, thereby following the Maliki opinion.

The object of the gift should be actually in existence and valuable. Tunisian Article 205 makes a gift of future property void. It must be an object of ownership negotiable and transferable, e.g. no valid gift can be made of water in the river, fish in the sea, or a flying-bird or mosque. It must not be inseparable from other property retained by the donor like fruits, trees or buildings without land.

It should be divisible and not part of joint property in order for the donee to be able to take possession.[10]

The Hanafis maintain that the gift of joint property is not valid. The Malikis, Shafiis and Hanbalis rule that gift of joint property is valid. The

8 *Ibid.*
10 Badran, *op. cit.* pp. 230–231.

Malikis go even further to say that a gift may be made for what may not be the object of sale, such as a runaway camel, fruits before being ripe, and usurped property.[11]

The Shias allow a gift of a joint property whether divisible or indivisible on taking possession thereof, provided in the latter case that the gift is of known magnitude.[12]

Egyptian Article 826 provides that: "Every co-owner in common is the absolute owner of his share. He may alienate his share and collect the fruits thereof and make use of his share provided he does not injure the rights of the other co-owner. . . ." The Iraqi Article 609/2 specifically provides that a gift of joint property is valid. Similarly, Kuwait Article 528. The form must denote the transfer of ownership forthwith. A gift is void if it is subject to a condition that does not actually exist, or if it is deferred to some time in the future. It cannot be in the interrogative as it then implies asking for offer or acceptance without asserting it.[13]

4. DEATH-ILLNESS

According to the Sharia, if a sick person, during death-illness, makes a gift to another, it shall not exceed one third of the estate unless allowed by the heirs. But if the donor makes a gift to one of his heirs, and then dies, and the rest of his heirs claim that the gift was made during death-illness, and the donee claims that the gift was made by the donor during good health, the donee has to prove his case. If he fails to do so, the gift shall be considered to have taken place during death-illness, and shall be governed accordingly, i.e. it will not be valid unless approved by the heirs.[14]

If the donor makes a gift during death-illness and then recovers from his illness, the gift shall be deemed valid. Modern Arab legislation follows suit (Arts. 916, Egyptian; 565, Jordanian; 877, Syrian; 920, Libyan; 1109, Iraqi; 529, Kuwaiti).

5. POSSESSION OF THE GIFTS

Some Sharia jurists take the view that the gift passes to the ownership of the donee on the completion of the contract, maintaining that taking

11 Sabiq, *op. cit.* p. 391.
12 Al-Hilli, *op. cit.* p. 127.
13 Al-Aqil, *op. cit.* p. 56.
14 For the definition of the death-illness and its effects on repudiation and inheritance, refer to Chapter 12, 5 and Chapter 6, 2.B.vi respectively.

possession thereof is not a condition of validity in contracts, such as in the case of sale. Ahmad ibn Hanbal, Malik and the Zahiris are of this opinion. Accordingly, if the donor or donee dies before delivery, then the gift will not be void because once the contract has taken place, the gift becomes the property of the donee. Abu Hanifa and Shafii, however, are of the opinion that taking possession is a condition for the validity of the gift. Without it, the donor is not under any obligation. If the donee or donor dies before delivery, the gift becomes void.[15]

Modern Arab legislation follows the view of Abu Hanifa and Shafii, however, and require that taking possession is a condition for the validity of the gift. Without it, the donor is not under any obligation. If the donee or donor dies before delivery, the gift becomes void[16] (Arts. 488/2, Egyptian; 456, Syrian; 477, Libyan; 603, Iraqi; 558/1, Jordanian; 509–510, Lebanese; 206, Algerian; and 525/1, Kuwaiti).

The emphasis on the need to deliver the gift and for the donee to take possession is further dealt with in Articles 493, Egyptian; 461, Syrian; 482, Libyan and 567, Jordanian.

6. REVOCATION OF A GIFT

Apart from the Hanafis and Shias, Islamic jurists are of the opinion that the revocation of a gift is not permissible, except if the gift is made by a father to his son. According to a Tradition of the Prophet, "It is not permissible for a person to make a gift or to revoke it except the father for what he gives to his son."[17] This ruling is held by the Hanbalis and the Shafiis who, by analogy, allow a mother to revoke a gift to her son provided that the father is alive. The Malikis make such a revocation subject to two conditions: that the donee has not married nor incurred a debt. The Zahiris rule out any revocation of a gift.[18] Notwithstanding this ruling, all jurists are unanimous that no revocation is possible for a gift made for charity.[19]

To this impediment the Hanafis add seven others in the absence of which the donor may wholly or in part revoke a gift unless he has not dropped his right of revocation within a specified agreement or in the terms of the gift contract. The seven impediments are:

15 Sabiq, *op. cit.* pp. 391–392.
16 *Ibid.* pp. 396–397.
17 Al-Aqil, *op. cit.* pp. 216, 217.
18 *Ibid.*
19 *Ibid.* pp. 220–228.

(i) if there is an inherent increase of the thing given involving an increase in the value thereof, e.g. land on which the donee has constructed a building; if the obstacle disappears, it renews the right of revocation;
(ii) if the donor or donee dies;
(iii) if the donee has definitely alienated the thing given; however, if such an alienation is only partial, the donor may revoke the gift as to the part remaining;
(iv) if the gift is made by one spouse to another, even if the donor wishes to revoke the gift after the marriage dissolution.
(v) If the gift is made for the benefit of a relative in a prohibited degree;
(vi) if the object given has perished while in possession of the donee; again, if the loss is partial, the right of revocation remains for the part remaining;
(vii) if the donee has supplied valuable consideration for the gift.[20]

These seven impediments for the revocation of a gift, plus the impediment regarding a gift made for charity making eight in total, are held by the Ithna-Asharis, although some allow a spouse to revoke a gift made to the other unless there is another impediment.[21] Some modern Arab legislators adopt the eight above impediments (Arts. 502, Egyptian; 470, Syrian and 491, Libyan). Iraqi and Jordanian Articles 623 and 579 add a further impediment, namely, a gift made by a creditor of a debt to a debtor. Kuwaiti Article 539 follows the Shafiis, ruling out the revocation of a gift from a mother to her child who is an orphan. Sarakhsi adds yet another impediment, i.e. a gift made to a child.

The Algerian Law of Personal Status, while adopting these general rules which are not mentioned expressly, but referred to generally under Article 222, allows both parents to revoke a gift to their child of whatever age unless the gift is made for the marriage thereof, as a guarantee for a loan or in settlement of a debt or if the donee has disposed of the object or changed its nature (Art. 211).

The Tunisian Law rules that if the donor sets a condition preserving his right to revoke a gift if he so wishes, the gift is valid and the condition void (Art. 209). Nevertheless, the donor (Art. 210) may apply for the revocation of his gift, without prejudice to a third party's duly acquired rights, and in the absence of impediments stated under Article 212, on any of the following grounds:

(i) If the donee fails to honour his obligations to the donor, provided such failure constitutes an act of gross ingratitude.

20 Al-Hilli, *op. cit.* pp. 129–131.
21 Al-Aqil, *op. cit.* p. 221.

(ii) If the donor becomes incapable to provide for himself a living standard befitting his social status or becomes unable to meet any maintenance he has to provide under the law.
(iii) If the donor begets a child who remains alive at the time of revocation.

Under Article 211 the right to apply for revocation on grounds of ingratitude lapses on the expiry of a year from the date of the fact of ingratitude or of becoming aware thereof and shall lapse in any event after 10 years of the fact.

Article 212 enumerates the impediments to the revocation as follows:

(i) If that is an inherent increase of the object involving an increase of the value thereof.
(ii) If the donee has alienated the object, but the donor may revoke the remaining part of the object, if any.
(iii) If the object has perished while in possession of the donee, whether through his own actions, through an event over which he has no control, or through usage. If only a part has perished, the donor may revoke the remaining part.

APPENDIX

Presentation Memorandum In the Matter of A Unified Arab Draft Law for Personal Status

The First Congress of the Arab Ministers of Justice (Rabbat 14-16/12/1977) stressed that the unification of legislations in Arab States is a national objective which must be fulfilled, and that the observation of the provisions of the Islamic Sharia is the safest and most fruitful way to achieve this objective.

The Ministerial Committee formed by the First Congress of the Arab Ministers of Justice following its meeting in the period from 4-7/12/1978 recommended that all efforts made on the Arab level must be combined to canonize the provisions of the Islamic Sharia, giving special priority to the legislation for personal status.

The Second Congress of the Arab Ministers of Justice (Sanaa 23-25/2/1981) stressed the importance of the unification of legislations concerning personal status in view of its impact to enrich private and public life of the Arab societies, and in order to found such legislation in the Arab States on the same basis and rules.

Article 2 of the Constitutional Regulations of the Council of Arab Ministers of Justice stipulates that the Council shall aim to reinforce and deepen Arab co-operation in the legal and judicial spheres, to support and sustain the joint effort to standardize Arab legislations in accordance with the decent provisions of Islamic Sharia, while taking into consideration the special circumstances of each Arab State, and to prepare plans and methods to achieve this objective and work towards the execution of such plans and methods.

The Sanaa plan to standardize Arab legislations approved by the Arab Ministers of Justice at their Second Congress stipulates that its aim is to provide a solid and stable foundation on which to build the unified Arab legislation in accordance with the provisions of the Islamic Sharia, while taking into consideration the specific social circumstances of each Arab country. The said plan included the drafting of a unified Arab law for personal status, the formation of a committee consisting of seven Arab experts specializing in Sharia and legal disciplines which was entrusted with the preparation of a unified Arab draft law for personal status, and to submit annual reports of their achievements to the Council of Arab Ministers of Justice.

The Committee briefed to prepare a unified draft Arab law for personal status held, over three years, seven meetings at the headquarters of the Secretariat General at Rabat-Kingdom of Morocco, each meeting lasted for 15 days. The preliminary meeting, on the 15-17/3/1982 was devoted to laying down the regulatory procedures for the work of the Committee, its annual meetings and the duration thereof, and to set a scientific methodology to prepare the draft and to draw the necessary steps to put into effect this methodology. During that preliminary meeting, the general outline of the draft was drawn, and each member of the Committee was briefed to prepare draft Articles for a section of the draft.

During the second, third, fourth, fifth and sixth meetings of the Committee, the draft Articles submitted by each member of the Committee were reviewed and discussed, together with the explanatory memorandum to the draft. The Committee finally drew the first formulation of the complete draft.

The seventh and last meeting of the Committee on 21/1/1985 to 4/2/1985 was devoted to reviewing all the Articles of the draft and the explanatory note thereto. After a revision in depth, and extensive deliberations, the Committee introduced certain modifications to the draft Articles and Explanatory Memorandum to put them in the formula it deemed the fittest within the context of the Sanaa plan for submission to the Council of Arab Ministers of Justice at its third session.

The Secretariat General, respectfully submitting to the Honourable Council this important draft with all the broad hopes attached thereto, and the major achievements expected therefrom as a superb model for the insightful conscious will, a pioneer step on the path of serious collective Arab effort and a cornerstone of major significance to build the edifice of Arab unity, does hope that the Honourable Council shall be able to adopt it in the nearest future as a contribution therefrom towards this positive endeavour to support and sustain the Arab co-operation march in the judicial and legislative spheres.

Submitted with respect to the Honourable Council for consideration.

Signed Mohammed Ash-Shadi – Secretary General to the Council.

OUTLINE OF THE ARAB UNIFIED DRAFT LAW FOR PERSONAL STATUS

Book One
Marriage

Book Two
Dissolution of Marriage

Book Three
Legal capacity and guardianship

Book Four

The Will

Part I – General Provisions
Part II – Essentials and Conditions
    Chapter 1 – The Form
    Chapter 2 – The Testator
    Chapter 3 – The Beneficiary
    Chapter 4 – The Object of the Will
Part III – The Will by Status Attribution
Part IV – The Impediments to the Will
Part V – The Mandatory Will
Part VI – Conflict of Legacies

Book Five

Inheritance

Part I – General Provisions
Part II – Classes of Heirs and Their Entitlement
    Chapter 1 – The Sharers
    Chapter 2 – The Agnates
    Chapter 3 – The Heirs as Sharers and Residuaries
Part III – Exclusions, Return and Increase
Part IV – Distant Kindred
    Chapter 1 – Classes of Distant Kindred
    Chapter 2 – Inheritance by Distant Kindred
Part V – Special Cases
    Chapter 1 – Akdariyya
    Chapter 2 – Almushtaraka (full brothers sharing with uterines)
Part VI – Miscellaneous Questions
Final Provisions

IN THE NAME OF GOD THE COMPASSIONATE
THE MOST MERCIFUL

THE UNIFIED ARAB DRAFT LAW FOR PERSONAL STATUS

Book One

Marriage

Part I

Betrothal

Article 1
Betrothal is the offer or promise of marriage. It shall include the reading of the Fatihah and the exchange of presents.

Article 2
Betrothal is not permissible of a woman in a permanent or temporary prohibited degree, or a woman betrothed to a third person as long as her betrothal stands.

Article 3
(a) Each of the parties to the betrothal may withdraw.
(b) The one who withdraws from the betrothal shall return to the other party the present given thereby if it is still existent, otherwise the like or the value thereof at the time of collection, unless otherwise dictated by custom.
(c) If the betrothal is terminated through death or through the occurrence of an impediment to marriage, no present shall be returned.

Article 4
If the termination of betrothal causes any injury, the party causing the injury shall be liable for damages.

Part II

General Provisions

Article 5
Marriage is a legal pact between a man and a woman with the objective of establishing a stable family under the patronage of the husband on foundations that guarantee for both of them to carry the burdens thereof in compassion and affection.

Article 6
(a) The spouses are bound by their contract conditions unless it is a condition which allows something forbidden or prevents something legitimate.
(b) If the contract is subject to a condition that runs contrary to its objective or intentions, the condition shall be void, but the contract shall remain valid.
(c) No condition shall be honoured unless it is expressly stipulated in the marriage contract.

Article 7
(a) Marriage shall be proved by an official document.
(b) Exceptionally and for a limited period, and in view of consideration of a specific fact, marriage may be proved by evidence or mutual declaration.

Article 8
The legal capacity for marriage shall be achieved through sanity with the boy reaching the legal age of majority, and the girl completing her eighteenth year of age.

Article 9
(a) The marriage of the insane or imbecile shall only be contracted by the guardian thereof having obtained permission by the court to that effect.
(b) The judge shall not grant permission for the marriage of the insane or imbecile except on the following conditions being fulfilled:
(i) the other party's acceptance to marry the insane or imbecile having been aware of the state thereof;
(ii) that the disease is not such as to pass to their posterity;
(iii) that the marriage would be beneficial to the insane or imbecile.
The two last conditions shall be ascertained under a report by a competent committee.

Article 10
The marriage of a person placed under interdiction on the grounds of prodigality shall only be contracted by the guardian thereof.

Article 11
If a person, having completed the fifteeth year of age, applies for marriage, the judge may grant permission thereof on ascertaining the applicants' suitability, subject to the consent by the guardian, who, on withholding such consent, shall be asked by the judge to give it within a specified period after which, if he fails to object, or objects unreasonably, the judge shall order the marriage.

Article 12
No minor, male or female, may marry before completing 15 years of age, without permission by the judge whenever there is a serious ground thereto, or its interest so requires.

Article 13
A person married under the two previous Articles shall acquire legal capacity for litigation in all matters related to marriage and the effects thereof.

Article 14
The marriage guardian is the agnate residuary by himself in the priority to inheritance. Should two guardians be of the same proximity in relationship, either may contract the marriage under the conditions thereof.

Article 15
The guardian must be a male, sane, adult, not under restrictions through pilgrimage or umra* and a Muslim, if the girl betrothed is Muslim.

Article 16
In the absence of the nearest guardian, should the judge deem that it would be detrimental to the marriage to wait for his consent, guardianship shall pass to the next in line.

Article 17
The judge is the guardian of anyone who has no guardian.

Article 18
The judge shall not contract the marriage of any person of whom he is the guardian, to himself, nor to any ascendant or descendant of his.

Part III

Essentials and Conditions

Article 19
The essentials of the marriage contract are:
(a) the spouses;
(b) offer and acceptance.

Chapter 1

The Spouses

Article 20
The spouses of legal capacity under the provisions of this law may contract their marriage and may appoint attorneys to act for them to that effect.

* Umra: the minor haj: pilgrimage to Mecca at times of the year other than during the proper haj season, at the end of the Hijra year in the month of Dhul-Hijja (the translator).

Article 21
(a) Marriage equality is a right of the woman and the guardian.
(b) Marriage equality shall be reckoned with at the time of the contract and shall be determined according to custom.
(c) The determination of age suitability between the spouses is the sole right of the wife.

Article 22
It is a condition for the marriage contract to be concluded that the woman shall not be in a permanent or temporary prohibited degree to the man.

Chapter 2

Offer and Acceptance

Article 23
The marriage contract shall be concluded through offer by one party and acceptance by the other of their own free will in terms which indicate it linguistically or according to custom. In the event of inability to talk, writing shall replace speech, and if impossible, then the understandable gestures.

Article 24
Acceptance should comply with the following conditions:
(i) that it shall be identical with the offer expressly or by implication;
(ii) that it shall occur at the same sitting as the offer;
(iii) that it shall be effective, together with the offer.

Chapter 3

The Prohibited Degrees

Section 1

Permanent Prohibited Degrees

Article 25
No person shall be allowed to marry any of the following blood relations:
(i) the ascendant thereof how-high-soever;
(ii) any descendant thereof how-low-soever;
(iii) any descendant of either or both parents how-low-soever;
(iv) the first generation of the descendants of grandfathers or grandmothers thereof.

Article 26
No person shall be permitted to marry the following in-laws:
(i) the spouse of any ascendant thereof, how-high-soever or a descendant thereof how-low-soever;
(ii) the ascendants of the spouse thereof, how-high-soever;
(iii) the descendants of his wife whose marriage he has actually consummated, how-low-soever.

Article 27
A descendant by adultry how-low-soever shall be in a prohibited degree to the parent thereof.

Article 28
A prohibited degree on grounds of kinship shall be prohibited on grounds of fosterage on the fulfilment of the following two conditions:
(i) suckling of the baby occurring during its first two years and prior to weaning;
(ii) that it is established that the fostering mother has given the baby a complete feed according to custom.

Article 29
A divorcee through *lian* shall be in a prohibited degree to her previous husband unless he admits he has lied.

Section 2

Temporary Prohibited Degrees

Article 30
The temporary prohibited degrees are:
(i) unlawful conjunction, that is for the man to have at the same time even during the iddat, two wives so related to each other that, if either of them had been a man, they would have been prohibited from marrying one another;
(ii) to have more than four wives at the same time, even if one of them was waiting during her iddat of a revocable marriage;
(iii) the wife of a third person;
(iv) the ex-wife of a third person during her period of iddat;
(v) the repudiated wife after three pronouncements of divorce whose ex-husband shall not be allowed to remarry except after the expiry of her iddat of another husband with whom marriage has actually been consummated under a valid contract.
(vi) a woman under religious restriction due to a pilgrimage or an urma.*
(vii) a woman not professing Christianity or Judaism if she is not Muslim;
(viii) a Muslim marrying a non-Muslim.

Article 31
(a) A Muslim may have up to four wives simultaneously unless he fears he cannot render them equal justice.
(b) No marriage to another wife may be contracted without permission by the judge. In order for such permission to be granted, the following conditions must be complied with:
(i) that there be a lawful interest;
(ii) that the husband be financially capable to support more than one wife;

*See previous footnote (translator).

(iii) that the woman be aware that her suitor is already married;
(iv) that the existing wife be informed that her husband is desirous to marry another woman besides her.
(c) No such permission shall be effective until it becomes conclusive.

Article 32
A woman may stipulate in her marriage contract that her husband shall not marry another woman. Should he marry another woman, the first wife shall be entitled to apply for the annulment of their marriage.

Chapter 4

The Contract Conditions

Article 33
For the marriage contract to be valid, it must comply with the following conditions:
(i) the presence of two witnesses;
(ii) no dower shall have been waived;
(iii) the consent of the guardian in the case of any spouse who does not possess legal capacity for marriage under the provisions of this law.

Article 34
The two witnesses must be Muslim, sane, of age, trustworthy, and must hear the offer and acceptance, and understand that the intention is marriage.

Article 35
The dower is the property given by the husband to express his willingness to marry.

Article 36
Everything that can be a lawful object of obligation is a valid dower.

Article 37
The dower is the sole property of the woman which she can dispose of the way she likes. Any condition to the contrary shall be void.

Article 38
(a) The payment of the whole or part of the dower may be prompt or deferred at the time of the contract.
(b) Under a valid contract, the whole dower shall be payable, and shall be confirmed on consummation or death. The deferred part of the dower shall become payable on death or separation unless it is otherwise stipulated in the contract. The divorced woman before consummation shall be entitled to half the dower if it was specified, otherwise the judge shall order for her the equivalent to half the dower of the equal.

Article 39
(a) The wife may withhold her consent to consummation until the prompt dower due to her is paid.
(b) Should the wife consent to consummation before receiving her dower from the husband, it shall be a debt on him to her.

Article 40
If a suitor gives his fiancée before the contract, property by way of dower, and then one party withdraws from the contract, or dies, what has been given shall be returned in itself, if it still exists, otherwise the equivalent or the value thereof at the time of receiving it.

Chapter 5

The Rights of the Spouses

Article 41
The mutual rights and duties of the spouses are:
(i) the lawful enjoyment by each spouse of the other;
(ii) the chastity and faithfulness of each spouse towards the other;
(iii) lawful cohabitation;
(iv) decent companionship and mutual respect and affection and the preservation of the welfare of the family;
(v) caring for the children and bringing them up in such a way as to secure for them decent rearing;
(vi) due respect by each spouse to the parents and nearest of kin of the other.

Article 42: The Wife's Rights vis-à-vis her husband:
(i) maintenance;
(ii) permission to visit her parents and her kin in a prohibited degree and to invite them to visit her at the matrimonial home according to decent custom;
(iii) to retain her maiden name;
(iv) not to interfere with her private property which she may dispose of freely;
(v) to avoid any physical or moral injury to her;
(vi) to observe justice between her and other wives should the husband have more than one.

Article 43: The Husband's Rights vis-à-vis his wife:
(i) to look after him and to obey his lawful orders of the household;
(ii) to look after, manage and take care of, the effects of the matrimonial home;
(iii) to care for his children by her and to suckle them unless there is any impediment.

Part IV

Form of Marriage

Article 44
(i) marriage is either valid or irregular;
(ii) a valid marriage is one which fulfils the essentials and conditions thereof;
(iii) A valid marriage shall have effect as from the time of its conclusion.

Article 45
(i) the irregular marriage is one which does not fulfil some essentials or conditions;
(ii) the irregular marriage shall have no effect before consummation.

Article 46
The irregular marriage after consummation shall produce the following effects:
(i) the lesser of the stipulated dower or the dower of the equal.
(ii) parentage and the creation of prohibited degrees on the grounds of affinity;
(iii) iddat;
(iv) maintenance so long as the woman is unaware of the irregularity of the contract.

Part V

Effects of Marriage

Chapter 1

Maintenance – General Provisions

Article 47
(a) Maintenance shall include food, raiment, housing, doctors and servants fees, medicines and all amenities of human life according to custom.
(b) The grounds for entitlement to maintenance are matrimony, blood relationship and a covenant.

Article 48
In the determination of maintenance, consideration shall be taken of the condition of the maintainer, the condition of the subject of maintenance, and the economic situation in terms of time and place.

Article 49
(a) Maintenance may be increased or reduced according to changing conditions.
(b) No action for increase or decrease of maintenance shall be heard before six months from the court order of paying maintenance, except under exceptional circumstances.

(c) The increase or decrease of the maintenance shall be ordered from the date of the legal suit.

Article 50
The continuous maintenance shall have a privilege over all other debts.

Article 51
The sustenance of the needy is a duty upon him who has excess.

Section 1

Maintenance for the Wife

Article 52
(a) The maintenance of the wife shall be a duty on her husband as from the time of a valid contract.
(b) The wife may contribute to the maintenance of the family if she has means.
(c) The wife who has means shall be under the obligation to maintain the family during the husband's insolvency.

Article 53
The wife shall not receive under a court order the maintenance of two years prior to the legal action, unless otherwise agreed upon between the spouses.

Article 54
During the examination of the maintenance action, the judge may order, at the request of the wife, a temporary maintenance for her, such an order being immediately enforceable under the law.

Article 55
The husband shall be under the obligation to provide maintenance for his wife in her iddat of divorce, repudiation or annulment, unless she is disobedient.

Article 56
The woman observing the iddat of death shall be entitled to live in the matrimonial home for the duration of the iddat unless she leaves it of her own free will.

Article 57
The wife shall not be entitled to any maintenance in the following cases:
(i) if she leaves the matrimonial home without a just excuse;
(ii) if she denies the husband access to the matrimonial home without a just excuse;
(iii) if she works outside her home without her husband's consent unless he prevents her from working arbitrarily;
(iv) if she refuses to travel with her husband without an excuse.

Article 58
The wife's maintenance shall lapse:
(i) on payment;
(ii) on discharge;
(iii) on the husband's death.

Article 59
The husband shall provide for his wife at his residence a safe accommodation befitting their condition.

Article 60
The wife shall live with her husband in the accommodation he provides, and shall leave the same with him unless she has stipulated otherwise under the contract, or unless the move is meant to cause her injury.

Article 61
(a) The husband may have, staying with his wife in the matrimonial home, his children from another wife if he is under obligation to maintain them, and his parents, provided no injury shall befall her as a consequence thereof.
(b) The wife has no right to have living with her in the matrimonial home her children from another husband unless they have no other guardian apart from her, or the husband consents thereto explicitly or by implication.
(c) The husband may withdraw his consent.

Article 62
The husband has no right to have living with his wife in the same matrimonial home another wife of his unless the first wife consents thereto. She may withdraw her consent whenever she likes.

Section 2

Maintenance for Relatives

Article 63
(a) The maintenance of the minor who has no means shall be incumbent on the father until the girl marries, and the boy reaches the age at which his like can earn a living and complete his sixteenth year of age, unless he is a student pursuing his studies with ordinary success, then until the completion thereof.
(b) The maintenance of the adult son who is incapable of earning a living because of a handicap or the like shall be incumbent on his father unless the son has property from which he can maintain himself.
(c) The maintenance of the daughter shall revert to her father if she is divorced, or if her husband dies, and she has no property.
(d) If the child's property falls short to provide adequate maintenance, the father shall be under the obligation to supplement the same to sufficiency under the previous conditions.

Article 64

The father shall be under the obligation to provide the cost for the fostering of his child if it is difficult for the mother to foster it, and that shall be by way of maintenance.

Article 65

(a) The child who has means, whether male or female, adult or a minor, shall be under obligation to provide maintenance for his parents if they have no property from which they can maintain themselves.

(b) If the parents property falls short of providing maintenance, the children who have means shall be under obligation to supplement the same to sufficiency.

Article 67

(a) The maintenance of the parents shall be shared by their children according to the latter's means.

(b) If the child provides maintenance for its parents on its own free will, it shall have no right to ask its siblings for a refund.

(c) If maintenance is provided following a court order, a child may demand its money back from each of them according to the court's order.

Article 68

If the son does not earn any surplus after the satisfaction of his own, his wife's and his children's needs, he shall be ordered to add his parents entitled to maintenance, to his family.

Article 69

The maintenance for every person entitled thereto shall be incumbent on his presumptive heirs among his relatives who have means in proportion to their inheritance share. If the presumptive heir is insolvent, maintenance shall pass on to the next in line to inherit with due regard to the provisions of Article 65 of this Act.

Article 70

If there are several persons entitled to maintenance, and the person on whom the maintenance is incumbent cannot provide maintenance for them all, then the wife's maintenance shall come first, followed by the children's maintenance, the parents' maintenance, and finally maintenance for blood relations.

Article 71

Maintenance for blood relations shall run as from the date of the legal action. The judge may order maintenance for children by the father for a prior period not exceeding six months before the legal action.

Section 3

Maintenance under a Covenant

Article 72
A covenantor who pledges to provide maintenance shall be bound to provide it to the covenantee whether the latter be adult or minor.

Article 73
Maintenance under a covenant shall run for the specified duration therefor. If the duration is not specified, the covenantor's word shall be accepted for the duration thereof.

Article 74
If the covenantor dies before the completion of the duration for the covenant, the maintenance shall not be taken from his estate for the remaining period unless the covenant was for a consideration.

Article 75
If the covenantor provides maintenance, it shall lapse on him on whom it is incumbent. If the covenantor does not provide maintenance, it shall pass to him on whom it is incumbent who shall be entitled to claim a refund against the convenantor for the amount he spent. No such refund can be claimed on the estate of the covenantor unless the covenant is for a consideration.

Article 76
The maintenance covenanted for a woman shall lapse if she marries.

Article 77
(a) The maintenance of an infant foundling of unknown parentage shall be incumbent on the finder thereof if he is capable to provide maintenance, and if the foundling has no means.
(b) If the father of the foundling or the person on whom it is incumbent to provide maintenance therefor is located and has means, the finder shall claim a refund of the maintenance he has incurred.

Chapter 2

Parentage – General Provisions

Article 78
Parentage can only be established through wedlock, acknowledgment, or evidence.

Section 1

Wedlock

Article 79

(a) The child shall appertain to the wedlock if the minimum term for pregnancy has lapsed since the marriage contract was concluded, and if it is not proven that the spouses could not have met.

(b) The parentage of the offspring of the consummation under the semblance of the lawfulness thereof shall be established if it is born within the minimum term of pregnancy as from the date of consummation.

Article 80

The minimum term for pregnancy is six months, and the maximum, one year.

Section 2

Acknowledgment

Article 81

(a) Acknowledgment of filiation even during the death-illness shall establish parentage under the following conditions:

(i) that the person who is acknowledged as a child be of unknown parentage;

(ii) that the deponent be adult and sane;

(iii) that the age-gap between the deponent and the acknowledged be such as to permit the truth of the acknowledgment.

(iv) that the acknowledged person confirms the acknowledgment if it is adult and sane.

(b) Confirmation of paternity is an acknowledgment of filiation issued by a man under the conditions stipulated in the previous paragraph.

Article 82

If the deponent is a married woman or counting her iddat, the parentage of the child to her husband shall only be established if he confirms her acknowledgment or if she produces evidence to the truthfulness thereof.

Article 83

The acknowledgment by a person of unknown parentage of paternity or maternity shall establish parentage if the acknowledged person confirms it, or if evidence to the truthfulness thereof is produced if the age gap so allows.

Article 84

Acknowledgment of parentage for any degree other than filiation, paternity or maternity, shall be binding only on a person other than the deponent by the confirmation thereby or through the production of evidence.

Article 85

No suit by the deponent's heirs to deny parentage after its being established through valid acknowledgment may be heard.

Book Two

Dissolution of Marriage

General Provisions

Article 86
Marriage is dissolved:
(i) by the husband's wish, in which case it shall be called repudiation;
(ii) by the spouses' mutual agreement and it is then called mukhalaa;
(iii) by court decree, in which case it is called divorce or annulment;
(iv) on the death of either spouse.

Part I

Repudiation

Article 87
(a) Repudiation is the dissolution of a marriage contract in the Sharia-set formula.
(b) Repudiation may occur by word of mouth, in writing and in the event of inability thereto, then by intelligible gesture.

Article 88
Repudiation shall be performed by the husband or an attorney acting on his behalf under a special power of attorney in the event of the husband's failure to be present in person, or by the wife if the husband has given her power to repudiate herself.

Article 89
(a) The person who performs repudiation must be sane and in possession of the power of choice.
(b) Repudiation by the insane, the imbecile, a person under alcoholic stupor, a person acting under duress, or any person who has lost discretion as a result of rage or otherwise shall be void.

Article 90
Repudiation can be only of a wife who has been married under a valid contract, and who is not counting her iddat.

Article 91
(a) Repudiation conditional on the ommission or commission of a deed shall be void.
(b) Repudiation through failing to honour an oath of repudiation or of the wife becoming a prohibited degree shall be void.
(c) A pronouncement of repudiation connected with a number by word of mouth or in writing or by gesture shall be deemed a single pronouncement.

Article 92
Repudiation is either revocable or irrevocable.
(a) The revocable repudiation does not terminate the marriage contract except after expiry of the iddat.
(b) The irrevocable repudiation shall terminate the marriage contract forthwith.

Article 93
Every repudiation shall be revocable except a pronouncement completing three pronouncements of repudiation, repudiation before consummation, repudiation for a consideration, and what is deemed under the law to be irrevocable.

Article 94
(a) Repudiation shall take effect through a declaration by the husband before the judge.
(b) The judge before hearing the declaration shall try to reconciliate between the spouses.

Article 95
A competent judge on the occurrence of repudiation shall order maintenance for the wife during her iddat, maintenance for the children, the person to whom custody is granted and access to the ward. Such an order shall be deemed immediately enforceable under the law. The person against whom the order has been given may appeal.

Article 96
(a) A divorced woman with whom marriage has been consummated is entitled to muta according to the wealth of the man and the condition of the woman.
(b) The woman repudiated may demand damages if the man has abused his right to effect repudiation.

Article 97
The husband may revoke repudiation so long as the repudiated wife is still in her iddat. Such a right cannot be waived.

Article 98
(a) Revocation of repudiation may be effected by deed, by word, or in writing, and in the event of being unable to do either, then by intelligible gesture.
(b) Revocation shall be confirmed and the wife shall be forthwith notified thereof.

Part II

Mukhalaa

Article 99
(a) The spouses may come to mutual agreement on the termination of the marriage contract through khalaa.
(b) The khalaa shall be for a consideration given by the wife.
(c) Khalaa shall be deemed an irrevocable repudiation.

Article 100
For the khalaa to be valid, the wife must possess legal capacity for giving and the husband legal capacity to effect repudiation.

Article 101
No khalaa shall be made for a consideration of a waiver to the custody of the children, or anything that concerns their rights. Should it be so effected, the khalaa shall be valid, and the condition void.

Article 102
(a) If a consideration is specified in the mukhalaa, what is so specified shall solely be binding.
(b) If no consideration is specified in the mukhalaa, the repudiation provisions shall apply.

Part III

Divorce

Chapter 1

Divorce for Defects

Article 103
Each spouse may apply for divorce on the ground of an incurable disease of the other, or a disease that would only be cured in more than a year, whether it is mental or organic, whether it has been suffered from before or after the contract, whether the other spouse knew it before consummation or after, and did not consent to it. However, if the disease is curable within a year, the court shall grant the spouse affected one year before ordering a divorce.

Article 104
Recourse shall be had to knowledgable specialist in order to determine the disease.

Article 105
Divorce on the ground of the other spouse's disease shall be irrevocable.

Chapter 2

Divorce on the Ground of Failure to pay the Prompt Dower

Article 106
(a) The wife with whom consummation has not occurred shall be granted a divorce decree on the ground of failure of the husband to pay her prompt dower in the following two cases:
(i) if the husband has no visible property from which to take the dower;
(ii) if the husband is visibly insolvent or of unknown condition, and the delay granted him by the judge to pay the dower expired without payment being effected.
(b) The wife with whom marriage has been consummated shall not be granted a divorce decree on the ground of failure by the husband to pay her prompt dower which shall remain a debt on the husband.

Article 107
Divorce on the ground of failure to pay the prompt dower shall be irrevocable.

Chapter 3

Divorce on the Ground of Injury and Dissent

Article 108
(a) Each spouse may apply to the court for a divorce on the ground of injury that renders the continuation of living together impossible.
(b) The judge shall try his utmost to reconcile between the two spouses.
(c) If the judge is unable to reconcile and the injury is proved, he shall order divorce with due consideration to the provisions of Article 112 of this Act.

Article 109
If injury is not proved and dissent continues between the two spouses and there is no way to effect a reconciliation, the judge shall appoint two arbitrators from their respective families if possible, otherwise of people whom he deems capable to reconcile, who shall take an oath to discharge their task in fairness and honesty, and shall have a delay for arbitration.

Article 110
(a) The arbitrators shall investigate the grounds of dissent and shall do their utmost to reconcile the two spouses.
(b) The two arbitrators shall submit to the judge a report on their endeavours and proposals showing the extent of injuries by each spouse to the other, or by one of them to the other.

Article 111
(a) The judge may approve the arbitrators' report or appoint two other arbitrators showing the reason for such a decision to undertake arbitration anew, pursuant to the procedures stipulated in the two previous articles.

(b) Should reconciliation prove impossible and dissent continue between the two spouses, the judge shall issue a divorce decree on the ground of the two arbitrators' report without prejudice to the provisions of Article 112 of this Act.

Article 112
(a) If the judge orders divorce for the wife with whom consummation has taken place on the grounds of injury or dissent, if the injury is wholly or mostly on the part of the wife, she shall lose her deferred dower, and the judge shall determine the amount she will have to return to the husband from the dower actually received. If the injury is mostly or wholly on the part of the husband, the dower shall remain the right of the wife.
(b) If the injured party claims damages, the judge shall order the same in proportion to the injury suffered.

Article 113
Divorce on the grounds of injury or dissent shall be irrevocable.

Article 114
If the wife applies for divorce before consummation and valid retirement and lodges with the court the dower she actually received and the costs incurred by the husband for marriage purposes, and the husband refrains from repudiating her, and the judge could not reconcile them, he shall order divorce.

Chapter 4

Divorce on the Grounds of Failure to Provide Maintenance

Article 115
(a) The wife may apply to the court for divorce if the husband refrains from providing maintenance for her without having visible property and without his insolvency being proved.
(b) No wife shall be granted a divorce decree from her insolvent husband before his being granted a delay not exceeding three months.
(c) The wife shall not be granted a divorce decree if insolvency was due to a cause over which the husband had no control, or if she knew of his insolvency before marriage, and did not object thereto.

Article 116
Divorce on the ground of failure to provide maintenance shall be revocable, but if complaint is renewed therefrom, the divorce shall be irrevocable.

Chapter 5

Divorce on the Ground of the Husband Going Absent or Missing

Article 117
The wife may apply to the court for a divorce decree on the ground of the absence of her husband whose address or place of residence is known even if he

has property from which she can take maintenance. However, she shall not be granted divorce before the husband being formally summoned and warned either to live with his wife, or to have her moving to him, or to repudiate her, giving him a delay of no less than four months and no more than one year.

Article 118
The wife of the missing or absent person whose address or place of residence is unknown may apply for divorce which shall not be ordered for her before the lapse of one year at least from the date of the husband going missing or absent.

Article 119
The wife of a convict against whom a prison sentence of no less than three years has been passed may apply for divorce which she shall not be granted before one year at least has lapsed since his imprisonment.

Chapter 6

Divorce on the Grounds of Desertion, Ilaa and Dhihar

Article 120
(a) The wife may apply for divorce if her husband has deserted her for no reason for four months or more, or if he has taken an oath not to cohabit with her for the said period.
(b) If the husband is willing to return or to cease deserting his wife, the judge shall grant him a reasonable delay after the lapse of which, if the husband has failed to return, the judge shall grant her a divorce.

Article 121
(a) The wife may apply for divorce on the grounds of dhihar.
(b) The judge shall summon the husband to expiate dhihar within four months from the date of the summons, and after the lapse of which, with the husband failing to do so, the judge shall order divorce.

Chapter 7

Common Provisions

Article 122
Divorce under Articles, 117, 118, 119, 120 and 121 shall be deemed revocable.

Article 123
While hearing a case for divorce, the judge shall take whatever temporary measures he deems necessary to secure maintenance for the wife and the children, and matters related to the custody of and access to the children.

Part IV

Annulment

Article 124
The marriage contract shall be annulled if it lacks any essential thereof or if it includes an impediment that runs against the exigencies thereof.

Article 125
The marriage contract shall be annulled if the wife is in a prohibited degree, or if an accident has occurred which prevents its lawful continuation.

Part V

Effects of Separation Between the Two Spouses

Chapter 1

The Iddat

Article 126
(a) The iddat is a waiting period observed imperatively by the wife without getting married following a separation.
(b) The iddat shall start from the day of the dissolution of marriage.
(c) The iddat shall start from the last act of cohabitation in the event of consummation with a semblance of its being lawful.

Section 1

The Iddat of Death

Article 127
(a) The wife whose husband under a valid contract has died, shall observe an iddat of four months and ten days if she is not pregnant.
(b) A pregnant woman whose husband has died shall have her iddat terminated on giving birth, or having an abortion, provided that the embryo shall be discernable.
(c) The woman with whom consummation has occurred with the semblance of its being lawful under an irregular contract or without a contract, shall observe the iddat of divorce if the man has died.

Section 2

The Iddat of the Non-Widow

Article 128
(a) The iddat for a pregnant woman shall terminate on her giving birth or with an abortion provided that the embryo is discernable.
(b) The iddat for the non-pregnant:

(i) Three complete menstrual courses for those who menstruate;
(ii) Three months for a woman who has not menstruated ever, or who has reached the menopause and her menstruation stopped. Should she see a menstruation before the expiry thereof, she shall resume the iddat for three courses.
(iii) Three months for the woman whose blood has not stopped if she has no known period. Should she have a period she remembers, she shall follow the same in counting the iddat.
(iv) The lesser period of three menstrual courses or a year for the one whose menstruation has stopped before reaching menopause.

Article 129
In all cases the iddat duration shall not exceed one year.

Section 3

The Overlapping of Iddats

Article 130
If the husband died and the woman was in an iddat of a revocable divorce, she shall pass to the iddat of death without counting the previous period.

Article 131
If the husband died while the woman was in an iddat of an irrevocable divorce, she shall complete the same, and shall not be bound to observe the iddat of death unless the repudiation occurred during the death-illness, in which case she shall observe the longer of the two terms.

Part VI

Custody

Article 132
Custody is the caring for the child, its education and upbringing without prejudice to the guardian's right for the purposes of guardianship of the person.

Article 133
The guardian must fulfil the following conditions:
(i) sanity;
(ii) majority;
(iii) honesty;
(iv) capability to bring up, maintain and care for the ward;
(v) freedom from infectious diseases.

Article 134
In addition to the conditions mentioned in the previous Article, the guardian shall comply with the following conditions:
(a) If it is a woman:

(i) to be in a prohibited degree to the ward if he is a male;
(ii) not to be married to a husband who is a stranger to the ward, and with whom marriage has been consummated, unless the court decides otherwise, taking into account the interests of the ward.
(b) If it is a man:
(i) to have living with him a woman who is fit for the custody of the child;
(ii) to be in a prohibited degree to the ward, if she is a female.

Article 135
If the woman guardian professes a faith different from that of the father of the ward, and she is not a mother of the ward, she shall lose her guardianship on the ward completing the fifth year of age, but if she is the mother thereof, her guardianship shall continue unless it transpires that she is exploiting her guardianship to bring up the ward in a faith different from that of the father.

Article 136
Guardianship shall run until the boy completes his fourteenth year of age, and until the girl marries and her marriage is consummated, unless the judge in all cases decides otherwise for the interests of the ward.

Articles 137
Guardianship is a duty of both parents for as long as matrimony sustains between them. On their separation, guardianship shall go to the mother, then the father, then the blood relations of the ward according to the following order, unless otherwise decided by the judge, for the interests of the ward:

the maternal grandmother of the ward, how-high-soever; then
its maternal aunt; then the maternal aunt of his mother; then
the paternal aunt of its mother; then
the paternal grandmother, how-high-soever; then
its sister; then
its paternal aunt; then
the paternal aunt of its father; then
the maternal aunt of its father; then
the daughter of his brother; then
the daughter of his sister.

In all cases, priority shall go to the full relation, then to the maternal, and then to the paternal.

Article 138
If the mother leaves the matrimonial home because of a dispute or otherwise, she shall keep the guardianship, unless the judge orders otherwise. If the ward is a suckling baby, the mother shall be obliged to take guardianship thereof.

Article 140
It shall be the duty of the father or other guardians of the ward to look after its interests, to discipline, guide and educate it, and the ward shall not spend the night with any person other than its female guardian unless otherwise ruled by the judge.

Article 141

The guardian who is entrusted with the custody of the ward may not leave the country with the ward without written consent by the guardian of the person of the ward. If the said guardian refuses to give such a consent, the matter shall be submitted to the court.

Article 142

Guardianship shall lapse in the following events:

(i) if any condition stipulated under Articles 133 and 134 of this Act is not complied with.

(ii) if the guardian entrusted with the custody of the ward settles down in a place where it is difficult for the guardian of the person of the ward to perform his duties;

(iii) if the person eligible for the guardianship keeps silent over claiming it for a year without an excuse;

(iv) if the new female guardian lives with the one who has lost her guardianship for any reason other than physical inability.

Article 143

The guardianship shall revert to the person who has lost it on the reason for losing the same ceasing to exist.

Article 144

(a) If the ward is under the guardianship of either parent, the other shall be entitled to visit it, and to receive it on visits, and to accompany it in a manner to be decided by the judge.

(b) If the parent of the ward is deceased or absent, the blood relations of the ward who are in a prohibited degree thereto are entitled to have access thereto in the manner decided by the judge.

(c) If the ward lives with a person other than its parents, the judge shall name the person who is entitled to visits by the ward from among its relations who are in a prohibited degree thereto.

Book Three

Legal Capacity

Status and Guardianship

Part I

Legal Capacity

Chapter 1
General Provisions

Article 145
A person shall enjoy full legal capacity to exercise his civil rights unless otherwise provided by the law.

Article 146
The age of majority is 21 calendar years.

Article 147
The following persons shall be deemed minor:
(i) a person who has not attained the age of majority;
(ii) the insane, the imbecile, the mentally deranged and the prodigal;
(iii) the missing or absent person.

Article 148
(a) The following persons shall be deemed lacking capacity:
(i) the minor, devoid of discretion;
(ii) the imbecile, the mentally deranged and the prodigal.

Article 149
The affairs of a minor shall be administered by his representative who is called according to the case the natural guardian *(waley)*, a testamentary guardian *(wasey mukhtar)*, a legal guardian (appointed by the judge) *(wasey el qadi)* or a curator *(qayyim)*.

Chapter 2

The Minor and its Various States

Article 150
The minor is a person who has not attained the age of majority. He may be of discretion or devoid thereof.
(a) The minor devoid of discretion in the meaning of this law is the person who has not completed 12 years of age.
(b) The minor with discretion is a person who has completed 12 years of age.

Article 151
(a) The dispositions of a minor devoid of discretion are utterly null and void.
(b) Dispositions of property by the minor possessing discretion are valid when wholly to his advantage, and void when wholly to his disadvantage.
(c) The dispositions of property by a minor possessing discretion which may be at the same time profitable and detrimental may be annulled if this is in the interest of the minor. Annulment cannot be claimed if the disposition is ratified by the minor upon attaining its majority or by the guardian or by the court in accordance with the law.

Article 152
(a) The father may grant his minor child possessing discretion absolute or restricted permission to administer its property or part thereof on attaining 15 years of age and showing good management sense. The father shall carry on with the supervision of his minor's dispositions.
(b) The father may withdraw or restrict permission when he deems this is in the interests of his child.

Article 153
The testamentary or legal guardian may, on approval by the judge, permit the minor with discretion to administer its property or part thereof on its completing fifteen years of age and showing good management sense.

Article 154
On the minor possessing discretion completing 15 years of age, and believing itself to enjoy good management sense, with the testamentary or legal guardian declining to grant it permission to administer its property or part thereof, the matter shall be referred to the judge.

Article 155
The minor who has been granted permission shall be deemed of full legal capacity within the limits of the permission granted.

Article 156
The person authorized by the judge or the testamentary or legal guardian shall submit to the judge regular accounts of his dispositions.

Article 157
The judge, testamentary or legal guardian, may cancel or restrict the permission if the interests of the minor so require.

Chapter 3

Actual and Deemed Majority

Article 158
The major is the person who has attained the age of majority unless he has been placed under interdiction on the grounds of any defect of legal capacity.

Article 159
The judge may deem the minor of age on reaching 18 years of age and proving it has good management sense.

Article 160
(a) The minor who has, or is deemed to have, reached majority, may ask for the annulment of the dispositions by the testamentary or legal guardian thereof which have occurred previously, wholly or in part, even after giving him general discharge.
(b) This right lapses after one year from the date of the minor administering its business following becoming or being deemed to have become major.

Chapter 4

The Defects of Legal Capacity

Article 161
The defects of legal capacity are insanity, mental derangement, imbecility and prodigality.
(a) The insane is the person wholly or intermittently devoid of reason.
(b) The mentally deranged is the person of little understanding, confused expression, and poor management.
(c) The imbecile is a person who can easily be defrauded in property transactions due to his naivete.
(d) The prodigal is a person who is unnecessarily wasteful or lavish.

Article 162
(a) Dispositions of property by the insane shall be valid during his remission and prior to being placed under interdiction, and shall be void otherwise.
(b) The dispositions by the mentally deranged, the prodigal and the imbecile, entered into after being placed under interdiction, shall be similar to those of a minor possessing discretion.
(c) The dispositions of the mentally deranged before being placed under interdiction shall be valid if his condition was not known at the time of contract and the other party was not aware thereof.
(d) The dispositions of the imbecile before being placed under interdiction shall be valid unless they were due to exploitation. Likewise the dispositions of the prodigal before being placed under interdiction shall be valid unless they were due to exploitation or collusion.

Article 163
A person placed under interdiction may institute on action on his own to lift interdiction.

Part II

Guardianship

Chapter 1

General Provisions

Article 164
Guardianship may be of the person or of property.
(a) Guardianship of the person deals with all that relates to the person of the minor.
(b) Guardianship of property deals with all that relates to the property of the minor.

Article 165
Guardianship of the person shall be invested in the father, then in the residuary in his own right following the order of the Inheritance Rules.

Article 166
Guardianship of property shall be invested in the father only.

Article 167
The guardian is required to be a major, sane, trustworthy and capable to discharge the duties of guardianship.

Article 168
A non-Muslim may not be a guardian of a Muslim.

Article 169
The guardianship shall cease if any of the conditions referred to in the previous two Articles is not fulfilled.

Chapter 2

Guardianship by the Father

Article 170
The father shall be the guardian of his child's property in terms of protection, disposition and investment.

Article 171
The guardianship of the father shall extend to the minor children of his son if their father is placed under interdiction.

Article 172
The father's dispositions shall be deemed valid in the following cases:
(i) to enter into contracts in the name of his child and the disposition of the property thereof;

(ii) to undertake commercial transactions on behalf of his child, but only so long as there is obvious advantage;
(iii) to accept lawful donations for the benefit of his child if they are free of disadvantageous obligations;
(iv) to spend from the property of his child towards those entitled to be maintained thereby.

Article 173
The acts of the father shall not be deemed valid unless the minor's interest therein is established in the following cases:
(i) if he bought the property of his child for himself;
(ii) if he sold his property to his child;
(iii) if he sold the property of his child in order to invest the value thereof for himself.

Article 174
(a) The dispositions by the father shall be void whenever it is established that they are not in the interests of the minor.
(b) The father shall be held liable in his own property for the gross mistake which resulted in damages to his child.

Article 175
The guardianship of the father shall be lifted whenever the judge is satisfied that the property of the minor becomes in danger due to the acts of its father.

Chapter 3

The Testamentary and Legal Guardian

Article 176
(a) The father may appoint a testamentary guardian (al-wasey al-mukhtar) for his minor or already conceived child, and for the minor children of his son placed under interdiction. He may revoke such appointments even if he has declared it irrevocable.
(b) If the minor has no testamentary guardian, the judge shall appoint for it a legal guardian to administer the property thereof with due regard to the minor's interests.

Article 177
The judge appoints a special or temporary guardian wherever the interest of the minor so requires.

Article 178
The testamentary or legal guardian is required to be:
(i) of full legal capacity;
(ii) trustworthy;
(iii) capable of discharging the duties of guardianship;
(iv) to have a lawful means for his livelihood;

(v) not to have been convicted of a crime of stealing, betraying a trust, misrepresentation, embezzlement, forgery, or any crime against decency or honour;
(vi) not to have been declared bankrupt unless he is rehabilitated;
(vii) not to have been dismissed from any testamentary or legal guardianship;
(viii) not to be an adversary in a legal dispute with the minor and no animosity to exist between them, nor any family differences that may threaten the interests of the minor.

Article 179
The testamentary or legal guardian is bound by the conditions and duties allocated thereto under the document appointing him as a testamentary or legal guardian unless these are contrary to the law.

Article 180
(a) The testamentary guardian may be a male or a female, natural or a juristic person, single or several, acting independently or with a supervisor.
(b) If there are several testamentary guardians, the judge may confine guardianship to one of their number as required in the interests of the minor.

Article 181
(a) Testamentary guardianship shall take effect subject to the acceptance of a testamentary guardian thereof.
(b) The discharge by the testamentary guardian of his duties shall be deemed an acceptance by him of his guardianship.

Article 182
The testamentary guardian shall not withdraw from the guardianship if he has accepted it expressly or by implication except for an emergency and with the approval of the judge.

Chapter 4

The Supervisor (al-nathir)

Article 183
If the father appoints a supervisor (nathir) to monitor the acts of the testamentary guardian, the supervisor shall discharge such a task as dictated by the minor's interests.

Article 184
The supervisor shall comply with the same conditions as the testamentary or legal guardian.

Chapter 5

The Acts of the Testamentary and Legal Guardian

Article 185
The testamentary or legal guardian shall administer and look after the minor's property and shall exert to that end the same care as if he is administering the property of his own children.

Article 186
The disposition of the testamentary or legal guardian shall be subject to the court supervision.

Article 187
The testamentary guardian and curator are required to submit periodical accounts for the administration of the minor's property.

Article 188
No testamentary or legal guardian may carry out the following acts without permission of the court:

(i) to dispose of the minor's property through sale, purchase, barter, partnership, pledge or any other disposition that transfers ownership or creates a real right;
(ii) to dispose of securities, shares or parts thereof or of any not insignificant or not perishable movables unless the value thereof is negligible;
(iii) to transfer the minor's debts or accept assignment thereto;
(iv) to invest the property of the minor for his own benefit;
(v) to lend or borrow the property of the minor;
(vi) to rent the real property of the minor;
(vii) to accept or refuse donations that are subject to conditions;
(viii) to spend from the money of the minor on those whose maintenance is incumbent thereon;
(ix) to pay for any liabilities that may exist on the estate or the minor;
(x) to acknowledge any right against the minor;
(xi) to accept settlement or arbitration;
(xii) to institute proceedings unless any delay in the institution thereof may result in damages to the minor or the loss of a right due thereto;
(xiii) to withdraw legal action or fail to resort to the procedures of appeal whether ordinary or extraordinary;
(xiv) to rent the property of the minor to himself, his spouse, an ascendant or descendant thereof, or to any person whom the testamentary or legal guardian represents.

Article 189
The judge or any official briefed to look after the minor's affairs shall be prohibited from buying or renting anything owned by the minor for himself, his spouse or any ascendant or descendant thereof, and shall also be prohibited from selling to the minor anything owned by him, his spouse or any ascendant or descendant thereof.

Article 190
The testamentary or legal guardian may ask for remuneration in consideration of his duties to be set as from the demand date.

Article 191
The testamentary or legal guardian, as the case may be, shall be civilly and criminally liable for any injury to the minor as a result of his negligence or breach of his duties.

Chapter 6

The Termination of the Testamentary or Legal Guardianship

Article 192
The appointment of the testamentary or legal guardian shall come to an end on the occurrence of any of the following events:
(i) his death or total or partial loss of legal capacity;
(ii) confirmation of his going missing or absent;
(iii) acceptance of his request to be released of his duties;
(iv) inability to discharge the duties of testamentary or legal guardianship;
(v) the minor being declared a major or attaining the age of majority in a state of sanity;
(vi) the removal of interdiction on the ward;
(vii) cession of the state of being missing or absent;
(viii) the recovery by the minor's father of his legal capacity;
(ix) the death of the minor.

Article 193
The testamentary or legal guardian shall be dismissed if he fails to comply with any of the conditions enumerated in Article 178 of this law.

Article 194
On the termination of his appointment, the testamentary or legal guardian shall hand over the property of the minor and all accounts and documents related thereto to the person concerned under the supervision of the judge within a period not exceeding thirty days from the date of the termination of his appointment.

Article 195
On the decrease of the testamentary or legal guardian, his heirs or the administrator of his estate shall notify the judge forthwith thereof in order to take adequate steps to safeguard the minor's interests.

Chapter 7

The Absent or the Missing Person

Article 196

(a) The absent is the person whose address or place of residence is not known.
(b) The missing person is the absent person who is not known to be alive or dead.

Article 197

If the absent or missing person has no agent, the judge shall appoint a guardian to administer the property thereof.

Article 198

Stock shall be taken of the absent or missing person's property on the appointment of a guardian, to be administered in the same manner as the minor's property.

Article 199

The state of being missing comes to an end on the occurrence of any of the following events:
(i) the return of the missing person, alive;
(ii) the confirmation of his death;
(iii) a court judgment of deemed death.

Article 200

The judge shall declare a missing person to be dead in the following events:
(i) if there is evidence of his death;
(ii) if a sufficient period lapses after the declaration of his being missing;
(iii) if he has gone missing in circumstances in which he is likely to perish and two years pass since his being declared missing.

Article 201

The judge shall in all cases investigate the possible whereabouts of the missing person by all means in order to ascertain whether he is dead or alive before declaring his death.

Article 202

The day on which the court declares a missing person to be dead shall be deemed as the date of his death.

Article 203

If the missing person has been declared dead by the court, and he reappears alive:
(i) he shall be entitled to the residue of his property with his heirs;
(ii) his wife shall return to him unless she has married and consummation has taken place.

Book Four

The Will

Part I

General Provisions

Article 204
The will is a disposition of property for no consideration to take effect after the death of the testator.

Article 205
(a) The will may be absolute or subject to a condition.
(b) If the will is subject to a condition that is contrary to the intentions thereof or the provisions of this Act, that condition shall be void.

Article 206
The will shall be executed within one-third of the estate left by the testator after paying all the charges attached thereto. A will may be valid if it exceeds one-third to the extent permitted by any of the adult heirs.

Article 207
Every disposition made by a person during the death-illness with the object of making a gift or favouring a person shall be governed by the rules applicable to wills, no matter what description has been given to such a disposition.

Part 2

Essentials and Conditions

Article 208
The essentials of the will are the form, the testator, the beneficiary and the object of the bequest.

Chapter 1

The Form

Article 209
A will may be made by word of mouth, or in writing, and if the testator is unable to do either, then by an intelligible gesture.

Chapter 2

The Testator

Article 210
(a) The will shall be valid if the testator possesses the legal capacity for making it, even if it is made during the death-illness.
(b) The testator may modify the will or revoke it wholly or in part.
(c) The disposition by the testator of the property assigned to the will shall be deemed a revocation thereby of the will.

Chapter 3

The Beneficiary

Article 211
The will shall be valid to a person to whom ownership can be duly transferred even if he is a non-Muslim.

Article 212
No will can be made to an heir unless it is allowed by the rest of the adult heirs, in which case it shall be executed from the portion of the heir who allowed it.

Article 213
(a) A will may be made for a specific person whether already in existence or expected to exist.
(b) A will may be made to a group of a limited or unlimited number.
(c) A will may be made for charity or places of worship, and for existing or expected charitable organizations.

Article 214
(a) For a will to a specific person to be valid, it must be accepted thereby after the death of the testator, or during the lifetime thereof, and remain accepted after the death of the testator.
(b) If the beneficiary is an embryo, a minor or a person placed under interdiction, the person entrusted with the guardianship of the property thereof may accept or reject the will after obtaining the judge's permission.
(c) A will made to a non-specific person may not be accepted or rejected by any person.
(d) Acceptance or rejection on behalf of juristic persons, organizations and foundations shall be by the legal representative thereof. If there is no such representative, the will shall be binding and effective.

Article 215
(a) The acceptance of a will need not be immediately on the death of the testator.
(b) Silence by the beneficiary for 30 days after being aware of the will shall be deemed an acceptance thereof.

Article 216
The beneficiary who possesses full legal capacity may reject the will wholly or in part.

Article 217
If the beneficiary dies after the death of the testator without having expressed acceptance or rejection, that right shall pass to the heirs of the beneficiary.

Article 218
(a) The ownership of the object bequeathed shall pass to the beneficiary on the death of the testator.
(b) The heir of the deceased among the beneficiaries shall represent the same before distribution.
(c) The object bequeathed shall be equally divided between the beneficiaries if they are multiple, unless the testator stipulates otherwise.
(d) If a will is made for twins unborn at the time of making the same, and one of them is born dead, the survivor shall be the sole owner of the object bequeathed.
(e) The heirs of the testator shall be entitled to the usufruct of the object bequeathed until the person entitled thereto comes to existence.

Article 219
(a) A will for an unquantifiable group that is to exist in future shall include those among them who are already in existence at the time of the death of the testator, and those who come to existence until their number is determinable.
(b) The number of the members of an indefinite group shall be determined on the death of the rest of their parents, or on loss of any chance of any survivor among them having posterity.
(c) On giving up hope of the existence of any one of the beneficiaries, the object bequeathed shall revert as part of the inheritable estate.

Article 220
The already existing members of an indefinite group which is determinable before the exact number is defined shall be entitled to the usufruct of the object bequeathed. The shares to the usufruct shall vary according to subsequent births and deaths.

Article 221
The yield of the object bequeathed for an unspecified group whose number cannot be determined shall be distributed among those existing among them with due regard to their respective needs. No share shall be allotted to anyone who died before division.

Article 222
A specified beneficiary shall be governed by the rules applicable to a non-specified beneficiary who can be determined to start with if they are both beneficiaries of the same will.

Article 223
The object bequeathed to a person unspecified shall be sold if there is fear of its getting lost or reduced in value. The proceeds of sale shall be used to purchase something beneficial to the beneficiaries.

Article 224
(a) A will made to places of worship and charitable or learned organizations shall be used to fund the administration, development, interests and beneficiaries thereof, and for other purposes, unless the expenditure is indicated through custom or circumstances.
(b) The yield of the object bequeathed for organizations which are expected to exist shall be paid to the nearest like thereto until they come to existence.

Chapter 4

The Object Bequeathed

Article 225
The object bequeathed must be owned by the testator and be meant for a lawful cause.

Article 226
(a) The object bequeathed may be of joint or specific ownership.
(b) The object bequeathed of joint ownership shall include all the property of the testator both actually existing and to exist in future.

Article 227
A will of a share of a jointly owned property shall be executed if a testator has specified an allocation thereof within the limits of one-third of his estate.

Article 228
(a) The specific object bequeathed may be immovable or movable property, fungibles or in specie, a substance or a utility.
(b) If the testator bequeathed a specific object for a certain person and then to another, it shall be equally shared by both unless it is proved that the testator's intention was to revoke the will for the first beneficiary.

Article 229
The object bequeathed may be a usufruct or a right to usufruct, a movable or an immovable property, for a determined or indeterminate period.

Article 230
(a) If the value of the specific property to which usufruct or the right to usufruct has been bequeathed is less than one-third of the estate, the substance shall be handed over to the beneficiary to enjoy the usufruct thereof pursuant to the will.
(b) If the value of the specific property of which usufruct or right to usufruct has been bequeathed is more than one-third of the estate, the heirs shall be given the choice between allowing the will or giving the beneficiary the equivalent of one-third of the estate.

Article 231
The beneficiary who has been bequeathed the usufruct of specific property may use or exploit it even in a manner otherwise to that stipulated in the will, provided no damage shall be caused to the substance.

Part 3

Will through the Attribution of Status

Article 232
In a will through the attribution of a status, a person who is not an heir shall be added to the heirs of the estate of the testator and shall be allotted a specific share therein.

Article 233
The person to whom a status has been attributed shall be entitled to the share of the heir whose status he has been granted whether it be a male or a female.

Part 4

The Impediments of the Will

Article 234
The will shall be void in the following events:
(i) the revocation by the testator of his will;
(ii) the loss of the legal capacity by the testator until the decease thereof;
(iii) the death of the beneficiary during the lifetime of the testator;
(iv) the beneficiary becoming a lawful heir to the testator;
(v) the rejection by the beneficiary of the will after the death of the testator;
(vi) the murder of the testator by the beneficiary deliberately and unlawfully, whether the beneficiary was a principal agent, an accomplice or has caused the death of the testator, provided that the murderer, on committing homicide, is sane, adult, and subject to criminal liability.

Part 5

The Mandatory Will

Article 235
If a child, male or female, dies before or simultaneously with its father or mother, the share that it would have inherited shall pass to the children thereof, male or female, according to the Sharia rules as a mandatory will provided that it shall not exceed one-third of the estate.

Article 236
The mandatory will shall be confined to the first generation of grandchildren, male or female, and in all cases, the share devolved on any of such grandchildren shall not exceed the share of any of the respective deceased children with any excess reverting to the estate.

Article 237
The grandchildren shall not be entitled to the mandatory will in any of the following events:
(i) if their grandfather or grandmother has attributed to them the status of a deceased child;
(ii) if they are heirs to the grandfather or grandmother or a son;
(iii) if the grandfather or grandmother during the lifetime thereof has made a gift to them in an amount equivalent to their share in the estate thereof with the intention that that be treated as mandatory will.

Article 238
If the grandparent has made a will to the grandchildren for less than what they would receive under a mandatory will, that share shall be increased to that extent. If the will is for more than that, the excess shall be subject to the consent of the adult heirs. If only some of them are made beneficiaries to the will, the remaining members shall be entitled to their share under a mandatory will.

Part 6

Conflict of Wills

Article 239
(a) The mandatory will shall always prevail over the voluntary testament.
(b) If one-third of the estate falls short of covering bequests of equal priority and the adult heirs have not allowed any excess of the said third, the beneficiaries' bequests shall be proportionally reduced. If one bequest relates to a specific object, the value thereof shall be shared with the beneficiary thereof receiving its share of the object and another its share of the remainder of the said third.

Book Five
Inheritance

Part I
General Provisions

Article 240
The estate is all property and rights left by the deceased.

Article 241
The estate shall be subject to charges which vary in priority according to the following order:
(i) the funeral expenses of the deceased according to custom;
(ii) the payment of the deceased's debts;
(iii) the execution of the mandatory will;
(iv) the execution of the voluntary will;
(v) the distribution of the residue of the estate among heirs.

Article 242
Inheritance is the mandatory succession to property and rights on the death of the owner thereof by those who are entitled thereto.

Article 243
The inheritance essentials are:
(i) the propositus *(al muwarreth)*;
(ii) the heir;
(iii) the estate.

Article 244
The grounds for inheritance are two, matrimony and blood relationship.

Article 245
The conditions for inheritance are that the propositus is dead in fact, or deemed to be dead, and the heir thereof at the time of the death, being alive in fact or deemed to be alive.

Article 246
There shall be prohibited from inheritance the one who murders the propositus deliberately and unlawfully, whether he is a principal agent or an accomplice, or has caused the death of the propositus, provided that the murderer is, at the time of committing the crime, sane and complying with the requirements of criminal liability.

Article 247
Difference in religion shall be a bar to inheritance.

Article 248
If two or more die and they would have mutually inherited from one another, without knowing which died first, none of them shall have any right in the other's estate.

Part 2

Classes of Heirs and their Rights

Article 249
The heir can be a sharer, a residuary, or both, or a distant kindred.

Chapter 1

The Sharers

Article 250
(a) The share is a prescribed portion for an heir in the estate.
(b) The shares are one-half, one-quarter, one-eighth, two-thirds, one-third and one-sixth of the estate, and one-third of the residue.
(c) The sharers are the parents, the spouses, the paternal grandfather how-high-soever, the valid grandmother (the non-uterine), the daughters, the daughters of a son how-low-soever, the sisters in general, the uterine brother.

Article 251
The half shall go to the following:
(i) the husband, provided the wife leaves no descendant entitled to inherit;
(ii) the daughter on her own, without any other descendant, male or female;
(iii) the daughter of a son, how-low-soever, on her own without any other descendant, or a son's child equal to or higher than her in degree.
(iv) the germane sister if she has no germane brother, nor another germane sister, nor a descendant that is an eligible heir to the deceased, nor a father nor a paternal grandfather.
(v) the consanguine sister on her own without a consanguine brother, nor a full brother nor a full sister, nor a descendant entitled to inherit from the deceased, nor a father, nor a paternal grandfather.

Article 252
The quarter shall go the following:
(i) the husband with the wife's descendant;
(ii) the wife even if more than one, if the husband has no descendant entitled to inherit.

Article 253
The eighth shall go to the wife, even if there are several, if the husband had a descendant heir.

Article 254
The two-thirds shall go the following:
(i) two or more daughters in the absence of a son of the deceased;
(ii) two or more daughters of the son how-low-soever their father may be, in the absence of a lineal child of the deceased, a son's son of the same degree as the daughter, or a child of a son higher than that;
(iii) two or more germane sisters in the absence of a germane brother, a descendant heir of the deceased, a father or a paternal grandfather;
(iv) two or more consanguine sisters in the absence of a consanguine brother, a full brother, a full sister, a descendant to inherit the deceased, a father or a paternal grandfather.

Article 255
One-third shall go to the following:
(i) the mother in the absence of an inheriting descendant of the deceased, or two or more of brothers or sisters of whatever side unless she inherits with a spouse and the father, in which case she shall receive one-third of the residue.
(ii) two or more uterine brothers in the absence of an inheriting descendant of the deceased, a father or a paternal grandfather. They shall share one-third between them equally, with the male receiving the same share as the female.
(iii) the paternal grandfather if he inherits with full or consanguine brothers or both being more than two brothers, or an equal number of sisters, in the absence of a sharer.

Article 256
One-sixth shall go to the following:
(a) the father with an inheriting descendant;
(b) the paternal grandfather in the following cases:
(i) if there is an inheriting descendant of the deceased;
(ii) if there are sharers when his share is less than one-sixth or one-third of the residue or if there is nothing left after their getting their shares;
(iii) with one sharer or more, and more than two brothers, or an equal number of sisters, whether full or consanguine, and one-sixth is more advantageous to him than one-third of the residue.
(c) the mother with an inheriting descendant, or with two or more brothers and sisters on whatever side;
(d) the valid grandmother, how-high-soever, one or more, provided there is no mother, nor a descendant thereto, nor a valid grandmother nearer to the deceased;
(e) the daughter or daughters of the son, how low their father is, with one lineal daughter or with one son's daughter higher if there is no son, nor a son's son, higher or in the same degree;

(f) the consanguine sister, one or more, with one full sister, if there is no inheriting descendant of the deceased, nor a father nor paternal grandfather, nor a full or consanguine brother;
(g) one uterine brother or sister in the absence of an inheriting descendant of the deceased, a father or a paternal grandfather.

Article 257
One-third of the residue shall go to the following:
(i) the mother with a spouse and the father in the absence of an inheriting descendant of the deceased, or two or more brothers or sisters on whatever side.
(ii) the paternal grandfather inheriting with a sharer, and more than two brothers or an equal number of sisters full or consanguine if one-third of the residue is more advantageous to him than one-sixth (of the whole estate).

Chapter 2
The Residuaries

Article 258
(a) A residuary is an heir whose entitlement to the estate is neither prescribed nor established.
(b) The residuaries are of three classes:
(i) a residuary in his own right;
(ii) a residuary through another;
(iii) a residuary with another.

Article 259
The residuary in his own right falls in various categories of different degree of priority according to the following order:
(i) the sons: these include the sons and the sons of a son how-low-soever;
(ii) the father: this includes the father and the paternal grandfather, how-high-soever;
(iii) the brothers: these include the full or consanguine brothers and their sons, how-low-soever;
(iv) the paternal uncles: these include the paternal uncles of the deceased whether they are full or consanguine brothers of the deceased's father, and the paternal uncles of the father, the paternal full or consanguine uncles of the paternal grandfather, how-high-soever, and the sons of the paternal full or consanguine uncles, how-low-soever.

Article 260
The residuary in his own right shall inherit the whole estate if there is no sharer, the residue thereof if there is any sharer, and shall inherit nothing if the prescribed shares exhaust the estate.

Article 261

(a) Among the residuaries, the order cited in Article 259 of this Act shall be adhered to, and if the relationship is of the same category, then the nearer in degree, and then the stronger blood relation in the event of equality in degree.
(b) The residuaries shall have equal rights to inheritance on being related to the deceased in the same category, degree and strength.

Article 262

If the paternal grandfather inherits with germane or consanguine brothers or sisters, whether there are sharers or not, the grandfather shall inherit as a residuary in the same way as if he were another brother of the deceased, unless one-sixth or one-third of the residue is more advantageous to him.

Article 263

(a) The residuaries through another are:
(i) one or more daughters with one or more son;
(ii) the daughter of a son how-low-soever, one or many, with one or more son of a son, whether of equal degree or lower, if she needs him to become a residuary herself and shall be excluded by such a male if higher;
(iii) the germane sister or sisters with the germane brother or brothers;
(iv) the consanguine sister or sisters with the consanguine brother or brothers.
(b) In these cases, the male shall receive the share of two females.

Article 264

The residuaries with another are the germane or consanguine sister or sisters with the daughter or the son's daughter, one or more, in which case the residuary with another shall have the same entitlement as the brother to inherit the residue and to exclude the other residuaries.

Chapter 3

Heirs as Both Sharers and Residuaries

Article 265

Those who inherit both as sharers and residuaries are:
(i) the father or paternal grandfather with the daughter or the daughter of a son how low her father is;
(ii) the husband, if he is the son of the paternal uncle of the deceased, shall receive his share as a spouse and his entitlement through his being her paternal cousin as a residuary.
(iii) the uterine brother or brothers if they are also the sons of the paternal uncle of the deceased, shall inherit as sharers, and shall receive their portion as paternal cousins as residuaries.

Part 3

Exclusion, Return and Proportional Abatement

Article 266
(a) Exclusion (hajb) is the loss to an heir of all or part of the inheritance as a result of the presence of another heir more entitled to inherit.
(b) Exclusion is of two kinds, total exclusion and reduction.
(c) An excluded person from inheritance may exclude another.

Article 267
A person barred from inheritance shall not exclude another.

Article 268
Return (rudd) is the case when the total shares of the sharers is less than the estate,* in which case the sharers' share shall be increased through return of the residue in proportion to their entitlement.

Article 269
The proportional abatement (aul) is the case when the total shares of sharers exceed the value of the estate* in which case their shares shall be reduced in the proportion of their entitlement.)

Part 4

Distant Kindred

Chapter 1

Classes of Distant Kindred

Article 270
Distant kindreds fall into four classes of differing degrees of priority to inheritance in the following order:
First Class: the daughter's children how-low-soever and the children of the daughters of a son how-low-soever.
Second Class: the uterine grandfathers and grandmothers, how-high-soever.
Third Class: (i) the children of uterine brothers and their children, how-low-soever;
(ii) the children of all sisters, how-low-soever;
(iii) the daughters of all brothers and their children, how-low-soever;
(iv) the daughters of all the brothers' sons, how-low-soever, and their children, how-low-soever.

* Deemed as the unity, the numerator less than the denominator (translator).
* Deemed as the unity, the numerator exceeding the denominator (translator).

Fourth Class: includes six categories with differing priority to inheritance in the following order:

(i) the uterine paternal uncles of the deceased and all his paternal aunts, (the father's relations) and his maternal uncles and all aunts (the mother's relations).

(ii) the children of those specified in the previous paragraph, how-low-soever, and the daughters of the deceased's full or consanguine paternal uncles, and the daughters of their sons, how-low-soever, and the children of the females mentioned, how-low-soever.

(iii) the deceased's father's uterine paternal uncles and all paternal aunts and maternal uncles and aunts of his father (the father's relations); all the paternal uncles and aunts, maternal uncles and aunts of the mother of the deceased (the mother's relations).

(iv) the children of those specified in the previous paragraph, how-low-soever, and the daughters of the deceased's father, full or half, paternal uncles, and the daughters of their sons how-low-soever, and the children of those specified, how-low-soever.

(v) the deceased's father's father's uterine paternal uncles and all the deceased's father's mother's paternal uncles, and the maternal aunts of the deceased's father's parents and their maternal uncles and aunts (the father's relations), and all the deceased's mother's parents, paternal and maternal aunts and uncles (the mother's relations).

(vi) the children of those specified in the previous paragraph how-low-soever, the daughters of the deceased father's father's full or half paternal uncles, and their sons' daughters, how-low-soever, and the children of those specified, how-low-soever, and so-on.

Chapter 2

Inheritance of Distant Kindred

Article 271

(a) Among the first class of distant kindred, the right to inheritance shall go first to those closest in degree to the deceased.

(b) If they are equal in degree of closeness, then the children of a sharer shall have priority over the children of a distant kindred.

(c) If they were all children of a sharer, or if none of them is a child of a sharer, they shall inherit together.

Article 272

(a) Among the second class of distant kindred, the first right to inheritance shall go to the closest in degree to the deceased.

(b) If they are of equal degree of closeness, priority shall go to the one related to a sharer.

(c) If they are equal in degree without any of them related through a sharer or if they are all related through a sharer, then if they are all on the father's or the mother's side, they shall inherit together. If they differ on the side of their relationship, two-thirds shall go to the father's relations and one-third to the mother's relations.

Article 273

(a) Among the third class of distant kindred, the first right to inheritance shall go to the closest in degree to the deceased.

(b) If they are of equal degree and some of them were the children of an heir, and some children of a distant kindred, the first category shall have priority over the second, otherwise priority shall go to the strongest blood relation to the deceased. Therefore anyone whose ascendant relates to the deceased through both parents shall prevail on another who relates through only one parent, and the one whose ancestor is related to the deceased through the father shall take priority over another who is related through the mother, and if they are of the same degree and strength of blood relationship, they shall inherit together.

Article 274

If in the first category of the fourth class specified under Article 270 of this Act, the heirs are exclusively the father's relations, namely the deceased's uterine paternal uncles and all his paternal aunts, or the mother's relations, namely all the maternal uncles and aunts of the deceased, the one with the strongest blood relationship to the deceased shall have priority. Thus anyone who is related through both parents shall have priority over another related through one parent, and the one who is related through the father shall have priority on another related through the mother. If they are equal in the strength of blood relationship, they shall inherit together. If both sides survive, two-thirds shall go to those relations on the father's side and one-third to those on the mother's side, and the share of each group shall be distributed as aforesaid.

Article 275

The provisions of the previous Article shall apply to the third and fifth categories.

Article 276

For the second category, the closest relationship shall have precedence over the more remote, even if it belongs to a different side, and in the event of equality and identity of the side, the stronger blood relation shall have precedence if they are all the children of a residuary, or of a distant kindred. If they differ, the residuary's child shall have precedence over the child of a distant kindred. On the side of relationship differing, two-thirds shall go to those relations on the father's side, and one-third to those on the mother's side, and each group shall have the shares divided among them as aforesaid.

Article 277

The provisions of the previous Article shall apply to the fourth and sixth categories.

Article 278
No account shall be taken of the multiplicity of the sides of relationship in respect of an heir of distant kindred, unless the side differs.

Article 279
In the distribution of the inheritance shares among distant kindred, the male shall receive the portion of two females.

Part 5

Special Cases

Chapter 1

The Akdariyya

Article 280
The grandfather shall be a residuary with the germane or consanguine sister who shall not inherit with him as a sharer except in the akdariyya cases, which is a husband, a mother, a grandfather and a germane or consanguine sister. In this case, the husband shall be allotted one-half, the mother one-third, the grandfather one-sixth, the sister a half which shall be added to the one-sixth of the grandfather, and the total shall be divided between them, with the grandfather receiving twice the share of the sister.

Chapter 2

The Mushtaraka

Article 281
The full brother shall inherit as a residuary, except in the mushtaraka, that is when a woman dies, leaving a husband, a mother or a grandmother, and a number of uterine brothers and full brother or brothers. In this case, the husband shall receive one half, the mother or grandmother one-sixth, and one-third shall be divided between the uterine and full brothers and sisters, with the male receiving twice the share of the female.

Chapter 3

The Malikiyya and the Semi-Malikiyya

Article 282
The grandfather shall not exclude the germane or consanguine brother except in the malikiyya or semi-malikiyya question. The malikiyya consists of a husband, a mother, a grandfather, uterine brothers or sisters and a consanguine brother. In this case, the husband shall receive one-half, the mother one-sixth and the grandfather shall receive the residue as a residuary.

The semi-malikiyya consists of a husband, a mother, a grandfather, uterine brothers and sisters and a germane brother. The husband shall receive one-half, the mother one-sixth, and the residue shall go to the grandfather as a residuary.

Part VI

Miscellaneous Questions

Article 283
(a) The missing person shall have set aside for him his share of the deceased's estate assuming that the missing person is alive. When he reappears alive, he shall receive his share. If he is ruled to be dead, his share shall be returned to the sharers entitled thereto at the time of the death of the propositus.
(b) If the missing person reappears alive after having been ruled by court as dead, he shall recover whatever is left in the possession of the other heirs of his share in the estate of the propositus.

Article 284
If the missing person is ruled by the court to be dead, his estate shall be distributed among his heirs. If he reappears alive, he shall recover what is left in the possession of the heirs of his estate, but shall not claim to recover what was lost in their possession.

Article 285
The embryo unborn shall have reserved for it of the estate the greater part on the assumption that it is male or female, and each other heir shall receive the lesser share under the assumption of maleness or femaleness.

Article 286
(a) If the share set aside for the unborn baby of the estate is less than its entitlement, it shall claim back the balance from whoever had more than its share among the heirs.
(b) If the share set apart from the estate for the unborn baby exceeds its due share, the excess shall be returned to those entitled thereto among the heirs.

Article 287
(a) If the deceased, during his life, has acknowledged parentage vis-a-vis a child, such an acknowledgment shall have no effect as far as the heirs are concerned, unless it fulfils the conditions of the validity thereof.
(b) If the deceased acknowledged parentage on behalf of another person under Article 84 of this Act, and has not renounced that acknowledgment, the beneficiary of the acknowledgment shall have a right to the estate of the deponent unless there is an heir thereto.
(c) If an heir acknowledges parentage to the propositus thereof of a third person without such an acknowledgment establishing parentage, the beneficiary shall receive its due from the share of the deponent only, unless it is excluded thereby.

Article 288
There shall be mutual inheritance rights between the illegitimate offspring and the child of lian and its mother and her relations.

Article 289
The hermaphrodite whose sex is unknown shall receive the lesser amount due for a male or female.

Article 290
(a) Exclusion by consent is an agreement among the heirs that some of them shall renounce their share in the estate for a given consideration.
(b) An heir who has entered into an agreement on exclusion by consent with another shall receive the latter's share, and shall replace him in the estate.
(c) If one heir concluded an exclusion by consent agreement with the other heirs, if it received its consideration therefor from the estate, its share shall be deducted from the estate and the shares of the remaining heirs shall remain as they are. If the consideration paid thereto was from their property, and the contract did not specify the modality of distribution of the share of the person who renounced his share, the said share shall be distributed among them in proportion to what each has paid, otherwise it shall be divided equally among them if the contribution of each heir to the consideration is unknown.

Final Provisions

Article 291
(a) The provisions of this Act shall govern all matters to which these provisions apply in letter or spirit.
(b) In the absence of a provision in this Act that is applicable, the judge shall decide according to the principles of Islamic Sharia most in conformity with the provisions of this Act.
(c) In all this, the courts shall seek guidance in the judicial Arab precedents and Islamic jurisprudence.*

*The whole Appendix has been translated by the author from the Arabic original.

Bibliography

A. IN ARABIC

I. Arabic Religious Texts

Al Quran
Saheeh-ul-Bukhari, 8 vols. (Cairo).
Saheeh-u-Muslim, 19 vols. (Cairo).
Both are anthologies of authenticated sayings of The Prophet.

II. Manuals and Monographs

ABDULLAH, Prof. Omar, *Ahkam-ush-Shariat-il-Islamiyya fil Ahwal-ish-Shakhsiyya* (Islamic Sharia Provisions on Personal Status), (6th ed., Alexandria, 1968).
ABDUL LATIF, Prof. Hassan Subhi Ahmad, *Ahkam-ul-Mawareeth Fish Sharia-til-Islamiyya* (The Inheritance Rules of the Islamic Sharia), (Alexandria).
ABIANI, Muhammad Zaid, Al-, *Mukhtasar Sharh il Ahkam ish Shariyya fil Ahwal ish Shakhsiyya* (A brief commentary on the Sharia Provisions on Personal Status by Muhammad Qadri Pasha), (Cairo, 1924 AD, 1342 AH).
ABUN NAJA, Shaikh Sharafuddin Musa Ibn Ahmad (died 960 AH), *Zaadul Mustaqni Fikhtisaar il Muqni* (A summary of the Hanbali Doctrine), (Cairo, 1398 AH).
ABU ZAHRA, Professor Muhammad, *Al Ahwal ush Shakhsiyya-Qism uz Zawaj* (Personal Status: On Marriage), (Cairo, 1950 AD, 1369 AH).
Sharh u Qanoon il Wasiyya (Commentary on the Wills Act), (2nd ed., Cairo, 1950 AD,1369 AH).
Akham ut Tarikaat i wal Mawareeth (On Estates and Succession), (Cairo 1963 AD, 1383 AH).
Muhadaraat fil Waqf (Lectures on Waqf).
Al Wilayatu alan Nafs (Guardianship of the Person), (Cairo).
Al Mirath u Ind al Jaafariyya (Inheritance according to the Jaafaris), (Cairo).
Al Kilkiyya wa Nathariyyatul Aqd Fish Sharia til Islamiyya (Ownership and the

Theory of Contract in the Islamic Sharia), (Cairo, 1977).

ALAMGIR, *Al Fatawa Alamgiriyya Almaarufa bil Fatawal Hindiyya* (Alamgiri Legal Opinions known as The Indian Legal Opinions), 6 vols. (Cairo, 1310 AH).

AQIL, Dr. Jamaluddin Taha Al-, *Aqd ul Hiba bayn al Fiqhi-l-Islami wal Qanoon-il-Madani* (The Gift Contract according to the Islamic Jurisprudence and the Civil Law), (Cairo, 1978).

BADRAN, Prof. Badran Abul Ainain, *Huquq ul Awlad-fish-Shariat-il-Islamiyya wal Wanoon* (The Children's Rights under the Islamic Sharia and the Law), (Alexandria, 1981).

Al Mawareeth wal Wasiyya wal Hiba (Inheritance, Will and Gift), (Alexandria).

BARDEESI, Professor Muhammad Zakariyya Al-, *Al Mirath u wal Wasiyya fil Islam* (Inheritance and Wills under Islam), (Cairo, 1964 AD, 1384 AH).

BAYLANI, Dr. Basheer Al-, *Qawaneen-ul-Ahwal-ish-Shaksiyya fi Lubnan* (The Personal Status Laws in the Lebanon), (Cairo, 1971).

GHANDOOR, Dr. Ahmad Al-, *Al Mirath fil Islam wal Qanoon* (Inheritance under Islam and the Law), (Cairo, 1966).

At-Talaq Fish-Sharia-l-Islamiyya wal Qanoon, Bahth Muqaran (Dissolution of Marriage under the Islamic Sharia and the Law - A Comparative Study), (1st ed., Cairo, 1967 AD, 1387 AH).

HANAFI, Ibrahim, *Qanoon ul Wasiyya* (The Wills Act), (Cairo, 1950).

HILLI, Shaikh Abdul Kareem Rida Al-, *Al Ahkaam ul Jaafariyya fil Ahwall-ish Shakhsiyya* (Jaafari Provisions on Personal Status) (Baghdad Muthanna Library, Cairo, 1947 AD, 1366 AH).

IBN HISHAM, Abu Muhammad Abd-ul-Malik (died 761 AH), *Sirat-u-Rasul-il-Lah* (A biography of the Apostle of God), (Cairo, 1936).

IBN u HAZM, Abu Muhammad Ali Ibn u Ahmad (died 456 AH), *Al Ihkam fi Usul-il-Ahkam,* (The Definite Opinion of the Sources of Jurist Rulings), 8 vols. (Cairo, 1345 AH).

Al Muhalla (The Decorated Book), (Cairo).

IBNU QAYYIM ALJOUZIA, Shamsuddin Abu Abdullah Muhammad Ibnu Abi (died 751 AH), *Zad ul Maad Fi Huda Khairil Ibaad* (On the Prophet's Traditions), 4 vols. 2nd ed., Cairo, 1369 AH).

Aalaam ul Muwaqqe'een An Rabb-il-Alameen (The Authoritative Expounders of Islam), 4 vols. (Beirut, 1973).

KASANI, Alauddin Abi Bakr Masud Al- (died 587 AH), *Badaia As-Sanaie fi Tarteeb ish Sharaie* (On the Classification of Sharia Laws), (Cairo, 1910 AD, 1328 AH).

MADKOOR, Prof. Muhammad Sallaam, *Al Wasaaya fil Fiqh il Islami, Wassiyyat ul Laah (Al Mirath) wa Wassiyyat ul Insan (Al Wasiyya),* (Testaments in Islamic Jurisprudence of God [Inheritance] and Man [The Will]), (2nd ed., Cairo, 1962).

Al Madkhal-ulilal-Fiqh-il-Islami, Tareekhuhu wa Masadiruhu wa Nazariyyatu-Hul-Amma (An Introduction to the Islamic Jurisprudence, its History, Sources and General Theories).

NAJI, Muhsin, *Sharh u Qanoon il Ahwal ish Shakhsiyya* (A Commentary on the [Iraqi] Personal Status Act), (Baghdad, 1979).

NAWAWI, Abu Zakariyya Yahya bin Sharaf An- (died 676 AH), *Minhaj ut-Talibeen* (The Method), (Cairo, 1357 AH).

QADI Khan - Fakhruddin Hassan ibn Mansur (died 592 AH), *Al Fatawa Al Khaniyya* (The Khaniyya Legal Opinions) (Published on the margin of Al Fatawa al Alamgiriyya, q.v.).

SABIQ, As SAYYID, *Fiqh us Sunnah* (The Sunni Jurisprudence), 3 vols. (Cairo, 1365 AH).

SABOONI, Dr. Abdur-Rahman As-, *Nizam ul Usra wa Hallu Mushkilatiha fi Dawa il Islam* (The Institution of the Family and the Solution of its Problems in the Light of Islam), (9th ed., enlarged and revised, Cairo 1983 AD, 1403 AH).

SANHOURI, Prof. Abdur-Rassaq Ahmad As-, *Alwaseet fi Sharh il Qanoon il Madani-l-Gadeed* (Intermediate Commentary on the new [Egyptian] Civil Code), 10 vols. (Cairo, 1952).

Masadir ul Haqq fil Fiqh il Islami (Diras a Muqarana) (Sources of Rights in Islamic Jurisprudence [A Comparative Study with Western Jursiprudence]), 6 vols. (Cairo, 1967).

SARAKHSI, Shamsul Aimma Abu Bakr Muhammad ibn Abi Sahl As- (died 438 AH), *Al Mabsut* (The Detailed Treatise), (Cairo, 1324 AH).

SHAFFI, Abu Abdullah, Ash- Muhammad ibn Idris (died 204 AH), *Al-Umm*, (The Main Source), 7 vols. (Cairo).

YAKAN, Zuhdi, *Alwaqf fish Shariati wal Qanoon* (Waqf under the Sharia and the Law), (Beirut, 1388 AH).

III. Statutes and Court Precedents

Algeria

The Civil Code, Prime Minister Order No. 75-58, of 26/9/1975 (20/9/1395 AH).

The Family Law No. 84-11, of 9/6/1984, 9/9/1404 AH.

Egypt

Act No. 25/1920, in respect of Maintenance and some questions of Personal Status.

Act No. 25/1929 in respect of Some Personal Status Provisions and the Explanatory Note thereof.

Major amendments to these two acts, especially on maintenance and divorce, were introduced under the Presidential Decree No. 44/1979. However, the said Decree, having been unduly promulgated by the President, was declared unconstitutional by the Egyptian Constitutional Court on 4 May 1985, but was adopted by the People's Assembly on 4 July 1985 under Law No. 100/1985.

Legislative Decree No. 78/1931, in respect of Regulations and Procedures of Sharia Courts. This Decree was extensively amended by:
Act No. 462/1955 on the Abolition of Sharia and Religious Courts.
Act No. 77/1943 on Inheritance.
Act No. 71/1946 on Wills.
Act No. 131/1952, on cases for Dismissal of Guardians of the Person.
Decree No. 119/1952 on Guardianship of Property.

Egyptian Court of Cassation

Majmouat-ul-Qawaid al Qanooniyya (Madani) (Compendium of Legal Rules [Civil]), vol. 1 (Cairo, 1940).
Al-Muhamaat (The Organ of the Egyptian Bar), year 15 (Cairo, 1934).
Mawsooat ul Ahwal ish Shakhsiyya (An Encyclopaedia of [Egyptian] Personal Status Laws), (Alexandria, 1985).
DIGWI, Muhammad Al-, a former President of the Egyptian Court of Appeal. *Al Ahwal ush Shakhsiyya Lil Misriyeen al Muslimeen fil Fiqh wal Qanoon* (Personal Status for the Muslim Egyptians, according to Jurisprudence and Court Precedents) (Cairo).

Iraq

The Civil Code under Act No. 40/1951.
The Personal Status Law No. 188/1959 as amended by Act No. 11/1963 and Act No. 21/1978.
KARAM, Dr. Abdul Wahid, *Al Ahwal ush Shakhsiyya fil Qanoon id Dowali l Khas il Iraqi* (Personal Status under the Iraqi Private International Law), (Baghdad, 1979).

Jordan

The Civil Code, Provisional Law No. 43/1976.
The Personal Status Law, Provisional Law No. 61/1976.

Lebanon

The Law on Obligations and Contracts 1932 (The Civil Code).
The Ottoman Family Law 1917 was promulgated by the Ottoman Sultan Muhammad Rashad on 25 October 1917, shortly before the collapse of the Ottoman Empire and the independence of the Arab States therefrom. It was not put into effect until the promulgation of the Decree No. 241 on 4 November 1942 on the Sharia Courts, in which Article 111 reads as follows:

> "The Sunni Judge shall rule according to the most authoritative opinion of the Hanafi Doctrine except in cases provided for in the Family Rights Law promulgated on 8 Muharram 1336 corresponding to 25 October 1917 in which cases the Sunni Judge shall apply the provisions of the said Law while the Jaafari Judge shall rule in accordance with the Jaafari Doctrine and the provisions in conformity with this Doctrine under the Family Law."

The said Decree was later abrogated by a new Law on 16 July 1962 which nevertheless has retained the above text of Article 111 under a new Article 242.

The Lebanese Druze Personal Status Act on 24/2/1948.

SAIGH, Nabeel Az-Zawahira As-, *Mausooat-ul-Ahwal-ish-Shakhsiyyati li Jamee-il Mazahib wal Adyan fi Surriyyat i wal Ordon wa Lubnan* (Personal Status Encyclopaedia for all religions and Denominations in Syria, Jordan and the Lebanon), (Damascus, 1984).

Morocco

Royal Decrees Nos. 343/57/1 and 379/157 promulgating the Personal Status Law.

Syria

The Civil Code, Decree No. 84/1949.
Decree No. 59/1953 on the Personal Status Law amended by Law No. 34/1975.

Tunisia

Personal Status Code Decree of 13/8/1956 AD, 6/1/1376 AH.
Decree of 18/7/1957 AD, 20/11/1376 on Guardianship.
Civil Status Act No. 3 of 1/8/1957 AD, 4/1/1377 AH.
Act No. 27 of 4/3/1958 AD, 12/8/1377 AH on Public Guardianship and Adoption, Compiled by Muhammad At-Tahir As-Senoussi, in *Mejelle of Personal Status* (Tunis, 1958).

B. IN ENGLISH

ANDERSON, Prof. J.N.D., *Islamic Law in Africa* (London, 1954).
BAILLIE, Neil B.E., *Digest of Muhammadan Law* (London, 1965).
BLACK, Henry Campbell, *Black's Law Dictionary* (5th ed., West Publishing Co., St. Paul Mimm, 1979).
GU, J., "Iranian Cultures" in *Encyclopaedia Britannica*, vol. 9 (USA, 1979).
JAFRI, S. Husain, M., *Origins and Early Development of Shia Islam* (London, 1979).
LEWICKI, T., "Al-Ibadiyya" in *Encyclopaedia of Islam*, vol. 3 (Leiden, 1971).
MANEK, Mohanlal Dayalji, *Handbook of Mahomedan Law (Muslim Personal Law)*, (Bombay, 1948).
M.S.M. "Islamic Theology and Philosophy" *in Encyclopaedia Britannica*, vol. 9 (USA, 1979).
MULLA, Sir Dinshah Fardunji, *Principles of Mahomedan Law* (3rd ed., Calcutta, 1933).

NASR, S.H., "Ithna Ashariyya" in *Encyclopaedia of Islam,* vol. 4, Fascicules 65-66, (Leiden, 1974).
F.R. "Islam" in *Encyclopaedia Britannica,* vol. 9 (USA, 1979).
SCHACHT, J., *An Introduction to Islamic Law* (Oxford, 1979).
TYABJI, Faiz Badruddin, *Muhammadan Law - The Personal Law of Muslims* (3rd ed., Bombay, 1940).
VESEY-FITZGERALD, Symour, *Muhammedan Law - An Abridgment According to its Various Schools* (London, 1931).
E.V. ZAMBOUR, "Dirham" in *Encyclopaedia of Islam.*

GLOSSARY

Abadis. Named after Abad At-Tanimi, a sect mainly based in Oman, North and East Africa, who derive their doctrine from the Quran, Sunna of the Prophets and the first two Patriarchal Caliphs, Abu Bakr and Omar, and the consensus of the community of Islam. Usually referred to by Arabists and Orientalists as "Ibadis" and considered by them as a Khariji sect, which the Abadis deny.

ahliyyat. Legal capacity.

ahliyyatul adaa. Literally, the capacity of execution, i.e. the capacity to contract, dispose and validly fulfil one's obligations.

ahliyyatul wujub. Literally, the capacity of obligation, i.e. to acquire rights and duties.

ahl-ul-kitab. Literally, the people of the Book: non-Muslims who believe in some holy scriptures: usually Christians and Jews. The Shias add the magis.

asaba. Literally, the agnates: the sons or the relations on the father's side: in inheritance, those who have no prescribed shares in the estate but take the residue left over after the sharers receive their prescribed portions. To that effect, the asaba are of three classes–(a) **asaba-bin-nafs,** i.e. in their own right; (b) **asaba-bil-ghayr,** who become asaba through another; and (c) **asaba maal-ghayr,** who become asabe or residuaries with another.

as-hab-ul-furud. The sharers.

aul. Proportionate abatement, in the event of the totality of shares in terms of fractions exceeding the unity.

bain bainoon kubra. Major irrevocable repudiation of marriage when the wife becomes temporarily (and under Tunisian law, permanently) prohibited for the husband to remarry following three pronouncements of repudiation.

bain bainoon sughra. Minor irrevocable repudiation of marriage when the husband may remarry his repudiated wife under a new contract, following one or two pronouncements of repudiation and after the lapse of iddat.

batil. Of a contract: void without any effect.

dhawul-arham. (From **rahm,** womb; those related through females). In the Sunni law of inheritance, the relations who are neither asaba (q.v.) nor sharers, e.g. the brothers' sisters or female cousins.

dhul ghafla ("dh" has the sound of "th" in "this"). The imbecile: a person who can be easily cheated in property transactions due to his naivete, legally considered of defective legal capacity.

fard. A prescribed share in the deceased's estate for the first category of heirs. pl. **faraid** or **furud,** hence **As-hab-ul-furud** q.v.

fasid. An irregular contract, which is defective but can have some legal effect under certain conditions.

hadana. Literally, caring. Custody by the mother or a woman, usually.

hadith. A saying. (See **Sunna**).

hajr. Interdiction: the status and act of imposing legal restrictions on the capacity to dispose of property.

hiba. Gift.

hijra, (migration). The Islamic calendar, starting from the emigration of the Prophet from Mecca to Medina in AD622. The hijra year is lunar.

iddat. (From **adda,** to count.) The period counted by a divorcee or a widow from the termination of marriage through divorce or death, during which she cannot re-marry.

ijma. Consensus: a source of Islamic jurisprudence.

ijtihad. Independent and informed opinion on legal or theological issues. Mujtahid: the Islamic thinker who gives such an opinion.

imamat. The doctrine of the leadership of the Islamic community and the subject of controversy between the Kharijis who believe that the Imam (the leader) must be elected by all Muslims irrespective of race, and the Shias, especially the Imamis or Ithna-Asharis who consider the imamat as a prerogativeof the House of Ali and his descendants, the Imam being the sole authoritative source of knowledge in legal and religious matters. (See also **Shia**).

istihsan. (From **istahsana** meaning to find preferable or more convenient.) A discursive device used by some jurists whereby preference is given to a rule other than the one reached by the more obvious form of analogy.

istis-hab. (From **istas-haba** meaning to find a link.) A methodological principle whereby a state of affairs known to have once existed is regarded to have persisted unless the contrary can be proven.

istislah. (From **istaslaha** meaning to seek the interest [of the Islamic community]. A methodological principle whereby public interest is deemed paramount in reaching a legal judgment.

Ithna-asharis. Literally, the Twelvers: the Shia sect which believes in twelve infallible Imams. (See **Shia**).

khilwat-us-sahiha (al). Valid retirement: the event of the husband and the wife, under a valid marriage contract, being together by themselves in a place where they are secure from observation.

khula. Release or redemption. Khul' is a dissolution of the bonds of marriage by the use of this word or its derivatives and for consideration which the wife pays or promises to pay.

lian. A form of irrevocable dissolution of marriage in which the husband affirms four times under oath that his wife has committed adultery and invokes the curse of God on him if he was telling a lie; the woman then affirms four times under oath that her husband is telling a lie, and invokes on herself the curse of God if he was telling the truth. Also called **mulaana.**

maatooh. A person mentally deranged and lacking legal capacity.

maazun. Literally, mutual cursing. (See **lian**).

madhoosh. Literally, the stunned: a person who has lost discretion because of rage or otherwise, to the point of becoming unaware of his uttering.

mahr (also called **sadaq** or **oqr**). The dower: a sum of money or other property which becomes payable by the husband to the wife as an effect of marriage.

Majnoon. Insane: a person considered of void legal capacity.

mandub. A desirable cause.

marad ul-maut. Literally, death-illness. A person in marad-ul-maut is suffering from a terminal disease ending in death.

Mejelle (Magazine). The Ottoman Civil Code compiled in AD 1877, AH 1293, based mainly on the Hanafi juristic schools. It remained until the 1950s the Civil Code of Syria, Iraq and Jordan.

muallq. Subject to a condition in the form of an oath or relegated to some event in the future.

mubah. A permissible cause.

mubaraat. Mutual discharge. (See **khula**).

mulaana. Literally, mutual cursing. (See **lian**).

munjaz. With immediate effect.

muta. Literally, pleasure. A form of temporary marriage recognized only by the Shia school, and considered as illegal by the Sunnis.

muta. Compensation paid to a woman by the husband who has arbitrarily divorced her.

mutawali. The administrator of the waqf who is merely a manager of the waqf.

nashiz. The disobedient wife who refuses to submit to the authority of her husband.
nafith ("th" as in "this"). Of a contract: effective.

oqr. Dower. (See **mahr**).

qayyim (al) (in Arab North Africa). The curator: a guardian appointed by the court for the minor who has no guardian.
qiyas. Analogy: a discursive method used by Islamic jurists whereby a judgment is derived from similar cases ruled upon under the Quran, Sunna or previously established ruling by unanimity.

raay. Literally, personal opinion. **As-Haab-ur-Raay:** a school of juristic thought which advocated the interpretation of the religious texts and analogy derived from precedents, as opposed to **As-Haab-ul-Hadith** who adhered to the Quran and the Prophet's traditions and refrained from judging any hypothetical question.
rud. Return: the converse of proportionate abatement (**aul** q.v.) when the total shares are less than a unity. The shares are then proportionately increased.

sadaq. Dower. (See **mahr**).
safeeh. The prodigal: a spendthrift who is unnecessarily wasteful or lavish, although endowed with sound mind. Considered of a defective legal capacity. (See also **dhul ghafla**).
Sahaba, (from **sahib** meaning friend). The Prophet's Companions; singular, Sahabi.
sahih. For a contract: valid and effective.
Sharia, (from **shara** meaning a path). The Divine Law of Islam.
Shia, (sect). The Followers of Ali and the People of his house, as contradistinct from the Sunnis who represent the orthodox and mainstream sect of Islam. The largest Shia denomination is the Ithna-Ashari, the official doctrine of Iran and of the Shias of the Arab Middle East and Pakistan. Also known as Jaafaris, after the sixth Imam and the first to codify the Shia law.
Sunna, (originally the trodden path). Traditions attributed to the Prophet. The Prophet's Sunna is usually divided into (a) verbal utterances (sunna qualia or hadith); (b) acts of the Prophet (sunna filia); and (3) the tacit assent of the Prophet (sunna taqririyya).

talaq. The dissolution of a valid marriage contract forthwith or at a later date by the husband, his agent or his wife duly authorised by him to do so, using the word **talaq,** a derivative or a synonym thereof.
talaq ala mal. A divorce for a pecuniary consideration. (See **khula** and **mubaraat**).
tamleek. The passing of property.

Umma. "Community"—Community of Islam, a generation of Muslims.

waqf. The waqf is the permanent dedication by a Muslim of any property in such a way that the appropriator's right is extinguished for charity or for religious objects or purposes. (Called **habous** in Algeria and Morocco).
waqif. Dedicator of the waqf.
wasey al-mukhtar (al). The testamentary guardian: a person appointed by the father in a testament to look after his children after his death.
wilayat. Guardianship: for marriage it can be with the right of compulsion (**wilayatul-ijbar**) or without such a right (**wilayatul-nadb**).

INDEX